Erasmus; His Life and Character as Shown in His Correspondence and Works
by Robert Blackley Drummond

Copyright © 2019 by HardPress

Address:
HardPress
8345 NW 66TH ST #2561
MIAMI FL 33166-2626
USA
Email: info@hardpress.net

Erasmus: His Life and Character as Shown in His Correspondence and ...

Robert Blackley Drummond

C 1198.140

HARVARD COLLEGE LIBRARY

FROM THE FUND OF
CHARLES MINOT
CLASS OF 1828

ERASMUS

DESIDERIUS ERASMUS.

ERASMUS

HIS LIFE AND CHARACTER

AS SHOWN IN HIS

CORRESPONDENCE AND WORKS

BY

ROBERT BLACKLEY DRUMMOND, B.A.

With Portrait

IN TWO VOLUMES

VOL. I.

LONDON
SMITH, ELDER, & CO., 15 WATERLOO PLACE
1873

All rights reserved

il 14.
und.
I.
5.

PREFACE.

AN ATTEMPT to do over again that which has been already done, is naturally thought to require some justification, and the justification almost inevitably takes the form of a disparagement of previous labourers in the same field—a disparagement which sometimes brings a severe but just retribution on the head of the new comer. The present writer is fortunately spared from taking any such invidious task upon his own shoulders. The standard lives of Erasmus in English are those of Butler and Jortin, the former of which Dean Milman, in his essay on Erasmus, has pronounced to be "a neat and terse, but meagre and unsatisfactory abstract" of Burigni's work. Of Jortin's life, the same authority, after admitting that "it contains much lively and pleasant remark, much amusing anecdote, many observations of excellent sense, conveyed in a style singularly terse, clever, and sometimes of the finest cutting sarcasm," remarks farther, "but never was a book so ill-composed; it consists of many rambling parts, without arrangement, without order, without proportion; it is no more than an abstract and summary of the letters of Erasmus, interspersed with explanatory or critical comments, and copious patches from other books." This is all very true; and yet it may be owned that, notwithstanding these defects, Jortin's work really makes the reader acquainted with Erasmus, which, after all, is the greatest merit a biography can possess. Other objections to it, as a book for the general reader, besides the undigested character of its contents, are that more than a third of it is in Latin; that, to say nothing of an occasional coarseness which unfits it for the drawing-room, the somewhat faded appearance of the paper and printing offends the eye accustomed to the sharp clear type of our own day; and lastly, that it is now comparatively rare.

Since Butler there has been no complete life of Erasmus in English, though Dean Milman's admirable sketch touches on most of the important points in his history, and judges fairly his character and position. If Mr. Seebohm's account of him, in his "Oxford Reformers," had embraced his whole life, although my estimate of him is somewhat different, I might have felt that my own labours had been anticipated. Other sketches, more or less partial, it is unnecessary to refer to; and I mention my own in the "Theological Review" (Nos. 18, 21, 23, and 30), only in order to thank the proprietors of that journal for their permission to make use of them in the present work.

Of foreign lives a brief but judicious estimate will be

found in the essay by the late Dean Milman already referred to, and I have no need to criticise them. I will only say that I have found advantage in consulting those of Müller, Hess, and Burigni. The large work, in two volumes, by M. H. Durand de Laur, entitled "Érasme, Précurseur et Initiateur de l'Esprit moderne," came under my eye only when my own was on the point of completion.

After all, Erasmus will ever remain his own biographer. To know the man, to understand his character, there is no better way than to read his works, and especially the two volumes of his Epistles. I have merely dipped my small cup into those abundant streams, and am not without hope that, whatever may be the defects of the work which I now venture to offer to the public, the translations which it contains from the letters and other writings of Erasmus may recommend it to those to whom the ponderous folios of Le Clerc are inaccessible, and that thus it may be the means of extending the interest in a man whose life has valuable lessons for our own times, and who indeed may be said, in many respects, to belong to this age rather than to his own.

ROBERT B. DRUMMOND.

February 25, 1873.

*** The Edition of Erasmus referred to in the following pages as *Er. Op.* is that of Le Clerc, in which also will be found the sketches of his life by himself and his friend Beatus Rhenanus.

CONTENTS

OF

THE FIRST VOLUME.

CHAPTER I.

State of Learning in the latter Half of the Fifteenth Century—Parentage of Erasmus—Early Education—Death of his Parents—School at Bolduc—Forced into a monastery—Takes the Vows—Friendship with Hermann—Early Compositions—Admires Laurentius Valla—Anecdote of the Convent—Deliverance 1

CHAPTER II.

Erasmus at Cambray—The University of Paris—Montaigu—Takes Pupils—Mountjoy—Grey—The Lady de Vere—Erasmus in Difficulties—Visits the Castle of Tornenhens—In Paris again—Vow to St. Geneviève—A Battle Royal—Satire on the Scotists . . 31

CHAPTER III.

Erasmus Visits England—Oxford—Linacre—Grocyn—Latimer—More—Wolsey—John Colet—Conversation on Cain's Sacrifice—Discussion with Colet—Letter to Fisher—Colet's Proposal—Erasmus in London—Introduced to Prince Henry—Leaves England . . 65

CHAPTER IV.

Misadventure at Dover—Letters of Erasmus—To the Provost of Burgundy—To Battus—To Tutor—To Battus again—To the Lady de Vere—Erasmus wants Money to go to Italy—Teaches Battus how to beg—Studies Greek—The "Enchiridion"—John Vitrarius, the Monk of St. Omer—Erasmus at Louvain—Panegyric on Philip of Burgundy—Letter to Colet—In England again 91

CHAPTER V.

Second Visit of Erasmus to England—Degree at Cambridge—Translations from Lucian—Acquaintance with Ursewick—Fox—Ruthall Warham — Fisher—More — Portrait of More—Departure from England 141

CHAPTER VI.

Inducements to visit Italy—Erasmus in Paris—Letter to Colet—To Linacre—To Wentford—Crosses the Alps—Turin—Adventure at Bologna—Paul Bombasius—Arrival at Venice—Aleander—Alexander, Archbishop of St. Andrew's—Richard Pace—Erasmus at Rome—Visit to Grimani—Returns to England 159

CHAPTER VII.

The Praise of Folly—Its origin and character—Analysis of the Work—Folly the Cause of Mirth—Satire on War—Hunting—Superstition—The Divines—The Monks—The Preachers—The Cardinals and Popes—Popularity of the Work—Attacked by Dorpius—Erasmus's Reply 184

CHAPTER VIII.

Erasmus at Cambridge—Ammonius of Lucca—Letter from Warham—The "De Copia"—Correspondence with Colet—The Cruelty of the School-room—Advice to a Courtier—Public Affairs—Correspondence with Ammonius—Pilgrimage to Walsingham—To the Tomb of Becket—Erasmus condemns War—Meeting with Cardinal Canossa 206

CHAPTER IX.

Letter to Ammonius—Erasmus refuses to return to Steyn—Adventure near Ghent—Visits Strasburg—Schelestadt—Basle—Acquaintance with Froben—Zasius—Zwingle—Œcolampadius—Pirckheimer—The Christian Prince—John Reuchlin—Letters to Raphael and Grimani—To Pope Leo X. 248

CHAPTER X.

The "Adages"—History of the Work—First Edition—Discussion with Polydore Virgil—Aldine Edition—Reprinted by Froben—Definition of a Proverb—Examples—Erasmus rails at Kings and Priests—The Sileni of Alcibiades—The Scarabæus 271

CHAPTER XI.

Laurentius Valla's Annotations on the New Testament—Erasmus edits the New Testament—Wrath of the Monks—Controversy with Faber—Latomus—Lee—Stunica—Caranza—Edition of St. Jerome—Spurious Works—Jerome's Life by Erasmus—Dedication to Warham 307

CHAPTER XII.

Erasmus at Bruges—Meeting with More—Invited to Ingoldstadt—Letter to Fisher—John Watson—Erasmus nearly made a Bishop—Invited to Paris—Budæus—Correspondence with him—Louvain—Atensis—Vives—College of Busleiden—Hutten—Death of Ammonius—Of Colet—English Dwelling-houses—Letter to Laurinus—To Beatus—Writings of Erasmus—The Complaint of Peace—The Paraphrase of the New Testament 361

Erratum.

Vol. i. p. 68, line 8 from bottom, *for* "Thomas" *read* "William" Latimer.

ERASMUS:

HIS LIFE AND CHARACTER.

CHAPTER I.

STATE OF LEARNING IN THE LATTER HALF OF THE FIFTEENTH CENTURY—PARENTAGE OF ERASMUS—EARLY EDUCATION—DEATH OF HIS PARENTS—SCHOOL AT BOLDUC—FORCED INTO A MONASTERY—TAKES THE VOWS—FRIENDSHIP WITH HERMANN—EARLY COMPOSITIONS — ADMIRES LAURENTIUS VALLA — ANECDOTE OF THE CONVENT—DELIVERANCE.

IN the middle of the fifteenth century the greater part of Europe was still wrapped in the darkness of the mediæval period, and scarcely a ray of the light which Italy had for some time enjoyed had yet found its way across the Alps. Such learning as there was, in the absence or scarcity of books, was necessarily confined to a few, while the mass of the people lived in the densest ignorance. The physical sciences scarcely existed, except in the spurious forms of alchemy and astrology, which, being conducted by false methods, and directed to impossible ends, contributed little to any real knowledge of nature. The physician, whose mind was strangely infected with fanciful notions about the influence of the stars and the atmosphere, and whose chief authorities were Galen and Aristotle, possessed few resources against the terrible plagues which every now and then swept through Europe, carrying off thousands of victims, and finding no obstacle in the overcrowded cities and houses built in disregard of every sanitary law. He could talk much of humours and fluids, but of the true constitution of the human frame, or the laws of organic life, he knew little or nothing. Belief in witchcraft, in demoniacal possession, in the horrors of *incubi* and *succubi*, in the magic power attached to the relics of saints, was universal, and the causes of unusual events were freely sought in supernatural agency, rather than in the processes of the natural world. Religion, too long divorced from practical conduct, consisted of a mass of lifeless ceremonies, while swarms of ignorant and fanatical monks wandered about, living upon the passions and superstitions of the multitude, but doing little service, it is to be feared, to God or man. The Bible, known even to the learned only in the Latin version, was otherwise a sealed book, being absolutely forbidden to the laity; and the noble literature of Greece and Rome was neglected by all save a few enthusiastic scholars. In Italy itself, where classical studies had been pursued with ardour since the beginning of the century, the light which shone so brightly at the luxurious courts of Florence, Ferrara, or Naples, was by no means generally diffused. The Church had long reached the climax of her power, and needed only the continuance of the ancient ignorance in order to make her sway perpetual. The great schoolmen, who, applying their subtle logic to the resolution of the deepest questions which can engage human thought, had done so much to maintain the intellectual activity of a time not yet ripe for more practical inquiries, had passed away; but the controversies they had raised remained behind, and their works, written in barbarous Latin, exercised the minds of the ingenuous youth at the universities, to the exclusion of the study of the classical models and the pursuit of physical science. Greek was only just beginning to be taught in the University of Paris, and printing, quite a recent invention, had still some time to wait before its influence could be widely felt. It was in this state of the world that Erasmus of Rotterdam was born. The story of his life, which it is my purpose to narrate, will show what part he bore in that great conflict, the issues of which, for his own age, were the triumph of letters and the Protestant Reformation, and of which the ultimate issue—still in the future—is the entire emancipation of the human mind from every form of intellectual and spiritual bondage.

Desiderius Erasmus, as he afterwards called himself, was born at Rotterdam, on the night of the 27th of October, in or about the year 1467.[1] His real name

---

[1] As we have the express testimony of Beatus Rhenanus, his intimate friend, that the year of Erasmus' birth is uncertain, and as Erasmus himself confesses this uncertainty more than once, it might seem useless to inquire further. See the Life, by Rhenanus, *ex Ep. ded. in fronte Operum Origenis, ab Erasmo recognitorum*:—"De anno quo natus est apud Batavos nobis non constat, de die constat, qui fuit ad quintum Calend. Novembres." Also *Er. Op*. iii. 508, A.: "Nam ipse nunc annum quinquagesimum secundum, aut ad summum tertium ago." As this was written before the 28th of October, in 1519, it gives us 1466 or 1467 as the year of Erasmus' birth, and in other passages of his works he himself points to the earlier of these two dates. His epitaph in Basle also gives 1466. On the other hand, 1467 is the date inscribed on the pedestal of the statue at Rotterdam, but whether

was Gerard, but as Gerard in the Dutch language means The Beloved, he followed the fashion of the times, and adopted its Greek equivalent "Erasmus," to which the Latin word "Desiderius," of similar import, was prefixed. Such names were not always formed with strict regard to philological law. For an old Roman, Desiderius would have been an impossible form, though the name was not unknown to mediæval Latinity, and Erasmus was afterwards aware that the Greek word he wanted was "Erasmius," not "Erasmus," and accordingly the name was given in its correct form to his godson, the son of Froben, the printer of Basle. He was equally unfortunate in the epithet "Roterodamus," which he usually appended as indicative of his birthplace. It ought to have been "Roterodamensis." He was the son of one Gerard, a native of Tergouw, and of Margaret, the daughter of a physician of Zevenbergen, in Brabant. Gerard belonged to a respectable family, and had received such culture as the times afforded; and as he is said to have been a man of mirthful temperament and fond of a joke, it must have been from

the magistrates of that city followed any independent or more certain evidence may be doubted. The different opinions that have been adopted vary from 1464 to 1469. The curious reader will find most of them in Burigni's note, or in Bayle. M. Ch. Ruelens, in his prefatory notice to the fac-simile of the *Silva Carminum*, adopts 1469.

As to the day of Erasmus' birth, there is a trifling discrepancy between the statement of Rhenanus, as quoted above, to the effect that he was born on the 28th of October, and the *Compendium Vitæ*, which gives October 27 ("natus est Roterodami in vigilia Simonis et Judæ Apostolorum"); but this need present no difficulty if we suppose that the event actually took place at the point where the two days meet, or, in other words, not far on either side of midnight.

That Erasmus was born at Rotterdam has never been doubted, except by the people of Tergouw, who have attempted to claim him as their own. See note in Burigni, vol. i. pp. 8 and 9, and Bayle, art. Rotterdam.

him rather than, as in the case of many celebrated men, from his mother, that Erasmus inherited some of his most remarkable traits. He was the youngest but one of ten brothers, and had been destined by his parents, Elias and Catherine, for the priesthood, those worthy people supposing that out of so large a number they owed at least one to God (such would seem to have been their own language); and if they forbade their son's marriage, they may be held in some degree responsible for the circumstance that their famous grandchild had to bear through life the mark of illegitimacy. For Gerard and Margaret, though there was the fullest intention of marriage on both sides, were never legally united. They, however, regarded their mutual obligations as inviolable, and remained faithful to the troth which they had secretly plighted before heaven. The young Gerard, or Erasmus, was their last, but not their only child. He had a brother, nearly three years older than himself, named Peter, after the maternal grandfather. What had become of this little Peter, or in whose charge he might be when the anxious mother fled to Rotterdam, in the hope of concealing the birth of a second infant, we are not informed; but doubtless he had found a welcome from the same good grandmother who was now willing to receive the new-born Gerard into her home. It would seem as if, after the birth of his first child, the elder Gerard had obtained the forgiveness of his parents by some kind of promise that his fault should not be repeated; for Margaret's pregnancy for the second time was followed by a burst of displeasure from the relatives on both sides, which led to his suddenly leaving home with the determination never to return. Having despatched to his parents and brothers a letter containing a drawing of two clasped hands, with the words "Farewell; I shall never see you more," he proceeded to Rome, where he maintained himself by copying manuscripts, that art, in which he possessed rare skill, not being yet superseded by the printing press. In this way he became a good classical scholar, and at the same time he applied himself to the study of law, intending probably to make that his future profession. Meantime the infant came into the world, and was taken home by its grandmother, whose heart must have relented towards Margaret also, and given her a shelter under the same roof. How long Gerard remained at Rome we are not exactly informed, but it was apparently after no long interval that an incident occurred which induced him to change his plan in life, and comply with the wishes of his friends. News reached him from home that the girl to whom he had attached himself was dead. Overwhelmed with grief, for his love for Margaret was fervent and unwavering, he now resolved on taking the fatal step which would render marriage impossible and all love for woman a sin. He gave himself up to religion, and submitted to ordination. Returning home some time afterwards, what was his astonishment and dismay to meet Margaret alive and well. The old people, in fact, had intentionally deceived him, in the hope that he would be induced to become a priest; and as their story produced the desired effect, it was no doubt artfully told. Strange power of superstition to make these people not only deliberately resolve that their son should sacrifice his natural affections on the altar of a mistaken piety, but fancy they were doing God service in carrying out their purpose by means of a wicked falsehood! Margaret never married. She remained true to her first love, and both parents watched faithfully over the early years of the children of their unfortunate union.

At four years old the little Gerard was sent to school with Peter Winckel, afterwards his guardian. There is a local tradition [2] that he was dull and slow at learning, and it is said that Dutch Vrows whose sons were more than commonly thick-headed used to comfort themselves with the name of Erasmus;—a very unlikely story, it must be confessed, first, because, according to the popular notion, stupidity is the normal condition of Dutch men,[3] and still more, it may be presumed, of Dutch children; and secondly, because even were it otherwise, no amount of dulness would be likely to be remembered in the case of a child just learning to read and write. And Erasmus cannot have remained very long at the school in Tergouw; for we learn that, while still a mere child, he was taken to Utrecht, to fill a place in the choir in the cathedral of that city. At the age of nine he went to Deventer, a thriving town on the Yssel, now, and perhaps then also, celebrated for its gingerbread (*Deventer Koek*), but more honourably known at that time as the seat of a somewhat celebrated school belonging to the "Brothers of the Common Life." This fraternity, not bound by

---

[2] See BAYLE, who denies its authenticity, and conjectures that it must have arisen from a misunderstanding of the *Compend. Vit.*—"primis annis minimum proficiebat in literis illis inamœnis, quibus natus non erat"—where, however, "inamœnis" clearly refers to the barbarous lesson-books of the times, and not, as Bayle supposes, to music, or some other exercise of singing-boys. M. Ch. Ruelens conjectures that the reference is to the vulgar tongue.

[3] The Dutch seem to have been always proverbial for their stupidity. In the *Praise of Folly*, Erasmus makes Folly speak of "Hollandi mei"—my Dutchmen.

indissoluble vows, differing from the mendicant orders in the fact that they did not beg, but, on the contrary, maintained themselves by manual labour, having at least a partial community of goods, and distinguished generally by their strict lives and fervent devotion, were among the earliest promoters of the revival of letters in Germany and the Low Countries, where they had many schools for the education of youth. That of Deventer, planned by Gerard Groot, and founded in the year 1400, seems to have been the first; and there Erasmus learned Latin and Greek as well as it could be taught through the barbarous handbooks then in use.[4] The Latin taught to the junior forms at least was the impure Latinity of the Middle Ages. The great authors of Greece and Rome were now easily accessible to the learned, but the manuscript copies and printed editions were as yet too rare to admit of their being thumbed by school-boys, for whom, moreover, it has always been thought necessary to make learning as disagreeable as possible. Printing in Greek had scarcely begun. There had not yet been published an edition of any Greek author. There was no such thing as a Greek grammar; that of Constantine Lascar was printed at Milan in 1476, but it was probably some time before it became known on this side the Alps. There was no such thing as a Greek lexicon: the very imperfect one of Craston appeared in 1480, after Erasmus had left Deventer.[5] Accordingly, it is not wonderful that our student was unable, when grown up and with his mind enriched with all the learning of Greece and Rome, to look back on these first years of his school life with much satisfaction. The studies, he says, were barbarous. "Heavens!" he exclaims in one

[4] HALLAM: *Lit. Hist.* i. p. 111. [5] HALLAM: *ubi supra*, p. 171.

of his essays, "what an age was that when, with a mighty show of learning, the stanzas of John à Garland used to be dunned into young men, accompanied by tiresome and laboured criticisms; when a great part of our time was wasted in composing, repeating, or learning the silliest verses!"[6] In the end, however, he had no reason to be dissatisfied with his progress; for before leaving school, which he did at the age of thirteen, he had the plays of Terence at his fingers' ends; or, according to another statement, the whole of Terence and Horace by heart. He had, besides, during the last year or two of his stay at Deventer, the advantage of occasional instruction in Greek from Alexander Hegius, the head master, who had himself learned that language from Rodolph Agricola, one of the principal restorers of learning in Germany.[7] Erasmus, indeed, does not give his master credit for any thorough knowledge of the Greek language, contenting himself with the somewhat doubtful praise that he was "not altogether ignorant of it;"[8] but this was said from the vantage-ground of very profound learning, and Hegius, in having any acquaintance with Greek, had the merit of knowing what at the time was known to very few. While at Deventer, it was the good fortune of Erasmus, as he esteemed it, to see Agricola, and no doubt he looked on that great scholar,

---

[6] *Er. Op.* i. 514, F.

[7] "Mihi admodum adhuc puero contigit uti præceptore... Alexandro Hegio Westphalo, qui ludum aliquando celebrem oppidi Daventriensis moderabatur, in quo nos olim admodum pueri utriusque linguæ prima didicimus elementa."—*Er. Op.* ii. 167, A. According, however, to the *Comp. Vit.*, it was only on holy days, when Hegius lectured to the whole school, that Erasmus had the opportunity of hearing him, and there is no reason to suppose that he learned much Greek before he began to study it for himself in maturer years.

[8] "Sed ne hic quidem Græcarum literarum omnino ignarus est."—*Er. Op.* iii. 1798, B.

then just returned from Italy, with wondering eyes. There is a story how Agricola, having asked to see the exercises written by the pupils of his friend Hegius, found that of Erasmus the best of all, and was particularly struck by the purity of the style, the aptness of the illustrations, and the ability displayed in the composition; and how he looked into his face, saying, "You will one day be a great man."[9] Another similar story tells much the same thing of John Sintheimius, or Zinthius, one of the best masters of the school, who is also said to have foretold the future eminence of his pupil. "Go on, Erasmus," said he, kissing him; "hereafter you will reach the highest pinnacle of learning."[10]

His studies at Deventer, however, were rudely interrupted, though not perhaps before he had learned all that the school could teach, by an outbreak of the plague. His mother, who had accompanied her son in order to watch over him, was one of the victims, and all the inmates of the house in which Erasmus lived were carried away. He of course returned to Tergouw.[11]

During this period of his life we may picture Erasmus as a quiet, thoughtful boy of delicate make, with the yellow hair and blue eyes of his country, fonder of his book or a discussion, grave or merry, with his schoolmates, than of their rougher sports; very precocious, and with abundance of that contempt which sharp boys always have for dullards; serious too, and disposed to a grave observance of all the little forms which religious parents taught their children in those days. Among

---

[9] VAL. ANDREAS: *Bibl. Belg.*
[10] BEAT. RHEN.: *Ep. Car. Cæs.*
[11] For the particulars of the parentage and childhood of Erasmus see the *Comp. Vit.* and the other sketches collected by Le Clerc: also the *Epistle of Baudius* in *Er. Op.* iii. 1916.

the Familiar Colloquies at least there is a charming dialogue, called " Youthful Piety," which describes a boy of this kind, and tells how, before he rises in the morning, he makes the sign of the cross, with his thumb, on his forehead and chest ; how, on his way to school, he looks into the church in order to salute Jesus and all the saints, and especially the Holy Virgin ; how careful he is to say grace before and after each meal ; and how, on going to bed, after having said his prayers, he places himself on his right side, with his arms folded across, so as to defend his breast with a figure of the cross, his right hand touching the left shoulder, and his left the right. Much of this, no doubt, may be fancy, but it is easy to believe that Erasmus has introduced some features from his own early recollections.

It was not long before Gerard followed Margaret to the grave, leaving his sons to the care of three guardians. Of the next few years of Erasmus' life we are fortunate in possessing an account from his own hands, in a letter which he wrote to the apostolic secretary with a view of procuring from Pope Leo X. a release from his monastic vows.[12] According to this letter, his father had left behind him a small property, part of which, however, was plundered by the relatives who stood by the bedside of the dying man, while of the remainder, which would still have been sufficient to secure the best education for the two boys, a considerable part was lost through the negligence of those to whose care it had been entrusted. Indeed, Gerard had been unfortunate in the selection of guardians for his sons. One of them was a merchant, and took very

---

[12] *Erasmus Rot. Lamberto Grunnio, Scribæ Apostolico.—Er. Op.* iii. 1821, *sqq.*

little trouble in the matter. The second before long died suddenly of the plague. The third—Peter Winckel, the schoolmaster of the place—seems to have been a mixture of the fanatic and the hypocrite. He was one of a class of persons, too numerous at that time, who made it a business of their lives to work upon the feelings of innocent boys and girls, to prevail upon them to enter the monasteries, using for this purpose all kinds of allurements, but taking care to select for their victims those who were likely to bring wealth to the Church. Upright and pious in the eyes of the world, he was at heart thoroughly selfish, a miser, and without any taste for literature. Erasmus and his brother were now ripe for the university; they were good grammarians and had gone through most of the logic; but the opportunity of sacrificing two such victims was not to be lost by the schoolmaster, who actually used to boast how many youths he had dedicated each year to the male and female saints who presided over the different monastic orders. So, fearing to send his wards where they might imbibe a worldly spirit and be encouraged to reject the yoke he was preparing for them, he resolved that they should go back to school. No wonder if Erasmus was disgusted. He had learned all that Deventer could teach him, and, young as he was, was looking forward with delight to the opportunities for more extended study which a university would afford. The school to which he was now consigned, at Bolduc in Brabant, though belonging to the same fraternity, had not the celebrity of Deventer. It is no wonder if Erasmus, looking back at the two years which he lost there, and anxious also to represent his own case in the strongest colours, did not give these places of education the best of characters. They were nothing more, in his estimation, than a kind of nursery from which the different orders of monks were replenished; and as that was the object which the "brethren" had in view, they paid more attention to disciplining their pupils—or *taming* them, as they called it—by blows and threats, than to the culture of their minds. The teachers, he adds, were chosen without regard to literary qualifications. Their libraries were for the most part destitute of classical works. The greater part of the day was spent in manual labour and prayers; and the result of all this was, that nowhere else were boys turned out worse taught or worse mannered. When Erasmus entered the school at Bolduc, he knew more than his teachers, one of whom, he says, was a prodigy of ignorance and conceit. Another, named Romboldus, was a kindly man, and took a strong fancy to him. He wished to prevail upon him to join the order, which he might have done without committing himself for life, as the vows were not perpetual. But Erasmus had no taste for it. Romboldus exhorted, entreated him; he bribed him with presents; he hugged and kissed him; but without effect. The boy answered, with more wisdom than belonged to his years, that he knew neither the kind of life he was asked to adopt nor his own mind, but that when he was older he would consider the matter.

In consequence of the plague having broken out in the school where they were, the two brothers were compelled to return home. Meantime their small property had been further impaired by the neglect, if not by the actual dishonesty, of their guardians. This circumstance made it peculiarly convenient to carry out the scheme which Winckel already had in view for them, the monasteries indeed furnishing, at that time, only too ready a means of disposing of young men who were likely otherwise to prove troublesome to their friends; and to a monastery, accordingly, it was determined they should be sent at once. Erasmus, however, had seen quite enough to suspect that the monastic life would not suit him, and resolved to resist. His first step was to secure an ally in his elder brother, who, being of a much weaker character, would have yielded, not, as he admitted, from religious motives, but from fear. "What a fool you are," urged Erasmus, "if for fear of men, who, at any rate, will not venture to strike you, you commit yourself to a kind of life of which you know nothing, and from which, once you have entered upon it, there is no retreat!" At length it was agreed that the question of the monastery should be deferred, and that in the meantime three or four years should be spent in study, Peter stipulating only that his brother would act as spokesman. A few days after, the guardian arrived, and with many professions of affection announced that he had been fortunate enough to find a place for them among the Canons Regular, of the order of St. Augustine, in their principal college of Sion, near Delft. Erasmus thanked him for his kindness, but added that he and his brother thought themselves too young and inexperienced to bind themselves to any particular plan of life. They had never been inside a monastery. They could not even guess what sort of a creature a monk was. They thought it far better to spend some years first in study, and then it would be time enough to consider the proposal. On receiving this answer, for which he was quite unprepared, Winckel fairly lost control of himself. He became frantic with rage. Though naturally of a gentle disposition, or appearing to be so, he could scarcely hold his hands. "So then," he cried, "I've thrown away my pains in begging such a capital place for you! You are a good-for-nothing fellow. I renounce my charge: see and provide yourself with the means of livelihood." He added that he would not even be responsible to those from whom he had been buying their food, and that their property was all gone. His threats drew tears from Erasmus, but could not move him from his purpose. Finding this to be the case, Winckel now called to his aid his brother guardian, a man of extraordinary suavity of temper. Quite a different method of persuasion was adopted. The boys were invited into the summer-house and desired to sit down; wine was called for; and after a friendly chat, the subject was again introduced. A charming picture was painted of monastic happiness; the ambition of the young men was appealed to; entreaties even were not spared. The elder brother gave way, and, notwithstanding the promises he had repeatedly made to stand firm, bent his neck to the yoke. Luckily for him, his constitution was as strong as his wit was heavy, and if there was nothing in his character to qualify him for a religious life according to any just notions of what it ought to be, he was much better adapted to consort with the ordinary monks of the time—to endure the dull routine of monastic life, and join in the heavy drinking-bouts by which its monotony was relieved—than the light-witted, eager student, Erasmus. He afterwards gave himself up to dissipation, and died unlamented by his brother, who found it difficult to trace in him any marks of a common parentage.[13] Erasmus, on the contrary, was of a delicate frame, and had been suffering for more than a year from a quartan fever. He was now just fifteen, and thus young and weakened by disease, he was plied with arguments and representations by all sorts of persons whom his guardian had stirred up to take his side in the contest. One drew a lovely picture of the peace and harmony of the monastic life, picking out exclu-

---

[13] In the letter to Grunnius, Erasmus, describing his brother under the name of Antonius, as he calls himself Florentius, gives him no very good character:—"Atque illi quidem pulchre cessit res. Erat enim ut ingenio tardus, ita corpore robustus, attentus ad rem, ibi vafer et callidus, pecuniarum furax, strenuus compotor, nec scortator ignavus ; in summa adeo minori dissimilis, ut supposititius videri posset. Nec enim unquam aliud fuit germano quam malus genius. Non ita multo post, hoc munus gessit inter suos sodales, quod Iscariotes inter Apostolos. Is tamen ubi vidit fratrem misere illaqueatum, tactus conscientiæ stimulis deplorabat, quod eum in nassam protractum perdidisset. Audis Judæ confessionem, et utinam ad illius exemplum sese suspendisset, antequam facinus hoc tam impium admitteret." The whole letter is written in a somewhat extravagant tone, as if the object were to prevail with the Pope by putting him in a good humour, and showing him what a clever fellow Erasmus was, rather than by convincing his reason by a temperate statement of facts. I might agree with Hess (*Erasmus von Roterdam*, vol. i. p. 26, note) that Antonius was really a school-fellow of Erasmus, whom he represents as a brother, did we not possess a letter inscribed, "Erasmus Domino Petro germano suo" (*Er. Op.* iii. 1859). Besides, in a letter written from Basle in 1527, Erasmus refers to the death of his brother in words which agree sufficiently with the bad character given of Antonius :—" Fratris germani mortem moderatissime tuli" (*Er. Op.* iii. 1053, E). How Hess can quote these words—unless he proposed to read "tulissem "—and at the same time deny the existence of the brother, I cannot understand. We find, too, from a letter of P. Merula, prefixed to vol. iii. of Le Clerc's *Erasmus*, that William Hermann dedicated a poem on the Praise of Friendship to Peter Gerard of Rotterdam, brother of Erasmus, " virum tum perhumanum, tum eruditissimum : " a fact which proves either the worthlessness of dedications, or that Peter, the son of Gerard, was not so black as his brother painted him.

sively the agreeable features. Another dwelt very pathetically on the dangers of this world, as if, says Erasmus sarcastically, the monks were out of the world; which, however, they would no doubt have us believe, since they paint themselves as safe in a stout ship, and all the rest of mankind as tossed about on the waves and ready to perish unless *they* reach out to them a pole or a rope. Another described the tortures of the infernal regions, as if, he again adds, there was no way to hell from the monasteries. Another tried to frighten him with monkish stories—for instance, of a traveller who sat down on the back of a dragon, mistaking it for the trunk of a tree: the dragon awoke, turned back his head, and devoured the traveller: *moral*, thus the world eats up its children;—or of a man who had left a monkish society, resisting all entreaties to remain, and been in consequence torn in pieces by a lion. Even at the age of fifteen, Erasmus was not likely to be much affected by stories such as these. Others tried a different sort, which perhaps were not any more to his taste; how there was a monk with whom Christ used to converse for some hours every day; how Catherine of Sienna enjoyed such intimacy with Christ her betrothed, that they used to walk up and down her bed-chamber and repeat prayers together by the hour. Unable to hold out continually against the pertinacity, rather than the arguments, of those about him, he at last began to waver. Just then he happened to visit another monastery belonging to the order to which he had been already recommended, that of Steyn, not far from Tergouw, and there he fell in with an old friend named Cornelius Werden, who had been brought up with him from childhood, had probably been a fellow-chorister with him at Utrecht, and had shared the same bed-room at Deventer. Cornelius had taken the hood, not from motives of piety, but for the sake of the ease and self-indulgence of the monastic life, and also because his parents were poor. He was some years older than Erasmus, but being dull and backward in his studies, and yet not, it would seem, without ambition to improve, he thought how useful his old companion might be made if he could once more have him at his side. For this end, therefore, he exerted all his eloquence. He described the peace, the harmony, the freedom of the monastery. It was a society of angels. There he would have an abundance of books and ample leisure for study. Induced by these representations and by a revived affection for the friend of his childhood, but still more because he was quite wearied out by the importunities of his guardians, who continued to threaten him with poverty and even starvation unless he would " renounce the world," as they phrased it, the poor youth at last took the leap, and became an inmate of the Augustinian house of Steyn. Still he did not abandon hope. A year must pass before he could be required to assume the dress of the order, and another before he took those vows which were to bind him to it for ever. He clung to the fond but delusive expectation, as it proved to be, that some happy chance would occur within that period to restore him to his liberty. Meantime, every indulgence was allowed him in order to reconcile him as far as possible to his new situation. The fasts were not strictly exacted, nor was he compelled to attend the midnight services. He had the society of companions of his own age. No one reproved, no one gave him advice; every one smiled upon him. His studies, too, made rapid progress. Sometimes he read to his friend a whole play of Terence in a single night, and within a few months they went together through several of the leading classical authors. These midnight lessons no doubt told upon his health, and, combined with what he had already endured and with the unwholesome situation of the monastery, may have laid the foundation of the diseases from which he suffered all his life; their effect, however, was unperceived or neglected at the time. And now the hour had arrived when the odious monkish dress must be put on. The guardians were summoned. Threats were once more resorted to. Cornelius, not wishing to lose so valuable a teacher, added his entreaties. Erasmus continued to resist, but, notwithstanding his protestations, he was compelled to submit and receive the Augustinian gown and hood. Another year went by not unpleasantly, the monks pursuing their former policy of showing their captive as much indulgence as was consistent with the rules of the house; but Erasmus only became more convinced than ever that he was unfitted both mentally and physically for a monastic life. He saw here no honour paid to learning; but, on the contrary, a disposition to extinguish eminent genius, and give the superiority to mere brute force. The prospect of spending his days among those coarse-grained men, and submitting to all their wearisome ceremonies, in a place where he would be obliged to pursue his studies in secret, though he might get drunk as openly as he pleased, was intolerable to him. Besides, with his delicate constitution, how was he to endure the fasts and watches which the superstition of the monks probably led them to observe with sufficient fidelity? His health required that he should eat often and in small quantities. He had the greatest dislike for fish, and even the smell of it gave him a headache. He could not go to sleep until late in the evening—the result, no doubt, of his own late studies—and if once disturbed, it was some hours before sleep would again visit him. But what could such considerations avail him now that he had actually "put his head into the noose?" The holy fathers saw that they had caught a prize, and they were resolved not to let it go. They represented these weaknesses as a device of Satan to undermine the faith of the young probationer, and assured him that if he would bravely overcome them, everything else would be easy and pleasant. They urged upon him that it would be a sin before Heaven, as well as infamous in the eyes of the world, should he now refuse to take the vows. It was too late to retreat; he had put his hand to the plough, and he must not look back: the assumption of the dress was itself a silent profession. They threatened him with the wrath of St. Augustine, who would assuredly avenge the insult offered him. They told him horrible stories, which even to Erasmus at the early age he then was may have sounded less absurd than they would to any schoolboy of our own day—how one man who had similarly gone back had fallen into an incurable disease, another had been killed by lightning, a third had died of the bite of a viper. Finally, they denounced him as an apostate. "Where will you go?" they cried. "You will never be able to come into the presence of good men; you will be execrated by monks and hated by the world." Nothing influenced him so much as the dread of shame. Besides, the force of circumstances was against him. He found himself quite helpless, without a friend to take his part. He did not know if he had a penny in the world. He had fought a hard battle, but for the present at least he was overcome. The fatal words were pronounced, and Erasmus was a monk.

Such is the spirited account which Erasmus himself has left—I have done little more than translate and abridge it—of his long resistance to the yoke of monasticism. It may seem surprising that a mere boy should have displayed so much wisdom, but it must be remembered he was a boy of extraordinary acuteness. Still one cannot help perceiving that he has made the most of his case. Possibly, subsequent experience was permitted to colour his narrative. Possibly his resistance was scarcely so determined, or his feelings so strong, as he chose afterwards to represent them. However that may be, the next half-dozen years of his life were spent in the monastery of Steyn, not without profit; perhaps also,—notwithstanding his dislike of the discipline which, now that he was caught, was strictly enforced,—not without some degree of inward satisfaction. One congenial spirit at least he met with here in William Hermann, with whom he formed a lifelong friendship. Both were animated by the same zeal for literature. They studied together, spending every spare hour by day or by night in reading the Latin classics. And such was their ardour that they even excited, it is said, some literary enthusiasm in the lazy, drunken herd in whose society their lot was cast. Erasmus, however, did not altogether escape the temptations incident to monastic life. Drunkenness he always detested; and perhaps no merit can be ascribed to him for avoiding a sin to which he had no inclination, and for which he was constitution-

ally unfit. But he confesses that he was at one time
"inclined to great vices,"[14] adding, that "if there had
been over him a superior of a truly Christian character,
and not one full of Jewish superstitions, he might have
been brought to yield excellent fruit." What those
great vices were, and how far his language implies that
he had yielded to temptation, the reader may be left to
decide. At all events, allowance should be made for a
strong expression; and if the monks were really as bad as
Erasmus describes them, the example he was compelled
daily to witness may fairly be pleaded on his behalf.

During his residence in the monastery, Erasmus, as
a young man full of classical enthusiasm, and anxious
to use every means of improving his taste, naturally
began to exercise his pen in various directions, and, like
other young authors, at first devoted himself chiefly to
the cultivation of the Muse; so much so, indeed, that it
was with some reluctance, he tells us, that he afterwards
turned to prose composition. According to his own
account, he left no species of verse unattempted. A
bucolic poem in imitation of Virgil, which was not
published till after his death, was written at Deventer
when he was not yet fourteen, and already gave evidence of imagination and command of language.[15] It
was probably in Steyn that he wrote, among other
similar effusions, a Sapphic ode in praise of the
archangel Michael,[16] of which he tells an amusing

---

[14] "Nec diffiteor me ad magna vitia fuisse propensum."—*Patri Servatio Erasmus.*

[15] *D. Erasmi Roterodami Bucolicon, lectu digniss. Cum scholiis Alardi Æmstelredami, cujus studio nunc primum et repertum et æditum est. Coloniæ ex. off. Heronis Alopecii, An.* 1539. *Er. Op.* viii. 561. For the title I am indebted to M. Ch. Ruelens, in his preliminary notice to the *Silva Carminum*, p. 18.

[16] *Er. Op.* v. 1321.

anecdote. The poem was written at the request of a certain important personage, priest of a church dedicated to S. Michael; but, although its style had been purposely restrained from any very daring flights of poetry, this gentleman was afraid to put it up on the walls of his church because he considered it so poetical that it was in danger of being mistaken for Greek! So, after all his trouble, the poem was sent back to the author, and with it, as compensation for the time he had spent upon it, the price of a bottle of wine. For this most liberal gift he returned his best thanks, but begged, however, to decline it, on the ground that it was much too handsome a present for such an humble person as himself.[17] His intimacy with Hermann, who was himself a poet of considerable merit, and afterwards became known to the world by a collection of odes and some other works, no doubt encouraged Erasmus in his efforts to excel in verse composition, and there remains to us an ode in honour of spring, composed in alternate couplets by the two friends as they strolled through the fields in the neighbourhood of the convent. We have also three satires by Erasmus, which he left in the hands of Hermann on his departure from Steyn, and which were printed several years afterwards at Tergouw, no doubt without the consent of the author.[18]

Fortunately Erasmus did not confine himself to attempts at verse composition. He was already laying the foundation of that brilliant prose style which, when

---

[17] *Cat. Luc.*

[18] *Herasmi Roterodami Silva Carminum antehac nunquam impressorum.* Gouda, 1513. The edition of M. Ch. Ruelens, of which only one hundred copies were printed, is a photo-lithographic fac-simile of the original. The poems in this volume have not been preserved by Le Clerc.

it became the vehicle of his great learning or his biting wit, was to make his name famous throughout Europe. Among youthful compositions in prose we have still a " Funeral Oration on Bertha de Heyen, a most excellent widow," to whom he had been frequently indebted for advice and consolation, as well as for more substantial assistance, and who had treated him with as much kindness as her own children.[19] But the most remarkable of these productions is the treatise on " Contempt of the World." [20] This essay, which attracted considerable attention during his lifetime, was written as an exercise when the author was barely twenty. It is interesting as showing how thoroughly his mind was imbued with the works of the great Roman writers, and how perfectly he had already formed his style by the study of the best models. It is clear that by this time he had Ovid, Virgil, and Juvenal at his fingers' ends, as well as Terence and Horace, and Cicero must have been a daily and nightly companion. This composition is interesting, too, as showing that Erasmus, when he pleased, could plead the cause of monasticism against " the world," and dwell eloquently upon the advantages it conferred. It would be rash, however, to infer from this that he was altogether reconciled to his situation— though the quiet of the monastery and the opportunities it afforded for study may probably have been some compensation for its restraints—or that he had not yet conceived his enmity to the system. As a rhetorician he would naturally wish to be able, when occasion required, to make the worse appear the better reason, and to support his adversary's side no less strongly than his own. Besides, he was not writing in his own name,

---

[19] *Er. Op.* viii. 552, E. [20] *De Contemtu Mundi. Er. Op.* v. 1239, *sqq.*

but in the name of a friend who had requested him to compose an address to a nephew whom he wished to persuade to take the hood. Nor, after all, does he conclude without some strong words against the monasteries. He ends with a vigorous passage, which may or may not have belonged to the essay in its original form, stating that many of them are mere schools of irreligion, in which it is impossible to live a pure or upright life; and finally reminds his reader that it will matter little whether he be a monk or no, provided he is a Christian.

The classical studies of Erasmus were naturally looked upon with great jealousy by the brethren of his order, who were accustomed to condemn all profane learning under the name of "poetry," and would raise the finger of warning against any one having a literary reputation, crying out "Beware; that man is a poet, he is no Christian!"[81] It was to expose such ignorant attacks, as well as to refute the more solid objections which might be urged by thoughtful men, that he began, when he was not yet twenty, a work entitled, "The Antibarbarians," which some few years afterwards he threw into the form of a dialogue and extended to four books. Of these, however, only the first remains, and that not in the original form.[82] It is an eloquent defence of classical learning; but, as we have it now, it is probably a great improvement on the first youthful composition, having been re-written when the author was advanced in life. Though the work becomes tedious to the modern reader who does not require to be convinced, he may discover from it the kind of arguments that were employed by

[81] *Er. Op.* ix. 1700, C.
[82] *Anti-barbarorum Liber Primus.* *Er. Op.* ix. 1691, *sqq.*

the enemies of learning. Classical studies were condemned as immoral and anti-Christian. The monks recommended that instead of resorting to the heathen poets—and under that designation they included Cicero and Livy no less than Virgil and Ovid—the student should derive his Latin from the Psalter, or from the barbarous grammars and handbooks which, under such ridiculous names as the Pearl, the Little Gem, the Garden of Roses, and so on, were then in favour. We find also that they relied a good deal upon such texts of Scripture as they could pervert to their purpose, and especially upon St. Paul's words, " Knowledge puffeth up."

Besides the Latin classical authors, the works of Laurentius Valla, and some of the other distinguished Italian scholars of the beginning of the century, were at this time read with avidity. Valla, as a denouncer of the usurpations of the Church, as an ardent promoter of classical learning, and as a critic of the New Testament, has been justly recognized as a forerunner of Erasmus.[23] The latter, when about eighteen, at the request of a certain schoolmaster, perhaps Peter Winckel himself, epitomized a work of Valla's designed to introduce the student to the niceties of the Latin language, and in consequence conceived the greatest admiration for the writer as absolutely unmatched for the subtlety of his intellect and the excellence of his memory.[24] The work shared the fate of some others of his youthful efforts,

---

[23] See MÜLLER, pp. 121, 122, where he draws out the parallel with much care.

[24] " Porro in elegantiarum observantiis nemini æque fidem habeo atque Laurentio Vallensi ; cui quem alium et ingenii acumine, et memoriæ tenacitate conferamus, non habemus."—*Er. Op.* iii. 1794, F.

by getting into print without his knowlege or consent, and in so corrupt a form, that in self-defence he was compelled to re-write it only two years before his death. His admiration for Valla involved him in a friendly controversy with a brother monk, Cornelius Lopsen of Tergouw, uncle to William Hermann, with whom he for some time carried on a pretty close correspondence.[25] Cornelius was a man of learning, but he probably desired to make learning subservient to the interests of the Church, and may even have dreaded the influence of the studies to which he was devoted. So at least we might infer from the fact that he was the author of a poem on the life of the Virgin, and entitled the *Mariad*, in no less than thirty books, which must now unhappily (or happily, as the reader may prefer) be counted among those works which the world has lost. The poet, as he himself informs us, had almost broken down at the termination of the sixth book, and as he contemplated the vastness of his enterprise, felt inclined to abandon it in despair. A young Canon Regular, however, of the name of Erasmus, whom he describes as strictly religious and the most accomplished man of his time in both verse and prose composition, encouraged him to persevere, constantly repeating to him that line of Virgil which tells us that labour conquers every obstacle.[26] Thus their friendship was cemented. Cornelius, replying to the praises bestowed upon Valla by Erasmus, does not fail to quote the witty epigram of Poggius :—

> Nunc postquam Manes defunctus Valla petivit,
> Non audet Pluto verba Latina loqui ;
> Jupiter hunc superis dignatus honore fuisset,
> Censorem linguæ sed timet ipse suæ.

---

[25] *Ep.* ccccvii.—ccccxix. App. pp. 16, 17), has disinterred those
[26] M. Ch. Ruelens (*ubi supra*, particulars. He points out (p. 25,

And in another letter, having called Valla "a croaking raven," Erasmus playfully threatens him with internecine warfare until he abandons that phrase, and substitutes for it the titles of "Attic muse" and "the marrow of persuasion." Another letter defends Valla from the charge of having been unduly severe in his criticisms, and claims for him the merit of having, "with vast industry, zeal, and labour, driven back the tide of barbarism, rescued literature from destruction, and restored to Italy the splendour of her ancient eloquence."

The correspondence with Cornelius proves that Erasmus had already formed that high appreciation of St. Jerome which he carried with him through life. He says he had found in Jerome's letters, the whole of which he had copied out with his own fingers, and which had supplied him with many a weapon against the assaults of the barbarians, a proof that vulgarity is not holiness, nor an elegant style the same thing with impiety.[27]

Thus, it will be seen, the years spent in the convent of Steyn were by no means unprofitable. They were, in fact, the best possible preparation both for the university and for that great conflict with the forces of superstition and ignorance in which the young Augustinian was to bear so conspicuous a part. The time has now almost come when the doors must be opened and

---

note), no less ingeniously than justly, that Aurelius, a surname of this Cornelius, is simply a Latinization of *van Gouda* (*Goud*, gold), while Aurotinus, which we find in the first letter from Erasmus, is another form devised by the latter.

[27] "Qui si Hieronymianas epistolas recte adspicerent, intelligerent utique rusticitatem sanctimoniam non esse; nec disertitudinem, impietatem. Quod autem ad eas lectitandas me invitas, habeo gratissimum. Jam olim tamen eas non modo legi, sed et quotquot sunt propriis ipse descripsi articulis, in quibus," etc. *Er. Op.* iii. 1795, E.

the captive released; but, meantime, there is one anecdote of convent life which has been frequently repeated, and which must not be passed over here; though whether it has been invented for lack of better material, or rests upon an authentic foundation, it would be unavailing to inquire. In the garden of the monastery, it is said, there grew a pear-tree bearing fruit of so fine a flavour that the prior thought it too good for any palate less refined than his own, and accordingly had given directions that it should be strictly reserved. It so happened, however, that Erasmus was also fond of pears, and was in the habit of going at night to rob the tree, which circumstance, occasioning a rapid disappearance of the fruit, induced the prior to resolve on lying in wait for the thief. So, early one morning he stationed himself at the window of his cell, and in the dusk detected one of the brethren in the tree feasting on the very choicest of his pears, but was unable to distinguish the features of Erasmus. The latter, hearing a noise, perceived that he was observed, and made haste to descend; but fearing lest the prior should follow him, he resolved to spare him the trouble, and at the same time save himself from punishment, by directing suspicion at once to an innocent person. He retreated at a leisurely pace, but limping as he went, and the prior, satisfied that he had discovered the culprit in the person of a lay-brother who was lame, forbore to pursue. When day came the monks were assembled; the limping brother was directly charged with the theft; the evidence, of course, was considered conclusive, and, in spite of his protests, the unlucky fellow was condemned to a severe penance.[28]

[28] LE CLERC, in *Bibl. Univ.* vii. p. 140, is the only authority for this story.

At last, after he had spent many years as an unwilling inmate of the convent of Steyn, apparently about the year 1491, deliverance unexpectedly arrived. Henry à Bergis, Bishop of Cambray, was intending to go to Rome to look for a cardinal's hat, and wished to take with him a scholarly man as his secretary and companion. It was precisely the opportunity that Erasmus longed for. Nicolas Werner, the prior of the convent, seeing how little suited he was by nature to the monastic life, had frequently advised him to seek some such opportunity, and now the Bishop of Cambray, having heard of his accomplishments, was anxious that his services should be secured. The consent of the Bishop of Utrecht, in whose diocese Steyn was situated, and of the general of the order, was obtained, and Erasmus bade farewell to the convent, leaving no regret behind save the inevitable separation from his dear friend Hermann. The Bishop, as it turned out, did not go to Rome, finding that he could not afford it; but he notwithstanding took the poor scholar under his protection, and promised him a pension to enable him to pursue his studies. This was intended to be paid, according to the custom of the time, independently of any services rendered. Such was the way in which literary men were supported in those days. The position would seem to us one of dependence; but where a munificent patron gave freely in acknowledgment of services so universally beneficial as those of literature, and exacted no return but a continuance of the same labour, there was nothing in it discreditable to either party. Erasmus, however, was unfortunate in his first patron: the Bishop was not wealthy, and the pension was not regularly paid.

CHAPTER II.

Erasmus at Cambray—The University of Paris—Montaigu—Takes Pupils—Mountjoy—Grey—The Lady de Vere—Erasmus in Difficulties—Visits the Castle of Tornenhens—In Paris again—Vow to St. Geneviève—A Battle Royal—Satire on the Scotists.

WHEN Erasmus entered the household of the Bishop of Cambray he was a young man of some four-and-twenty, of small but well-built and elegant person, with a pleasant expression of countenance, and of grave deportment, as became his profession. His blue eyes, light brown or yellowish hair, and fair complexion marked his German origin. His voice was thin and weak, but his pronunciation was beautifully accurate. The expression of his face might indicate something of natural timidity, while the pointed nose and large flexible mouth, which must have been much the same then as they were afterwards when Holbein drew them, marked the shrewd observer and the keen humourist. His naturally delicate constitution had not been strengthened by the discipline of a convent or the unhealthy influences to which it had been exposed among the marshes of Holland; and all through life he was subject to and easily affected by slight external changes, as of food or climate.[1] He was by this time, as we

[1] "Corpusculo satis compacto et eleganti, sed quod esset tenerrimæ complexionis, et minimarum etiam rerum mutatione, puta vini, cibi

have seen, an accomplished Latin scholar, and could already write that language probably with more elegance than any of his contemporaries. Of Greek he knew little, perhaps not more than the mere elements of the grammar, not having resumed its study since his boyhood. He had as yet gone through no systematic training in theology, though we may presume that his desultory reading in the convent library had embraced many of the Fathers, and at all events we know he had some acquaintance with Jerome and Augustine. Above all, he had not yet studied the scholastic philosophy, so essential in those days to the thoroughly equipped theologian; and, accordingly, being disappointed for the present in his hopes of going to Italy, he naturally sought the nearest university, that of Paris, in order to complete his education, the Bishop furnishing him with funds for the journey. His want of a university training, however, was no hindrance to his taking priest's orders; he was ordained by the Bishop of Utrecht, in whose diocese Steyn was situated, on the 25th of April, 1492.[2] At Cambray the sweetness of his manners and the charms of his conversation won him many friends, among whom are particularly mentioned James Battus, subsequently a frequent correspondent, and Anthony à Bergis, the Bishop's brother and Abbot of St. Bertin.

cœlive, facile offenderetur ... Cute corporis et faciei candida, capillitio in juventa sufflavo, oculis cæsiis, vultu festivo, voce exili, lingua pulchre explicita, cultu honesto et gravi, qui Cæsareum Consiliarium, Theologum et Sacerdotem deceret." Beat. Rhen. *Ep. Car. Cæs.*

[2] VAL. ANDREAS: *Bibl. Belg.* *Er. Op.* ix. 1573, A. The biographers of Erasmus give this date as Feb. 25, 1492 (Müller, p. 160, &c.); but the words of Valerius Andreas are: "Anno 1492, v. Kal. Maias, die S. Marco sacro, Sacerdos factus est." This would properly give April 27, but St. Mark's day is April 25.

The University of Paris was at this time one of the most renowned schools in Europe. Nevertheless, very little had been accomplished there for the revival of letters or the promotion of liberal studies. Rhetoric—which was understood to include the study of the classical writers, as well as the art of graceful composition—having been long almost entirely neglected, had for some years past been respectably represented by Robert Gaguin, the author of a history of France, and a man not indeed of very profound learning, nor by any means perfect as a writer of Latin, but of elevated mind and noble character. Since 1458 there had been a Greek chair, and the first professor, Gregory of Tiferno, was now replaced by George Hermonymus of Sparta, according to Erasmus, a most incompetent teacher.[3] In 1489, just two or three years before the arrival of Erasmus in Paris, three foreigners, Faustus Andrelinus, Jerome Balbus, and Cornelius Vitellius, requested permission to give lessons in *belles lettres*, and obtained it, with the restriction, however, suggested by the jealousy of the scholastics, that it should be for only one hour in the evening. Andrelinus, an Italian, and the best known of the three, was a man of loose life and boundless vanity, who, in order to fill his class-room, undertook to give lectures on the sphere, the canon law, and other subjects of which his knowledge was extremely insufficient; and when he lectured upon his proper subjects, of which he may be supposed to have known something—he was himself an indifferent poet, and when only twenty had

[3] "Lutetiæ tantum unus Georgius Hermonymus Græce balbutiebat, sed talis, ut neque potuisset docere si voluisset; neque voluisset, si potuisset."—*Cat. Luc.*

been crowned Laureate at Rome—he sought to gain applause by ill-timed jests rather than by a serious endeavour to communicate knowledge and taste;[4] so that on the whole the advantages held out to the student desirous of liberal culture were not very great. On the other hand, the scholastic philosophy still reigned supreme, as it had done for upwards of two hundred years. The Nominalists, who must be regarded as representing in that age the freer side of speculation, having been proscribed for some time by Louis XI., though again permitted to teach, did not enjoy much influence. The Realists, in their two divisions of Thomists and Scotists—the followers of St. Thomas Aquinas and the followers of Duns Scotus—filled the schools, and the principal seat of the Scotist philosophy was the College of Montaigu, in which the poverty of

[4] " Nam Faustus Andrelinus alioqui carminibus magna cura pangendis intentus, defunctorie profitebatur, jocis quibusdam magis festivis quam doctis, plausum rudium auditorum captans. Gaguinus obeundis legationibus ad exteros Principes occupatus erat, in istis studiis non ita prorsum absolutus ; nec docebat publice."— Beat. Rhen. *ubi supra*. Crevier (*Histoire de l'Université de Paris*, vol. iv. p. 249) says that Gaguin gave lessons in rhetoric, but he may, no doubt, as Rhenanus says, have ceased to lecture publicly before the arrival of Erasmus. He was certainly looked up to as the principal restorer of humane learning in the University of Paris. Erasmus himself says, in writing to him : " Testis abunde est hoc celebratissimum Gymnasium urbis Parisiorum, cujus tu florentissime alioquin studia primus Latinarum litterarum opibus decorasti, pulcherrimoque incremento eloquentiæ, quam unam adhuc desiderare videbantur, adauxisti."— *Er. Op.* iii. 1818, C. Erasmus gave Andrelinus a very bad character after his death. " Cum Faustum dico, multa tibi succurrunt, quæ nolim literis committere. Qua petulantia solitus est ille in Theologorum ordinem debacchari ? Quam non caste erat illius professio ? Neque cuiquam obscurum erat qualis esset vita. Tantum malorum Galli doctrinæ hominis condonabant, quæ tamen ultra mediocritatem non admodum erat progressa."—*Er. Op.* iii. 535, F. Conf. Bayle, and Crevier, iv. 439.

Erasmus compelled him for a time to seek a home. This college, occupying, it is said, the site on which the Library of St. Geneviève now stands, opposite the Panthéon, was founded in the year 1314, but derived its chief celebrity from a poor priest named John Standonck, who was appointed Principal and Rector successively in 1483 and 1485, and who, having found the college in the utmost state of dilapidation, built a chapel and a library, and lodgings for eighty-four bursars, for whose subsistence he also provided. Standonck had himself in youth struggled with the extremest poverty, maintaining himself at the university by discharging the most menial offices in the house of St. Geneviève, while at night—it is said, the only time he had for study—he would mount the church-steeple, in order to read by moonlight. Thus trained, his sympathies were naturally with the scholar of humble means, and he saw with sorrow that the bursaries founded for the poor were frequently appropriated by those who were well enough able to pay for their own education. On becoming Rector of Montaigu, partly to remedy this abuse by deterring wealthy young men from the college, partly, no doubt, because he himself had faith in the good effects of ascetic discipline, he subjected his pupils to the hardest possible life, and to the most humiliating practices. They were compelled to observe all the fasts of the Church, and for any breach of discipline the punishment was cruelly severe. They rose early and attended frequent mass. They had to work in the kitchen, serve in the refectory, sweep the hall, the chapel, the dormitory, the stairs.[5] At table flesh-meat was an unknown luxury, and the supply even of bread was strictly

[5] Crevier, vol. v. pp. 20—25.

limited. The only approach to substantial fare was eggs, and these were usually rotten. Quantities of them, however, were devoured. Those who were thirsty had to fetch bad water for themselves from the well, or if a little wine were allowed it was such wretched stuff as to be scarcely drinkable. The accommodation at night was even worse: the beds were hard and damp, the bed-rooms were on the ground without flooring, only sprinkled over with a thin coating of plaster-of-Paris, and some of them even in such evil neighbourhood that to sleep in them was certain to be followed either by death or by some deadly disorder.[6] In this wretched place Erasmus passed some time—he could not have endured it very long—and among such associations it is no wonder if he did not fall in love with the Scotist philosophy. He would no doubt have discovered its barrenness without any such assistance, but memories of rotten eggs and bad wine may have lent a sting to the invectives which he was ever afterwards ready to pour out upon its professors.

The effect of this bad living on the sickly frame of the delicate student was, as may be supposed, an accession of disease, which compelled him once more to seek shelter under the roof of the friendly Bishop.[7] There he was kindly received, and a letter, which evidently belongs to this second visit to Cambray, gives an interesting account of the state of his feelings. He had been suffering severely, he informs his correspondent, Arnold, perhaps More's friend, for a month and a half from a nocturnal fever, which had well-nigh carried him off. "There is nothing I wish for now," he continues, "but that time may be given me to devote

[6] *Coll. Fam.*, 'Ιχθυοφάγια.   [7] *Compendium Vitæ.*

myself entirely to God, weep over sins which I committed when I was yet without wisdom, familiarise myself with the Holy Scriptures, and spend my time in reading and writing. This I cannot do in the retirement of a monastery. For I am the most delicate creature in the world; my health will not bear either watchings or fastings, or any discomforts, even at its best. Here, where I live in such luxury, I am continually falling ill; what would become of me among the diseases incident to the monastic life? I had resolved this year to go to Italy, and give some months to theology at Bologna, and there take my Doctor's degree, then, in the year of Jubilee, visit Rome, and, having done so, return to my brethren and settle with them. But I fear I shall not be able to carry out this plan.[8]

He did not go to Italy at present, being prevented by the state of his health, which made him shrink from the fatigue of the journey, and by his poverty. The Bishop, he complains, gave very stingily, being much more liberal in his promises than his performances, and so on his recovery, after paying a short visit to his native country, he returned to Paris,[9] resolved thenceforth to pursue his studies independently, and maintain

---

[8] *Ep.* iii. The reference to the year of Jubilee, which would be 1500, as near at hand, shows that the date 1490 affixed to this letter is too early. It is, probably, at least a few years later.

[9] The biographers of Erasmus have generally assumed that he went to Paris for the first time in 1496, thus giving him five or six years at Cambray, and only one or two for his university studies previous to his first visit to England (*see* Müller, p. 161; Butler, p. 43; Hess, p. 42), relying no doubt on the fact that the first letter we have from Paris bears the date 1496. But this, besides being intrinsically improbable, is at variance with the statement of Erasmus himself, that he had written the treatise, *De Conscribendis Epistolis*, at Paris, about thirty years ago. (See Preface in vol. i. to that treatise.) This statement being

himself by private tuition. By this time he had enough of friends to have no difficulty in obtaining pupils. The University of Paris was frequented by students from all parts of Europe, and it was no small advantage to parents to find a scholar like Erasmus to whose care they could entrust their sons. Such work, though, perhaps, a little below his ambition, suited him admirably. His extensive reading and tenacious memory furnished him with ample materials for literary conversation, and all but the dullest must have felt the contagion of his enthusiasm. Indeed, Erasmus must have been the most delightful of preceptors. Not only was his heart in his work, not only did he seek to make learning as attractive as possible by investing it with all the graces he had gathered in various fields of literature, but he seems to have conceived strong personal attachments to the young men put under his charge, treating them more as companions and equals than as pupils while they were with him, and keeping up correspondence with more than one of them after they had returned to their homes. The first connection which he formed of this kind, however, turned out very unhappily. He was induced to enter the household of an old man who had two young noblemen living with him, and who professed an ardent love of literature and an intention of taking holy orders. After a stay of some months a quarrel took place, with the result that Erasmus was turned out and obliged to seek a home elsewhere. From that time forth the unfortunate old

made in 1522, shows that he was at Paris as early as 1492, and I accordingly assume that he went there immediately after, perhaps before, his ordination, and that his stay with the Bishop of Cambray was not prolonged much beyond a year.

man became the object of the most virulent abuse on the part of his former instructor.[10] He appears in several of the letters of this period, and is described as so hideous a monster, physically and mentally, that it is a wonder how any one could ever have approached him. As he had both wealth and influence he was an object of real dread. He is nowhere mentioned by name, but always introduced with a certain air of mystery, and on one occasion with a request that what is said of him may not be repeated. His offence seems to have been that he had found fault with the conduct of Erasmus, and circulated calumnious reports regarding it. Probably, he was one who affected an austere piety —he is described as a consummate hypocrite,—and complained of some slight deviation from the monkish standard of virtue. Possibly there may have been lapses of conduct which furnished ground for serious accusation. Or there may have been nothing more than intense mutual dislike arising from complete in-

---

[10] *Ep.* vi. xx. xxxii. I cannot accept the conjecture of Burigni that this old man was no other than the Bishop of Cambray. How could Erasmus speak of him as intending to take orders (*Er. Op.* iii. 33, D), or how could he speak of himself as having been his preceptor ("docuit hominem aliquot menses." *Ib.*)? Besides, there is no evidence that Erasmus had any serious quarrel with his patron, and we find him afterwards writing to him in the most friendly terms (*Ep.* lvi.). I am more inclined to suspect that the subject of Erasmus' invectives was the noble Englishman referred to by Beatus Rhenanus (*ubi supra*).— "Quumque vitam collegiaticam duriorem experiretur, non invitus emigravit ad Anglum quemdam generosum, adolescentes duos generosos secum habentem;" and this perfectly agrees with *Ep.* xx., from which it appears that Thomas Grey was an inmate of this old man's house. If, however, we are to disregard the particulars just referred to, and to suppose that they are mentioned merely as a blind to avert suspicion from the real person, it would seem to me more reasonable to fix on Standonck than on the Bishop of Cambray.

compatibility of temper and of tastes. At all events, reports were in circulation which gave Erasmus great pain, and by which even friends were deceived. And when at length a letter reached him from his old companion, William Hermann of Tergouw, upbraiding him with his conduct, his misery was complete. He replied asserting his innocence, but his language shows that he was at this time—partly, no doubt, in consequence of ill health—almost in a state of despair.

"I may, indeed, dear William, preserve my innocence as I do, but I cannot help what people may say of me. I care more what you think of me, you whom I value (so may God love me) beyond any one else in the world. What was the meaning of that letter of yours in which you seemed to find fault with my conduct? Would you know, then, how Erasmus lives here? He lives—nay, I know not if he can be said to live; but if so he lives in the greatest wretchedness, and quite worn out by calamities of every kind; surrounded by plots, deserted by his friends, the sport of fortune. Nevertheless, he lives in perfect innocence. I know you will scarcely believe me. You are thinking of the Erasmus of old times, and of my liberty, and all my brilliant prospects. But if I could only speak to you I could easily convince you. If you wish, then, to form a correct idea of Erasmus, imagine no light-headed reveller or debauchee, but one plunged in affliction, perpetually weeping, hateful to himself, who now neither wishes to live nor is permitted to die; in short, one entirely miserable—not, however, through any fault of his own, but from the unkindness of fortune, and cherishing also the warmest possible affection for you." [11]

[11] *Ep.* xv.

But it was not long before he recovered his usual good spirits. After leaving the household of the old man, he undertook the tuition of two young countrymen of his own, named Henry and Augustine, of whom the former soon became a special favourite. A letter supposed to be written by Henry to his elder brother Christian—himself a former pupil and now engaged in business—gives a charming description of a life devoted to the pursuit of literature. The letter is really the composition of Erasmus himself. It represents Christian as appearing to his brother in a dream, and asking after his welfare. Henry, in reply, tells how fortunate he has been in securing the companionship of so kind and accomplished a teacher. " I have Helicon itself within the walls of my bed-chamber," he exclaims, and then he proceeds at some length to give an account of his studies, not forgetting to bestow many praises upon his preceptor. It is clear, from this letter, that Erasmus knew how to mingle pleasure with his instructions, and aimed to excite in his pupils the same ardour for learning which he felt himself. During their walks among the vineyards on the banks of the Seine, he would entertain them with stories from the classics, or declaim in eloquent commonplace against the meanness of business and in praise of learning, telling them that was the only lasting riches which fortune could neither give nor take away, that it increased by use instead of diminishing, &c.; that, in short, "without it we are not even men." Literature was not only the business of the day, but its sole occupation. " At dinner we talk of nothing but books, and our suppers are made palatable with literature. When we go to walk our conversation is still about books, and even in our games we cannot quite forget them. We converse about them until sleep steals over us, and then our very dreams are learned; when we waken in the morning we begin the day with letters." [12]

Among the pupils of Erasmus in Paris were some young English noblemen, one of whom (William Blunt, Lord Mountjoy) conferred upon him a pension of one hundred crowns a year, and remained his attached friend through life. Mountjoy had been page of honour to Prince Henry, afterwards Henry VIII., and they had studied history together.[13] He was now a young man of the most amiable manners and of great promise, and so admirable a scholar that his letters were read aloud in the University class-rooms as models of Latin composition.[14]

Another was Thomas Grey, son of the Marquis of Dorset. Grey lived in the household of the old man already described, and consequently ceased to be a pupil when the quarrel took place. Erasmus, who is never sparing of flattery, describes him in a long letter to himself, in which he laments his unhappy fate in being condemned to associate with such a monster, as a young man of beautiful person and highly-gifted mind.[15] Another letter shows the interest he continued to take in his studies. He warns him to avoid immoral writers, and to choose only the best, amongst whom he mentions especially "Virgil, Lucan, Cicero, Lactantius, Jerome, Sallust, Livy." The last sentence of this letter illustrates the difficulties under which writing was sometimes carried on in those days: "For want of ink, I have written with mulberry juice."[16]

[12] *Ep.* xxxii.
[13] *Er. Op.* iii. 1360, A.
[14] CREVIER, vol. iv. p. 441.
[15] *Ep.* xx.
[16] *Ep.* xxi.

Nor would Erasmus, however straitened for money, consent to spend his time on those who were likely to do no credit to his teaching. He declined most advantageous offers from another young Englishman, who, being in priest's orders, had refused a bishopric on the ground that he did not possess the necessary learning for so high an office. Being in the enjoyment of an ample fortune, he might easily have dispensed with the revenue attached to the see; but the King would not accept his excuses, and being informed that he must be ready within a year, he applied to Erasmus to become his instructor. For a short time he was an inmate of his household, where he paid him the utmost attention, and offered him one hundred crowns for a year's tuition, besides a benefice within a few months, or a loan of three hundred crowns if he wished to purchase a benefice immediately. But to these promises Erasmus turned a deaf ear. He was resolved not on any account to sacrifice either his studies or his liberty; for, as he told Werner, to whom he wrote giving an account of this affair, he had not gone to the University either to teach or to make money, but to learn.[17]

During the years thus spent at Paris in classical reading and tuition, Erasmus continued to vary the monotony of his life by an annual visit to his own country, and by occasional excursions elsewhere, which were not merely prompted by his restless disposition, but rendered necessary by the uncertain state of his health. It would not, indeed, have been safe to remain in Paris during the summer months. That terrible scourge of

---

[17] *Ep.* cli. App. Knight seems to have been mistaken in identifying this "adolescens" with James Stanley, Bishop of Ely, who was then an old man. See Seebohm, *Oxford Reformers*, p. 227, note.

those times of which we hear so often, the plague, broke out year after year in the great centres of population, and carried off its appointed number of victims. And accordingly each season our student set off for Holland, no doubt finding the sea voyage, much as he disliked it, exceedingly beneficial, and glad to renew his intercourse with the few friends at home who sympathized with his labours.[18] Wherever he went he made friends among those interested in the progress of learning, and if they were able to show their interest by conferring substantial favours upon students, no modesty deterred him from making known his wants. He had probably not been very long at Paris before he made the acquaintance of Gaguin, from whose learned library it is interesting to find him borrowing a Macrobius,[19] and of Faustus Andrelinus, with whom he was speedily on terms of intimacy. In honour of both these men he wrote some Latin verses of no great merit, which have been included among his collected works.[20] At Orleans he gained the friendship of James Tutor, an ecclesiastical lawyer, with whom he stopped upon one occasion for three months, and whom he describes as a man of wonderful integrity and of no common learning. But his dearest friend at this time—that is, previous to his first visit in England in 1497 or 1498—was Battus, who was then residing in the castle of Tornenhens, in the island of Walcherin, the seat of Anna de Borselle, or Bersala, Lady de Vere. The Marchioness de Vere was the youthful widow of Philip, bastard son of the Duke of Burgundy,[21] and Battus was tutor to her son

---

[18] "Ob pestilentiam ibi multis annis perpetuam, singulos annos redeundum est in patriam."—*Comp. Vit.*

[19] *Ep.* lxxxiv.
[20] *Er. Op.* i. 1217, 1218.
[21] BAYLE : art. *Bersala.*

Adolphus and his two sisters. From Battus she had heard what a wonderful man Erasmus was, and had expressed a strong desire to see him. The result was an invitation to the castle, which was eventually accepted, and turned to good account. Her misfortunes, however—the precise nature of them does not appear—prevented this lady from doing as much for the cause of letters as she desired.

The following letters, which I have re-arranged according to the internal evidence of their chronology, give a lively account of this journey, undertaken in the depth of winter, and of the preparations for it:—

Erasmus *to* Battus.[22]

"*Paris, Nov.* 29, 1498 [? 1496].

"It is no secret to me, most excellent Battus, how disappointed you are that I have not come immediately, especially as things have turned out so much better than either of us ventured to hope. But when you have heard my reasons, you will cease to wonder, and you will find that I have consulted for you no less than for myself. I can hardly tell you how much pleasure your letter has given me. I am already picturing to myself the joy of our meeting; with what freedom we shall chat together, on what intimate terms we shall live with the Muses! How I long to escape from this odious slavery! 'Why, then,' you ask, 'do you delay?' You shall see that I have not acted unadvisedly. I had not expected the news so suddenly. There is due me here a small sum of money—if any sum can seem small to me. I have some agreements with certain persons unfulfilled, which I could not

[22] *Ep.* xxxi.

abandon without loss; I have just begun a month with the Count; I have paid the rent of my room; I have something on hand with Augustine; I know not what has become of my boy's books; I have received neither letters nor money in his favour, and our accounts are open to dispute. You perceive, my dear Battus, that I cannot leave all these things without loss. . . . There is no need that I should suggest to you, my dear Battus, for I know your fidelity and good-will, to look after both my interests and my dignity. I am somewhat terrified at the idea of a Court; and I am aware what an awkward kind of fellow I am: but I am glad that my lady is so well-disposed towards me. But what were the feelings of the clerical gentleman? Did he give any ground for hope? Could there be anything colder? I would rather have had a definite sum named in your letter, than that you should speak of a very large one. I will not indeed urge against you Virgil's line—

> Varium et mutabile semper
> Femina,

for I do not reckon her a woman, but credit her with the spirit of a man. How many are there, however, in your neighbourhood who take an interest in our literary pursuits? Who is there that does not hate all learning? . . . There is sent me a hired horse that might be bought for a farthing, and a sum for travelling expenses, not merely small, but really amounting to nothing. Is it likely, my dear James, that so cold a beginning will turn to any warmth in the end? When shall you have a more honest or reasonable cause for begging on my account than now, when I am to be summoned from this city and from the profitable employments in which I am here engaged? I could not come on foot for such a sum; how then could I come with two companions and on horseback? If, however, you do not like that the journey should be paid for by my lady, as I think is the case, I should object much more to your paying for it, as that would be most unfair. What could be more inconsistent with the description you have given of me, than to fly off at the first beck, especially on such conditions? Who would not think me either wanting in stability or a fool, certainly a most wretched creature? If I did not love you most tenderly, my dear Battus, and so much that the happiness of meeting you will be a compensation for any inconveniences, these things would deter me from my purpose; but they have no effect upon me. I only entreat you to remember my *dignity*. 'What then,' you will ask, 'are your ideas on the subject?' I will tell you. I will make every preparation here, collect my writings, and settle my affairs. You will, meantime, transcribe what I send. You will give me an accurate account of your feelings by the boy who, I am told, is coming here to study; then, when you have copied the Laurentius, after three weeks or so, you will return it by the same boy—I mean Adrian, who will both bring back Laurentius, and with it a sum for my expenses and a letter containing a definite invitation; a sum, remember, worthy my acceptance. For as to coming at my own expense, I cannot do it, because I have nothing; and it would not be fair that I should, because I am leaving behind me a very good means of livelihood. Besides, I wish you would send a better horse, if possible. I don't want a magnificent Bucephalus, but one on which a man need not be ashamed to sit; and you know I must have two horses, for I have determined in any case to bring my servant with me: the second one, accordingly, I intend for the groom. You will easily persuade my lady of this. You have the best of causes; and I know the eloquence with which you can make the best causes of the worst. But if she shall object to do it: how, pray, can she give a pension, if she refuses to pay the expense of a journey? These are the reasons why our meetings must necessarily be deferred.... There is no need for me to suggest to you what you should say to my lady in my name. Farewell, my dear Battus."

ERASMUS *to* WILLIAM, LORD MOUNTJOY.[23]

"*The Castle of Tornenhens, Feb.* 3, 1497.

"I HAVE at length arrived in safety, in spite, as it would seem, of the powers of heaven and hell! What a dreadful journey! Don't talk to me of Hercules or Ulysses; henceforth I can despise them both. Juno, always unfriendly to poets, fought against me. Again she petitioned Æolus; nor was she content with storms, but waged war upon me with all the arms of heaven—the bitterest cold, snow, hail, rain, mists, in short everything you can think of in the shape of bad weather. She used these weapons now singly and now all at once. On the first night a sharp frost coming on suddenly after a prolonged shower, had made the road extremely difficult; add to this an extraordinary depth of snow, then hail, then more rain, which as soon as it touched the ground or a tree was congealed into ice. The ground was everywhere crusted over with ice, but this presented no smooth surface, but rose up here and there in little hills ending in the sharpest possible points. The trees

[23] *Ep.* vi.

were clothed with ice, and so overloaded with it, that some of them touched the ground with their tops, some had their boughs torn off them, some had their trunks snapped in the middle, while some were completely rooted up. Some of the country-people, old men, vowed that they had never seen anything like it before in their lives. Meantime our horses had to go now through heaps of deep snow, now through thorn-bushes crusted with ice, now through furrows doubly difficult, as they had been first hardened with frost and afterwards sharpened with ice; now over a crust covered with snow, which was too soft to bear a horse, but hard enough to cut his hoofs. What do you suppose were the feelings of Erasmus in such a state of things? If the horse was astonished the rider was equally so; and as often as the animal pricked his ears my spirits sank; as often as he fell down upon his knees my heart leaped up. One moment I was overpowered with fear to think of the fate of Bellerophon, the next I began to curse my own rashness in trusting my life, and my learning too, to a dumb animal. But listen to something which you might believe was borrowed from the veracious narratives of Lucian if it had not happened to myself, Battus being witness.

"When the castle was in sight I found everything crusted over with ice. And such was the violence of the wind, that on that day one or two men were thrown down and lost their lives in consequence. It was blowing, however, in my back. So I allowed myself to be carried down the slope of the hill, sailing over the surface of the ice, and guiding my course with a stick, which served me for a rudder. A new kind of navigation! Almost the whole way I met no one, and no one followed me, so furious was the storm. Not until the fourth day, and hardly then, was the sun to be seen. One advantage however I derived from such overwhelming calamities, that there was less reason to be afraid of robbers; and yet I was afraid of them, as men with money in their purse must always be. There is my journey, most noble youth, and if it was full of hardship, everything that followed was perfectly smooth. I arrived in safety at the house of Anna Marchioness de Vere. How shall I describe to you the politeness, the kindness, the liberality of this lady? I know that the amplifications of rhetoric are looked upon with suspicion, especially by those who are not unpractised in the art. But believe me, in this case, I exaggerate nothing; rather the reality far surpasses the power of my art. Never has nature produced a lady more modest or wise, fairer or more kind. And shall I say all in a single word? She has been as kind to me beyond my deserts as that old man was injurious contrary to my deserts. She has loaded me with as great obligations, though they were called forth by no services of mine, as he did with insults, after he had received the greatest benefits. What shall I say of my Battus, the simplest, most affectionate soul in the world. Now I begin to hate those ingrates. To think that I should have been a slave so long to such monsters! Oh! that I should not sooner have become acquainted with you from whom fortune has separated me before friendship had united us This I wrote when I was preparing to set out for my native country; after that I shall be with you forthwith, and revisit my beloved Paris; and perhaps I may arrive before this letter. Of the proposal that we should live together, however, I can write nothing certain. We can determine when we meet, according to the convenience of both. Assure yourself that the man does not live who loves you better than your friend Erasmus. Battus also, the partner of all my loves and hates, has an equal affection for you. Take good care of your health, my dear William."

The next letter, dated about a week later, is from Antwerp, and is addressed to his friend Battus. Such of the allusions as do not explain themselves must be left to the ingenuity of the reader :—

ERASMUS *to* JAMES BATTUS.[24]

"*Antwerp, Feb.* 12, 1497.

"How does my pleasant and most trusty friend, Battus? If Lady de Vere, once your patroness, but now mine also, is well, and if everything prospers with her, it is as I wish and trust. I cannot tell you in writing if I dared, and I dare not if I could, how I long to know whether she has gone away yet, and whether she has taken with her her dearest possessions. You happy man, beloved by heaven, if you have steered clear of those rocks, and can enjoy without envy your happiness which seems to me to be complete! The virtue of my lady, to whom I doubt not all the gods are favourable, gives me confidence that you will. That has happened in her case, my dear Battus, which often does in yours, that I begin to love and admire more ardently when I am absent. Good heaven! her frankness, her courtesy in one of her high rank, her gentleness, notwithstanding her great wrongs, her cheerfulness in the midst of so many cares. Then her firm-

[24] *Ep.* viii.

ness, the perfect innocence of her life, her kindness to literary men, her affability to every one. So I am quite sure, my dear Battus, you are the luckiest of men if you can have her as your patroness as long as possible, and that you will, I have no doubt, if you repay her kindness to you as you are doing by reciprocal good offices.

"We have arrived safely at Antwerp. Augustine has preceded us to Paris with his companions: he promised he would wait there for me for some days. So that I think I must make haste, not to lose the advantage of such good companionship. I have no advice to give you; for I know your diligence in my affairs, and so great is the goodness of your most generous mistress towards me, that I blush to think I have been loaded with so much kindness by one to whom I have never rendered any service. It must be my task, however, to consider most carefully how I may show that her kindnesses have not been altogether thrown away upon me. I will return to you immediately, if heaven will. I pray that I may find you all safe and well, her particularly, on whom all our hope and all our welfare depends. You need not wonder at my writing bearing marks of haste, for I wrote this on board when we were just about to start, and while every one was in a great bustle about me. Farewell. My best wishes to your mistress's son, a most amiable youth, and his sister, whose resemblance to her brother and mother I think very striking. Please to greet your friends by name, in my name."

He did not, however, return immediately; and the next letter will show why.

ERASMUS *to* BATTUS.[25]

"*Paris, May* 2, 1499 [? 1497].

"I HAVE already written two letters to you, one of which I entrusted to a stranger: the other has been lost, and it was a very long one, so I will tell you everything as briefly as I can. I had an unfortunate journey. My knapsack, which was tied to my saddle, fell off, and could not be found after a long search. I had in it a shirt, a linen nightcap, ten gold pieces which I had taken out that I might be able to change them should I have occasion for it, and my prayer-book. The person I had entrusted with my money on leaving home has squandered it disgracefully, lending part and spending part on himself. Henry, to whose wife I had given a loan, has gone off to Louvain, and his wife has followed him. A third, a printer, got money in my name during my absence for paper, he says, I had bought, and will not return a halfpenny. I find, my dear Battus, that a large sum has slipped away, and has become smaller than you would believe. I sold the horse, having kept him about fourteen days, for five gold pieces; he was unsound in his feet. I have put off my journey, not merely because I have no means for it, but principally on account of losing my prayer-book. I live with the Count on the old terms, in which I have shown myself not at all exacting in order that I might feel more at liberty; he is fond of me and pays me every attention. I am extremely

---

[25] *Ep*. liii. The reference to Faustus Andrelinus in this letter would imply a still earlier date than that which I suggest, if we could believe Crevier (vol. iv. p. 439), that Andrelinus was obliged to fly for his life to England in 1496. But *Ep*. lxv. (see below, p. 86) shows that Andrelinus had never been in England as late as 1498 at least.

intimate with Faustus and another new poet; with Delius I have the keenest contests. I am devoting myself entirely to books, collecting my scattered compositions and preparing new ones. I allow myself no leisure time, so far as my health permits, which I find has been somewhat impaired by fatiguing journeys. Such is the present state of my affairs; now I will tell you briefly what my plans are for the future.

"I have resolved to put off my Italian journey till August, if I can meantime provide all that such an undertaking requires. The Count has also determined to visit Italy himself if his mother will allow him; but not for another year, nor has he said a word about taking me. I remember how finely I was before disappointed in a hope of this kind; and if I am to wait here a year, when shall I see my dear Battus again? I cannot tell you how my heart longs for your companionship. So that it seems better to hasten my departure as much as I can. I am remodelling my work on the composition of letters, and when it is finished will send it you; it is to be dedicated to your pupil Adolphus. . . . Pray try, my dear Battus, that we may live together at Louvain as soon as possible, and complete what you have begun. I am ashamed to say how much my loss annoys me. Farewell."

The treatise on letter-writing, referred to above, was not dedicated to Adolphus, nor was it published for many years afterwards. In the preface to the edition published at Basle in 1522, Erasmus says he had written it at Paris about thirty years ago for an Englishman who was going away upon a long journey, and that it was only in consequence of its having appeared in England without his sanction that he took the trouble of revising and publishing it. There were incorporated in it two declamations, which he wrote for his pupil, Lord Mountjoy, about the same time with the original sketch, one in commendation of the married state, the other against it. Mountjoy, when asked how he liked the first, merrily replied, "So much that I think of marrying immediately." "But wait," said his preceptor, "till you have read the other side." "Nay," retorted his lordship, "that I leave to you." And he not only kept his word, but Erasmus adds that at the time he tells this anecdote (1524) he had had three wives and might not improbably marry a fourth.[26] For Adolphus Erasmus wrote a brief exhortation to the pursuit of virtue, from which it would seem that he was then, in the year 1498, working hard at Greek, and had already made some acquaintance with Homer in the original. Along with this composition he sent him some prayers which he says he had written for him at the request of his mother and by the advice of Battus, by the diligent use of which he might both improve his style and avoid those "military prayers" in which courtiers delight, and which are very unlearned and very superstitious.[27]

While he was in Paris an incident occurred which curiously illustrates the way in which Erasmus was already beginning to look at the superstitions of his Church. On one occasion he was laid up with a fever, and having vowed to St. Geneviève, the patroness of Paris, that in the event of his recovery he would write a

[26] *Cat. Luc.*
[27] *Erasmi Epistola de Virtute Amplectenda.—Er. Op.* v. 65, sqq. *Pæan Virgini Matri dicendus, compositus in gratiam Dominæ Veriensis.* —*Ib.* 1227. *Obsecratio ad Virginem Matrem Mariam in rebus adversis, per Desiderium Erasmum Roterodamum.*—*Ib.* 1233.

poem in her honour, on his restoration to health, he proceeded to give an account of the miracle, as well as of another of a more public nature, in a style half-serious, half-humorous, which could not have been altogether satisfactory to the prior of his convent, to whom the letter containing it was addressed. "I recovered," he says, "not by the aid of the physician whom I called in, but of St. Geneviève alone, a most noble virgin, whose bones are deposited in the convent of the Canons Regular here, and daily bristle with prodigies. The interposition was very condescending on her part, and very beneficial to myself. I am afraid the rain with you must have put the fields quite under water; at least, it has rained here for nearly three months without ever stopping. The Seine has burst its banks and inundated the city. St. Geneviève's coffer, however, was carried to Notre Dame, the Bishop and the whole university walking in solemn procession. The Canons Regular led the way, the Abbot himself and all his monks walking with bare feet, while four of them, who were stripped to the skin, supported the coffer. Ever since we have had most lovely weather." [28]

Such a way of handling the subject, however, notwithstanding its tone of concealed irony, was probably not inconsistent with some degree of faith, or half-faith, in the power of the saint. Certainly Erasmus would not have denied the value of her interference, though it is probable he would not have wished always to dispense with the aid of Dr. William Cop, the accomplished Basle physician, whose acquaintance he made about this time. The vow to St. Geneviève—no very difficult one for Erasmus to keep—was duly fulfilled.[29]

[28] *Ep.* cliv. App. [29] *Divæ Genovefæ carmen votivum.*—*Er. Op.* v. 1335.

Two other letters may be inserted here, as illustrative of Erasmus' life as a student in Paris. One is an amusing description of a domestic scene. In the other he takes his revenge on the Scotists and their "harsh and crabbed" philosophy.

ERASMUS *to* CHRISTIAN.[30]

"*Paris*, 1497.

"ATTIC honey, hail! I wrote nothing all yesterday, on purpose, because I was enraged. Now, don't ask with whom, for I tell you it was with yourself. 'What had I done?' Well, I was just afraid such a cunning fellow as I know you to be, must be laying a trap for me. In fact I had my suspicions about that box of yours, lest it should let out upon me a swarm of evils, as it is said Pandora's did on Epimetheus; but when I had opened it, I was angry with myself for my suspicions. 'Why did you not write to-day then?' you will ask. I was exceedingly busy. 'And what may have been your business, pray?' I was at a dramatic exhibition, and a very entertaining one too. 'Was it a comedy,' you will ask, 'or a tragedy?' Whichever you please: only none of the actors were dressed for the stage; there was but one act; the chorus had no flutes; the players wore neither sock nor buskin, but were barefooted; there was no dancing; the stage was the ground; the boxes were my dining-room; as the plot thickened there was a deal of noise, and the *denouement* was noisy in the extreme. 'What kind of a farce is this you are inventing for my entertainment?' Nay, Christian, I am reporting a fact. The exhibition I saw was the mistress of the house, fighting valiantly

[30] *Ep.* xix.

with her domestic servant. The trumpet had sounded long before the battle, that is to say, there was a vigorous scolding match between them. In this they came off equal, neither of them gaining a triumph. It took place in the garden, while I looked on from the dining-room window in silence, though not without laughing. But hear the catastrophe. After the battle the maid came up to my bed-room to make the beds. While talking to her I praised her courage in having been a match for her mistress in screaming and abuse; but added I was sorry she had not been as brave with her hands as with her tongue. For the mistress, a powerful virago, who might have been taken for a female athlete, every now and then pounded the poor girl's head, who was not nearly so tall as she was, with her fists. 'Have you no nails,' said I, 'that you should quietly submit to that?' She answered, with a smile, that what she wanted was not so much spirit as strength. 'Do you think,' said I, 'that the issues of war depend so much upon strength? The great thing in every encounter is a plan of operations.' She asked what plan I had to suggest. 'When she next attacks you,' said I, 'immediately tear off her cap;' for the women of Paris have a strange fancy for wearing black caps: 'that done, fly at her hair.' As I said this in joke, I supposed it would be so understood. However, at supper-time up comes a stranger quite out of breath; he was King Charles's herald, vulgarly called Gentil Gerson. 'Come, my masters,' cries he, 'you shall see a bloody spectacle.' We ran with all speed, and found mistress and maid struggling with one another on the ground. With difficulty we parted them. How bloody the battle had been was evident from the result. Scattered on the ground, here lay the cap, there a veil, while the ground was covered with balls of hair; so cruelly had they mauled one another. When we sat down to supper, the mistress told us in great wrath how boldly the girl had behaved. 'When I was going to chastise her,' said she, that is, to pound her with the fists, 'she immediately pulled my cap off my head.' I perceived that I had not spoken in vain. 'That done,' she continued, 'the vixen brandished it in my face'—that wasn't part of my advice; 'then,' said she, 'she pulled out all the hair you see here!' She called heaven and earth to witness that she had never met with so small a girl who was at the same time so vicious. We remarked on the chances incident to human life and the uncertain issue of war. Meantime I congratulated myself that the dame did not suspect that I had any hand in the matter, otherwise I, too, should have found that she had a tongue. But enough of fun; now for more serious matters. You have undertaken to outdo me in two things, writing letters and sending presents. In the first, you clearly confess yourself beaten, having begun to fight with me by the hands of another. Have you the impudence to deny it? I should think not, if you have any shame. The other contest I have not even begun, but surrendered at once. In letters you are far surpassed; nay, you do not fight at all, except like Patroclus in the arms of Achilles. In presents I am unwilling to enter the field with you. A poet with a merchant? Not a likely thing! But ho, there! I challenge you to a fairer fight. Try whether you can first tire me with presents or I you with letters. Such a warfare were well worthy of a poet and of a broker. If you have any courage, put on your armour, and farewell!"

ERASMUS *to* THOMAS GREY.[31]

"*Paris*, 1499 [? 1497].

"THAT I have now for some time discontinued my old custom of writing is no ground for alarm. Though truly

Filled with anxious fear is love,

I have not grown cold in love. 'What then?' you will say. I have unlearned the habit of writing. 'What has happened that Erasmus has lost his pen?' Something wondrous strange, and yet true. I, that famous old Theologian, have lately become a Scotist; which thing, if you love me, pray Heaven may turn to good. We are so buried in the dreams of your countryman (for Scotus, contended for by many countries as Homer once was, is claimed in particular by England), that methinks we should hardly waken though Stentor was roaring in our ears. Canst thou write thus, you will say, while sleeping so sound? Σίγα, βέβηλε (Silence, profane fellow), you have not the least notion of a theological sleep. Many not only write when they are asleep, but go after the girls and get drunk and συκοφαντοῦσιν (play the sycophant). I find by experience that many things are possible which are incredible to those who have not experienced them. I once thought the sleep of Epimenides more than a fable; now I don't wonder at it at all, as I have myself had the same experience. Here, I am sure enough, you will say, 'What the deuce fables art thou talking of?' Though thou art one of the profane, who must be kept far from the sacred shrines of theology, yet see how I love thee, for I will unfold to thee so great a mystery.

[31] *Ep*. lxxxv.

There was once a certain Epimenides, the man who wrote that the Cretans are all liars, a Cretan himself, and who yet, in that respect, told no lie. It was not enough for him that he lived to extreme old age, but long after his death his skin was found with the marks of letters upon it. Some say it is preserved to this hour in the sacred temple of Scotist theology, the Sorbonne, and that it is esteemed of no less value there than it was in old times in Crete, or than the Sibylline books were at Rome. At all events, they are said to seek responses from it whensoever their syllogisms fail them, nor can any one get a sight of it unless he has borne the title M. N. (Magister Noster) for fifteen whole years. Should any other cast profane eyes upon it, forthwith he is struck blind as a mole. That what I say is no nonsense is proved by that very old Greek proverb τὸ Ἐπιμενίδιον δέρμα (the skin of Epimenides), by which they meant anything of an abstruse nature and inaccessible to the vulgar. He also published theological books, for he was particularly distinguished in the profession of theology, albeit prophet and poet are the same. In these books he tied such syllogistic knots that he could never untie them himself; he collected such mysteries as he would never have been able to understand had he not been a prophet. Once he is said to have gone out of the city for the purpose of taking a walk, because there was nothing that pleased him at home. At length he entered a very deep cavern, whether he was oppressed with heat, and desired to enjoy its cool shade, or was weary and sought repose, or because, having wandered from the path (for even theologians sometimes wander), he was afraid of the wild beasts which the approach of night might rouse from their lairs, or, what is most likely, in quest of a suitable place for meditation. Then, as he was biting his nails, and buried in deep thought about instants, quiddities, and formalities, sleep crept over him. You will not believe it, I know, if I say he did not waken before the evening of the following day, though even drunkards sleep longer. What will you say, then, when I tell you that that theological sleep was prolonged, as authors unanimously agree, to the forty-seventh year; and they say that it is no mystery that he did not cease to sleep either sooner or later? A man quite dead, you will say. On the contrary, I think Epimenides was well off to have come to himself at all. Most of the theologians of our time never waken, and when they are sleeping as soundly as if they had been dosed with mandragora, they fancy their minds are most active. But let us return to the wakening of Epimenides. Having rubbed his drooping eyelids, and not being quite sure whether he was awake or asleep, he went out of the cave; then, when he saw how changed was the whole face of the surrounding country by so great a lapse of time, the beds of rivers removed, woods here cut down and there grown up, plains swelled into hills, hills sunk into plains, while the very moss growing over the entrance to the cavern, and the thorn-bushes in the neighbourhood, were no longer the same, the man began to doubt whether he was himself. He goes to the city, and here everything is new: he recognizes neither the walls, the streets, the money, nor the people themselves; dress, manners, and speech are all changed. So swift is the revolution of human affairs. He addresses every one he meets, 'Ho! friend, do you not think I am Epimenides?' The other, supposing he has been made a fool of, replies, Ἐς κόρακας, 'Look for a stranger.' So he walks about, the laughing-stock of the town, for some months, until he falls in with some companions, very old men, by whom he is recognized. But come, dear Thomas, what think you Epimenides was dreaming of for so many years! What else but those most subtle subtleties of which the Scotists are now so proud? For that Epimenides has come to life again in Scotus I should not hesitate to swear. What if you should see Erasmus sitting κεχηνότα (with open mouth) among those holy Scotists, while Gryllardus delivers a prelection from a lofty chair? If you should see his brow contracted, his eyes fixed, his face full of anxious thought? You would say he was another man. They say that the mysteries of this learning cannot be understood by one who has any commerce whatever with the Muses or with the Graces. If you have acquired any knowledge of polite literature you must unlearn it; if you have drunk from the waters of Helicon you must spew them up again. I am doing my utmost not to say anything in pure Latin, to abandon all grace and wit, and I think I am succeeding: there is hope that they will at length acknowledge Erasmus. But to what purpose is all this, you will say. That you may not hereafter expect anything from Erasmus that savours of his old studies or habits, remembering among whom I live, among whom I sit every day: so look out for another playmate. But, lest you mistake me, most sweet Grey, I would not have you interpret these things as said against theology, for which, as you know, I have always entertained the greatest respect: I only wished to have a joke at the expense of certain theologians of the present generation, whose brains are rotten, their language barbarous, their apprehension dull, their learning thorny, their manners rude, their life a mere scene of hypocrisy, and their hearts as black as hell."[32]

Erasmus had spent five or six winters at the University of Paris, pursuing those studies which were necessary for his degree in arts, and making some acquaintance, how much against the grain we have just seen, with the scholastic divinity; he was known by various compositions in prose and verse to a daily increasing circle of influential and admiring friends, and was looked on as one of the most rising scholars of the day, when his friend Mountjoy proposed to him that he should accompany him to England. The opportunity of being presented at the English Court, and of making the acquaintance of the learned men of that country, of whom there was a few now beginning to be known, was not to be lightly thrown away, even though his cherished purpose of visiting Italy must again be deferred, and his lordship's proposal was therefore cordially accepted.

[32] For the last vigorous sentence, I am indebted to Dr. Knight.

CHAPTER III.

Erasmus Visits England—Oxford—Linacre—Grocyn—Latimer—More—Wolsey—John Colet—Conversation on Cain's Sacrifice—Discussion with Colet—Letter to Fisher—Colet's Proposal—Erasmus in London—Introduced to Prince Henry—Leaves England.

The biographers of Erasmus following the dates of his letters, which, however, are by no means to be implicitly relied on, have generally fixed on 1497 as the year of his first visit to England, and then make him re-visit it, after his return to Paris in 1498. This is certainly not improbable, but as there is no evidence in the letters, beyond the untrustworthy dates, of two visits to England at this time, I think it preferable to assume that he first crossed the Channel in the summer or autumn of 1498, and remained in this country about a year and a half, leaving it, as we shall see, early in 1500.[1]

The universities were of course the principal attractions for him in England, and to Oxford accordingly he

---

[1] That Erasmus spent part of the year 1498 in Paris is clear from the date affixed to his treatise *De Virtute Amplectenda* (*Er. Op.* v. 72, D.). On the other hand, we have a letter (*Ep.* xcii.) dated Paris, January 27, 1500, and written on the anniversary of his leaving England. But as the *Adages* certainly belong to the year 1500, and as we know that they were printed as soon as possible after his return to Paris, it is clear that for 1500 in the letter referred to we must read 1501. This gives us January 27, 1500, as the date of his departure from Great Britain.

repaired at once, carrying with him letters of recommendation to Father Richard Charnock, Prior of the Canons Regular of St. Augustine (to which order, it will be remembered, he himself belonged) and head of St. Mary's College. In external aspect, Oxford did not at that time differ very widely from its present appearance. Its noble Colleges, most of which are older than the Reformation, were there, only fresher and more beautiful than they are now; and yet even then the sentiment of antiquity was not wanting for those who remembered that the University dated—such at least was the common belief—from the reign of King Alfred. Its beautiful academic gardens, " studious walks and shades," then as now invited to meditation. But although Oxford has retained to the present hour so much of its mediæval character, it was yet to a considerable extent peopled by another world; it was a very different set of ideas that circulated among its students. Monks of various orders—black Benedictines or Augustinians and grey Franciscans—might be seen mingling with the scarlet robes of the Doctors and the gay colours of the Bachelors. Among those learned men the language of Chaucer was probably seldom heard. Corrupt Latin—at this time, however, gradually becoming purer as the ancient classics were more studied—was the universal medium of communication in the world of letters, and Erasmus, who was obliged to apologize to one of his Dutch correspondents for writing to him in Latin on the plea of his imperfect acquaintance with *his own* language, had no difficulty in making himself understood at Oxford. The old *Trivium*, embracing Grammar, Dialectics and Rhetoric, and the *Quadrivium*, comprising Music, Arithmetic, Geometry, and Astronomy, were believed to complete the circle of the Arts; but these studies were pursued not by any independent method, but only as they were presented in wretched mediæval handbooks or bad Latin versions of the Arabic translations of Aristotle. The great Latin classics were beginning to be read by more enterprising students, but the corrupt writers of the Middle Ages still swayed the class-rooms, aided by the grammars of Priscian, and Boethius was preferred to Cicero and Horace. As for Greek, it was almost unknown. Ten years before the arrival of Erasmus, some Italians had visited Oxford and given lectures on that language, but without any marked success. Already, indeed, it was regarded with some suspicion, but not yet with the dislike and hatred which it subsequently provoked, when with the growing freedom of the human mind it came to be spoken of by the adversaries of learning as the fountain of all heresies. It need scarcely be added that at Oxford as at Paris, the scholastic philosophy—that grand attempt to establish the theology of the Roman Church on the basis of logic, and reconcile Aristotle with St. Augustine—still reigned supreme. Nominalists and Realists, Thomists and Scotists, still divided the field between them; still disputed with unabated enthusiasm about instants, essences and quiddities; still discussed with unflagging interest whether the Deity could have taken the form of any creature but a man,[2] whether the Pope was greater than St. Peter, whether the Virgin Mary was instructed in the liberal arts. One man, indeed, was already raising a modest protest against this so-called

---

[2] I put the question in a form that may be as little shocking to the reader as possible. Erasmus states it thus:—" Num Deus potuerit Diabolum aut Asinum assumere."

philosophy; but had its advocates understood the signs of the times, had they foreseen that they were about to be assailed, not with their own weapons, in the use of which they were probably skilful enough, but with the far more deadly shafts of endless raillery and wit, of vast learning and indomitable industry, they might well have trembled at the name of Erasmus.

At Oxford, Erasmus met with at least a few congenial spirits, interested in the same studies with himself, filled with the same contempt for monkish ignorance and stupidity, and looking forward with the same hopes to the triumph of learning. One of these was Thomas Linacre,[3] afterwards physician to Henry VIII., the most painstaking of scholars, the most accurate of grammarians, a man of very varied learning, and one of the first to go from this country to Italy for the purpose of acquiring a knowledge of Greek. Another was William Grocyn, who, along with Linacre, had returned a few years before from Italy, where both had studied Greek at Florence under Demetrius Chalcondyles and Politian, and who was now giving public instructions in that language.[4] There too was Latimer, also an excellent Grecian, an accomplished theologian, a man of eminent ability and of " more than virgin modesty."[5]

On this visit to England Erasmus also met, and was at once captivated by, young Thomas More, the future Lord Chancellor, then a young man in his twenty-first year,[6] of the most amiable disposition and the most winning manners, and an enthusiastic student of the

---

[3] " Vir exacti quidem, sed severi, judicii."—*Er. Op.* iii. 250, A.
[4] *Ib.* 294, D, E.
[5] *Ib.* 378, E.

[6] It seems to be now an established point that More was born in February, 1478. See Appendix C. to Seebohm's *Oxford Reformers*.

new learning. The famous story of the first meeting of these two great wits—how Erasmus, struck by the conversation and the talents of the brilliant young lawyer, exclaimed in ecstacies, "*Aut tu es Morus aut nullus;*" to which the other retorted, "*Aut tu es Erasmus aut diabolus*"—is, I am afraid, one of those many good stories of which it is safest to remark, *se non è vero è ben trovato*.[7] There is no doubt, however, that they were mutually delighted with one another, and entered into a life-long friendship. It must have been in London that they first met, as More had been removed from Oxford by his father, who was alarmed lest the study of Greek should give him a distaste for the legal pursuits for which he was destined, and possibly make him a heretic, upwards of two years before. At Oxford Erasmus may have seen, and, perhaps, been introduced to, another future Chancellor of England, and a munificent patron of learning; but a man much less lovable than More, and in every way of quite an opposite stamp of character. Thomas Wolsey was then bursar of Magdalen College. It does not appear, however, that Wolsey took much notice of the foreign scholar, nor does the latter mention him in any of the letters which we have of his written at Oxford. But the man who possessed most interest for Erasmus and exercised most influence over him was Colet, afterwards Dean of St. Paul's and founder of St. Paul's School. Of this eminent man it will be necessary to subjoin a somewhat fuller notice, for which we are chiefly indebted to his warm admirer and friend, the scholar of Rotterdam.

[7] Mr. Seebohm, however, seems inclined to accept this story, and shows that the occurrence is at any rate not impossible. *Oxford Reformers*, p. 113.

John Colet was born in London in the year 1466, the eldest, and, at the time that Erasmus first made his acquaintance, the only survivor, of a family of eleven sons and as many daughters. His father was Sir Henry Colet, an eminent citizen, and twice Lord Mayor, of London. Sent to Oxford at the age of seventeen, he went through the regular course of study, and distinguished himself in every branch, not only giving much time, as was required of him, to the scholastic philosophy, but reading Cicero with the utmost eagerness, and making himself master of Plato and Plotinus. He was besides an excellent mathematician. Having taken his degree of M.A., he went abroad about the year 1493, visiting France first and afterwards Italy. Before this, however, he had determined to enter the Church, and indeed already, according to the evil practice of the times, had been presented, though he was not even in deacon's orders, to no less than three livings and one prebend. In Italy he devoted himself entirely to the study of theology; and the works of the Fathers, especially Ambrose, Cyprian, Origen, and Jerome, whom he greatly preferred to Augustine, were read with enthusiasm, while the works of the schoolmen, though much less to his taste, were not neglected. Nor did the young divine altogether despise the literature of his own country. Colet desired to prepare himself for preaching the gospel to the people, and as Erasmus tells us that he polished his language by studying the writings of those who had done for England what Dante and Petrarch did for Italy (probably Erasmus had just heard the name of Geoffrey Chaucer at Oxford), we may be sure he had taken some deep draughts from the "well of English undefiled." On his return to England,

Colet again took up his residence at Oxford, and immediately began a course of public and gratuitous lectures on the Epistles of Paul. The lectures at once attracted notice. Boldly throwing off the trammels of the scholastic divinity and approaching the subject naturally and rationally, Colet treated the Epistles as actual memorials of the apostle and his age, and not as a mere armoury of theological weapons; and such freshness and interest did he succeed in imparting to the subject, that, although he had not yet taken any degree in theology, perhaps, however, partly because he was known rather to despise such degrees, the Doctors and Dons came crowding to hear him, bringing their note-books in their hands.[8] It might well be suspected that some of his audience were led by other motives than curiosity or the desire of profiting by his instructions. To have been in Italy was itself a suspicious circumstance; to be opposed to scholasticism was worse; and, besides, Colet was known to have little respect for the University degrees in theology. He was, moreover, not entirely innocent of Greek, though his knowledge of that language was by

---

[8] The reader will find a fuller and very interesting account of these lectures in Mr. Seebohm's *Oxford Reformers of* 1498. That Colet's theology was founded on a much more natural interpretation of Scripture than that of the schoolmen is clear. But whether it had come wholly under the dominion of common sense, even according to the standard of that age, the following passage from Knight's *Life of Colet* may perhaps render doubtful:— "In his comment on 1 Cor. vi. he doth scarce allow going to law; and in the viiith chapter of the same Epistle he allows not marriage to be lawful; but only as a remedy *contra incontinentiam*. . . . Nor did he think it necessary that Christians should marry for the begetting of children; *for that* (saith he) *might be left to the* Gentiles.—*But what if the* Gentiles *should be converted?*— *Then* (saith he) *the Kingdom of God was come; then would the world be* Sanctus et animo et corpore; *then would the end be and God all in all,*" &c.—Introd. p. xii.

no means extensive. It does not appear, however, that any heresy was found in his lectures. The degree of Doctor of Divinity was eventually conferred upon him unsolicited, and he accepted it, says Erasmus, rather to comply with the wishes of those who thought him worthy of it than as having himself desired it.[9]

When Erasmus arrived at Oxford, the first to welcome him, after Father Charnock, was Colet. He was then thirty-one years of age, of a tall and elegant person, the sweetest manners and the utmost purity and simplicity of life. He told his friend, surely with some little exaggeration, that he had been naturally of an exceedingly proud disposition, most impatient of wrong, with a strange propensity to love, luxury and sleep; fond of mirth and pleasantry, and not altogether free from covetousness; but so strenuously had he fought against those vices with the aid of philosophy, the study of divinity, watching, fasting and prayer, that he had preserved himself pure from all worldly stains. As a student he was indefatigable, in his pleasures extremely moderate; and it was only when he entered into conversation with ladies, or engaged in an encounter of raillery with the wits of the University, that he permitted his natural mirthfulness to overcome his acquired gravity. It was seldom, however, that he went into mixed company, and when he did he contrived to sit beside some grave divine with whom he might converse in Latin, so avoiding the light or worldly talk of the dinner-table. He took particular pleasure in the society of children, and used often to recall how Christ had compared them with angels, and exhorted his disciples to imitate them.[10]

[9] *Ep*. ccccxxxv.   [10] *Ib*.

The first interchange of civilities between the two scholars was by letter. Colet wrote a warm greeting to Erasmus, telling him he had heard of him in Paris, and had been shown a letter of his which excited his curiosity, and gave him the impression of having been written by a man of great learning and wide general knowledge. "But," he adds, "what particularly recommends you to me is, that the reverend Father whose guest you are told me yesterday that in his opinion you are a most excellent man and endowed with singular goodness." Then, after a few more complimentary phrases, the writer concludes, as is natural, by expressing his anxiety to do what lies in his power to make the visit of Erasmus as agreeable to him as he feels sure it will be advantageous to England. The reply of Erasmus is much longer, much more elaborate, more profuse of compliments, and with a greater affectation of modesty. The praise of a man like Colet, he says, is of more value to him than that of a whole host of the illiterate. Yet so far from making him feel proud, it humiliates him to be told he possesses those qualities which he venerates in others, but is conscious of wanting himself. He will not, however, find fault either with those who so affectionately recommended him, or with Colet's readiness to receive their recommendation, since it is natural for a humane man to think well of strangers, and of a kindly one to give ready credence to friends. Accordingly he values his judgment as friendly, though he cannot approve of it as true; not because he thinks his correspondent an incompetent judge, inasmuch as he knows him to be a man of remarkable discernment, nor suspects him of flattery, since he is not ignorant of the simplicity of his nature, but because he was misled

by his own extraordinary candour and modesty to listen too favourably to the praises of others. But lest his friend should complain that he had been imposed upon with bad goods, Erasmus volunteers a portrait of himself, which he says will be the more true to life in proportion as he knows himself better than any one else:—
"You will find a man of small fortune, or rather none at all; without ambition, but most ready to return affection; with but a slight tincture of letters, it is true, but still a most ardent admirer of them; who has a religious veneration for excellence in others, but has none of his own; who may be easily surpassed in learning by any one, but in fidelity by none: simple, open, frank, unskilled alike to affect and to dissemble; of small but unimpaired ability, sparing in his speech; in short, one from whom you have nothing to expect but good-will." England, he continues, has such attractions for him chiefly on account of its abundance of learned men, "among whom I count you by far the first." And then the letter concludes with a description of Colet's style. "Nor shall I now describe, most excellent Sir, how much I have been charmed and delighted with your style, so smooth, so calm, so unaffected, flowing from your well-stored mind like a fountain of purest water, equal, uniform, clear, simple, full of modesty, with no violations of taste, no complicated or obscure sentences; so that I cannot be wrong in thinking I see in your letter as it were an image of your mind. You say what you mean, you mean what you say. Words born in the heart, not on the tongue, follow the sense spontaneously, not the sense the words. Finally, with a happy ease, you pour out without trouble what it would cost another the utmost labour

to express. But I will forbear to praise you, lest I should offend one who has shewn me such kindness. I know that they are most unwilling to be praised who of all men most deserve it. Farewell." [11]

Both these letters were more artificial than any one would think of writing now, but that was to be expected from men writing a learned language, and conscious that every word would be criticised. They were, however, the beginning of a friendship which ended only with death. It was probably not long after this that Erasmus was present at a College dinner-party—described by him in a letter to a friend who was to have been there—at which Colet presided, when a discussion arose as to the cause of Cain's rejection. Colet maintained the fanciful notion that Cain's offence consisted in the distrust of the Creator's goodness, and confidence in his own industry, which he showed in becoming the first tiller of the ground, while Abel, content with the spontaneous produce of the earth, was a keeper of sheep; a more rational interpretation, however, it must be confessed, than that of the popular orthodoxy of our own day. What view Erasmus adopted is not said; only he and the rest of the company opposed Colet, who, however, was a match for them all. According to the account of Erasmus, he was transported with enthusiasm, his tone changed, his eyes flashed, his face was transfigured, he seemed like one inspired. The discussion had lasted long, and was becoming too hot to be agreeable, when Erasmus brought it to a close in the happiest way. Nimbly changing sides—no doubt his friend's arguments had really convinced him—he proceeded to narrate a story which he pretended to have

[11] *Ep.* xi. and xli.

found in an old moth-eaten manuscript, in which he made Cain's laborious toil, and the greediness by which it was prompted, a part of his offence, but added thereto a theft perpetrated on the produce of Eden by the connivance of the angel that guarded its gates. Colet had no doubt laid himself open to ridicule by seeming to make industry a sin ; but the strong point of his position was, that Cain was rejected for something wrong in his own conduct or motives, and not, as was probably maintained on the other side, for having offered a bloodless sacrifice. And here Erasmus came effectually to his aid. The fable is told with all its author's graces of rhetoric, but if it has not been extended and adorned, as is probable, for the entertainment of his correspondent and the admiration of posterity, the hearers must have begun to yawn before it was concluded. It produced, however, the desired effect of restoring peace. The end, which is all that need be inserted here, is, that God, seeing how Cain delighted in toil, resolved to give him more than enough of it, and accordingly sent among his crops armies of ants, weevils, toads, caterpillars, mice, birds, and all sorts of destructive creatures, to attack them in every stage of their growth. " Cain endeavoured to appease God by an offering of fruits, but finding that the smoke would not ascend, he perceived that God's anger was fixed against him, and accordingly abandoned hope."[12] The friend for whom this account was written was John Sixtine, of Friesland, another scholar who had studied beyond the Alps, and who afterwards obtained preferment in the English Church.[13]

On another occasion Erasmus took the part of the scholastics against Colet, and maintained it, notwith-

---

[12] *Ep.* xliv.   [13] KNIGHT's *Life of Colet*, p. 218.

standing his great, perhaps excessive, respect for the learning of his opponent; and this time it so happened that the divines were on that side which would be now generally allowed to be the side of reason and common sense. The subject of discussion was the agony of Christ in the garden, and the words in which he seemed to pray that he might escape from death—"O my Father, if it be possible, let this cup pass from me." The received explanation at that time was, that "Christ as true man, being in that hour unsupported by the aid of his divinity, shrank from the appalling suffering which was then at hand, through that infirmity which he had assumed along with many other imperfections of our nature;" and that explanation Erasmus adopted so far as to maintain very decidedly the presence of this human weakness, though he was willing to allow that there might be various meanings in the sacred text, the Word of God being manifold. Colet, on the other hand, argued that it was inconsistent with the great love of Christ to pray that he might escape that death which he had before so earnestly desired for our sakes, and that it was absurd in the extreme to suppose that while so many martyrs had not only met the most cruel tortures without fear, but had welcomed them with joy, their love conquering all sense of pain, Christ, who was love itself, and had come into the world for no other end than by his own death to deliver us who were subject to death, could have shrunk either from the shame or the pain of the cross. Accordingly, Colet would refer the sorrow of Christ to anything rather than fear of death; and his opinion, which he supported by the authority of Jerome, who, he said, had alone seen the truth on this question, was, that "our Saviour Jesus prayed for nothing else than that his death, which he desired should be the salvation of the whole world, might not be ruinous to the Jews." This most unnatural interpretation Erasmus discussed at great length in a treatise, written in the form of a letter to Colet, in which he set forth with great candour and learning the arguments which had been urged on either side in the conversation of the preceding afternoon. His argument in this short disputation, as he calls it, which he amplifies with any amount of rhetorical language and illustrates with great wealth of classical allusion, may be very briefly stated.[14] Christ, in taking upon him the nature of man, took with it also all those imperfections which, though they are among the consequences of the first sin, are not themselves sinful. Such are hunger, thirst, fatigue and so forth, and amongst these is the fear of death. If it is argued that a brave man does not fear death, it may be answered that fortitude does not consist in insensibility to danger, but in overcoming the natural dread of approaching evils so far as to encounter them manfully, and that both Homer and Virgil describe their heroes as showing all the outward signs of terror. If it is argued that Peter, a sinful man, was possessed by so deep a love for Christ that he lost all sense of fear and was ready to lay down his life for his sake, and that it is therefore monstrous to attribute to Christ the fear of death and at the same time the most absolute love, it is ingeniously replied that, while in us one feeling flows in upon and absorbs another, in him each power of mind and body discharged its natural function independently of all others,

---

[14] *Desiderii Erasmi Roterodami Disputatiuncula de tædio, pavore, tristitia Jesu, instante supplicio crucis*, etc.—*Er. Op.* v. 1265.

so that the love for mankind which made Jesus willing to ascend the cross, and the fear of death which made him shrink from it, existed side by side, neither feeling intruding upon or diminishing the other. That so many, both heathen and Christian, martyrs should have embraced death with alacrity and even joy, is felt to be a great difficulty, and full justice is done by Erasmus to the argument thence in his opponent's favour; and his answer, that the martyrs were endowed with fortitude through another's virtue, not their own, whereas Christ in the moment of suffering was deserted by his divinity, is from the rational point of view less satisfactory than most of his reasoning. Erasmus, however, is so far from granting to Colet that his own view takes anything from Christ's love, as to maintain that it even enhances it. For, whereas Christ took upon him the nature of man of his own accord, it was his love for mankind which prompted him to assume that very weakness through which he shrank from death, and in this light "the more imperfections you attribute to him (saving those which are sinful or unworthy), the more you will illustrate the love of the Saviour." And Erasmus finally is carried so far as to assert that Christ had assumed "a bodily frame than which there was never any other more sensitive to cold, heat, fatigue, want and pain, and a soul in all its faculties of the very keenest feeling." It is noteworthy, as indicating the theological position of both men, that this treatise nowhere suggests the view which at once occurs to the mind as the received orthodoxy of our own day—namely, that the agony was occasioned, not by the anticipation of death, even of a death fraught with all the significance of the crucifixion, but by the foreknowledge that the vials of

God's wrath were about to be poured out on the sufferer. Erasmus does indeed regard the death of Christ as a ransom for the world; but his language is cautious and reverential, and as far as possible removed from the revolting extravagances which Luther afterwards wrote upon the same subject. "It was fitting," he says, "that that death should be as bitter as possible which was paid for so many deaths, which was to wash away the sins of the whole world." His doctrine appears to have been—and it was probably that of Colet also—that Christ by his life and sufferings provided "an inexhaustible treasury of merits," sufficient not only to blot out original sin, but to leave a surplus which might be applied to the expiation of our daily faults. As regards the question between them, Colet was not convinced by the arguments of his friend. He wrote a courteous note, thanking him for the pleasure he had derived from his very long but most agreeable letter, and acknowledging the accuracy with which he had remembered their conversation, and his learning and eloquence. He declared, however, that he still retained the opinion he had imbibed from Jerome, and enclosed the first instalment of his reply. In this he merely disputes the preliminary position of his friend, that the Scriptures are susceptible of a variety of constructions, maintaining that their fruitfulness consists not in their yielding many senses, but in their yielding one true one. A note from the hand of Erasmus himself intimates that the correspondence on Colet's part was continued, but the remainder has been lost.[15]

The *Disputatiuncula de tædio et pavore* has another than a theological interest, as indicating the progress

[15] *Er. Op.* v. 1294, A.

Erasmus had at that time made in the study of Greek. No doubt he was now busy at Greek with the assistance of the Oxford Grecians; and Greek words here and there throughout the treatise show that neither he nor his correspondent was entirely ignorant of the language; but two circumstances would seem to indicate that to the writer Greek literature was still to a great extent a *terra incognita*. After quoting several passages from the Æneid in illustration of his argument that insensibility to danger is no mark of a brave man, he adds, "the same thing has been noticed by the learned in the Homeric poetry," nor is there in the whole composition any quotation from a Greek author. We know, however, that he had at least begun the study of Homer, and there are also signs of some degree of familiarity with Plato, though this need not necessarily be in the original. But the most remarkable circumstance is, that he seems to be quite unacquainted with the Greek Testament; for not only does he invariably quote it in Latin, but he actually founds an argument on the pronoun *iste* (not the exact equivalent of τοῦτο) in the words, *Transeat a me calix iste*. Such is the force of habit, that he actually forgets, and expects his opponent to forget, that the New Testament was written in Greek, and quotes the Vulgate as though it had all the authority of inspiration! But, after all, this need not have been an oversight. If Erasmus and Colet might have hesitated to affirm that the Vulgate was inspired, at all events it was customary to argue from its texts as if there were no original to appeal to beyond it.

Notwithstanding such differences as these—which, indeed, were only sufficient to cement their friendship—there were at least two things in which there was complete sympathy between Erasmus and Colet. These were dislike of the monastic system and enmity to the schoolmen. Colet, whose mind had been more systematically directed to the study of divinity than that of Erasmus, was probably the first to revolt from the ingenious subtleties which constituted the theology of those days; and in this respect he would seem even to have exercised some direct influence on the mind of his more accomplished and less cautious friend. He used to say, Erasmus tells us, but only in the presence of those on whom he could rely, that he considered the Scotists, who were vulgarly credited with extraordinary acuteness, dull and stupid fellows; for to dissect minutely the words and sentences of others, and criticise now this point and now that,—that, he said, was the mark of a barren understanding. But for some cause or other— probably he had lost much time in reading the ponderous folios which contain his works—he was still more severe upon Aquinas. Upon one occasion, when Erasmus was praising the great schoolman, especially his *Aurea Catena*, which he thought was a valuable aid to the understanding of the Bible and the Fathers, Colet avoided expressing any opinion; but in another conversation, on the renewal of the subject, fixing his eyes upon him to discover whether he was serious in his recommendations of Aquinas which he was now urging with vehemence, and perceiving that he was speaking from his heart, he exclaimed, as if he had been suddenly inspired, "Why do you preach to me of a man like that, who must have had boundless arrogance, else he would not have been so rash and presumptuous as to define all things; and much of the spirit of the world, else he would not have contaminated the whole doctrine of Christ with his own profane philosophy?" Erasmus was struck with his friend's enthusiasm, and forthwith began to study the writings of Aquinas. The result was, that the esteem in which he had hitherto held them was soon greatly diminished.

In such friendly discussions as these, in listening to Colet's lectures and studying Greek under Linacre, Erasmus spent about a year at our great English university, which, however, he would leave, during the holidays, for an occasional visit to London. He was delighted with the country and with everything he saw there, but especially with his Oxford friends, and this delight he expresses in the most enthusiastic style, in a letter written from London to Robert Fisher, probably another of the young Englishmen whose acquaintance he had made in Paris, and who was now in Italy. "I should have been long ago where you are," so it runs, "had not Lord Mountjoy, just as I was ready to set out, carried me off to England. For to what place would I not follow a young man so accomplished, so kind and so amiable? God love me! I am ready to follow him even to hell! You certainly gave me a very full and most graphic description of him, but, trust me, he is every day outgrowing both your description and my own good opinion of him. But how do you like our England, you will ask? If you think my word worth anything, dear Robert, believe me when I say that I never liked anything so much. I have found here a climate as delightful as it is perfectly healthy; moreover, so much learning and culture, and that of no common kind, but recondite, exact and ancient, Latin and Greek, that I now hardly want to go to Italy, except to see it. When I listen to my friend Colet, I can fancy I am listening to Plato himself. Who but must admire Grocyn, who is nothing short of a complete encyclopædia of knowledge? Did ever any one possess such taste, so acute, polished, and searching, as Linacre? Has nature ever produced a mind gentler, sweeter, or more richly gifted than that of Thomas More? Why need I review the rest of the catalogue? It is marvellous what a thick crop of ancient learning is springing up all through this country—an inducement to you to hasten your return. The Count so loves and remembers you, that there is no one of whom he speaks oftener or of whom he would rather speak. Farewell. In haste." [16]

Colet would gladly have persuaded Erasmus to remain in Oxford, and with this view he urged him to undertake a course of lectures on the Pentateuch, or Isaiah, or some other book of the Old Testament, similar to those which he himself was giving upon the Pauline Epistles, and he even reproached him with a dereliction of duty in declining the task. It was not, however, to the mind of Erasmus just then to settle down at Oxford, nor, much as he loved and admired Colet, would he give up for his sake his purpose of visiting Italy and devoting himself to the study of Greek. He had come to England to learn rather than to teach, and his own studies were as yet far from complete. Moreover, he was no doubt conscious of possessing powers which, when they attained their maturity, would raise him to a far higher position than that of a teacher of youth at an English university. Fortunate is it for the world that he did not accede to the proposal. He would, indeed, have made an admirable professor, but, had he now settled down to professorial work, would

[16] *Ep.* xiv.

he have had time to edit the Greek Testament and write the other works by which he prepared the way for the Reformation? He might, indeed, have united with Colet in fighting the battle of Scriptural theology against the unprofitable subtleties of scholasticism, but it was more to his taste to encounter the old system openly, with all the resources of his wit and learning, on a field where he might win the admiration of the world, than to undermine it by means of lectures delivered to Oxford students; and if he had accepted his friend's invitation, where would have been the *Encomium Moriæ*? In truth, the thing was out of the question. The life, the movement of the new age, was, as it were, impersonated in Erasmus. His mind was far too restless, his genius too ambitious to permit him to look on a lectureship in a university as in any way fulfilling the purpose of his life. So he excuses himself on the plea of insufficient knowledge. "How," he asks, "can he teach others what he does not know himself?" Colet had begged him to try and impart some warmth to the studies of the place during these cold winter months; but how can he warm others when he is himself shivering all over? He had never intended to remain at Oxford, so that it is unjust to reproach him with having abandoned what he had never undertaken. Colet, it seems, would have been satisfied, had he at least consented to give lectures on poetry and rhetoric; but as the other was above his strength, so this, he says, fell below his purpose. In short, he must presently return to Paris, and waits only for the winter to relax its severity.[17] Before the end of January in the new year (1500), this plan was carried out. He parted with

[17] *Er. Op.* v. 1263, 1264.

Colet, however, probably before Christmas, and proceeded to London, where he spent some weeks in visiting his friends.

And now, leaving behind the learning of the University, we must follow our versatile theologian for a moment into different scenes; for, in London or its neighbourhood, it would seem, by his own account, he spent the time most merrily, the gayest of the gay, associating with great men and courtiers, laughing, feasting, kissing the fair, and bowing to every one. "We have made some progress in England," he assures Andrelinus, in a letter written in the very best of spirits, evidently from the midst of these gaieties. "Your old acquaintance Erasmus has become a tolerable huntsman, no bad rider, and a most accomplished courtier; he makes a good bow and wears a pleasant smile; and all this in spite of nature. . . . If you knew the wealth of Britain, you would put wings on your feet and fly hither; or, if your gout prevented you, you would certainly wish to be a Dædalus. For, to mention but one thing out of a number, there are here ladies divinely beautiful, the kindest and most fascinating creatures in the world, far before the Muses whom you worship. There is, besides, a custom which it would be impossible to praise too much. Wherever you go, every one welcomes you with a kiss, and the same on bidding farewell. You call again, when there is more kissing. If your friends call on you, they kiss you, and when they take their leave kisses again go round. You meet an acquaintance anywhere, and you are kissed till you are tired. In short, turn where you will, there are kisses, kisses everywhere. And if you were once to taste them, and find how delicate and fragrant they are, you would certainly desire, not for ten years only, like Solon, but till death, to be a sojourner in England."[18]

Before his departure it was the good fortune of Erasmus to be introduced to Prince Henry, afterwards Henry VIII., who was then, however, the Duke of York, his elder brother, Arthur, Prince of Wales, being still alive. He was staying with Mountjoy on his estate at Greenwich, when More, accompanied by another young lawyer named Arnold, came to visit him, and inviting him to accompany them on a walk to a neighbouring village, which he did not name, carried him away to Eltham, where the royal children were receiving their education. They were playing in a large hall when Erasmus and his friends entered; Henry, a manly little fellow, just nine years old, was standing in the middle, and received the visitors with princely courtesy. His elder sister Margaret, who afterwards married James V. of Scotland, was on one side, and Mary, then a child of four, on the other. Arthur was not present, and Edmund was an infant in his nurse's arms. Presently More put into the hands of Henry a composition of his own, and Erasmus, having nothing of the kind ready, was not a little annoyed that he had not been forewarned of the purpose of their walk, and the more so when the Prince during dinner sent him a slip of paper challenging him to a proof of his literary powers. Three days passed before he was able to respond; but by that time he had produced an elaborate poem, in alternate hexameter and iambic verse, in praise of England, Henry VII., and the royal children.[19] The verses are what might be expected from a man thoroughly imbued with classical literature, but without

[18] *Ep.* lxv.   [19] *Cat. Luc.*

much genius for poetry. England is, of course, described as the finest country in the world, and with the finest climate. Henry is the best of kings, great in war but inclined to peace, more patriotic than the Decii, more pious than Numa, more eloquent than Nestor, with ability superior to Cæsar's, and liberality greater than that of Mæcenas, parsimonious in nothing save the blood of his subjects. The praise bestowed on the young Prince is more moderate. A few graceful lines acknowledge his love of learning, and his resemblance to the father whose name he bore. The poem was accompanied by a letter to the Prince, in which he was entreated to accept an offering, which, however unworthy, was in its nature better and more enduring than any of the gifts of fortune.[20]

Erasmus sailed from Dover on the 27th of January, not, we may be sure, without regret at parting with his new friends. If, indeed, apart from his studies at Oxford, he had gained nothing by his visit to England but the friendship of two such men as Colet and More, his journey would have borne ample fruit. Of the latter there will be an opportunity of speaking more at length on the occasion of his second visit to this country. In the meantime there was no one for whom he had conceived a higher admiration than John Colet. The two men resembled one another in many respects, and yet each possessed qualities which the other wanted—a circumstance which, perhaps, had the effect of drawing them still more closely together. They agreed very largely in their opinions, their tastes, their love of learning, and their dislike of scholastic subtleties. But if Colet found in Erasmus far greater intellectual vigour, profounder

---

[20] *Ode Erasmi Roterodami de laudibus Britanniæ*, etc.—*Er. Op.* i. 1215.

learning, more extensive knowledge of the world than he could pretend to, and a biting humour which he did not possess, Erasmus found in him, on the other hand, a deep earnestness, a gravity and holy fervour which were not in his own nature, and of the want of which he may have been conscious. Colet, moreover, seems to have been a little of the ascetic. When he went to London he gave up suppers, and he seldom drank anything but beer, or partook of more than one dish. His friend, on the contrary, being of a sickly frame, required pampering, and the self-denial of others is not always the less admirable if we are unable to share in it. There is no reason to suppose that Erasmus first learnt from Colet that dislike of scholasticism which ever lent vigour to his pen. Through his influence, we have seen, his judgment underwent some modification in regard to one of the great leaders of that philosophy with whose worth he had previously had little acquaintance. But as for the vulgar herd of theologians of his own day, the bitter experiences of his early life, the strict discipline and loose morality of Steyn, the damp bedrooms and rotten eggs of Montaigu, had taught him to hate both their life and their doctrine. There was, however, one respect in which his English friend would seem to have exercised a distinct influence over his mind. Erasmus had not, indeed, so far escaped the influence of his age and his monastic training as to suppose that any study could compete in importance with theology; yet his natural tastes might, probably, have led him to give secular learning at least an equal place in his regard. The spirit of Colet may be traced in the absolute devotion to divinity which he sometimes expresses. When he writes to this friend he puts himself on the defensive, endeavouring to show that he looks upon his excursions in profane literature as little better than trifles of which he would gladly free himself, or at the best as preparatory to his graver studies, and that his whole heart is in theology.

CHAPTER IV.

MISADVENTURE AT DOVER—LETTERS OF ERASMUS—TO THE PROVOST OF BURGUNDY—TO BATTUS—TO TUTOR—TO BATTUS AGAIN—TO THE LADY DE VERE—ERASMUS WANTS MONEY TO GO TO ITALY—TEACHES BATTUS HOW TO BEG—STUDIES GREEK—THE "ENCHIRIDION"—JOHN VITRARIUS, THE MONK OF ST. OMER—ERASMUS AT LOUVAIN—PANEGYRIC ON PHILIP OF BURGUNDY—LETTER TO COLET—IN ENGLAND AGAIN.

ON his departure from England Erasmus met with a misadventure which caused him considerable annoyance and which he did not easily forget. There was a law at that time that no one should take more than a certain very small quantity of coin out of the realm; but Erasmus, having been told by his friends Mountjoy and More—the latter, who was then a student in Lincoln's Inn, ought certainly to have known something of the law—that this regulation applied only to British money, and all the little cash he possessed being French, supposed he had nothing to apprehend. On his arrival at Dover, however, he found out his mistake. The customhouse officers relieved him of all his money save the legal sum, which was, probably, barely sufficient for his travelling expenses.[1] In his difficulty he had recourse to his friend Battus, with whom we find him spending a couple of nights before proceeding to Paris,[2] and who,

---

[1] *Cat. Luc.*   [2] *Ep.* lxii.

no doubt, provided him with the necessary means for continuing his journey. On his way he met with another adventure, of which he gives a detailed narrative in one of his letters, having had a narrow escape of being robbed and murdered near Amiens. He and a young Englishman who was travelling with him had hired horses at a road-side inn, and soon saw reason to suspect the groom who accompanied them. Their alarm was increased when the innkeeper himself, on some flimsy pretext, joined the party, and reached its height when they found themselves compelled to sleep in the same room with this suspicious couple. The night, however, passed without accident, and the next day the attempt to extort money failed, owing to the poverty of the travellers.[3]

It is impossible, and, if it were possible, it would perhaps be hardly worth while, to trace all the wanderings of Erasmus during the next half-dozen years. It may suffice to say that he lived principally at Paris, Orleans, and in the Low Countries, and spent his time in studying Greek, running away from the plague, dreaming of Italy, and begging hard from his patrons to supply him with the means of going there. We have seen how kindly he was received at the Castle of Tornenhens, and what a favourable impression was made upon him by its amiable and accomplished mistress, Lady de Vere. It was to this lady, failing the Bishop of Cambray, that he now chiefly looked for the means of carrying out his cherished scheme of visiting Italy and taking his doctor's degree in one of the universities of that country. The following extracts from his letters give some account of his doings for the

[3] *Ep.* lxxxi.

next year or so, and they serve also to illustrate his character better than any words in which his biographer could attempt to describe it. They show us Erasmus painted by himself, and if they prove that his efforts to extort money were by no means dignified nor even altogether creditable, the reader will make what allowance he pleases for a time in which it seemed the natural state of things for literary men to be dependent on wealthy patrons. It may be added that the more elaborate letters of Erasmus were doubtless regarded both by himself and by those to whom they were addressed as models of Latin composition, and as having, therefore, a distinct money value.

ERASMUS *to* NICHOLAS, *Provost of Burgundy.*[4]

Paris, 1498 [? 1500].

"SUCH is my regard for you that, measured by that, any letter of mine would be short; but I am so busy that, measured by my occupations, any, however short, would be extremely long. The ancients used to call poets and men of letters allegorically swans; and not, I think, without reason: for the feathers of the bird are not purer than the poet's heart; both are sacred to Phœbus; both delight immensely in limpid streams and well-watered meadows; and both possess the gift of song. In our days, however, it seems, both have lost their voice, at least in this latitude, and do not regain it even when death draws near. The reason is, I imagine, that the swan, as the natural historians tell us, sings only while the western breezes blow. Can we wonder, then, that all swans should be mute just now, when there are so many north and south winds, but no zephyrs? For the

[4] *Ep.* xxiv.

British Aquilo has taken away not only my money but my voice, as effectually as any wolf that had seen me first.[5] But zephyrs breathe only at the approach of spring. Wherefore, kind Provost, if you will be the spring to my patroness, Lady de Vere, and she will breathe on me as the west wind, I will be a swan to you both, and will pour out such melody in your praise that remotest posterity shall hear it. There is no need for me to explain this riddle, seeing that I am writing to an Œdipus, and not to a Davus. Farewell."

ERASMUS *to* JAMES BATTUS.[6]

Paris, 1499 [? 1500].

"MAY you enjoy, my dear Battus, that health which I want. Since my return to Paris my health has been very delicate; the great fatigues of my winter journey having been succeeded by constant study, so that I have merely changed, not discontinued, my labours. Besides, this season of the year is not only trying in itself, but is especially unfavourable to my constitution. For I remember, as long as I have lived in France, not a Lent has gone by without giving me an illness. Lately, too, having changed my residence, my new quarters disagree with me so much that I feel unmistakable signs of that nocturnal fever which two years since very nearly sent me below. I fight against it with all the care I can and with the aid of the doctors, but have hardly escaped; for my health is still very uncertain. Should that fever again attack me all would be over, my dear Battus, with your friend Erasmus. However, I have good hopes that I may recover, with the

---

[5] It was a popular superstition that a man meeting a wolf was struck speechless, if the wolf saw him first.   [6] *Ep.* xxix.

help of St. Geneviève, whose kind aid I have more than once experienced; especially as I have got, in William Cop, not merely a very experienced, but also a kind and attentive physician, and, what is very uncommon, a cultivator of the Muses. . . . I am preparing a volume of adages, which I hope will be published after Easter; a work, I assure you, of some length, and requiring infinite toil. For I have collected about eight hundred proverbs, partly Greek and partly Latin; and I intend to dedicate the work to your pupil Adolphus. I am glad you are hastening to my lady, and particularly that you have been invited. Nor do I doubt that she has invited you partly on my account, for I wrote her a history of the whole affair in bad French. Accordingly I must maintain myself another month on borrowed money, until I get some good news from you; but for this I should have returned thither myself. I beg of you, my dear Battus, to show your former spirit. I know you can do anything if you will only try. But there is one thing in your conduct that I do not like, that ever since I wrote you an imaginary letter from England, you think I invent everything. Yet in that letter, which you think I wrote from my imagination, may I die if I invented anything. So abandon that unjust suspicion and do not suppose that I write anything, especially to you, which does not come from my heart. It is my intention, as soon as I have finished this work, to make every effort to complete the dialogue,[7] and to devote this whole summer to writing books. In autumn I shall, if possible, visit Italy, and take my doctor's degree; see you, in whom is my hope, that I am provided with the means. I have been giving

[7] The *Anti-Barbarians*, no doubt. See *ante*, p. 25.

my whole mind to the study of Greek, and as soon as I get money I shall buy, first, Greek books, and then clothes. Farewell, my dear Battus, and do not forget your friend Erasmus. Once my health is mended I shall neglect nothing."

ERASMUS *to* JAMES TUTOR.[8]

Paris, 1498 [? *Vere*, 1500.]

"I INTENDED going straight to you from Paris, dear Tutor, and there is nowhere I would go more gladly. I had got together a little money, too, not to be a burden on you; but hearing there was disease there also, I was compelled to alter my course and come here. At Antwerp I paid a visit to your excellent parents, and found them, as I expected, very like yourself. I was in Holland about two months, not settled, but constantly running about and drinking, as dogs do in Egypt. For my part, I would rather live among the Phæacians. Our gentle friend William [Hermann?] I found it impossible to stimulate to study, and so I left him with such feelings that even now I am sensible of no loss in parting from him. I upbraided him in your name so strongly that we almost quarrelled. If Epicurus himself could be born again and see their manner of life, he would think himself a sour stoic. We sailed from Dordrecht the day before the beginning of Lent, and were in the greatest danger. While stopping several days in Zierikzee on my boy's account, who had begun to feel a little feverish after the voyage, I was near being taken ill myself, only I fled from Zeeland, which to me is hell, as quickly as I could. I paid my respects to the Bishop; but, as usual, he invented new excuses

[8] *Ep.* xxxv.

for not giving anything. With Lady de Vere things were in such a state that I could neither speak to her without danger, nor go away without grave suspicion. You know the affair of the Provost, who is now in prison, while my lady is under surveillance. Accordingly, being without hope in that quarter, for I think it a wretched thing to be in suspense, I have come straight to my friend Battus. He is the only person here that I like. I am studying Greek, but alone, for Battus has no time for it, and, besides, prefers Latin. I intend casting anchor here for one or two months, and then I shall go wherever the winds call me. You are, no doubt, expecting to hear how kindly his Reverence has welcomed me now that I am in the neighbourhood. I have nothing to write about this, my dear Tutor, for the Euripus is not affected by so many tides as this man's mind. A little before my arrival he was so eager about it that he despatched Lewis with all haste to Holland to summon me, and gave me, besides, two gold pieces for the expenses of my journey. But when I came he showed so much coldness you would have thought it a miracle. So I think I need not care for these fluctuating admirers. My lady, meeting me by accident in the street, offered me her hand, and with such a very kind look as seemed to show that she still retained her former good-will towards me, though I scarcely venture to hope so, so wide-awake are the watch-dogs, which, in this case, are the wolves also. Accordingly, Erasmus is now taking care of himself, and is clothed in his own feathers. With a view to visiting William, or rather to making him a Grecian, I took a great bundle of books with me to Haarlem, but which was greater, the expense or the toil and danger, I do not know. At all events, both were thrown away. I lost by that journey twelve crowns and one friend. For I find I before imposed on myself about him; but I shall be made wise by blows, as boys are, and use my wisdom for myself rather than others. That is all, my dearest Tutor, that I have to tell you of your friend Erasmus. . . . I think of visiting Italy this autumn, or rather I dream about it, for I see no gleams of hope in any quarter. . . . Farewell."

ERASMUS *to* JAMES TUTOR.[9]

"*Tournay*, 1499 [? *Vere*, 1500].

"THE day before writing this I had already entrusted another messenger with a letter for you, but in case there should be any accident, I thought it safer to add a second by the present one, not in the same words but with the same theme. I have spent more than six weeks in Holland at very great expense; and never was time so completely thrown away. My boy's illness delayed me again in Zeeland several days, which was not only very wearisome, as I was in a hurry elsewhere, but also attended with great danger to my health. For I have never felt any climate more severe or less suited to my constitution. Everything else, my dear Tutor, has fallen out as usual with your friend Erasmus. The Bishop of Cambray is what he has always been. The Lady de Vere has been unfortunate, and needs to be aided rather than burdened. I am now resting in the arms of my friend Battus and surrounded by books; and not altogether without you, so often is the name of Tutor mentioned:—there is no subject on which I am more ready to converse, or to which Battus listens more eagerly. He loves you; he is all on fire, he longs to see

[9] *Ep.* LIX.

you. Believe me—if you believe anything I say—I find so much hypocrisy and treachery in human friendships—I do not mean merely common ones, but even in the most devoted attachments—that I have no wish to try any new ones. Battus is the only man in whom I have found good-will as constant as it is sincere. He is a friend I do not owe to fortune, seeing that virtue alone recommended him; nor am I afraid that fortune may take him from me. For why should he cease to love me in my affliction, who began to love me when I was in the deepest affliction? You, most learned James, resemble him not only in your name, but in your extraordinary frankness and simplicity. Accordingly, such is my feeling towards you both, that if your faith (which the powers of heaven avert!) should deceive me, I should cease to have any faith in faith itself. My health, thank heaven, is pretty good, and somewhat more steady than it was. I have almost transferred my allegiance from the Roman to the Greek Muses, nor shall I rest until I have arrived at the goal of mediocrity. My heart desired more than I can tell you to remove into your household; for I saw that, without any expense to you, I could enjoy your society—and there does not live a more charming man than you—and at the same time give you the benefit of mine; but I was deterred by the pestilence, which drove me from Paris and sent me into this banishment. For what is there to keep me here but Battus alone, whom I cannot have entirely to myself because he is compelled to give up a great part of his time to the slavery of a Court? . . . I have searched for a Greek grammar with the greatest care, that I might buy it and send it you; but there was not one to be had, neither Constantine's nor Urban's. . . .

Now I will tell you what my plans are for the future. I sometimes think of revisiting Britain to spend a month or two with Colet in discussing points of theology; nor am I unaware how much advantage I might derive from that project, only I am terrified for the dangerous rocks on which I formerly made shipwreck. I have the same longing to visit Italy as ever; but, as Plautus says, 'it is not easy to fly without wings.' I am kept from France by the plague. In Holland the climate agrees with me, but I dislike those Epicurean revels; then look at the people, how dirty and uncivilized they are, what a hearty contempt they have for study, while learning is quite unprofitable and brings the greatest odium on its possessor: which would be my case most of all, as all my friends seem to require, though they say nothing, that I should return strengthened, and, as it were, fully armed against the arrogance of the unlearned. I am waiting, accordingly, with no fixed plan, ready to steer wherever the favouring winds shall call me. If you can see more clearly, or foresee more wisely, in your friend's case than he can himself, aid me with your advice. Whatever may happen with you which you think I ought to know, be sure to write me. Farewell, with kind regards to all your household."

ERASMUS *to* BATTUS.[10]

"*Paris*, 1498 [? 1500].

"THE day on which I wrote this letter I intended setting out for Orleans. There is never wanting some bad genius to interrupt our studies. I was indeed more disposed to come to you, both because I should be nearer to my own country, and because an opportunity seemed

[10] *Ep.* xxxvi.

to be presented to me for aiding or at least encouraging your studies. But many objections occurred to me as to there being a suitable place for me to stay at; for though I approve of that which you pointed out in Peter's house, I have a scruple there, as you know; not that I fear either for my continence or my character, but lest any suspicious rumour should in consequence reach the ears of my friend Peter. For the vulgar, as you are aware, and particularly courtiers, hate the men of letters, and very freely attribute to us what they do themselves. Besides I thought there might be some who would wonder at my going thither so often. Finally I thought of your coldness; especially as I remembered that your advice to me to take refuge there was cold and timid. And I do not know that you now care even for literature, since you have been seized with a new kind of love, in which coaxing fosters desire, while a surfeit occasions no disgust. You know what I mean. It is no secret to me that you have become more attached to William, and that you give all your thoughts to making provision for him—a thing which I am so far from grudging that I consider I am indebted to you for it. But to desert me, after having laid the foundations of my fortune—what do you call that but to expose to destruction your own children? My lady provided William with a splendid outfit for his journey, and sent me empty away, though he was returning to his own country, while I was leaving mine; though he was going to drinking parties and I to my books. You will reply that the lady is rich enough to confer favours on both. But you are not ignorant of the ways of courtiers, you know the caprices to which women are subject: however I am silent. However that may be, if I am robbed of what was promised me, I am glad my friend William will be the gainer. If, on the other hand, I am mistaken in my suspicions, which I hope may be the case, and you are the Battus you used to be, induce my lady to fulfil her promises, and besides to give me a living; that you may suppose is given to yourself and not to me: for thus you will have contrived to have a church living without being a priest. I will tell you why I desire this so much. I wish to leave France. I wish to live in my own country. This I see will be better for my fame and more favourable to the preservation of my health. For my friends there think I live away from home willingly for the sake of freedom: those here suspect that my countrymen do not want me, and that I live here as it were in exile. Lastly, if there were no other reason, there is this very weighty one, that I should see you and my friend William very often. . . . . I have written more fully to the Lord Provost, and have sent him a copy of my Adages, also William's Odes, and my own foolish verses on the Cottage of the Nativity, printed some time ago. . . . . I intend taking my Doctor's degree if either Mountjoy or my lady send me anything; but if not I will give up all hope of that honour and return to you upon any terms. I have had quite enough of France. Farewell, most excellent Battus."

ERASMUS *to* BATTUS.[11]

"*St. Omer*, 1499 [? 1500].

"I SEE you are angry at my letter, which you say was written 'morosely;' I think *jocosely*, or, if there was any gall, it was not directed against you, but was rather

[11] *Ep.* lx.

the effusion in your presence of a most just and proper feeling of grief. Even if I acknowledge having sinned, the matter is not yet simplified, seeing that there has been no thought either of my ruined state, or of your good fortune. For it does not become a man who is in the deepest affliction to wish to be thought funny, much less saucy and forward, but to be humble, especially before one whom fortune favours and to whom you are in debt. . . . . Henceforth I will love my Battus as a friend and benefactor, and as a learned man. I will serve him as a preceptor, as my king, in whose power it is both to destroy and to bless. I will even consent to your beating me if hereafter you find a word in my letters, I will not say saucy or impudent, but that is not altogether flattering and suppliant; such as might become a slave who only fears the cross. I owe you besides a debt of gratitude, my worthy patron, for having aided my memory and reminded me of your high station. Now I will reply to your very kind letter in order, and I beg of you to hear me calmly. In the first place I will abandon completely that habit of mine of writing 'morosely.' And if you think it is not enough to have repented of my error, I refuse no punishment, if you will only take me back into favour, not such as I enjoyed formerly—I am not so impudent as to ask that;—the most I can hope is to enjoy the lowest degree of it. That the Provost heartily wishes me well I admit is no merit of mine. Your regard for me, which led you to recommend me to so great a man, I humbly acknowledge. As to your promise that you would faithfully and zealously plead my cause to my lady, what shall I, on my part, promise you in return for your kindness? What can I promise but myself?

Yet I have been long in the number of your slaves. Your sending me William's letter seemed to me much the same as bidding me go and hang myself on the next tree. I have been long aware that it is all over with me since he stepped into my shoes. Why, however, should I find it so hard to bear an evil which I have drawn down upon myself by my own folly? Now, if you should even crucify me I will bear it, though I think that would be more tolerable than to see William preferred before me. This one thing I beg on my knees—I conjure you by your own good fortune, and by the anger of the gods against myself—do not, if you are determined to destroy me, subject me to prolonged suffering. . . . . In inviting me to the castle, if the plague should drive me hence, you have restored, O merciful Battus, my hope of life. Why should I not throw myself prostrate and kiss your feet? I see you wish me to be saved, you do not wish me to perish of hunger. For what punishment could be either more bitter or more disgraceful? My worthy patron, the plague is already at the door; I long to fly to that blessed castle, more than I long to go to heaven. But you will pardon my timidity: I am afraid your anger has not entirely cooled. When I am quite sure of that, I will then leave this altar of refuge. . . . . Farewell. I shall be hungry enough here, as I deserve to be."

ERASMUS *to* ANNA BERSALA.[12]

"*Paris, Jan.* 27, 1500 [? 1501].

"ANCIENT literature has preserved for the admiration of posterity the fame of three Annas—the sister of Dido, whose surname was Perenna, and who, according

[12] *Ep.* xcii.

to the belief of antiquity, was translated to heaven for her extraordinary self-devotion ; the wife of Elkannah, of whom it is praise enough to say that when an old woman she became, by the favour of God, the mother of Samuel, that most holy priest and incorruptible judge ; and, lastly, the mother of the Virgin and grandmother of Jesus, God and man : so that she certainly needs no trumpeting. And the first of these the Roman Muses have consecrated to immortality. The second derives her nobility from the Hebrew annals. The third is adored by the piety of all Christians, and celebrated in the eloquent writings of Rodolphus Agricola and Baptista of Mantua. Oh ! that my pen were gifted with the power to make known to posterity your character, so affectionate, so pure, so chaste, that you might be numbered as a fourth Anna with the other three. And so it should be, were my poor abilities but equal to your virtue. I am, indeed, inclined to believe that that name has been given to you, as Maro says, not without the will and consent of heaven, so many qualities do I perceive that you have in common with them. They were most noble ; but what can this realm boast more illustrious than your ancestors ? They were renowned for their piety, and your piety is most acceptable to heaven. Their patience was sorely tried by affliction : in that, too, you resemble them more than I could desire, for your integrity and virgin simplicity were, I must say, most deserving of everlasting prosperity. What, however, can you do ? Here is Fortune's old game, to exalt the unworthy and bring misery on the guiltless. But thou, my patroness,

> . . . ne cede malis, sed contra audentior ito
> Quam tua te fortuna sinat.

But although, on account of my extraordinary affection for you, or rather filial love (for I owe all my welfare to her by whose kindness I am enabled to live among books, without which I could not live at all), I feel your misfortunes most acutely. Yet this consideration affords me great comfort, that such storms are sometimes sent by kind heaven, not to crush or overwhelm, but to give occasion for virtue to shine forth with greater splendour. Thus did the virtue of Hercules, Æneas, and Ulysses gain lustre. Thus was the patience of Job proved. I am, therefore, less grieved that you suffer these evils than rejoiced to see how well you bear them. And you bear them with so much patience that I, who am a man, I may almost say, born to misfortunes, strengthen myself by your example (for I will speak without reserve) more than by any derived from ancient literature : yes, for a whole year I have been pursuing my way with both winds and tide against me, and under a frowning heaven. . . . . Your rank, indeed, one would have thought was almost above the caprices of Fortune, and yet she sometimes clutches at you to humble you ; but against me she displays such unvarying spite—in this only false to her character— that she must be supposed to have conspired against my studies. It occurs to me as I write—for to whom shall I disclose my unhappiness if not to her who alone is both able· and willing to apply the cure?—I say it occurs to me that this is the anniversary of the day on which I made shipwreck of my little all, the earnings of my studies, on the shore of Britain. From that day, as I remember, Fortune has exposed me to an unvarying succession of misfortunes until this very hour ; for as soon as the British Charybdis had thrown me up upon this continent, I was greeted by a fierce storm, followed by the most fatiguing journey I ever experienced; then I had the knives of robbers presented at my throat; then fever; afterwards the plague, which, however, only put me to flight, did not seize upon me. Add to these, the domestic cares which life produces every day in abundance. But I am ashamed (God love me!) that I, who am a man, having at my command all the resources of learning, and armed with the precepts of philosophy, should be thus alarmed, while you, a woman by nature, and, by the indulgence of Fortune, born in the highest station, and brought up in the midst of luxury, bear your misfortunes with a spirit far from womanish; because, too, I was resolved, in spite of the blustering of Fortune, not to abandon the cause of literature, nor be cast down, so long as I could look to you as the cynosure of my eyes. For not even Fortune can take literature from me: the little money that my leisure demands, your wealth, which is equal to your goodwill, can easily supply. . . . There are two things which I find are very necessary for me: to visit Italy, in order that the little learning I possess may derive some authority from the celebrity of that country; and to obtain the title of Doctor. Both things, indeed, are mere bosh; for, as Horace says, those who cross the sea do not immediately change their character, nor will the shadow of a great name make me one whit more learned than before; but as the times go, you must conform to custom, since no one is thought learned—I do not mean by the vulgar only, but even by the foremost literary men—unless he is styled Master, notwithstanding the prohibition of Christ, the king of theologians; though, in ancient times, no one was deemed learned because he had purchased the title of Doctor, but they were called doctors who, by the publication of books, had given a clear proof of their learning. But, as I have said, it is to no purpose to act a good part which every one would hiss. So I must put on the lion's skin, in order that those who judge a man, not from his books, which they do not understand, but from his title, may be persuaded that I have some literature. . . . . These are the monsters with whom I have to contend, and to show myself another Hercules: wherefore, if you will arm your Erasmus, that he may fight with these portents with equal courage and authority, not only I, but the cause of letters, will be indebted to you . . . Farewell; and think favourably of my Muses."

In two other letters to Battus, he becomes still more pressing, and seems inclined to quarrel with his friend because he has not yet procured him the means of accomplishing his long-cherished intention of visiting Italy. In the first,[13] after complaining bitterly of a miserable eight francs which he had just received, he continues:—

"May I die if I ever wrote anything with such repugnance as those flatteries which I have addressed to my lady, to the Bishop [of Cambray], and to the Abbot [his brother]! . . . A year has already passed since the money was promised, and meantime you still put me off with hope, telling me not to despair, and that you will do your best for me, till I am quite sick of such phrases so constantly dinned into my ears. Finally you deplore my lady's misfortunes. You seem to me to be sick with

[13] *Ep.* lii.

another person's disease. She neglects her property, and must you forsooth take it to heart? She trifles away her time and her money with her ——, and must you growl out, 'She has nothing to give away?' One thing I see plainly enough, that if she gives nothing on these pretexts, she will never give anything, for great people never want excuses of that kind. It were a mighty matter indeed, if, when such immense sums are going to sheer waste, she were to bestow on me a couple of hundred francs! She has plenty to give for the keep of those villanous cowled blackguards—you know whom I mean—and she has nothing to maintain the independence of one who might write books worthy of immortality, if I may make that small boast about myself. She has fallen, it is true, into many difficulties, but that is her own fault, if she chose to take up with that handsome bumpkin, rather than with some person of grave and sober character, as became both her age and her sex. I foresee far greater inconveniences if she does not change her mind, though I do not write this with any feeling of enmity to her, for I love her, as I am bound to do, seeing how kind she has been to me. But what would it be to her fortune, I beg you to consider, if I should receive two hundred francs? Why, if that sum were given me, after seven hours' time she would never miss it. All that is wanted is that the money should be procured, if not from herself, from her banker, so that I may get it here in Paris. You have already written a great many letters to her upon this matter, but you only give hints and throw out inuendoes. Nothing could be more unavailing. You ought to have waited for a fairly good opportunity, and then boldly pressed home the request which you had before cautiously hinted; and this is what you must still do. May I die if you do not prevail, once you have made the attempt courageously."

To judge from the next letter,[14] Battus may have written that he found a difficulty in approaching the subject, and Erasmus accordingly sends him, from Orleans, whither he has removed in the meantime, the most explicit instructions as to the best mode of proceeding.

"Tell my lady," he says, "what a modest man I am, and that my nature will not permit me to discover my wants to herself. You may write, moreover, that I am just now in the very greatest want, because this flight to Orleans has been a great expense to me. For I was obliged to leave those from whom I was deriving some income. Say that the Doctor's degree cannot be taken with more honour anywhere than in Italy, and that Italy cannot be visited by a man in a delicate state of health without the greatest expense, especially as it is not possible for me, with my literary reputation, whatever that may be worth, to live meanly. Point out how much more honour I shall bring my lady by my learning than the other divines whom she maintains; for they deliver vulgar harangues, while my writings will live for ever; they, with their ignorant platitudes, are listened to in one or two churches, while my books will be read by Greeks and Latins, ay, by every nation throughout the wide world. Say that such unlearned divines may be met with everywhere in crowds, while my equal can scarcely be found in the course of many centuries; unless, perchance, you are too scrupulous to tell a few white lies for your friend. Next point out that she will

[14] *Ep.* xciv.

be no poorer, if, while so much of her wealth is most disgracefully squandered, she spends a few gold pieces on the restoration of the corrupt text of St. Jerome and the revival of true divinity. Having enlarged upon these points, as your taste directs, and written at length of my character, my intentions, my affection for my lady, and my modesty, you can add that I have written to say that I want two hundred francs, which would be simply paying my next year's pension at once. This, Battus, is by no means a pretence; for to visit Italy with one hundred francs, part of which indeed is already spent, I should not think safe, unless I want again to enter into some one's service. Rather than do that may I die first! Then how little difference it can make to her whether she makes me a present now or after a year, while to me it is all important? Next prevail with her to procure some church living for me, in order that, on my return, I may be able to settle down quietly to my books. Nor be satisfied with persuading, but give her as good a reason as you can invent why she should promise me the first of many that she has, if not the best, at all events a tolerable one, which I may exchange for another whenever there shall be a better at her disposal. I am aware that there are many applicants for livings; but you can say that I am the only man whom, if she compares with all others, &c. You know how you have been accustomed to lie profusely for Erasmus."

All these urgent entreaties would seem to have failed of their purpose; no such sum at least was forthcoming as enabled Erasmus to prosecute his intention of visiting Italy. A year or two afterwards we find that he lost his friend Battus by death, while the Lady de Vere contracted a marriage far below her station.[15] The Bishop of Cambray, who had quite cast him off some time before, was also removed by death; and Erasmus wrote three Latin epitaphs upon him and one Greek one, for which he tells his friend Hermann, he received only six florins; so that the Bishop, he adds, preserved his character for stinginess even in death.[16] It is clear that Erasmus—and the retort is not unfair—endeavoured to obtain from the dead what he had been unable to extort from the living.

The foregoing extracts show that, notwithstanding his unsettled life, Erasmus was all this time diligently pursuing his study of Greek, of which he was determined to make himself a master. Finding little benefit from the instructions of George Hermonymus of Sparta, he became his own teacher, and in order to perfect himself, he adopted the plan of translating from Greek into Latin. In this way he translated a declamation of the sophist Libanius and two others by an unknown author, which he dedicated to the Chancellor of the University of Louvain, and received for them ten gold pieces, a present which seems to have satisfied him, and afterwards, as we shall see in due time, several pieces by Lucian, a writer whom he particularly affected, some of Plutarch's Moral Essays, and the Hecuba and Iphigenia in Aulis of Euripides. Whether, after all, he ever became a perfect Grecian may be doubted; or rather it is certain that while he soon acquired that familiarity with the language which a man of his talent and industry could not well miss, and which enabled

---

[15] "Battum mors ademit, vel venenum potius. . . . Dominam Veriensem matrimonium plus quam servile eripuit."—*Er. Op.* iii. 1837, D.

[16] *Er. Op.* iii. 1837, C.

him to read and even write it with ease, he never possessed that thorough accuracy which greater advantages or greater care might have bestowed, and which one man at least of that age—Budæus—is said to have possessed.

Meantime other studies were not neglected. The collection of Adages spoken of in the first letter to Battus,[17] was actually published in the year 1500; but as that was but the foundation of one of the most important works of Erasmus, I reserve any further notice of it for a future chapter. Another work demands our attention here; a little religious treatise or handbook of piety, which was composed under the following circumstances: Erasmus was on a visit, one summer, to the Castle of Tornenhens, whither he had fled for refuge from the plague, when he made the acquaintance of a military man, whose company he found agreeable enough, but whose conduct was known to be licentious in the extreme. This man had a wife of extraordinary piety who was extremely concerned for his salvation, and who accordingly begged Erasmus to put down in writing a few things such as he thought might waken in him some sense of religion. He complied and made a few notes, which he afterwards elaborated at leisure while residing at Louvain. The work, when finished, was shown to some learned friends, who expressed their strong approbation, and it was accordingly published. It is a work of some importance for the biography of Erasmus, because it shows the theological position which he took up from the very first; how freely he treated questions touching on the most fundamental doctrines of the Church, how thoroughly practical he sought to make religion, and how boldly he

[17] See above, p. 95.

assailed what he regarded as the superstitions of his time. This will appear sufficiently from the following review.

The *Enchiridion*, or, Christian Soldier's Dagger,[18] as this treatise was called, is a charming little work, written in that easy flowing style of which its author was now a master, and combining in the most skilful way the wisdom of the heathen sages with the teachings of Scripture. Some might think it too much leavened with ideas borrowed from the philosophy of Greece and Rome, and it was probably upon that account that it incurred the charge of being deficient in unction; but for all that, it is full of sound sense and practical piety. Little stress, indeed, is laid upon those points which the Catholic Church regarded as fundamental, and although the Fall of Man and his Redemption by the Cross are incidentally referred to, it is clear that the heart of the writer is in the practical lessons which he desires to inculcate. His idea of human nature is almost wholly Platonic. Man, he says, consists of soul and body, which at first acted together in perfect harmony, and would have continued to do so, had not the serpent sown the seeds of contention between them. Since that time there has been perpetual warfare between the two, the spirit striving against the flesh and the flesh against the spirit. But the consequences of the first sin would not seem, in the estimation of Erasmus, to have affected the essential nature of the soul, which is still spoken of as divine, and as retaining a consciousness of its heavenly origin. "But that divine principle, which, bearing

---

[18] *Enchiridion Militis Christiani.*—*Er. Op.* v. 1. Enchiridion means a handbook, or a dagger. That the latter is the translation intended by Erasmus is evident from his own words: "Enchiridion, hoc est, pugiunculum modo, quemdam excudimus," &c.

sovereign sway within us, ever counsels us to our good, remembering the source whence it has come, admits no baseness nor impurity." [19] The spirit, or inner man, or the law of the mind, of which Paul speaks, is explained to be identical with the reason of the philosophers; and thus it is implied throughout this treatise, that man, so far from being utterly incapacitated for good, as Augustine taught and as Luther was presently to teach, does instinctively, in virtue of his higher nature, seek those things which are above. The end of all human effort, however, is Christ; and the way to Christ is faith. But by Christ we are told to understand "no unmeaning word but love, simplicity, patience, purity; in short, whatever Christ taught." And by faith is signified, not that self-abandonment to a Divine Saviour, not that trust in another's righteousness—which, according to many, is its very essence—but simply belief that God's promises and threats, as revealed in Scripture, are true; belief that in another world sin will be punished and virtue rewarded. In short, Erasmus clearly teaches that the only way of salvation is that of self-denial, self-conquest, and virtue. How far he was from being prepared to accept at this time what was soon to become the great Protestant doctrine of faith without works, is apparent from a passage in which, speaking of the troubles of life, he says, "these will all be added to the sum of thy merits if they find thee in the way of Christ." That he never accepted it will appear sufficiently hereafter.[20]

[19] "Anima, generis ætherii memor, summa vi sursum nititur, et cum terrestri mole luctatur."—*Er. Op.* v. 13, A. "At consultor ille divinus, sublimi in arce præsidens, memor originis suæ, nihil sordidum, nihil humile cogitat."—*Ib.* 14, D.

[20] "Fides unica est ad Christum janua. . . . Sic prorsus habeto, nihil tam verum esse . . . quam quæ

This doctrine that there was a possibility of merit on the part of man, and that the troubles which he was called upon to sustain in the pursuit of righteousness would be counted to him as merits, was, of course, perfectly in accordance with the teaching of the Roman Church. Whether it is true or not, or in what sense true, is, at least to the unprejudiced thinker, quite another question; but it is one on which the biographer is not called upon to give judgment. No one doubts that the doctrine of merits gave birth to a great number of abuses, and was involved with a great deal of superstition. And these abuses and that superstition, Erasmus, here, as upon every occasion that offered, set himself to expose. Pilgrimages, fasts, the worship of saints, respect for relics, he does not venture to condemn; but urges that they should be regarded merely as the means of piety, and not as an end in themselves. "The most acceptable worship," he says, "which you can offer to the Virgin Mary is to endeavour to imitate her humility. If you must adore the bones of Paul locked up in a casket, adore also the spirit of Paul which shines forth from his writings." "You honour the image of Christ's face carved in wood or stone, or painted upon canvas, how much more religiously ought you to honour the image of His mind expressed by the art of the Holy Spirit in the Gospel writings." "You gaze with mute

legis in his literis quas cœleste Numen, hoc est, veritas, inspiravit," etc.—*Ib.* 21, E. F. Compare the whole passage. "Sed ut certiore cursu queas ad felicitatem contendere, hæc tibi quarta sit regula, ut totius vitæ tuæ Christum, velut unicum scopum præfigas, ad quem unum omnia studia, omnes conatus, omne otium ac negotium conferas. Christum vero esse puta, non vocem inanem, sed nihil aliud quam charitatem, simplicitatem, patientiam, puritatem, breviter quicquid ille docuit."—*Ib.* 25, A.

wonder on a tunic or handkerchief which is said to have belonged to Christ, and yet when you read the oracles of Christ your eyes droop with sleep." We shall have ample opportunity of noticing hereafter the exposures by Erasmus of the manners and practices of the monks, but the following tolerably strong passage may be given at present:—" I am ashamed to say how superstitiously most of them observe those petty ceremonies which were instituted by men no better than themselves, and yet which had originally a very different purpose in view; how much hatred they display in exacting them from others, how confidently they rely upon them, how rashly they make themselves judges of other people's conduct, how contentiously they uphold them. By these acts of theirs they think they can merit heaven, and if it so happens at any time that they have shown some zeal in their performance, they fancy themselves equal to Paul or Anthony. Then they begin to exercise a most haughty censorship over the lives of others, following that ignorant rule, as the comic poet calls it, of thinking nothing right but what they do themselves. When, however, they have grown grey in the observance of the rules of their order, after all you shall find that they have nothing of the temper of Christ, but are altogether unspiritual, and steeped to the lips in certain unsocial vices; peevish creatures to live with, and scarce supportable even to themselves; if their charity is cold their anger is hot enough; their hatred is most obstinate, their language most virulent; in carrying on a quarrel they will never let themselves be beaten, and they are ready to fight for any cause however trifling; and altogether they are so far from the perfection of Christ, that they have not even those common virtues which either natural reason, or experience, or the precepts of the philosophers enable the heathen to acquire; indocile, intractable, quarrelsome, sensuous, they turn with disgust from the words of Holy Writ; they never shew a kindness to any one, but are full of foul suspicions towards others, and vainly conceited of themselves. Is this the result of the labours of so many years, that, though filled with every vice, you should think yourself the best of men; that instead of a Christian you should be a Jew, serving the beggarly elements only in order that you may have glory, not in secret before God, but openly before men?"

Again, urging the virtue of charity, he exclaims, "Tell me not this is charity, to be constant at church, to prostrate yourself before the images of the saints, to burn wax-candles, and to chant prayers. God has no need of these things. What Paul calls charity is to edify your neighbour, to esteem all men members of the same body, to think all are one in Christ, to rejoice in the Lord at your brother's welfare as if it were your own, to remedy his misfortunes as if they too were your own; to correct the erring gently, to instruct the ignorant, to raise the fallen, to comfort the cast-down, to assist them that are in trouble, to succour them that are in want: in fine, to direct all your powers, all your zeal, all your care to this end; to do good in Christ in all to whom you can do good, in order that, as he was neither born, nor lived, nor died to himself, but gave himself wholly for our advantage, so we also may serve our brother's needs and not our own. Were this so, there would be no kind of life more happy or more pleasant than that of those who have set themselves apart for the service of religion; which now on the contrary we find to be severe and toilsome, and filled with Jewish superstitions, nor free from any of the vices of the outer world; in some respects it is even more deeply stained."

Thus did Erasmus boldly expose the inner life of the monasteries which he knew by experience so well. Nor, probably, did the monks consider it any mitigation if he pleaded that he attacked vices only, not men. The good, he truly said, would be glad to be admonished in the things which pertain to salvation. But those who knew how well they deserved his severity, and still more those who, without knowing it, yet deserved it, were sure to be filled with that rage which never forgets and never forgives. But in attacking the superstitions of the Church, Erasmus does not by any means spare the outside world. He laments that as regards morals there was never even among the heathen a more corrupt age than that in which he lived. "But," he adds, "as to their faith, let them look to it themselves. This at least is most unquestionable, that faith without moral conduct corresponding to it, is not only of no avail, but increases the sum of damnation." "True probity is utterly despised; riches, no matter by what means acquired, were never so highly esteemed as they are at present." "Poverty is considered the worst misfortune, and the lowest disgrace." "Such is our way of venerating and expressing the doctrine of Christ, that nothing is now deemed more utterly mean and contemptible, indeed mad, than to be truly and heartily a Christian; as if Christ had either lived in vain upon earth, or Christianity had changed its character, or did not apply equally to all men." Truly, an awakening was needed for the age of which such things could be written. No doubt there are always moralists to lament that their own time is the most corrupt that has ever been; and the complaint that wealth is the standard of virtue often means no more than that the needy philosopher is not asked to dinner by the rich fool, whom he professes to despise. Nevertheless, it will not be denied that as regards the corruption of religion at least, and the prevalence of superstition upon the one hand and hypocrisy on the other, the half-century preceding the Reformation surpassed most others.

It is worth while to remark that in the work at present under our notice we meet with that tendency to allegorize Scripture which always marks the first revolt against the letter; a tendency which may be traced in St. Paul himself in reference to the Old Testament, and in Origen and some of the Fathers in reference to various parts of the Bible. Erasmus warns his reader against the literal acceptation of Scripture, exhorting him to break the hard and bitter husk so as to reach the sweet kernel—the spiritual sense—which is concealed within, and quoting with special emphasis the words of Christ, "It is the Spirit which quickeneth; the flesh profiteth nothing." He accordingly recommends those interpreters who depart farthest from the literal sense, the principal of whom, after Paul, are Origen, Ambrose, Jerome, and Augustine. "For I perceive," he adds, "that our new-fangled theologians adhere too closely to the letter, and employ themselves in discussing captious questions of divinity, rather than in unravelling the mysteries of the Word, as if that was not true which Paul writes, that our law is spiritual." To give one or two instances of the way in which this allegorizing tendency is applied, the manna which the children of Israel ate in the desert is said to signify the knowledge of the ancient law; and the meaning of the word in Hebrew, "What is this?" indicates the duty of continual investigation. So the frequent mention in Scripture of wells, fountains, and rivers, is designed to commend to us the diligent search after the mysterious meanings which lie concealed under the literal narrative. Incidentally, Erasmus suggests a figurative interpretation for the miracle at Cana, where he says that Jesus at the marriage-feast turned the water of the cold and insipid letter into the wine of the spirit. Such a notion would now be called neological. Erasmus called those who adhered to the letter, neoteric. It is, perhaps, unnecessary to observe that all this was, as a matter of course, perfectly consistent with the acceptance of the truth of Scripture as history. The spiritual significance might as well be supposed to underlie the actual facts as the narrative which records them.[21] Only it will be seen that the way was thus opened for doubts, which might be applied more or less extensively, as to the truth of the narrative as a record of actual facts; and when Erasmus, in another passage, gives it as his opinion that the whole account of the creation is, so long as we look no deeper than the surface, not a whit better than the story of Prometheus and the fire stolen from heaven, we may feel satisfied that he did not in his own mind believe the world to have been made precisely in the manner described in the book of Genesis.

This excellent little work, though it failed, as may

---

[21] This, indeed, is the express teaching of St. Thomas Aquinas, from whom, probably, Erasmus derived it. "Respondeo dicendum quod auctor sacræ Scripturæ est Deus, in cujus potestate est ut non solum voces ad significandum accommodet (quod etiam homo facere potest) sed etiam res ipsas."— *Summa. Theol.* Pars I. Quæst. I. Art. x.

be supposed, to reform the character of the person for whose benefit it was originally composed, and though for some time after its publication it was comparatively neglected, eventually, as soon as its merits became known, attracted great attention, and ran rapidly through many editions.[22] Some, as I have already remarked, complained that it wanted unction, and, undoubtedly, it has not much of the oily phraseology which that word suggests. Erasmus himself has not hesitated to record the jesting remark of a learned friend, that "there was more religion in the book than the author," a remark which he allowed to be both witty and true, pleading, however, that it was unfair to blame him if, while sincerely desiring to lead a pious life, he had not always succeeded in the attempt. On the other hand, he could afford to despise those who condemned his work as wanting in learning, and said that

---

[22] "Libellus erat aliquamdiu neglectus. Mox mire cœpit esse vendibilis, idque potissimum commendatione quorundam Dominicalium, quorum aliquammultos nuper alienavit addita Præfatio ad Paulum Volzium Abbatem, virum moribus, ut si quis alius. pure Christianis."— *Cat. Luc.* "Ubi video toties jam excusum formulis, semper velut novum efflagitari."—Præf. ad Paul Volz. According to Brunet, the first edition of the *Enchiridion* appeared in a collection entitled *Des. Erasmi Lucubratiunculæ. Hantwerpiæ, opera Theodori Martini,* 1509, in 4to., which has been several times reprinted at Strasburg, Basle, and elsewhere, from 1515 to 1535. This, then, I suppose, is the earliest extant edition, and marks the date when the work began to be in demand. But the *Enchiridion* bears the date 1501; and unless there had been an edition then or soon afterwards, Erasmus would hardly have complained that it was for some time neglected; neither would he refer to it in writing to Colet, in 1504, as a work which Colet must have known (*Er. Op.* iii. 95, D.). We have besides an express statement of Erasmus to the effect that the *Enchiridion* was first published at Louvain twenty-two years ago (*Er. Op.* iii. 873, D); this statement occurring in a letter dated 1525, gives the year 1503 as the date of the original edition.

any schoolboy could have written it, because it handled none of the Scotist questions, as if there were no learning apart from those subtleties. It was enough for him, he adds, if it enabled men to pass their lives in Christian peace, even though it might not prepare them for the disputes of the Sorbonne. For his own part, he had no wish to add one more to the already far too numerous commentaries on the sentences, or summaries, of divinity, in which every question was defined with a minuteness which absolutely precluded the exercise of the individual reason. Such a work as "The Christian Soldier's Dagger" could not be very acceptable to the monks, and it is not strange if a fanatic like Ignatius Loyola found it far too sober for his fiery religion—he maintained, it seems, that the perusal of it cooled his piety—and consequently forbade it to his order. It is more to the purpose that it was commended by a scholar like Budæus, and found favour with the future Pope Adrian VI., who was then Principal of the University of Louvain.[23] It was subsequently condemned by the Sorbonne as heretical; but was translated, nevertheless, into German, Italian, French, Spanish, and English. The first English translation (1533) is believed to be by William Tyndale.

Among the learned men who encouraged the publication of the little treatise described above, was a Franciscan monk, John Vitrarius, with whom Erasmus became acquainted at St. Omer, and whose character he has sketched as a parallel to that of Colet, "to whom," he adds, "he was, in my opinion, in no respect inferior, except that, owing to the restraint of his profession, he was unable to do so much good." We have

[23] *Er. Op.* iii. 873, E.

already been introduced to the English priest, let us now make the acquaintance of the monk of St. Omer, another man who exercised some influence upon Erasmus when comparatively a young man.

"He was," he says, "about forty years old when I first knew him; and he immediately took a fancy to me, notwithstanding the difference in our characters. He had great influence in the best circles, and was high in favour with many of the nobility, being a man of tall and graceful person, very talented, and with that elevated tone of mind which is the essence of true politeness. As a boy he had acquired the Scotist learning, which he neither absolutely condemned, as it contains some good things meanly expressed, nor, on the other hand, did he set a high value upon it. But after having read Ambrose, Cyprian, and Jerome, it was astonishing how distasteful it became to him, in comparison with the writings of those Fathers. He admired no author in religious literature more than Origen; and when I expressed my surprise that he should like the writings of a heretic, he replied with astonishing vivacity that it was impossible to believe that a mind which had produced so many learned works, written with so much fervour, was not possessed by the Holy Spirit. But although he by no means approved of the monastic life, into which he had either entered of his own accord when too young to know better, or had been seduced by others—many a time has he said to me that it was a fool's life, rather than a religious one, to sleep, waken, and go to sleep again, to speak and be silent, to go and come, to eat and leave off eating, all at the sound of a bell, doing everything according to human prescriptions, rather than according to the law of Christ; adding that there could be nothing more unjust than equality among persons so very unequal, especially as men of heavenly mind, and born for better things, were often quite lost from having to observe so many ceremonies and human regulations, or even through the envy of the meaner spirits around them; yet he never advised any one to cast off his profession, nor did he himself make any attempt of the kind, for he was prepared to bear all things rather than give offence to any; in this also following the example of his favourite apostle, St. Paul. There was, moreover, nothing so unjust which he would not endure with the greatest cheerfulness for the sake of preserving peace. The books of Scripture, especially the Epistles of Paul, he had studied so carefully that no one could be more intimately acquainted with his own finger-nails than he was with Paul's writings. Indeed you had only to repeat a word or two, no matter from what part, and he would immediately go on to the end of the Epistle without a single mistake. He knew a great deal of St. Ambrose off by heart; and it is scarcely credible how much he could remember of other orthodox Fathers—a power which he owed partly to a naturally tenacious memory, partly to assiduous study. Once when I asked him in a familiar conversation how he prepared himself when he was going to preach, he replied that he was accustomed to open Paul, and continue reading him until he felt his heart begin to burn; then he stopped and prayed fervently to God, until he was warned that it was time to begin. He did not divide his sermons—which is done to such an extent by the majority of preachers that one might think it was forbidden to do otherwise—whence it happens that the division so often becomes quite meaningless. Indeed all that careful division only takes from the warmth of the address, and by discovering the art diminishes the impression of the preacher's sincerity. But Vitrarius, by never breaking the flow of his discourse, contrived to connect the sacred Epistle with the reading of the Gospel, so that the hearer returned home both instructed and with an inward zeal for religion. He neither made use of extravagant gesticulations, nor, like many preachers, stormed and roared, but with perfect self-possession uttered his words in such a way that you could see they came from an ardent and simple but sober mind : nor was he so long as to cause weariness ; he did not try to show his learning by various quotations, like other preachers, who put together centos from Scotus, Thomas, or Durandus, or from the works on the civil and canon law, or from the philosophers or poets, in order that the multitude may think they know everything. His whole sermon was full of Holy Scripture, nor would he quote anything else. What he said came from the heart ; he was inspired with an incredible zeal for drawing men to the pure philosophy of Christ.

"In labours such as these he was ambitious of the glory of martyrdom ; and once, as I learned from his most intimate friends, he had obtained from his superiors permission to visit countries in which Christ is either unknown or not worshipped in the right way, thinking he would be happy if, in this service, he should gain the martyr's crown. But on his way he was recalled by a voice which seemed to come from heaven, saying, 'Return, John ; thou shalt not fail of martyrdom at home.' He obeyed the divine behest, and found it true what the voice had spoken. There was then a sisterhood in which the religious discipline was so completely subverted, that it was much more of a brothel than a convent; and yet there were among the nuns a few who were both susceptible of reformation and wished for it. While he was endeavouring by frequent sermons and exhortations to bring them back to Christ, eight of the most desperate of their number conspired, and having kept watch for him, drew him into a secret place, and then put their handkerchiefs round his neck and tried to strangle him; and they would have succeeded in their impious purpose had they not by chance been interrupted. He was already half dead, and it was with difficulty that he recovered his breath; yet he never made any complaint of this matter, not even to his most intimate friends, nor did he at all relax the efforts which he was making for the conversion of those nuns; nay, he did not even look at them more sternly than was his wont. He was acquainted with the author of this conspiracy—he was a Dominican divine, the Suffragan Bishop of Boulogne, a man who openly led a wicked life—yet he never uttered a reproach to him, though there was no class of men whom he disliked more than those who, professing to be the leaders and teachers of religion, alienated the people from Christ by their character and impious doctrine. Sometimes he would preach seven times in one day, nor did he ever lack words and learning when his theme was Christ. His whole life indeed was an eloquent sermon. He was cheerful and by no means ungenial in company; yet without the faintest spark of levity or frivolity, still less of gluttony or intemperance. He would direct the conversation towards learned subjects, and very often towards religion, especially if any one visited him, or he was making a call anywhere. Or if he was going on a journey he had rich friends who sometimes set him on a mule or a horse, that he might talk more comfortably, and then, breathing more freely, this excellent man would bring forth treasures that no gems could purchase. He sent no one from him sad; nay, no one ever left him without being the better of his company and feeling a deeper love for godliness. He was the most disinterested of men, and never in any particular was he governed by his appetite, by ambition, avarice, pleasure, hatred, envy, or any other evil passion. Whatever happened he returned thanks to God, nor did he know any greater pleasure than to kindle men's hearts with the love of gospel religion. Nor were his efforts vain; he had gained many to Christ, both men and women, whose death proved how much they differed from the common run of Christians; for you might have seen his disciples meeting death with the greatest cheerfulness, and on its approach singing in a way that proved their hearts to be touched with the spirit of God: while others, having performed the usual ceremonies and made the customary protestations, gave up the ghost, perhaps believing, but perhaps not. Ghisbert, the excellent physician of that town, one who constantly cultivated true piety, who was present at the deathbed of many of both schools, is a witness of this fact. He had converted also some of the members of his own fraternity, but not many; just as even Christ could not do many miracles in his own country; for they usually prefer those who by their teaching bring plenty of meat to the kitchen, rather than those who win many souls to Christ. While, however, this pure spirit—a temple truly worthy of Christ—abhorred vice in every form, there was nothing more deeply repugnant to it than licentiousness, so that the faintest allusion of an improper kind was an offence to it, while immodest language was absolutely intolerable. He never declaimed violently against the vices of the world, nor revealed any confessional secret; but he would draw such a picture of virtue, that every hearer might discover, by the contrast, his own faults. In giving advice he showed extraordinary wisdom, integrity, and skill. He did not very willingly listen to secret confessions; yet he was in this most observant of charity: anxious and repeated confessions he openly disapproved. For superstition and ceremonies he had little respect, and he would eat any meat that was set before him, but always moderately and with giving of thanks: his dress had nothing to distinguish it from that of others. He was accustomed sometimes to make a journey for his health whenever he felt himself unwell. Accordingly, one day, when he was saying his morning prayers with a friend who accompanied him, he felt sick, perhaps owing to his fast of the day before: he went into the nearest house and took some food; on resuming the journey he began to pray, and his companion thinking he must begin all over again from the beginning, because he had taken food before the prayers of the first hour were finished, he replied with energy, that they had committed no sin, and that, on the contrary, God would be a gainer. 'Before,' said he, 'we were languid and exhausted, but now we will sing spiritual songs to God with cheerfulness, and he will be pleased with our sacrifices because they are offered by a cheerful giver.' I was then living with Anthony à Bergis abbot of St. Bertin, and as he did not dine till the afternoon, finding myself unable to endure so long a fast—it was the season of Lent—

especially as I was deeply engaged in study, I was accustomed to take a warm drink before dinner to sustain my stomach till dinner-time. When I asked him if that was permissible, he looked at the lay companion whom he had with him at the time to see if he was offended, and replied, 'You would commit a sin if you were not to do so;—if for the sake of a morsel of food you were to discontinue your sacred studies, besides injuring your health.'

"When Pope Alexander, in order to increase his gains, had doubled the Year of Jubilee, and the Bishop of Tournay had purchased the indulgence at his own risk with ready money, his commissioners made every effort not merely to secure the Bishop against loss, but even to bring him in a handsome return for his outlay. The first that were invited to give their aid in this matter were, of course, the most popular preachers. Our friend seeing that what had formerly been given to the poor would now be differently applied, though he did not express his disapproval of the Pope's offer, yet said nothing in its favour. But he did express his disapproval of the poor being defrauded of their customary alms, and condemned the silly credulity of those who thought their sins would be pardoned if they put their money in the box. At last the commissioners offered him one hundred florins towards building the chapel which was then in course of erection in his convent, on condition that if he would not recommend the Papal indulgences, he would at least conceal his objections. 'Away,' cried he, 'with your money, ye simoniacal priests! Think you I am one who will suppress the truth of the Gospel for money? If that is a hindrance to your gains, I ought to have more care for souls than for your pay!' Conscience-smitten, they gave way for the moment to the evangelical zeal of his reply; but meantime, quite unexpectedly, a sentence of excommunication was posted up at early dawn, which, however, was torn down by a citizen before it became much known. He, nothing daunted by these threats, continued teaching the people and celebrating the mass with great calmness, nor did he betray any fear of such an anathema because it was threatened him for preaching Christ. Presently he was cited to appear before his bishop, the Bishop of Boulogne; he obeyed, and went with only one companion, having no anxiety on his own account. The citizens, however, had mustered a body of horse on the road, lest he should be drawn into some trap, for what crime will not the accursed love of gold urge men to perpetrate? The Bishop objected to him some articles extracted from his sermons; but he answered courageously, and satisfied him. A little while after he was summoned again, when more articles were objected; having answered these also, he asked why his accusers were not present to accuse him at their peril, adding that he had already come twice to show his respect for his Bishop, but he would not come a third time if he were similarly summoned; he had better work to do at home. Thus he was left to himself, either because there was no pretext for doing him an injury, or because they feared a popular disturbance —the better part of the people being much attached to him on account of his virtue, though quite without his seeking their favour.

You will now ask, I am sure, what was the end of this man? He offended not only the commissioners, but also some of his brethren, not because they could find fault with his life, but because it was too good for their interests. All his anxiety was for the salvation of souls; but in making provision for the kitchen, in extending the convent walls, and enticing into them young men of property, he was not so active as they would have wished. He did not, however, altogether neglect these cares, especially so far as they were necessary, though he did not pay the extravagant attention to them which is often done. He had once made an enemy of one Thynnus, a courtier, a man of most immoral life, who had committed many adulteries, and quite neglected his own wife, a lady of good birth and the mother of several children. It so happened that she also was seduced, whereupon he immediately threw her off for the first slip, though he had so often pardoned his own lapses. The lady went from bad to worse, and at length fell into the extreme of misery. Vitrarius tried everything to reconcile husband and wife, but to no purpose; and finding him quite hardened and inflexible, whether he appealed to his respect for the marriage tie, to his love for his and her children, or to his conscience, seeing that he had given occasion, by so many adulteries and by neglect, to his wife's sin, left him as one of whom there was no hope. This man, a little afterwards, sent a quarter of pork to the convent, as he had been accustomed. But John, who was at that time purveyor, had given orders to the porter not to take anything in without calling him, and on the arrival of the present, having been called, he said to the servants who carried the pork, 'Take back your burden whence you have brought it; we do not receive the Devil's gifts!' Accordingly, though they knew very well that his life and doctrine were full of evangelical piety, yet as he did not look after the interests of the larder, he was desired to resign his office, which he did most willingly; and there was chosen in his place one whom I know, procured from some other monastery, who was as different from the other as he could possibly be; in short, he seemed to me to be one to whom no wise man would care to trust his cabbage-garden. I know not whether he was thrust upon them by those who wanted to get rid of him, or whether they thought he would prove fit for their purpose. As, however, from the influence of his example a few others were found who showed more zeal for promoting Christian piety than for storing the larder, they removed him to a convent of nuns in Courtray, where he ended his days in peace, teaching, consoling, and exhorting, having left behind him some books of extracts which he had made in French from the ecclesiastical writers, and which I doubt not corresponded to his life and conversation. And yet I hear that he is now condemned by some who think there is great danger if the people should read anything save the fables of the Church histories or the dreams of the monks. There lives still a spark of his doctrine in the breasts of many, whom if you compare with others, you would say that the latter were not Christians, but Jews. In such contempt was this remarkable man held by the members of his own order, whom the Apostle Paul, if he had had him as a colleague, would, I doubt not, have preferred even to Barnabas or Timothy."

In the winter of 1503-4, Erasmus was in Louvain, stopping at the house of John Paludanus, the orator of the university. It was in compliance with the solicitations of Paludanus that he wrote and afterwards delivered, in the Ducal Hall at Brussels, on the 6th of January, 1504, a congratulatory address to "Philip, Prince of Burgundy, son of the Emperor Maximilian, on his happy return from Spain."[24] It was with much reluctance that Erasmus undertook this office. His timid nature must have shrunk from so public a display, and, while it was necessary that he should praise the Prince, he feared to incur the charge of being a flatterer. Nor did he escape this accusation. He could only defend himself by appealing to the example of the ancient panegyrists, who, under the pretence of eulogy, had clearly no other object than to encourage to virtue; a defence which, he maintained, would justify him in the eyes of impartial judges, even though his panegyric had been addressed to a Phalaris or a Sardanapalus, whereas, in truth, it was addressed to a young man in whose character great virtues already appeared, and of whom the best hopes might be entertained for the future. Flattery on such an occasion is, perhaps, unavoidable, and, at any rate, in this address Erasmus ascribes to this young prince almost all possible virtues; but, in telling him all that he was of good and great, he at least showed him what he ought to be. Ever consistent in his hatred of war, and in the belief that it is a crime against heaven and humanity, he did not fail to point out that there were other and nobler paths to greatness than that of military glory. The panegyric was published, and dedicated to Nicholas Rutier, Bishop of Arras. The Prince was highly pleased with it, gave a handsome reward to the poor scholar, and wished to prevail upon him to remain at his Court. But this

[24] *Desiderii Erasmi Roterodami Panegyricus Philippo Burgundionum Principi dictus.—Er. Op.* iv. 505.

would have suited Erasmus even less than a professor's chair. After another year or two, finding himself still without the money he so much needed, he determined again to visit England, where he had already some wealthy friends not unwilling to assist his studies, and where he might hope by his presence to acquire many more. Meantime, the following letter was written to Colet, partly to renew his acquaintance and congratulate him on his appointment to the deanery of St. Paul's, partly, as will be seen, to ask his assistance in looking after the money he thought he ought to be getting for some copies of the Adages.

ERASMUS *to* JOHN COLET.[25]

"*Paris*, 1504.

"IF either our friendship, most learned Colet, had sprung from vulgar causes, or your character had ever seemed to have anything vulgar about it, I at least should have some apprehension lest, owing to so long and so wide a separation, it might not, indeed, have quite died out; but, at any rate, grown cold. As it is, since my admiration for your remarkable learning and love for your piety have recommended you to me, while I am recommended to you by your hope, perhaps, of finding the same qualities in me, or, rather, by your belief that I possess them, I do not think I need fear, although we see it commonly happen, lest, being out of

---

[25] *Ep.* cii. Colet, it would seem, was appointed to the Deanery of St. Paul's sometime in 1504, though he did not receive the temporalities till May, 1505 (*Oxford Reformers*, p. 138). When the Doctor's degree was conferred upon him we are not informed; but if it was at or before his appointment, the date of this letter may be correct, and it otherwise agrees with the contents.

your sight, I should be, on that account, less in your heart. But that now for several years no letters have come from Colet, I would fain persuade myself was owing to your occupations or to your not knowing exactly in what part of the world I might be—in short, to anything rather than forgetfulness of your friend. As, however, I have neither the right nor the wish to expostulate with you on your silence, I the more earnestly beg and entreat you to steal from your studies and business a little leisure in which to address me sometimes in writing. I wonder that none of your commentaries on Paul and the Gospels have yet seen the light. I am not, indeed, ignorant of your modesty, but even that should be overcome and laid aside out of regard for the public advantage. On the title of Doctor and the honour of the deanery, and some other ornaments which I hear have been spontaneously conferred upon your virtues, I do not congratulate *you*, who I know will gain nothing from them but more labour, so much as those on whose behalf you will bear them—so much indeed as the honours themselves, which, methinks, are then only worthy of the name when they are conferred on one who deserves and yet has not sought them. I cannot express to you, most excellent Colet, how I am devoting myself with all my power to sacred literature, how I loathe everything which calls me away from that, or even retards me in the pursuit. But the unkindness of fortune, who constantly regards me with the same look, was to blame, that I was unable to disentangle myself from these trifles. With this intention, accordingly, I went to France, that, should I be unable to finish them, I may somehow throw them aside. Then I shall be free to devote myself with my whole heart to the study of the Scriptures, in which I mean to spend all the rest of my life. Yet three years ago I attempted something on the Epistle of Paul to the Romans, and finished, without interruption, four volumes,[26] intending to go on had not certain matters called me away, the chief of which was that here and there I found myself deficient in Greek. Accordingly, for about three years, I have been wholly occupied with Greek literature, and I do not think I have altogether wasted my time. I began also to learn Hebrew, but deterred by the strangeness of the language, and at the same time because neither the life nor the genius of man is sufficient for so many studies, I gave it up. I have read a good part of the works of Origen, and I think I have gained something from this teacher; for he discovers as it were the sources, and indicates the methods, of theological science.

"I send you a trifling literary present of some of my shorter lucubrations; amongst which you will find that discussion we had in England on the agony of Christ, though so changed you will scarcely know it. The remainder, containing your answer and my reply, could not be found. The *Enchiridion* I wrote not to display my genius or eloquence, but solely as a remedy against the error which makes religion depend on ceremonies, and an observance, almost more than Judaic, of bodily acts, while strangely neglecting all that relates to true piety. I attempted, moreover, to teach a kind of Art of Piety, after the manner of those who have composed rules for self-discipline; all the rest I wrote against the grain, particularly the Pæan and the Obsecration, works which were dedicated to the good

---

[26] "Quatuor volumina." What quantity this may indicate I am unable to say:—probably four sheets.

will of my friend Battus, and the kindness of Anna, Marchioness de Vere. I had so much distaste for the Panegyric that I do not remember having ever done anything more completely under protest. For I saw that this sort of thing cannot be done without flattery. Nevertheless I used a new kind of art, to be very free in my flatteries, and very flattering without losing my freedom. If you want any of your lucubrations printed, only send me a copy, and I will attend to everything else and have it printed without fault. I wrote lately, as no doubt you remember, about the hundred copies of my Adages, which were sent into England at my expense three years ago. Grocyn had written to me that I might rely on his faith and diligence to do everything to have them distributed to my satisfaction. Nor do I doubt he has fulfilled his promise, as he is of all Britons the most honest and the best. You will condescend then to lend me your aid in this matter by admonishing and urging forward those by whom you think the business ought to be completed. For there can be no doubt that after such a time the books must be sold, and the money must have come to somebody: just at present it would be of more use to me than ever before. For I must try by some means to have some months to myself, in order to extricate myself from the labours which I have undertaken in profane literature, which I was hoping would have been this winter, had not so many hopes disappointed me. Nor can this liberty, namely of a few months, be purchased except for a considerable sum. Wherefore I beseech you to lend me what aid you can, now that I am extremely anxious to apply to sacred studies, and save me from that department of literature which has quite ceased to have any charms for me. I must not ask my friend, Count William Mountjoy; yet methinks he would not act amiss if he were to render me some aid of his own goodness, either on the ground that he has always been such a patron of my studies, or because one of my works was undertaken at his suggestion and inscribed to his name—I mean the Adages. For I regret the former edition, both because, by the fault of the printers, it is so full of errors that one might think it had been purposely corrupted; and because, at the instigation of certain persons, I precipitated a work which now at last begins to appear to me jejune and poor since I have studied the Greek writers. I have, therefore, determined to mend both my own fault and that of the printers in a second edition, and, at the same time, to benefit students by a most useful work. But though meantime I am engaged on a matter which is, perhaps, humbler, yet, while I am busy in the gardens of the Greeks, I pluck many flowers as I pass along, which will be of use hereafter even in the study of the Holy Scriptures. For this one thing I know by experience that in no department of literature are we anything without Greek. For it is one thing to conjecture, another to judge; one thing to believe your own eyes, another to believe other people's. Lo, to what a length my letter has grown! But it is love, not any fault, that makes me so talkative. Farewell, most learned and most excellent Colet.

"I am anxious to know what has become of our friend Sixtine; moreover, what Principal Richard Charnock, your dear friend, is doing. To secure safe delivery of anything you may write or send address it to Christopher

Fisher, a devoted friend of yours and patron of all literary men, in whose family I am stopping."

No answer is extant to this letter, nor is there anything more to record of Erasmus till we again meet him in England. He left Paris apparently towards the close of 1505, and on the first day of the new year we find him once more in London.

CHAPTER V.

SECOND VISIT OF ERASMUS TO ENGLAND — DEGREE AT CAMBRIDGE —TRANSLATIONS FROM LUCIAN—ACQUAINTANCE WITH URSEWICK — FOX — RUTHALL—WARHAM — FISHER— MORE — PORTRAIT OF MORE—DEPARTURE FROM ENGLAND.

THE second visit of Erasmus to England was a short one, lasting only about half a year. It was long enough, however, to enable him to renew his intercourse with his old friends—More, Grocyn, Linacre, and Colet, and to acquire some new ones. It would seem, too, that he took this opportunity of visiting Cambridge for the first time, and that he was made bachelor of divinity of that university.[1]

[1] "The greatest master of the antiquities of this university is pleased to say no more than that Desiderius Erasmus had his grace at Cambridge in the year 1506, to commence B.D. and D.D. at the same time, performing his exercise and satisfying the beadles ; and was afterwards admitted the Lady Margaret's Professor, *circa annum* 1511."—*Knight*, p. 88. Probably, however, a previous statement (quoted by Knight from Dr. John Caius or Keys) that he " had his grace to be bachelor of divinity " (p. 86) without any mention of D.D., is more correct ; for in his doctor's diploma, which he obtained at Turin this same year, Erasmus is called " a *bachelor* well deserving in the said faculty of sacred theology." A statement of More's, too, seems decisive of the point that Erasmus was not a D.D. of either English University. " Jam Oxonia Cantabrigiaque tam carum habent Erasmum, quam habere debent eum, qui in utraque diu cum ingenti scholasticorum fruge, nec minore sua laude versatus est ; utraque eum ad se invitat, utraque eum in suorum Theologorum numerum (quoniam eo honore alibi est insignitus) transplantare conatur."—*Apol. pro Moria Erasmi. Er. Op.* iii. 1896, B.C.

It has been already noticed that he employed himself occasionally in making translations from the Greek authors, as the best way he could find of gaining familiarity with that language. And these labours, as constituting his literary stock in trade, and, indeed, often his only means of livelihood, he of course endeavoured to turn to account in the usual way. Lucian had hitherto been his favourite, and in the light sarcasm and pleasant humour of that writer he found much that was congenial to his own nature. Erasmus, indeed, could not be more severe on the monks than Lucian on the would-be philosophers of his day, nor more successful in turning them into ridicule; but he certainly followed hard in his footsteps, nor can he refuse to acknowledge a debt to the witty satirist of Samosata. While stopping at the castle of Hamme, of which Mountjoy was governor, about two years before, he had sent a translation of the "Mycillus" to Christopher Ursewick, for many years recorder of London, and chaplain and almoner to Henry VII., in promoting whose succession to the throne he had done faithful service, and by whom he was frequently entrusted with important business. Ursewick might, had he desired it, have risen to the highest position in Church and State, but being without ambition, he refused the Bishopric of Norwich, and preferred a life of religious retirement at Hackney, where he was now spending his days in peaceful seclusion.[2] He had previously conferred some favours on Erasmus, and the latter sent him this dialogue as a proof of his gratitude. The dedication is particularly interesting, as containing a fine estimate of Lucian. "He revived," says Erasmus, "the wit of the old comedy, but without

[2] KNIGHT's *Life of Erasmus*, p. 78.

its abusiveness. It is marvellous with what graceful dexterity he touches every subject, turning all things into ridicule, and leaving nothing unscathed by his wit. Never does he make even a passing allusion but he must couple with it some sarcasm. For the philosophers he entertains the most cordial hatred, and, above all, for the Pythagoreans; the Platonists, also, he detests for their sophisms, and the Stoics for their intolerable pride. At these last he cuts and thrusts, attacking them with every kind of weapon; and always justly: for what can be more odious or less tolerable than wickedness when it wears the mask of virtue? Hence they called him blasphemer, which means an evil speaker; and no wonder if they did so, seeing how unmercifully he thrust at their sores. Even the gods do not escape his satire, but are ridiculed with equal freedom; and for this he was branded with the title of atheist—a name, however, which was creditable rather than otherwise, seeing that it was given him by the impious and the superstitious. He flourished (it is supposed) about the time of Trajan, but certainly does not deserve to be counted among the Sophists. Such is the grace of his style, the felicity of his invention, the elegance of his wit, the sharpness of his satire; so delicate are his allusions, so easily does he pass from grave to gay, from lively to severe, so amusing is he when he is most instructive, so instructive when he is most amusing; while he paints the manners, the passions, the pursuits of mankind as with a pencil, making us see them before our eyes rather than merely read of them, that no comedy, no satire that ever was written, can be compared with his dialogues, either for the pleasure or for the instruction which they afford." Such is the description which Erasmus gives of the writer whom he himself most resembled; nor does he, on this occasion, conclude without flinging a sarcasm at the scholastic divines. After begging his friend to read attentively this witty dialogue, he continues: "You have here a cock talking with a cobbler, his master, more ludicrously than any professional jester, and yet more wisely than the vulgar herd of divines and philosophers in their schools, who, with a noble disdain of more important matters, dispute about pompous nothings."[3]

And now we find him forwarding the *Toxaris*, or "Friendship," to Dr. Richard Fox, Bishop of Winchester, as a new year's gift, not without a pretty plain hint that such presents are usually blessed to him that gives as well as to him that takes.[4] Probably, Erasmus, having only recently arrived in England, was not aware that this Dr. Fox had done all he could to ruin his friend More, having, as Roper tells us, "pretended great favour towards him, and promised that, if he would be ruled by him, he would not fail but bring him into the King's favour again; meaning, as it afterwards appeared, to cause him thereby to confess his offence against the King, whereby his highness might with the better colour have occasion to revenge his displeasure against him." More fortunately escaped the wiles of the crafty Bishop, having received a hint of his purpose from his friend Whitford, Fox's chaplain, who warned him not to follow his master's counsel, "for my lord," said he, "to serve

---

[3] *Er. Op.* i. 243, *sqq.*

[4] "E priscorum usque sæculis mos hic in hæc nostra tempora deductus est, Amplissime Pater, ut Calendis Januariis, principe ineuntis anni die, munuscula quæpiam missitentur. quæ nescio quid lætioris ominis afferre creduntur, tum ad quos abeunt, tum illis ad quos redeunt." —*Er. Op.* i. 213-214.

the King's turn, will not stick to agree to his own father's death."[5] Erasmus, in his dedication to Fox, takes occasion to lament the decay of friendship among Christians, observing that "Christianity is nothing but true and perfect friendship, dying with Christ and living in Christ," and ends with begging him to continue his love and assistance as of old. Whether the patronage of this Bishop proved very profitable may be doubted, as we have no mention of any presents received from him; nor indeed was the example of Henry VII.'s court favourable to the purpose which Erasmus had principally in view in this visit to England. The Bishop of Winchester, however, evidently continued to take an interest in him, for we find him complaining that he was such a stranger with him, and so seldom came to his house; and on another occasion he indulged in a joke at his expense, saying he had thought Erasmus had received a benefice, and on being informed that he had not, but that he was hoping for one, he asked with a laugh if he could live on that hope.[6]

Probably he was more successful with Thomas Ruthall, Secretary to the King, who was very kind to him afterwards as Bishop of Durham. To him he dedicated the "Timon," observing that it might seem strange that he should send the "Misanthropist" to a man so well known for his extraordinary philanthropy, but it was the only piece he had in his possession at the moment.[7] He also sent him at another time, perhaps before coming to England, three other dialogues, the "Cynic," the "Necyomanteia," and the "Philopseudes," accom-

[5] ROPER's *Life of More*, pp. 8, 9.
[6] *Er. Op.* iii. 113, A., 114, C.
[7] This dedicatory letter is dated in Le Clerc (*Er. Op.* i. 255) Londini, MD.IV., but I presume it ought to be MD.VI.

panied by a letter, in which, apropos of the last-named, he takes occasion to condemn the gloomy and superstitious fables which are commonly told with so much confidence and authority, and one of which—a story, too, whose absurdity is exposed in this very dialogue—deceived even the sober judgment of St. Augustine. Erasmus cannot help suspecting that the great majority of these fables were invented by the worst of the heretics, who merely wished to amuse themselves with the credulity of simple people, or else to destroy the credit of true Christian history. "What inspired Scripture," he adds, "guarantees to us as history, in that we must put implicit trust; but all other stories we must receive with great caution and judgment, or else reject them, if we desire to be free from empty confidence and superstitious terror."[8] This letter proves that Ruthall, who is described as a man of distinguished learning and great wisdom in the transaction of affairs, was imbued with the more liberal tendencies of the age. Erasmus would not have written thus to a bigot.

But by far the most important friendship which he formed at this time was that of William Warham, Archbishop of Canterbury and Lord Chancellor of England, to whom he dedicated his Latin translation of the Hecuba of Euripides, and who afterwards proved one of his kindest and most liberal patrons. His first impression, indeed, of this Prelate was not altogether favourable; for on the presentation of the Hecuba, the Archbishop repaid the compliment with what he thought a very insignificant present, and he and his friend Grocyn, who had accompanied him, had a good laugh

---

[8] *Ep.* cccclxxv. App. The translations of these three dialogues are not included in Le Clerc's edition.

together in the boat, as they were rowed away from the palace at Lambeth, in trying to account for this niggardliness on the part of a man of such reputed generosity and wealth. Grocyn, who would seem to have known the ways of the world better than his friend, suggested, what was no doubt the true explanation, that the Archbishop must have suspected that he was not the first to whom the Hecuba had been dedicated. "And how," asked the aggrieved scholar, "can such a suspicion have entered his head?" "*Quia sic soletis vos*," was the reply—"Because such is the practice of you literary men." Determined to show that in his case at least the suspicion was groundless, Erasmus had his Hecuba printed as soon as he got back to Paris, and having added to it a translation of the Iphigenia in Aulis, on which he had employed himself at Cambridge, he dedicated both to Warham, and thus secured his friendship and patronage. "In this way," he says, "I revenged myself for Grocyn's wit, though I had at that time no intention of re-visiting Great Britain, nor any thought of ever asking another favour from the Archbishop. So great was my pride, notwithstanding my humble fortune." [9]

Warham was now about fifty-five years old, and had recently succeeded to the primacy on the unexpected death of Archbishop Dean. He was an Oxford man, a doctor of the civil and canon law, and had practised as a lawyer in the Court of Arches.[10] He gained distinction by going on several important embassies, and conducting the King's affairs with prudence and success; and he was a favourite with Henry VII., who was

---

[9] *Cat. Luc.*
[10] HOOK's *Lives of the Archbishops of Canterbury*, vol. vi. p. 157.

wise enough to know when he had found a good servant. According to Erasmus, who was never tired of praising Warham, and for whom, indeed, he seems to have entertained the sincerest affection, he was "a theologian, not in name, but in reality." Notwithstanding his many avocations, "he yet found time," he continues, "to observe most religiously the prescribed hours of prayer, to say mass almost every day, besides attending two or three services, to try causes, to receive embassies, to advise with the King about any matter of importance which might have arisen at court, to visit the churches of his diocese in the event of anything having occurred requiring his superintendence, besides often receiving in his palace as many as two hundred guests; while all the leisure he could find was given to reading." Erasmus mentions it as a remarkable circumstance—and it throws some light on the manners of the dignitaries of the Church in those days—that the Archbishop gave no part of his time to hunting, gambling, or frivolous talk, but preferred before all such pleasures an hour's quiet reading or conversation with some learned friend. "Though he sometimes entertained bishops, dukes, and counts, still his dinner was always over within an hour's time; and although his rank required him to keep a sumptuous table, he was himself so incredibly simple in his tastes that he never touched the luxuries which were set before his guests. He seldom tasted wine, but drank, even at the age of seventy, a very thin beer, and even that in very small quantities. Besides, though hardly tasting anything, he kept the whole table in good humour by the courtesy of his looks and manners, and his pleasant genial talk. He preserved, however, the same perfect sobriety and composure after as before dinner. He abstained altogether from suppers ; or, in the case of familiar friends, in which number I was reckoned, he would, indeed, take his seat at the table, but touched scarcely anything : if there was nobody with him, he would devote the usual supper-hour either to prayers or to reading. And as he was himself full of pleasantry, which, however, he never permitted to pass the bounds of good sense and good-nature, he also enjoyed the jests of his friends ; only scandal and abuse of others he detested like the poison of a serpent. Thus did that excellent man make the days abundantly long, of whose shortness so many complain." [11]

Thus wrote Erasmus of this eminent man, after his death, and when no more favours were to be expected from him. In his letters he frequently speaks of him as his Mæcenas: and there is no doubt that his love of learning (in which, however, he does not seem to have been personally distinguished [12]), as well as his liking for a joke, led him to be extremely liberal to the needy Dutch scholar. If the latter did not visit him again before leaving London, as would follow from his own statement, and if he was disappointed at the result of his first visit, he afterwards became most intimate with him, and received many proofs of his bounty. It was most likely about the same time that he made the acquaintance of the amiable and excellent John Fisher, Bishop of Rochester, who eventually died so nobly, for conscience' sake, on Tower Hill, not many days before his friend Sir Thomas More. Fisher is described by Erasmus as a man " not only of admirable integrity of

[11] *Er. Op.* v. 810, 811.
[12] " Quam non vulgaris eruditio" (*Er. Op.* iii. 118, D), is the most Erasmus ventures to say of him on that point.

life, but of profound learning," and one who had ever shown him remarkable kindness.[13] And in another place he says of him, "Either I am greatly mistaken, or he is the only man with whom there is no one of this age that can be compared either for integrity of life, or for learning, or for greatness of mind; Canterbury," he adds, "is the only exception I can make."[14]

Of all his English acquaintances, however, there was none for whom he cherished such an affectionate regard, or in whose company he took greater pleasure, than his young friend, Thomas More. In the year 1506, More, who had recently married, having decided not to take monastic vows as he once intended, was living in retirement, being then under the shadow of the royal displeasure for his manly resistance in Parliament to Henry VII., and was devoting all his time to literary pursuits; and Erasmus was often at his house in Bucklersbury, when they studied together their favourite authors, or amused themselves with making epigrams on bad kings and hypocritical monks. In this kind of composition Erasmus tells us he was less successful than in any other, though he used sometimes to practise it during his walks, or sitting at table over the walnuts and wine; nevertheless, his epigrams were collected by some too partial friends and printed along with More's at Basle.[15] One day More suggested that they should both write a declamation in reply to Lucian's "Tyranni-

---

[13] *Er. Op.* iii. 118, B.
[14] *Ib.* 102, D.
[15] "Nullo in genere me minus exercui, quam in Epigrammatis, et tamen interdum inter ambulandum, aut etiam in compotationibus lusimus aliquot, diversis temporibus, quorum nonnulla ab amicis nimium mei nominis studiosis collecta sunt, et edita Basileæ; quoque magis riderentur, adjunxerunt Thomæ Mori Epigrammatis, in hoc genere felicissimi."—*Cat. Luc.*

cide," which Erasmus had translated; they did so, and that of the latter was sent with a short dedicatory epistle to Richard Whitford, chaplain to the Bishop of Winchester, from whom, doubtless, it had its reward.[16]

Thus did these congenial spirits pass their days, mingling study with amusement, and many a good laugh, to be sure, they must have had together, as anything occurred to strike the humour of the one or of the other. It was apparently at this time, when they were both somewhat unsettled, that Erasmus enjoyed the closest intimacy with More, though, as we shall find, he had several opportunities afterwards of renewing their intercourse, and it is not strange if he conceived a warm attachment to so truly loveable a character; for so simple, genial, amiable, and yet truly high-minded a man as Sir Thomas More has seldom, if ever again, been known among Englishmen. Years afterwards, when More was a privy councillor, and high in favour with Henry VIII., Erasmus drew his portrait in one of the most characteristic and interesting of the many sketches which he has left of his celebrated contemporaries. It is contained in a letter to Ulrich von Hutten (1519), who had expressed a wish to have some such description of a man of whom he had heard so much, and, with some omissions, is as follows:—

"To begin," he says, "with that part which is least known to you, he cannot be called a tall man, and yet neither is he remarkably little. But so perfect is the symmetry of his form, that you never think whether he is short or tall. He is of a fair complexion, his face fair

---

[16] "Descripseram Declamationem Lucianicæ respondentem contra Tyrannicidam, huc provocante Thoma Moro, tum studiorum sodali."—*Ib.*

rather than pale, though by no means ruddy, except that a very faint flush overspreads it; his hair is blackish-brown, or, if you like it better, brownish-black, his beard thin, his eyes bluish with spots here and thére, a mark of great talent, and considered in England the sign of an amiable temper, though our countrymen prefer black eyes. They say there is no sort of eyes less subject to disease. His face is a picture of his mind, and always wears a pleasant and mirthful expression, now and then passing into a laugh; and, truth to say, he is more inclined to pleasantry than to gravity and dignity, though as far as possible from folly and buffoonery. His right shoulder has the look of being somewhat higher than his left, especially when he is walking—the fault not of nature but of habit, as is the case with many of our peculiarities. In the rest of his person there is nothing very striking except that his hands are rather coarse, that is to say, in comparison with the general beauty of his person. He was always from his childhood very negligent of everything relating to personal adornment. . . . His health is good rather than robust, yet sufficient for any labours worthy of an honest citizen; and he suffers from no diseases, or at any rate from very few. There is reason to hope he will be long-lived, since his father is a very old man and enjoys a wonderfully vigorous and hearty old age. I have never seen any one less dainty in his choice of food. Until he was grown up he liked to drink water best—a custom which he had from his father. But not to offend any one in this matter, he would deceive the company by drinking beer, and that as thin as water, and often plain water, out of a tin cup. Wine—it being the custom then for people to invite one another to drink out of the same cup—he would touch with the tips of his lips, that he might not seem absolutely to refuse it, and at the same time because he wished to accustom himself to common things. He preferred plain roast beef, salt fish and brown bread well raised, to what most people call delicacies, though he by no means abstained from everything that gives harmless pleasure even to the body. He was always fond of everything with milk in it, and of fruit; eggs he regards as a luxury. His voice is neither loud nor very shrill, but penetrating, with no softness or melody; and yet he speaks distinctly: for although he takes pleasure in all kinds of music, he does not seem to have been gifted by nature with a voice for singing. His speech is wonderfully precise and articulate, neither too rapid nor at all hesitating. He dresses very simply, and wears no silk or purple or gold chains, except when it is impossible to avoid it. He is exceedingly regardless of those ceremonies by which most people judge of good manners, and as he exacts them from no one, he is not anxious to show them to others; yet he understands them perfectly if he chooses to practise them. He thinks it effeminate, however, and unworthy of a man to spend a great part of one's time on such trivial concerns. . . .

"One might suppose he had been expressly formed for friendship, so sincerely does he cultivate, and so tenaciously adhere to it. Nor is he afraid of having too many friends, though Hesiod condemns it. In fact, he is ready to strike up acquaintance with everybody; and while he is thus by no means fastidious in his choice of friends, he is ever most kind in showing them hospitality, and most constant in retaining them. If by chance he falls in with any one whose faults are past cure, he takes an opportunity of dismissing him quietly, thus untying rather than rudely breaking the bonds of friendship. But when he finds any who are truly sincere and of congenial temperament, he is so fond of conversing with them and telling them stories, that you would fancy he considered this the greatest pleasure of life; for he has an utter abhorrence of ball, dice, cards, and other games with which most gentlemen beguile their hours of leisure. Moreover, while he is inattentive to his own interest, he is most diligent in looking after the business of his friends. In short, whoever wants a perfect pattern of true friendship, cannot possibly do better than take it from the example of More. In company he possesses such rare courtesy and sweetness of manners as would cheer any heart, however sad, or alleviate the tedium of any situation, however disagreeable. From his boyhood he was always as fond of jokes as if he had come into the world for no other purpose; yet he never went the length of scurrility, nor could he bear to utter an unkind word. When a lad, he both wrote farces and acted in them. So great is his love for pleasantry, especially if it be sharp and really clever, that he would enjoy a joke even at his own expense; and this led him, when he was a young man, to amuse himself with writing epigrams; indeed, it was he who instigated me to write my 'Praise of Folly,' which was as much in my way as for a camel to dance. There is nothing, however, in the world, not even in the most serious business, from which he will not extract amusement. In company with learned and sensible men he finds pleasure in intellectual converse; but among fools or silly people he amuses himself with their folly, nor do the most foolish people annoy him, so extraordinary is his power of adapting himself to every character. With ladies, and even with his wife, he does nothing but laugh and joke. You might fancy him a second Democritus, or rather that philosopher, the disciple of Pythagoras, who, walking up and down the market-place with vacant mind, calmly surveys the busy throng of buyers and sellers. No man is less influenced by the opinion of the world, and yet, on the other hand, there is no one who has more common sense. One of his greatest pleasures is to observe the form, the instincts, and the dispositions of different animals ; and there is hardly any kind of bird which he does not keep at home, besides other rare animals, as the ape, the fox, the ferret, the weasel, and such like. Besides, if he hears of any foreign, or otherwise interesting, curiosity, he at once buys it ; and every corner of his house is so filled with these things that, wherever you turn, something or other worth looking at attracts the eye ; and so his own pleasure is renewed as often as he sees others pleased."

Erasmus then proceeds at some length to sketch his friend's life, noticing his early inclination to the priesthood, his lectures on St. Augustine, his two marriages, his children, and the happiness of his home. " No man," he continues, " was ever less greedy of filthy lucre. He has set aside for his children what he thinks enough for them, and the remainder he spends lavishly. When he was living by his practice at the bar, he gave to every one the truest and most friendly advice, looking to their advantage rather than his own ; and he would persuade many to compose their differences, telling them that would be less expensive than going to law. If he could not succeed in that, seeing there are some people who delight in litigation, he would then point out how they might have their differences settled at the smallest possible expense. For several years he was a judge of civil causes [Under-Sheriff] in the City of London, where he was born—an office which, as it has few duties connected with it (the court sits only on Thursdays till noon), is yet esteemed one of the greatest honour. No one ever despatched more cases, no one ever acted with greater integrity: he often returned to the suitors the fees due by law. . . . If difficult cases demand a judge of special wisdom and gravity, More decides them so as to please both parties; and yet never was he prevailed on to receive a bribe from any one. Happy would it be for the world if every king could employ such ministers of justice as More. Nor has he, in consequence of his elevation, become too proud to remember his humble friends; and amid the pressure of business, he yet finds time now and then to return to his beloved studies. Whatever power he has in virtue of his rank, whatever influence he enjoys through the favour of his sovereign, he uses it all for the good of his country and for the good of his friends. At all times he was most anxious to confer favours without distinction, and always leaned in a marvellous degree to the side of mercy; and now, when he has more power, he indulges this spirit the more freely. He helps some with money, protects others by his authority; others he advances by his recommendations, while he aids with his advice those whom he cannot otherwise assist, and never sends any one from him dissatisfied. You would suppose More was the public patron of all poor men. He thinks it a great gain to himself to have

relieved the oppressed, set at liberty the embarrassed
or perplexed, or recovered the friendship of any one
who was estranged from him. No one can be more
ready to do a kindness, no one less exacting in looking
for its repayment. Now, though he is in so many
respects at the very pinnacle of good-fortune, and
although good-fortune is usually accompanied by pride,
I have never yet met with any one who was more
entirely free from that vice."[17]

Such, then, was this admirable man, as he im-
pressed himself on the observant eye and retentive
memory of the scholar of Rotterdam. Except by the
same pen, it is not often that a portrait has been drawn
so elaborately worked out, so minute in its details, so
true in its colouring, so telling in its general effect, and
so accurate in every particular. It is clear that many
parts of the description apply admirably to Erasmus
himself; and this enables us to understand how it was
that these two men found one another so mutually
attractive. If More could not pretend to compare with
his friend in extent of learning, or perhaps even in
breadth of thought, he was certainly his superior, as he
was the superior of every one, in simplicity of character
and pure-minded integrity. Both, however, were full of
humour and of good-humour; both were ardent lovers
of learning; and both were agreed that ignorance and
hypocrisy were legitimate subjects of ridicule. Both
men, moreover, were sincerely religious; and Erasmus
adds, in his letter to Hutten, that "More diligently
cultivated true piety, at the same time that he was a
complete stranger to all superstition." On this last
point, however, he afterwards corrected himself, and

[17] *Ep.* ccccxlvii.

while mentioning, to the credit of his clemency, that during his chancellorship no one was executed for heresy, he more truly observes that "if he inclined to either extreme, it was to superstition rather than to irreligion.[18] In a letter to Budæus, two years after that to Hutten, Erasmus specially commends More's three daughters, Margaret, Elizabeth, and Cicely, and it may be hoped that his acquaintance with these excellent ladies led him, universal satirist as he was, to think somewhat more highly of female capacity than would seem to have been his wont. He tells how they each wrote him a letter without help or correction from their father, and how pleased he was both with the excellence of the style and the good sense of the matter. "Believe me, Budæus, I never saw anything so admirable."[19] This, however, belongs to a much later period than that of which we are now speaking, when More had only just married his first wife.

And now at last, by hard, earnest work, by diligent soliciting from wealthy patrons, by careful husbanding of his small means, Erasmus finds himself in possession of a sufficient sum to pay for his journey to Italy, and secure the desired Doctor's degree. Once more in the early summer of 1506 he leaves the shores of England, this time, we may believe, for we hear of no misadventure, having taken such precautions as enabled him to escape the harpies of the custom-house. We must now follow him first to Paris, and then across the Alpine snows to Turin, to Venice, to Bologna, and to Rome.

[18] *Er. Op.* iii. 1811, A. [19] *Ep.* dcv.

CHAPTER VI.

INDUCEMENTS TO VISIT ITALY — ERASMUS IN PARIS — LETTER T COLET — TO LINACRE — TO WENTFORD — CROSSES THE ALPS — TURIN — ADVENTURE AT BOLOGNA — PAUL BOMBASIUS — ARRIVAL AT VENICE — ALEANDER — ALEXANDER, ARCHBISHOP OF ST. ANDREWS — RICHARD PACE — ERASMUS AT ROME — VISIT TO GRIMANI — RETURNS TO ENGLAND.

ITALY, the birthplace and the home of Latin literature, renowned throughout the world for her antiquities, her libraries, her arts, and her learning; the one country where the old classical memories had never completely died out, and where they had first recovered their influence; the country of Cicero and Horace, of Dante and Petrarch, of Valla, and Poggio, and Politiano, was the promised land of the cis-Alpine scholar. To be recognized by the Italians was his great ambition; and after he had studied in their schools, conversed with their learned men, and carried back to the chill regions of the North something of their Ciceronian elegance and Greek learning, then only could he venture to look upon himself as better than a barbarian. Already an Agricola, a Reuchlin, a Linacre, a Grocyn, a Colet, had crossed the Alps, and carried back to their own countries the fruit of their Italian studies; and although the scholar of Rotterdam sometimes fancied he had found in Oxford every advantage he could hope from Italy, he was never satisfied until he, too, had visited the acknowledged centre and source of reviving literature. For the Churchman, too, Rome, the seat of the Papal Court, could not but have its attractions; and while the main object of Erasmus was exclusively literary, visions of high preferment may sometimes have floated before his mind. Indeed, even as a literary man it was important for him to visit Rome. He knew that he had a fierce battle to fight with the ignorance of the monkish orders; and therefore to secure for himself and for the cause which he represented the friendship and favour of Popes and Cardinals, was a matter of no inconsiderable importance.

Such may have been the feelings which inspired him as he left the shores of England. Three letters from Paris, where he would not, in all probability, at that season—the middle of June—remain more than two or three days *en route* for Italy, are sufficiently characteristic to be worth translating. They will serve also as an introduction to what follows:

ERASMUS *to* JOHN COLET.[1]

"*Paris, June* 19, 1506.

"I CAN scarcely tell you with what various feelings I have left Britain and returned to France. For I find it by no means easy to decide whether I am more rejoiced to see my old friends in France once more, or sorry to leave behind my new acquaintances in England. For this I can truly say, that there is no entire country where I have found so many sincere, learned, kind, and distinguished friends, adorned with every virtue, as in the single city of London; where they were all so eager to pay me kindness and attention, that it is impossible for me to prefer any one before the rest, and I must

[1] *Ep.* civ.

needs love all alike. It is impossible that the loss of such friends should not grieve me: but, on the other hand, I am comforted by my own thoughts, which enable me to represent them to my mind as if they were actually present, and indulge the hope of revisiting them speedily, never again to leave them until death shall part us. To bring this about soon and without trouble, I rely upon your love and kindness to do what you can along with my other friends. I cannot tell you how pleased I am with the disposition of Baptista's children, so modest, teachable, and diligent in learning; by which I am led to hope that they will both fulfil their father's expectations and repay my attention, and hereafter do great honour to Britain. Farewell."

ERASMUS *to* THOMAS LINACRE.[2]

"*Paris*, 1506.

"I HAVE arrived in Paris, and am well in every respect, except that on the four days' voyage I caught cold, and was taken with a troublesome malady which just at this moment is giving me a horrible headache. The glands are swollen under my ears on both sides, my temples are beating, and both my ears ringing. And meantime there is no Linacre here to relieve me by his skill. So much has my resolution to visit Italy already cost me. For never in my life did I resolve on anything so firmly as that I would on no account trust myself to the winds and waves when it was possible for me to travel by land. The French must think I have risen from the dead, for a report, with some appearance of authenticity, and which no one contradicted, had got abroad here that Erasmus was gone to heaven. This rumour, I imagine, grew

[2] *Ep.* cv.

by some mistake out of the death of that Frenchman, Milo, who, like myself, leaving France, had gone into the family of Mountjoy, and a few days afterwards was taken with the plague and died. To this mistake, however (for as to the omen I nothing regard it), I owe this at least that I have enjoyed in my lifetime a foretaste of what they will say of me after my death. I am so charmed with France since my return, that it is doubtful whether Britain, which has given me so many and such excellent friends, more flatters my disposition, or France, which for old acquaintance' sake, also, from the liberty which I énjoy here, and lastly, from a special favour and affection which this country has always shown me, is ever most delightful. So that I have, in this way, two pleasures equally great: that of thinking of my British acquaintances, especially those whom I may hope to see soon again, and that of revisiting my French friends. You could not help laughing if you knew how greedily my little Greek has been expecting from me the δῶρον (gift) which I promised in return for his Cyprian pens; how often he reminds me of the δῶρον, how often he finds fault that it has not been sent. In sooth, 'tis delightful thus to mock a gaping crow. The stupid fellow does not see that I wrote in this sense, πέμψω δῶρόν τι ἄξιόν σου, (I will send thee a gift worthy of thee,) that is, something paltry. My new task of bringing up Baptista's children I hope will turn out well. For I find them boys of excellent capacity, modest, teachable, and already possessed of sense beyond their years. That Clysto, their attendant, is the most guileless, the most amiable, the kindest of men. Farewell, most learned and most genial preceptor; and write oftener to me, though it be briefly, only write."

Erasmus *to his friend* Roger Wentford.[3]

"*Paris, June* 19, 1507 [? 1506.]

"Among the many very dear friends I have made in Britain, you, my dear Roger, are one of the first to come to my thoughts, you who have so constantly loved me, or delighted me by your acquaintance, so helped me by your friendly offices that to whatsoever part of the world the fates shall carry me, I shall take with me the most agreeable recollections of my friend Roger. And I wish your fortune would afford you so much liberty that you could accompany us into Italy; you would have all Erasmus whom you have already made, if I may use the word, your own-est in many ways. My journey turned out very well, except the sea voyage, which was hateful. For four nights we were at the mercy of the winds and waves, in consequence of which I have been seized with a pain in the head, which, however, I hope to get rid of soon. You would wonder how much I am charmed with France, which is the more delightful to me because it is so long since I have seen it. My chief regret for England is that I have left so many friends behind me; such learned, upright, affectionate, kind, agreeable people, and to whom I am indebted for so many favours. Among them you must be put in the first rank. So take care to continue unchanged in your love for Erasmus, while I, in my turn, will endeavour every day to surpass myself in my affection for Roger. Farewell."

Baptista Boier, the father of the children referred to in these letters, was chief physician to King Henry VII.; and Erasmus, without being their teacher, had under-

[3] *Ep.* cvi.

taken to exercise a general superintendence over the studies of his two sons, John and Bernard, and to accompany them as far as Bologna. Their attendant, Clysto, did not long merit the high opinion which he entertained of him, but proved a quarrelsome and disagreeable person. On the way across the Alps he fell out with the courier of the King of England, who had been sent with the party as their protector. From the most violent abuse the two proceeded to blows, and even drew their swords upon one another; but fortunately the quarrel passed off without serious consequences, and when it was made up in the evening over a glass of wine as suddenly as it had commenced, Erasmus, who had at first thrown the blame upon only one of the two, lost all confidence in the stability of their characters, and found that they were both equally odious to him. This made the rest of his journey extremely unpleasant to him, and indeed he would have broken the connection at once had it not been for his obligations to Baptista, which, however, prevented him from doing so before the end of a year.[4] For the present he found consolation, as there was now no one with whom he cared to converse, in composing a poem on the evils of old age.[5]

If the poetical effusions of Erasmus are generally not of much value, some exception may be made in favour of this poem, which no one can read without admiration; and if the glorious scenery of the Alps failed to impress the mind of that age with a sense of the sublime and the terrible—and no doubt it appeared to the eyes of the present traveller and his companions,

---

[4] *Cat. Luc. Er. Op.* iii. 1397, F.
[5] *Carmen ad Gulielmum Copum Basiliensem de senectutis incommodis.*—*Er. Op.* iv. 755, *sqq.*

a scene of merely wild and unpleasing desolation—it may at least be supposed that the pure air of the upper regions was capable of inspiring an otherwise unpromising subject. We may admire here fancy, variety, beauty, invention : whoever looks for deeper or grander qualities will undoubtedly be disappointed. The picture too is interesting with which this poem presents us, of the learned monk, seated on his mule, struggling through the Alpine snow, already, though barely forty, thinking himself an old man, his head sprinkled with grey hairs and his chin fast becoming white ; such had been the effects of incessant work and (in youth at least) unwholesome food, upon a constitution naturally delicate.[6] The poem was actually written in the saddle, and then copied out at the inn where the party stopped for the night.

At Turin, where he must have remained for some weeks, the degree of Doctor of Divinity was conferred upon Erasmus by the University, on Friday, 4th of September, 1506.[7] We have seen that in pressing his claims upon Lady de Vere he had told her that to take such a degree was his principal object in wishing to visit Italy. Now, however, he had either changed his mind, or he had some reason or other for giving a different representation of himself; for we find him writing to Servatius, one of the Steyn brethren and afterwards prior of the convent, that he had taken the degree

---

[6] "Nunc mihi jam raris sparguntur tempora canis,
      Et albicare mentum
  Incipiens, jam præteritis vernantibus annis,
      Vitæ monet cadentis,
  Adventare hiemem, gelidamque instare senectam."
—*Er. Op.* iv. 756.

[7] See copy of diploma in *Epistolæ Familiares Des. Erasmi Roterodami ad Bonif. Amerbachium, I.V.D. ac Prof. Basil. cum nonnullis aliis ad Erasmum spectantibus.*—*Basiliæ*, 1779.

contrary to his own inclinations and at the instigation of his friends; and that the main object of his journey was the study of Greek.[8] Perhaps he was afraid Servatius might retort, "Why not take your doctor's degree in your own country, at Louvain?" or more probably Servatius had a contempt for University degrees of any kind, as we know he was one of those who could see nothing good beyond the walls of his convent.

Italy was at this time by no means in the state in which a lover of learning and a friend of peace would have wished to find it. The warlike and ambitious Julius II. was now on the Papal throne, and, in league with the Emperor Maximilian and Louis XII. of France, was making every effort for the recovery of the dominions of the Church. On his arrival in Bologna, Erasmus found the city threatened by an interdict, which was to be removed only on condition of the surrender of Bentivoglio and his sons, the leaders of the party opposed to the Papacy. Julius had advanced as far as Imola, while on the other side a French army was lying at Modena, ready, at a word from the Pope, to move forward and set fire to Bologna and put the inhabitants to the sword. Under these circumstances Erasmus wisely withdrew to Florence, but returned on hearing a report, which turned out to be well founded, that the Bentivoglios had been expelled and taken by the French. He was back just in time to witness the Pope's triumphal entry into the city. On the 10th of November Julius entered Bologna, and the next day went in triumphal procession to the cathedral of San Petronio,

[8] "Doctoratum in sacra Theologia nuper accepimus, idque plane contra animi mei sententiam, ac precibus amicorum expugnati."—"Italiam adivimus, Græcitatis potissimum causa."—*Er. Op.* iii. 1871, C, D.

where he celebrated mass. His reception was of the most splendid kind. The carpeted streets were spanned by thirteen triumphal arches, greeting the Pope as "the liberator of the city," while tapestries and pictures, trees and flowers, and even roses—a wondrous sight at that season of the year—adorned the houses on either side of the way; and the incense which curled up from the sumptuous altars which stood at intervals along the streets, might well have seemed to be in honour of the warlike priest, who, carried on a throne beneath a splendid canopy of brocaded cloth of gold, formed the centre of attraction, rather than of the God whose minister he professed to be.[9] That sight, the sight of the High Priest of Christendom celebrating a triumph with a magnificence worthy of a heathen conqueror, made a deep and most painful impression on at least one of the many thousands who were assembled to witness it. The monk from Rotterdam never forgot, and never lost an opportunity of expressing his disapproval of an act so unfitted to the character of the head of the Christian Church.

It was at Bologna that Erasmus, by his own account, met with an adventure which induced him to abandon his monkish habit, and exchange it for that of the secular clergy. The dress of his order, which, it would seem, varied somewhat in different countries, was either a rochet, or else a simple scapulary of white linen over the cassock, and that surmounted by a black hood or gown. Erasmus had obtained leave from the Bishop of Utrecht to wear without scruple either of these dresses, according to the custom of the country in which he might happen to be, and, finding on his way

[9] RAYNALDI *Ann. Eccl.* ann. 1506, § 29. *Er. Op.* iii. 1871 C, D.

through Italy, that the dress of the canons regular was universally the black gown with the scapulary underneath, and not, as at Paris, merely a black hood over a white rochet, he at once conformed to the general custom. Now, at Bologna it so happened that, during an outbreak of the plague, the physicians in attendance on patients attacked by that disease had been ordered to wear upon the shoulder a white napkin, to warn the passers-by from contact with them; and Erasmus, one day pushing along the streets quite regardless whether he touched any one, was mistaken for a physician by some young rakes, who drew their swords upon him, and would have attacked him had not a lady, seeing his danger, called out that he was only a priest. Another day he was again set upon with sticks and abuse, and from that time forth accordingly he concealed the scapulary, applying to the Pope for a dispensation to wear the dress of his order or not as should seem good to him; a request which was readily granted, provided only he would still wear a priest's habit.[10] Such is the pleasant story, usually received by his biographers with all seriousness, with which Erasmus sought to impose on the good Father Servatius, when, some time after having become prior of the convent, he endeavoured to

[10] "Semper antehac usus sum cultu Canonicorum, et ab Episcopo Trajectino, cum essem Lovanii, impetravi, ut sine scrupulo uterer scapulari lineo, pro veste nigra integra, et capitio nigro, pro pallio nigro, juxta morem Lutetiorum. Cum autem adirem Italiam, videremque toto itinere Canonicos veste nigra uti cum scapulari, ne quid offenderem novitate cultus, veste nigra illic uti cœpi cum scapulari," &c.—*Rev. Pat. Servatio Erasmus.* I hope I shall not be thought too sceptical in questioning the truth of this story. The only authority I can adduce in my favour is the writer of the *Critique de l'Apologie d'Erasme de M. l'Abbé Marsolier*, who treats it as a "conte badin," p. 70; but this would naturally be the view of the enemies of Erasmus.

prevail on the wandering sheep to abandon the vain pursuit of worldly learning, and return to his brethren at Steyn, reproaching him at the same time, no doubt, with having even discarded the monastic dress. If the same story was used in seeking the dispensation from Julius, we may be sure the Pope laughed at it rather than examined its truth. For who could believe that, in a city like Bologna, wholly given up to superstition, in which there were no less than twenty-two monasteries, and at least one belonging to the Canons Regular,[11] a monk dressed scrupulously according to the fashion of the place could possibly be mistaken for a physician; or that a scapulary, which would appear as two narrow strips of white beside the black gown, and retreating under it, bears any resemblance, except in whiteness, to a handkerchief suspended from one shoulder *above* the gown of the wearer? Before all, who could believe that Erasmus would remain a day in a city in which the plague had broken out? However that may be, there can be no doubt that the dispensation which he applied for was at once granted by the Pope, if not upon any solid grounds, in consideration of his literary merits;— otherwise, indeed, he would have been excommunicate— and it was afterwards confirmed by Leo X.

By far the most distinguished among the professors at the ancient University of Bologna at this time, and the only man of note whose friendship Erasmus seems to have acquired there, was Paul Bombasius, public Professor of Greek, a man of the most varied learning and the most engaging manners.[12] He afterwards

[11] UGHELLUS, *Italia Sacra*. t. ii. c. 6.

[12] Erasmus has noticed Bombasius in the most flattering terms in the *Ciceronianus* (*Er. Op.* i. 1010, F.), and more fully in the *Adages* (I. vi. 1). See also Bayle.

withdrew from the service of literature, in order to devote himself to public affairs, and removing to Rome, became secretary to Cardinal Pucci. We find him, while there, many years afterwards, assisting Erasmus in his Greek Testament, by ascertaining for him the reading of the Vatican manuscript in one or two passages of John's First Epistle. He eventually lost his life during the sack of Rome, in the Pontificate of Clement VII., having been overtaken and killed by a party of soldiers as he was endeavouring to make his escape to the castle of St. Angelo.

In the society of this learned man Erasmus took great delight, discussing with him questions of criticism, in which he derived much advantage from his nice taste, and consulting him in reference to the important work which he was now preparing—the new and greatly enlarged edition of his collection of the Adages of the Ancients. At this work he had been labouring for the last eight years, and it probably occupied most of the time which he spent at Bologna. He was there rather more than a year,[13] with the exception of a short visit to Rome in the spring of 1507, when he witnessed another spectacle similar to that which had so shocked him on his arrival at Bologna, when on the 28th of March, the Pope, seated on a mule, went in triumphal procession through the streets of his capital, celebrating his victory over the enemies of the Church. When his work was sufficiently advanced to permit him to think of publication, he wrote to Aldus Manutius, the celebrated printer of Venice, to know if he would undertake to print it, and having received a favourable reply, he packed up his manuscripts and proceeded to Venice, where he

---

[13] "Egit paulo plus quam annum Bononiæ."—*Comp. Vit.*

must have arrived towards the close of the year 1507, or in the beginning of 1508. Aldus had never seen him before, and on his arrival at the office, without announcement, being just then occupied with correcting the press, he kept him standing some time, supposing he was merely one of the many visitors attracted thither by idle curiosity; but as soon as he learned who he was, he welcomed him most warmly, and received him into the house of his father-in-law, Andreas Asulanus, with whom he himself lived.[14] There Erasmus occupied the same room, and indeed it would seem the same bed—for in those days beds were few even in rich men's houses—with Jerome Aleander, who was afterwards so notorious in the history of the Reformation, and of whom Luther, not very scrupulous in his treatment of enemies, has drawn so black a picture, describing him, without any good ground, as a Jew by birth, "though it is certain," he adds, "that he was not a Pharisee, as he did not believe in the resurrection of the dead, but lived as if there were no future life and without any restraint upon his evil inclinations."[15] When Erasmus met him he was about twenty-eight years of age, and was an excellent scholar, possessing, besides Greek and Latin, the rare accomplishment of a good knowledge of Hebrew. He is said to have had a most extraordinary memory, and to have been able to repeat by heart anything which he had once read. He would seem to have been very friendly with Erasmus as long as they lived together, and although they eventually became enemies, the latter never forgot the agreeable hours they had spent together over their books and their wine. Aleander did not

---

[14] BEAT. RHEN. *Ep. Car. Cas.*
[15] See BAYLE, and the passage from Luther which he quotes.

remain much longer at Venice, as that same year he was invited by Louis XII. to a Professor's chair in the University of Paris.

With Aldus, Erasmus lived on terms of the pleasantest intimacy, and the printer would sometimes playfully anticipate the time when they should both be old men, saying in a trembling voice, "How do you do, Erasmus?" and then replying in a still more attenuated tone—albeit Erasmus was some twenty years younger— "If you are well, so am I." But these moments of relaxation were snatched with difficulty from days and nights of incessant toil. For about nine months Erasmus worked so hard that, as he says himself, he had scarcely time to eat. If his enemies were to be believed, he found time to drink; for *they* said, and on the authority of Aldus himself, that though he usually did as much work in a day as most men would accomplish in two, he made Aldus pay for it by indulging to excess in his good wine, and they even alleged—but this was certainly a calumny—that he was sometimes lying drunk while others were at work.[16] Erasmus never concealed that

---

[16] J. CÆS. SCALIGERI *pro M. Tullio Cicerone contra Desid. Erasmum Roterodamum. Oratio I. Tolosæ*, 1620. Scaliger's evidence, of course, is not of much value (for who would believe mere vituperation?); but his statement in his second oration is so particular and so moderate, that it may seem to deserve some credit. "Aldum præterea Manutium Romanum optimum ac simplicissimi pudoris virum, recuperandorum soceri sui prædiorum causa qui sese Mantuam recepisset, tum videre, tum audire, memini, hæc eadem majore tui, quam tu ipse faceres, verecundia, narrantem: Plus operis abs te uno factum die, quam quantum abs quovis alio biduana opera exigi consuevisset. Verum hoc neque sibi gratis, neque tibi incommode evenisse dicebat. Id enim temporis quod ab onere superesset, excubantibus aliis in opere, te Monembatici vini pretiosi indulgentia reponere solitum." This, however, means little more than what I have said in the text, that Erasmus liked

he enjoyed his wine, and was even particular about its quality; but there is certainly no evidence that he ever drank to excess. Further particulars connected with the publication of the Adages I reserve for another place, where I shall give a full description of that work. At Venice Erasmus published also a revised edition of his translations of Hecuba and Iphigenia in Aulis, and edited for Aldus, Terence and Plautus.

His experience at Venice was in one respect unfortunate, for it was there that he was first attacked by the stone, from which he suffered cruelly during the rest of his life.[17] The winter of this year was passed at Padua, whither he went at the invitation of Alexander, the youthful Archbishop of St. Andrews, and son of James IV. of Scotland, who wished to have the benefit of his assistance in his studies. Of this young man, who, notwithstanding the high ecclesiastical office which he held, was only eighteen years of age, Erasmus has left a pleasing picture in his Adages. He was of heroic stature and extremely handsome, as his father also was, very dignified in his carriage, of a most gentle and amiable temper, and so devoted to study that even at meal-times he would have a priest to read aloud to him some useful book. Erasmus instructed him in Greek, and in Latin composition; and wrote for him several

---

a good glass of wine, and that was not discreditable to him, especially considering that wine of some sort was then considered a necessary of life even in the monasteries.

[17] "Interim mihi cum calculo malo nondum noto res erat."—*Er. Op.* ii. 405 C. "Nec oblitus sum nostræ pristinæ consuetudinis; nec si velim oblivisci, sinat calculus, quem istic primum collegi, meque subinde repetens, Venetiæ commonefacit."—Letter to Asulanus (Basil. 15 Cal. April, 1523), communicated to Burigni by Cardinal Passionei, and printed for the first time in his *Vie d'Erasme*. This is not the only place where Erasmus uses the singular, *Venetia*, instead of the plural, *Venetiæ*.

rhetorical exercises, one of which, a consolatory discourse upon death, was afterwards published. He made his own way through the books of the canonical law and their barbarous commentators. The afternoon was usually given to music and singing, or literary conversation; and if any time could be spared from other employments, it was devoted to the reading of history, of which he was especially fond. In short, all his time was spent in study, except what was required for sleep and religious exercises. His was a high-souled nature, far above every vulgar passion, yet without pride. He was extremely sensitive, but capable of great self-control, and deeply religious without being at all superstitious. This amiable young man, who might have been an honour to literature, fell, a few years afterwards, on the fatal field of Flodden, fighting by the side of his father.[18]

[18] "Cæsus est una cum fortissimo patre filius, et filius eo patre dignissimus Alexander Archiepiscopus, titulo divi Andreæ, juvenis quidem viginti ferme natus annos; in quo nullam consummati viri laudem desiderares. Mira formæ gratia, mira dignitas, heroica proceritas, ingenium placidissimum quidem illud, sed tamen ad cognitionem omnium disciplinarum acerrimum. Nam mihi fuit cum eo quondam in urbe Senensi domestica consuetudo: quo tempore a nobis in Rhetorum præceptis Græcanicisque literis exercebatur," &c. "Animus sublimis, et a sordidis istis affectibus procul semotus; sed ita ut nihil adesset ferocitatis, nihil fastidii. Nihil non sentiebat, permulta dissimulabat: nec unquam ad iracundiam poterat incitari."—*Er. Op.* ii. 554, B—E. It will be observed that Erasmus says nothing here of having been invited by the Archbishop to Padua, nor, indeed, does he anywhere say that he knew him there at all. His silence may, perhaps, throw some doubt on the accuracy of Beatus Rhenanus (*Ep. Cæs. Car.*), whom, however, I have followed in the text. Erasmus has noticed this prince only once in his correspondence, where he mentions that he was so near-sighted he could not see to read unless the book was held close to his nose (*Ep.* dccclxxiv). It is interesting to compare with the description of Alexander by Erasmus the equally elaborate picture of his

At Padua Erasmus probably attended the lectures of Marcus Musurus, of Crete, who was then Professor of Greek in the university, and whom he describes as so indefatigable in his work, that he scarcely permitted four days in the year to pass in which he did not give a public lecture. Musurus was a man of great learning, and a much better Latinist than most of the Greeks who came westwards. He afterwards taught Greek at Venice, and eventually, having been invited to Rome by Leo X., was created Archbishop of Malvozia in the Morea, a dignity, however, which he did not long enjoy, as he died almost immediately afterwards, in the year 1517.[19] At Ferrara he made the acquaintance of Richard Pace, afterwards Colet's successor as Dean of St. Paul's, with whom he maintained a warm friendship throughout life. He was, indeed, on one occasion very angry with him, because, in a book which was quite unworthy of his learning, he had several times introduced Erasmus, and spoken of him as a needy person and one hated by the theologians. Erasmus declared that he could not see the wit of this, if it was meant for wit, as he was on the best terms with all the leading divines of the day, and had an ample income, which he might easily increase to any extent if he chose to take a part in public affairs; nor, on the other hand, could he suppose that he was in earnest. He recommended him, through More, not again to transgress in the same way, but to confine himself to translating Greek.[20] However, the offence was forgiven, and Erasmus heartily sympathized

---

father by the Spanish Ambassador at his court, Don Pedro de Puebla. See Burton's *History of Scotland*, iii. pp. 213-215.

[19] See BAYLE, and the passages from Erasmus there quoted.
[20] *Ep.* cclxxv. cclxxxvii. App.

with him in the persecutions he underwent from Wolsey, and wrote him an affectionate letter of congratulation on his release from the Tower.[21] From Padua Erasmus removed to Sienna, where he resided some months with his pupil Alexander, and where he parted from him, proceeding thence to Rome, which he may have reached early in the spring of 1509. The young archbishop, who had received a summons from his father to return home, presented him, on his departure, with several rings, among which was one which subsequently gave rise to some discussion, and was made the ground of a silly calumny against Erasmus. This was a seal-ring engraved with the head of the god Terminus—a youth's head with long hair, with the name inscribed below—which its new owner continued to make use of, to the end of his life, as his common seal, having added the inscription, *Concedo nulli.* These words, of course, were seized hold of by the enemies of Erasmus, as though he were speaking of himself, and thereby asserting universal superiority; and in his old age he found himself compelled to write an apology for his seal,[22] his explanation being that the inscription was to be read not of himself, but of the god Terminus, thus, *Concedo nulli Terminus,* meaning that death is the great enemy whom no one can resist. The truth was, he says, he accepted the ring as an omen of the near approach of death, and in order to preserve this thought in his memory, he added the inscription and used it as his seal.

At Rome he was warmly received by all who were

---

[21] *Ep.* mxcvii.

[22] *Desiderii Erasmi Epistola Apologetica de Termini sui inscriptione,* Concedo nulli.—*Er. Op.* x. 1757, *sqq.*

then most eminent in rank and learning; and though it would seem that he remained there only a few months, he had time, nevertheless, to form some valuable friendships. He was particularly intimate with Raphael, Cardinal of St. George, and he was of course introduced to the Cardinal de' Medici, who did not forget him when he became Pope Leo X. Among other learned men, Scipio Carteromachus, of Pistoia, whom he had first met at Bologna, and who is described by Erasmus as a most accomplished scholar, but so unostentatious that, unless pains were taken to draw him out, he might have passed for one completely ignorant of letters, was then residing at Rome; and Erasmus tells how this learned man would often call at his lodgings of an afternoon to enjoy an hour's conversation, and how they frequently shared the same table, and sometimes even the same bed.[23]

Another of the cardinals who showed him great favour, but whose acquaintance he made only as he was on the point of leaving Rome, was Dominic Grimani. He was only once at his palace, but of this visit he has left so graphic a description that it must not be omitted. "I had been more than once invited to converse with him," says Erasmus, "I think through Peter Bembo, but so little liking had I at that time for paying my court to the great, that I went at last for shame of refusing, rather than from any inclination. Neither in the court-yard nor in the entrance-hall was there a creature to be seen: it was then the afternoon. I gave my horse to the servant, and went upstairs alone. I entered the first, the second, the third room; still no one to be seen, and not a door shut; I could not help

---

[23] *Er. Op.* x. 1750, F.

wondering at the solitude. I came to the last room, and there I found only òne person, a Greek, as I thought, a physician, with his head shaved, standing at the open door. I asked him what the Cardinal was doing. He told me he was inside, talking with some gentlemen; and as I said no more, he asked me my business. 'I would have paid my respects to him,' said I, 'if it had been convenient, but as he is engaged, I will call again.' As I was going away I stopped at a window to look at the view, when the Greek came back to me, and asked whether I had any message I wished to send to the Cardinal. 'There is no need,' said I, 'to disturb him, I will come again soon.' At last he asked me my name, and I told him. As soon as he heard it, before I was aware, he hurried in, and presently returning, desired me not to go, and in a few minutes I was admitted. The Cardinal received me, not as a man of his rank might have received one of my humble condition, but as if I had been an equal. A chair was placed for me, and for more than two hours we conversed together, nor would he even permit me to be uncovered, which was a wonderful condescension in a man of his exalted rank. Among many very learned remarks, in which he showed that he had already formed the plan, which I hear he has since executed, of collecting a library, he advised me not to leave Rome, a place where men of genius were sure to find encouragement. He invited me to come and live under his roof and share all his fortunes, adding that the climate of Rome, being warm and moist, would agree with my constitution, and particularly the part of the city in which he had his palace, which, he said, was built by one of the Popes, who had chosen that site for its healthiness.

After a long conversation, in which we both took our share, he sent for his nephew, who was already an archbishop, and a young man of extraordinary genius. As I offered to rise, the Cardinal would not let me, and said, the disciple ought to stand in the presence of his master. Then he showed me his library, consisting of books in every language. Had I been so fortunate as to have known him sooner, I would never have quitted that city, where I found far more favour than I deserved; but I had made up my mind to go, and I had so far committed myself that it would scarcely have been honourable to remain. When I told him I had received a summons from the King of England he ceased to press me, but begged me not to doubt that his promises were sincere, nor to judge him by the standard of other courtiers. He let me go most unwillingly; but when he could not detain me, seeing that I was anxious to take my leave, he made me promise to call once again before leaving the city. I am sorry to say, however, I did not do so; for I was afraid his eloquence might prevail with me to make me change my mind." [24]

Notwithstanding what Erasmus says here, it is not probable that he ever seriously thought of settling at Rome, or that his residence there was very satisfactory to him. We are told, indeed, that he was offered the office of penitentiary, to which a considerable emolument was attached, if he would remain; [25] but as this office can be held only by a cardinal, it is more probable that it was merely spoken of for him, or promised at some future more or less remote, than that he had

---

[24] *Ep.* mclxxv.
[25] BEAT. RHEN. *ubi supra.* This fact, I believe, is nowhere mentioned by Erasmus himself.

actually the option of declining it. Nor was the court of Julius II., who was just then meditating war upon the Republic of Venice, for the recovery of the domains of the Church, likely to be very congenial to the tastes of the peaceful scholar. The Pope, indeed, was a patron of literature, but, full of ambitious schemes, he probably had not much time to bestow on the German ecclesiastic, who seems ever to have regarded his memory with horror. There is no evidence that Erasmus enjoyed any degree of personal intimacy with Julius; only one incident, which he has himself recorded, would show that he was willing to do what lay in his power to conciliate favour. At the request of the Cardinal of St. George he wrote a treatise against the war, to which he gave the name of *Antipolemus*, but very soon afterwards, as the Pope's intentions became more evident, he was induced to write another in its favour. We may well believe that in the former he was much more in earnest than in the latter, but it is not much to his credit that he should have consented to write the second at all. The only excuse that can be offered for him is that on the mere political question he had, perhaps, really no opinion whatever; and it need not be doubted that the piece in favour of the war, which, with the other, has been lost, was qualified with earnest denunciations of war in general, which he always cordially detested. The second oration carried the day, Erasmus somewhat naïvely tells us, which was no great wonder considering it expressed the views at which the Pope had already arrived.[26]

Erasmus, who, it must be confessed, was rather fond of regarding himself, and wished others to regard him,

[26] *Cat. Luc.*

as an ill-used man, would fain have us believe that in leaving Rome he yielded to the most pressing solicitations from his English friends, and went relying on promises which were never fulfilled. By his own account —but this statement was made a great many years afterwards—he was so taken with the simplicity, the sobriety, the high culture, and the kindness of the Italians, that he had quite made up his mind to settle at Rome, and would have done so had he not been irresistibly drawn back to England by the most splendid promises.[27] Of these promises, however, there is very little trace except in his own letters. Mountjoy, writing to him from Greenwich on the 27th of May, does, indeed, assure him that he will be welcomed at the English court by the new king, who had already given proof of his fondness for literature, and speaks in general terms of the favour and the riches he may expect. He also speaks in glowing terms of the bounty of Henry's nature, contrasting so favourably with the niggardliness of his father's reign. But the only definite promise he makes is in the name of the Archbishop of Canterbury, who, he says, will give him a benefice if he returns. Besides, this letter is not an invitation to Erasmus, but a reply to two letters of his which have unfortunately been lost, but in which, it is clear from Mountjoy's answer, he had complained that the climate of Italy did not agree with his health, as well as of other misfortunes, the nature of which can be only conjectured.[28] The truth seems to be that, finding that he was not likely to gain anything by a longer stay in Italy, and hearing

---

[27] "Idque adeo fecissem, nisi promissis montibus aureis in Angliam fuissem retractus verius quam revocatus."—*Er. Op.* x. 1750, E.

[28] *Ep.* x.

that the Prince of Wales, in whose good graces he already stood high, had succeeded to the English throne as Henry VIII., he began of his own accord to turn his thoughts once more towards his friends in London, and wanted only a very little encouragement to return to them. Besides the letter from Mountjoy just described, he had also received a very friendly one from Henry himself, shortly before his accession, written with his own royal fingers;[29] a very great honour, no doubt; but this letter, which still remains,[30] however flattering, certainly contains no invitation to England, and no promises, and, on the whole, it would seem that the "golden mountains" of which Erasmus was fond of talking existed principally in his own imagination. The one definite promise made to him was, as we shall presently see, strictly fulfilled.

It may be presumed, though there is no positive evidence of it, that Erasmus left Rome shortly after receiving Mountjoy's letter, which indeed was accompanied by a note for ten pounds, five from himself and five from Archbishop Warham, to pay the expenses of his journey. Crossing the Alps from Como to Coire, he proceeded by way of Lake Constance to Strasburg, and so down the Rhine to his native Holland, whence, after a short visit to his friends at Antwerp and Louvain, he sailed for England.[31] And thus ended his first and only visit to Italy. The majestic scenery of the Alps, the bright Italian sky, the arts, the antiquities of that classic region, seem to have made but little im-

---

[29] "Rex ipse paulo ante patris obitum, quum essem in Italia, scripsit ad me suapte manu litteras amantissimas."—*Rev. Pat. Servatio Erasmus.*

[30] *Ep.* ccccli. App.

[31] BEAT. RHEN. *ubi supra.*

pression on his mind. Once only does he speak of Venice as the most magnificent city in the world.[32] But it was not for these things that he travelled. He had made many friends among the learned and the great, and in any difficulties into which he might fall hereafter through his zeal for letters he could rely on some powerful support. He had improved his knowledge of Greek. He had published an important work. He had extended his reputation as one of the most learned men of his day, and he was now carrying back to the barbarous lands north of the Alps all that Italy could bestow upon the scholar. Thus for his own purposes, and for his life's work, his journey had not been unprofitable.

[32] *Er. Op.* iii. 506, D.

CHAPTER VII.

THE PRAISE OF FOLLY—ITS ORIGIN AND CHARACTER—ANALYSIS OF THE WORK—FOLLY THE CAUSE OF MIRTH—SATIRE ON WAR—HUNTING — SUPERSTITION — THE DIVINES — THE MONKS — THE PREACHERS—THE CARDINALS AND POPES — POPULARITY OF THE WORK—ATTACKED BY DORPIUS—ERASMUS'S REPLY.

WHEN we next meet Erasmus he is once more in London, and again forming part of the family circle of his dear friend Sir Thomas More. As he was riding across the Alpine snows this friend had been much in his thoughts; and how odd it was, it had occurred to him, that the wisest and wittiest man that he knew should bear a name which in Greek signifies the Fool. And then, no doubt, he had begun to think how many real fools there were in the world, and what various forms folly assumed. His own experience and reading furnished him with abundant examples; and before his journey was at an end, a kind of declamation, in which, under pretence of eulogizing folly, he might turn all classes of men into ridicule, had worked itself into some sort of shape in his thoughts.[1] Arrived in London, he seized his pen, and in about a week's time had completed one of the famous satires of the world.

[1] "Superioribus diebus quum me ex Italia in Angliam reciperem. . . . visum est Moriæ encomion ludere. Quæ Pallas istuc tibi misit in mentem? inquies. Primum admonuit me Mori cognomen tibi gentile, quod tam ad Moriæ vocabulum accedit, quam es ipse a re alienus."—*Enc. Mor. Præf.*

Such was the origin of the *Encomium Moriæ*, or Praise of Folly,[2] one of the best known, as it is also one of the most characteristic, of its author's compositions: and, although he himself always spoke of it as a piece which he had merely dashed off for the amusement of his friends, and even went so far as to express regret that he had ever written it, it really contains, in a short compass, his whole philosophy of man—all that he ever wrote on the abuses of his time, on the superstitions of monks, and the pride of kings. Abounding in wit and eloquence, and displaying great knowledge of the world and keen observation of men and things, it has also its deep and serious meanings underneath the light satire that plays upon the surface. Naturally it reminds us of Lucian more than any other writer, in the contempt, mirthful rather than fierce or indignant, which it affects to pour out upon human life and on all human occupations. Nor does Erasmus fall greatly short of his model. His humour is scarcely less rich, the shafts of his ridicule are as sharp, the images which he presents to the mind are as ludicrous, as in the writings of that great master of satire. The idea of the piece is ingenious and original. Folly, personified, pronounces her own panegyric, and shows, by various humorous examples, that mankind are indebted to her for all the happiness they enjoy. On the whole, she sustains this difficult part with admirable skill, except when she now and then forgets for a moment that her sole duty is to praise, and becomes too earnest in her denunciations of the follies of the world. And if the piece is fairly open to the charge of being sometimes

[2] Μωρίας Ἐγκώμιον, *id est Stultitiæ Laus: Erasmi Roterodami Declamatio.*—*Er. Op.* iv. 405.

a little rambling, the character of the speaker may surely plead an ample apology.

This little work, though insignificant in bulk, yet exercised such an influence at the time of its appearance, and is so important for illustrating the genius of its author and the sort of work he tried to do in the world, that it will be necessary to notice it at some length. An analysis of its contents will best explain its character and significance.

Folly, who, as we have seen, delivers the harangue, at once boldly introduces herself as the sole cause of mirth in heaven and among men, who spreads joy over every countenance, however sad before, just as the sun, when he "shows his jolly golden face to the earth," sheds new bloom and the freshness of youth over nature. She then claims the right of trumpeting her own praises, and calls upon all to prick up their asses' ears to hear her. Having announced her name and parentage, she declares herself to be a goddess, and, indeed, the very chief of divinities, inasmuch as she is the authoress of the greatest blessings to humanity. For she not only gives life itself, but also all the pleasures of life. Who knows not that man's childhood is by far the most delightful period of his existence? And why? Because he is then most a fool. And next to that his youth, in which folly still prevails; while in proportion as he retires from her dominion, and becomes possessed, through discipline and experience, of mature wisdom, his beauty loses its bloom, his strength declines, his wit becomes less pungent, until at last weary old age succeeds, which would be absolutely unbearable, unless Folly, in pity of such grievous miseries, gave relief by bringing on a second childhood. Nature herself has kindly provided for an abundant supply of folly in the human race; for since, according to the Stoic definitions, wisdom means only being guided by reason, whereas folly, on the other hand, consists in submitting to the government of the passions, Jupiter, wishing to make life merry, gave man far more passion than reason, banishing the latter into one little corner of his person, and leaving all the rest of the body to the sway of the former. Man, however, being designed for the management of affairs, could not do without a small quantity of reason; but in order to temper the evil thus occasioned, at the suggestion of Folly woman was introduced into the world—"a foolish, silly creature, no doubt, but amusing and agreeable, and well adapted to mitigate the gloom of man's temper by familiar intercourse." Woman owes all her advantages to Folly. The great end of her existence is to please man, and this she could not do without folly. If any one doubts it, he has only to consider how much nonsense a man talks to a woman whenever he wishes to enjoy the pleasures of female society.

It is now shown that friendship, love, marriage, success in life, are all dependent on the aid of Folly, which blinds us to the faults of others as well as to our own. Then comes a fine piece of satire on war, which Erasmus always detested. "Is not war," asks Folly, "the very source and fountain of all famous deeds? And what, I should be glad to learn, can be more foolish than, for any insignificant cause, to engage in a contest from which both parties invariably carry away more hurt than advantage. I say 'carry away,' for no one thinks of those that perish. And when the armies have been set in array, all bristling with steel, and the trumpets have brayed aloud, what is the use, pray, of your wise men, who are quite exhausted with study, and whose thin and frigid blood scarce serves them to draw their breath? Stout, well-fed men, are what you want, with plenty of courage, but as little as may be of intellectual power. Unless you would choose to have Demosthenes for a soldier, who, following the advice of Archilochus, had hardly come in sight of the enemy when he threw away his shield and fled, as cowardly as a soldier as he was wise as an orator. But counsel, it is said, is very important in war. Yes, in the general, I admit; but even then it must be military, not philosophical, counsel; with this exception, it is by parasites, scoundrels, robbers, assassins, ploughboys, clowns, debtors, and such like dregs of mankind, that this glorious business is carried on, and not by candle-light philosophers."

Wise men, Folly proceeds to argue, are quite useless for all the purposes of life, as is proved by the case of Socrates, who, when he attempted to discharge some public function, only succeeded in making himself ridiculous. The wise are, indeed, a bad race, but it has been observed that those who devote their lives to study are generally unfortunate in their children, nature thus kindly providing that this curse of wisdom may not be propagated too far. The wise man, moreover, is the most miserable of beings; while, on the other hand, no one is so happy as a fool. Fools have no fear of death, they are not tortured by conscience, they are not terrified by the fables of hell, they are not afraid of ghosts, they are not haunted by the apprehension of impending evils nor distracted by the hope of future blessings. They are so beloved by the greatest monarchs that some cannot even dine or pass an hour without them. Besides, fools only are simple and truth-telling; and what is more praiseworthy than truth? The fool speaks out whatever is in his mind, whereas the wise man has two tongues, with one of which he tells the truth, with the other speaks only what the occasion may seem to demand. But here the philosophers object that madness is the greatest of all miseries, and extraordinary folly is nearly allied to madness. This is a great mistake. Madness, so far from causing misery, is, on the contrary, by the delusions to which it gives rise, generally productive of happiness. And it may be doubted whether there is any one who does not suffer from madness, though, where the disease is very common, it goes by some other name.

"Such are they who despise all amusements compared with hunting, and swear that that hideous blowing of horns and baying of dogs gives them more pleasure than anything else in the world. Their enjoyment, however, is at its height when the game comes to be slaughtered. Bulls and wethers a clown may butcher, but your stag must be lanced by none but a gentleman. Taking off his cap and dropping down on his knees, with a knife made for the purpose (for it would never do to perform just the same operation with a common instrument), he most religiously cuts certain parts in a certain order, and with certain gestures. Meantime, the company, standing round in perfect silence, look on with wonder and awe, as if some new sort of sacrifice was going to be offered, although they may have seen the sight a thousand times before. And whoever has the good luck to taste a bit of the flesh thinks that not a little nobility has entered into his constitution. Thus, though by their continual slaughtering and eating of game they almost degenerate into wild animals themselves, yet they fancy all the time they are living like kings."

We have seen that in one of his letters from England Erasmus claims to be a first-rate huntsman; and unless he had been at least once in at the death, he could scarcely have given so humorous a description of the operation.[3] After noticing two or three other classes of madmen, Folly next shows off the vulgar credulity of the time. "But that class of men," she proceeds, "is altogether of our kidney, whose sole delight is to hear and tell lying stories of miracles and prodigies, and who can never have enough of fables about spectres, spirits, ghosts, the place of future punishment, and a thousand such wonders; which are all believed the more willingly as they are remote from truth, and in the like proportion tickle the ear with a more agreeable itching. Such fables are not only wonderfully useful for relieving the tedium of the hours, but they are also very profitable, especially for priests and preachers. Nearly allied to these, again, are they who have permitted the no doubt foolish, but still agreeable, persuasion to possess them, that should they see a wooden image or painting of St. Christopher Polyphemus,[4] they will not die that day,

---

[3] It is interesting to find that More agreed with Erasmus on this point, and that in his *Utopia* he assigns the business of hunting and butchering to slaves. "The Utopians," he says, "look upon hunting as one of the basest parts of a butcher's business, for they account it more decent to kill beasts for the sustenance of mankind than to take pleasure in seeing a weak, harmless, and fearful hare torn in pieces by a strong, fierce, and cruel dog."

[4] The pictures of St. Christopher often more nearly resembled Virgil's

"Monstrum horrendum, informe, ingens, cui lumen ademptum,"

than the gentle saint who carried the infant Christ.

or that whoever shall salute a carving of St. Barbara will return safely from battle, or whoever meet Erasmus[5] on certain days, with certain tapers and certain prayers, become suddenly rich. Now, forsooth, they have invented a George Hercules too, like another Hippolytus. His horse, most religiously adorned with trappings and studs, they all but worship, and to swear by his brazen helmet is an oath for a king. But what shall I say of those who flatter themselves with the pleasant delusion that they can grant pardon for sins, and who measure the periods of purgatory, as it were, with time-pieces, meting out centuries, years, months, days, hours, as if by a mathematical table where there could be no possibility of error? or of those who, trusting to certain little magic marks and prayers which some pious impostor invented either for amusement or with a view to gain, promise themselves wealth, honours, pleasures, abundance, unfailing health, and a green old age, and in the other world a seat next Christ himself,—which, by the way, they would not wish to reach for a long time yet; that is, not till the pleasures of this life, however much against their will and however closely they may have clung to them, shall nevertheless have flown—then they would wish those heavenly joys to follow? Here is a man—say a merchant, or a soldier, or a judge—who thinks that by payment of a single coin out of his robberies, all the vileness of his life may once for all be swept away, and imagines that so many perjuries, lusts, fits of drunkenness, so many quarrels, impostures, perfidies, acts of treachery, can be redeemed as by contract—ay, and so redeemed that he may now return to a new round of crime. But could any frame of mind

[5] Not the author, but a saint of that name.

be more foolish—I mean happier—than theirs who by the daily recitation of those seven verses from the Psalms promise themselves more than supreme happiness? And these magic verses some jesting demon, who was not, however, so cunning but he could be taken in, is believed to have pointed out to St. Bernard, the poor devil having been entrapped by the saint's art.[6] And these things, which are so foolish that I am almost ashamed of them myself, are nevertheless regarded with approbation, and that not merely by the vulgar, but even by the professors of religion. . . . Now, if in this state of things any odious wise man were to rise up and proclaim what is doubtless true,—Thou shalt not perish miserably if thou livest well; thy sins will be forgiven, if to thy money thou addest hatred of thy misdeeds, and after that tears, watching, prayers and fasts, and changest thy whole manner of life; such and such a saint will bless thee if thou wilt endeavour to follow his example:—I say, if the wise man should bray out such truths as these, behold of how great happiness he would rob mankind, and into what confusion he would plunge them!"

Erasmus now proceeds to attack in succession various classes of men, including merchants, grammarians and schoolmasters, poets and scholars, lawyers, philosophers, monks, and theologians. On the two last, of whom he knew most and who presented the greatest number of points for attack, he is particularly severe. "The divines perhaps it might be better to pass by, seeing they are an extremely supercilious and irritable race, lest, if provoked, they may rush upon me in a

---

[6] The saint threatened that if he did not show him the verses in question, he would read the whole book of Psalms every day.

body, armed with six hundred conclusive arguments, and force me to recant; and should I refuse they would forthwith raise the cry of heresy. For that is the thunder with which they terrify all who are unfortunate enough to incur their hostility. It is true there are none who are less willing to acknowledge themselves dependent on my bounty; but for all that they are deeply in my debt, as it is I who bestow upon them that self-love by which they are able to fancy themselves caught up to the third heaven, and to look down on the rest of mankind as if they were so many sheep feeding on the ground; and indeed they pity their miserable condition, while they are themselves protected by so vast an array of magisterial definitions, conclusions, corollaries, propositions explicit and implicit, and have so many loop-holes of escape, that no chains, though they should be forged on the anvil of Vulcan, can hold them so fast but they will contrive to extricate themselves; for which purpose they are provided with a number of fine distinctions with which they can cut all knots more easily than the sharpest axe, and with a vast supply of newly-invented terms and words of prodigious length. They are extremely ingenious too in explaining the profoundest mysteries of divinity; as, by what process the world was created and fashioned; through what channels the plague spot of original sin was transmitted to posterity; in what manner, by what degrees, and in how long a time, Christ was made perfect in the Virgin's womb; how accidents can subsist in the consecrated wafer without any substance in which to inhere. But these are comparatively trivial questions. There are others which they think worthy of great and illuminated theologians, as they call them, and for the discussion of which they exert all their faculties. Such are the following,—whether the divine generation required an instant of time for its completion; whether there is more than one filiation in Christ; whether the proposition, God the Father hates the Son, is a possible one; whether God could have taken upon him the form of a woman, of the devil, of an ass, of a cucumber, or a flint-stone. Then, supposing he had taken the form of a cucumber, how he could have preached, worked miracles, or been crucified? What Peter would have consecrated if he had celebrated the eucharist while Christ's body was hanging upon the cross? Whether at that time Christ could have been called a man; and whether after the resurrection it will be possible for us to eat and drink,[7] * as we do now, to guard against hunger and thirst. And there are a thousand other niceties, far more subtle than these, about notions, relations, formalities, quiddities, ecceities, which no one can possibly see, unless indeed he be as sharp-sighted as Lynceus, so as to discover in the thickest darkness what in reality has no existence whatever.

"Consider next those tenets of theirs which are so strange and absurd that the dogmas of the Stoics, which are generally looked upon as paradoxes, seem in comparison quite natural and intelligible; for example, that it is a smaller crime to commit a thousand murders, than for a poor cobbler to put a stitch in a shoe on the Lord's-day; or that it were better to destroy the whole

---

[7] It may be worth noticing that the passage which I have marked thus *, and what follows in the Latin down to "At interim ipsi felicissime sibi placent," &c., does not occur in the oldest edition, nor in that of Aldus of 1515, where the reading is, "edere aut bibere licebit? Video, ridetis jamdudum tam frivolas Theologorum argutias. At ipsi felicissime," &c.

world than to utter even the most innocent falsehood. And these exceedingly subtle subtleties are made more subtle still by the several sects of their schoolmen, the Realists, Nominalists, Thomists, Albertists, Occamists, Scotists, whose doctrines are more involved and intricate than the windings of the Labyrinth; nor have I yet named all their schools, but the principal ones only; in all of which there is so much learning and so much abstruseness, that methinks the Apostles themselves would need a new out-pouring of the Spirit before they could engage in controversy with these new divines. Paul no doubt had a full measure of faith; yet when he says that faith is the substance of things hoped for, the evidence of things not seen, his definition is little in accordance with the rules of the Masters of Arts. And though he had an abundance of charity, yet he does not divide or define this virtue in by any means a logical manner in his thirteenth chapter of First Corinthians. The Apostles too were in the habit of consecrating the Host, which they surely did most religiously; and yet if they were questioned as to the 'terminus a quo' and the 'terminus ad quem,' the nature of transubstantiation, how the same body can be in different places at the same time, the difference between the attributes of the body of Christ in heaven, on the cross, and in the sacrament of the mass; at what moment of time transubstantiation takes place; whether the prayer through which it is effected is a discreet quantity having no permanent *punctum*, they would not, I fancy, have answered with as much acumen as our Scotists now display in their dissertations and definitions. They were well acquainted with the mother of Jesus; yet which of them has demonstrated in the philosophical style of some of our divines, that she was preserved immaculate from original sin? Peter received the power of the keys from Christ himself, who certainly would not have trusted him had he been unworthy; and yet I doubt much whether he understood how it was possible for a man who has no knowledge to have the key of knowledge; at least he has nowhere touched upon that subtle question. They baptized all nations; and yet they have nowhere taught us what is the formal, material, efficient, and final cause of baptism; nor is there any mention in their writings of a delible and indelible character in that sacrament. They worshipped indeed; but in the spirit, following no other rule but that of the Gospel, 'God is a Spirit, and they that worship him must worship him in spirit and in truth.' But it does not appear that it was then revealed to them that they must adore in one and the same act Christ himself in heaven and his image painted upon a wall, with two fingers stretched out, his hair uncut, and a circle with three marks on it round his head. To understand these mysteries requires six-and-thirty years to be spent in the study of Aristotle's physics and the doctrines of the Scotists." *

More follows in the same strain, but we pass on to the attack on the monkish orders.

"Next in happiness to the Divines are those who call themselves Monks, and claim to be in a special sense religious, though both names are utterly false; for as to the latter, a considerable number of them have no religion whatever, and as to the former, the word Monk means 'solitary,' whereas they are so thick that we meet them at every turn. Now, I cannot conceive what state could be more wretched than theirs, were it not that I befriend them in so many ways. For though this class of men are held in such execration by everybody that it is thought unlucky even to meet them by chance, they are nevertheless immensely in love with themselves. In the first place, they think it the height of piety to have so little taste for learning as to be unable even to read. In the next place, when they roar out in church, with voices harsh as the braying of a donkey, their daily count of Psalms, the notes of which they follow, to be sure, but not the meaning, they fancy they are charming the ears of the saints with the divinest music. There are some of them, too, who make a good profit out of dirt and mendicity, begging their bread from door to door with a great deal of noise; nay, they press into all the public-houses, get into the stage-coaches, come on board the passage-boats, to the great loss and damage of the regular highway beggars. And that is the way in which these most sweet men, by their dirt, their ignorance, their brutal vulgarity, and their impudence, imitate the Apostles — so they have the assurance to tell us. Nothing, however, can be more pleasant than to observe how they do everything by rule, as if there were certain mathematical principles laid down for their guidance, which it would be the height of impiety to transgress. Thus, they must be very particular as to the number of knots with which their sandals are tied, the colour of their girdles, the distinctive shape of the habits of their respective orders and the stuff of which they are made, the number of cords of which their belts are twisted, the form and capacity of their hoods, the breadth of their skull-caps, the length of time they may devote to sleep. Now, who does not see how impossible it is to preserve this uniformity, where there is so great a variety in the persons and the dispositions of men? And yet for the sake of these trifles they not only look down on all the rest of the world, but they despise one another, and though they profess to be inspired by apostolic charity, they are ready to fill the world with confusion if a gown be girt on the wrong way, or be a little too dark in colour. You may see some of them so extremely scrupulous that they will wear their outer garments of nothing but hair-cloth, while they have the finest material next their skin; others, on the contrary, with linen outside and wool inside; and yet others who would no more touch money than they would poison, though all the time they are free enough with wine and women. In short, they are all animated by a marvellous zeal for creating as much diversity as ever they can in their rule of life; nor do they study so much to be like Christ as to be unlike one another."

The preachers, with their gesticulations, their contortions of countenance, their affected changes of voice, are next turned into ridicule. Even the highest dignitaries of the Church are made to smart under the lash. Erasmus lectures the Cardinals on their duties, and finally lays hands on the supreme Pontiffs themselves. No situation, argues Folly, could be more wretched than that of the vicegerents of Christ, if they endeavoured to imitate Christ's life — namely, his poverty, toil, doctrine, his cross, his contempt for life; which they would do if they had the smallest particle of wisdom. As it is, however, they leave all the labour to Peter and Paul, who have plenty of leisure for it, while they reserve for themselves the pleasures and the splendours of their office. And here Erasmus found it impossible not to remember some of the scenes he had witnessed in Italy. He refers to the then reigning Pope in the boldest and most personal way, speaking of "decrepit old men, who nevertheless put on all the ardour of youth, and spare no expense, regard no toil, provided they can subvert law, religion, and peace, and turn the whole world upside down." It would be interesting to find that Erasmus maintained here the same generous doctrine of religious toleration which was sometime afterwards propounded by his friend More in the Utopia. This perhaps was hardly to be looked for in a work so purely satirical, but in the later editions of the "Praise of Folly" there was inserted a story which showed at any rate that the author was far from thinking the stake the most satisfactory refutation of false doctrine. At a certain theological discussion some one asked what authority there was in Scripture for burning heretics, whereupon an old, sour-looking divine arose, and answered with some warmth that it had been commanded by the Apostle Paul in the words, "A man that is a heretic after the first and second admonition reject." As no one could perceive the force of the argument, he at length explained that the Latin word *devita* (reject) signified *de vita tollendum hæreticum* (a heretic must be put to death). Some laughed, while others thought the argument conclusive, and he then proceeded to quote the text "Thou shalt not suffer a witch to live," where the Latin word is *maleficus* (an evil-doer). "Now, every heretic is an evil-doer;" *ergo*, &c. The story, it would seem was a true one, which Erasmus had from Colet, and the scene took place in St. Paul's Cathedral.[8]

[8] See Erasmus's note on *Tit.* iii. 10. Mr. Seebohm is, no doubt, right in referring this occurrence to the Convocation of 1512. *Oxford Reformers*, p. 248 and notes.

The declamation concludes in truly orthodox style with a copious citation of Scriptural texts in commendation of Folly; and the free way in which Scripture is handled, and even the most sacred names introduced, while it shows certainly great want of taste, if not even want of reverence, might reasonably have given offence to persons who were neither very superstitious nor very bigoted. The age, however, was one in which there was hardly any reverence and a great deal of superstition and bigotry. Yet Erasmus afterwards became sensible of this error, and acknowledged that he ought at least to have forborne from introducing the name of Christ in a humorous composition like the *Moria*.

Such, then, was this remarkable work—remarkable not merely for its inherent excellences, which, however, are such as to entitle it to a high place among compositions of its class, but still more as being, in that century at least, the first decisive trumpet-blast summoning the friends of light and learning to gird on their armour, and heralding the advance of that reforming spirit with which the Papal power was destined ere long to engage in deadly and terrible encounter. As the work proceeded it was read to More and other congenial friends, by whom it was received with applause. Erasmus, if we may trust his own statement, made apologetically many years afterwards, valued it too slightly to think of publishing it. He had written it, he said, when he was kept indoors for a few days by an attack of the gravel, before his books had arrived, and when, in fact, he was too ill to enter on any more serious study: possibly, he really shrank from the hostility which he must have foreseen it would arouse. Any objections he may have had were, however, disregarded by the friends who encouraged him to complete his undertaking. Through their agency a copy of the work—an imperfect one—eventually found its way to Paris and was there printed.[9] The little book was received with immense favour, especially among people of influence, and within a very few months went through no less than seven editions. Kings, bishops, archbishops, and cardinals, Erasmus assures one of his correspondents, were delighted with it, and Leo X. read it through from beginning to end.[10] It was first printed, it would seem, in 1511.[11] In 1514 Froben printed an edition at Basle, with a commentary by Gerard Listrius, a young physician of that city, and an intimate friend of the author, from whom, no doubt, he received his instructions, the object of the commentary being evidently not merely to explain the frequent classical

---

[9] *Er. Op.* ix. 3, D, E. *Conf. Cat. Luc.* — "Moriam lusimus apud Thomam Morum, tum ex Italia reversi, quod opus quum mihi sic esset contemtum, ut nec editione dignarer (nam aderam Lutetiæ, quum per nescio quos pessimis formulis depravatissime excuderetur), tamen vix aliud majore plausu exceptum est, præsertim apud Magnates : paucos tantum monachos, eosque deterrimos, ac theologos nonnullos morosiores offendit libertas."

[10] *Er. Op.* iii. 275, B.

[11] The *Encomium Moriæ*, having been written far on in 1509, could scarcely have been printed before 1510, and probably was not printed until 1511. The earliest edition which has a date is that of Schurer, printed at Strasburg in 1511. I have also seen in the Imperial Library (as it then was) in Paris a very old black-letter copy, badly enough printed to justify the description of Erasmus, "pessimis formulis depravatissime," and which may probably be one of the original edition. It has neither date nor printer's name. There is, indeed, no appearance of this edition being derived "ab exemplo non solum mendoso verum etiam mutilo " (*Er. Op.* ix. 3, E.) ; but is it not possible that this statement was merely intended to reconcile the subsequent enlargements which were made on the original work with the contempt in which Erasmus always professed to hold it?

allusions, but to blunt the edge of some of the more pungent sarcasms. Aldus printed a neat edition in 1515, and it was afterwards reprinted several times by Froben, having received some considerable additions from the hand of the author. Every one knows the humorous illustrations by Holbein, the originals of which are still preserved in the public library of Basle, and opposite one of which, representing himself, Erasmus wrote, in Latin, "Ah! if Erasmus were still like that, he would certainly marry." The "Praise of Folly" has been translated into most European languages, and a French version by George Haloin appeared as early as the year 1517. For a copy of this we find Erasmus inquiring with some curiosity; but when he received it he was by no means pleased with the performance, the translator having taken what liberties he chose with the original, and added to it or omitted passages to suit his taste.[12]

Such a work as the "Praise of Folly" could not fail to rouse opposition and dislike. Yet it was a considerable time before the monks broke silence. Probably their dull brains did not at first apprehend the fact that they were turned into ridicule, or they contented themselves with denouncing the impieties of this second Lucian over their cups. Indeed, Erasmus himself tells us that the *Moria* was not understood except by a few until the appearance of Listrius's Commentary; but "when," he adds, "it was translated into French, then even those who couldn't read their Psalter understood it."[13] Besides, it would be a matter of some difficulty to attack with any chance of success a man who had corresponded with the King of England, and who num-

[12] *Ep.* cclxiv. cclxxxiv. [13] *Ep.* cclxiv.

bered so many of the most eminent dignitaries of the Church among his personal friends. It was clear that against a person of such consideration no mere vulgar clamour would avail. The most politic course would be to appeal to his own good feeling, to allow his eminent merits as a scholar, and at the same time expostulate with him gently on his faults. This was the course which was eventually followed. The University of Louvain found a champion in a young divine named Martin Dorpius, who was prevailed on to write to Erasmus to remonstrate with him on the publication of what he called "the unlucky *Moria*." Dorpius, accordingly, who was a young man of very amiable temper, and not obstinately opposed to true learning, addressed Erasmus, whom he had known personally at Louvain, in a very respectful and complimentary style, telling him how unfortunate it was for his own fame that such a book should have appeared at the very time that he was beginning to be held in admiration by all the most eminent lawyers and theologians. Erasmus took the letter in good part, and in reply assured his correspondent that though he was every day receiving letters from learned men saluting him as "the sun" and "the moon" of Germany, and loading him with all sorts of flattering titles, none of them gave him so much pleasure as the expostulatory letter of his dear Dorpius. He then entered on a long and elaborate defence of himself, protesting that his sole object in all his works was to do good, and that the *Moria* simply attempted under another form to do the same thing which the *Enchiridion* had aimed to accomplish in a more serious spirit. He challenged Dorpius to name any one whose character he had blackened or on whom he had cast the slightest aspersion. And as to his having alienated the whole order of divines, he denied it altogether; for since the publication of the *Moria* he had never met with any hostility, except on the part of a few of that class who hate all literature; on the contrary, were it not that it might seem arrogant to do so, he could name men of the highest rank in the Church, distinguished for their piety and learning, and some of them even bishops, who had never received him so cordially before, and who were much better pleased with his book than he was himself. He declared, indeed, that he himself did not set the slightest value upon it; that he was astonished at its success, and that he considered none but sacred studies deserving of the name of literature. He even condescended to say that he almost regretted the publication of the *Moria;* but his regret was either not very sincere, or did not last very long, for the little work continued to appear with the author's sanction, and with several additional passages not found in the earliest editions.[14] Dorpius, far from being pacified by the very flattering letter of the illustrious scholar, who had praised "his heavenly temper, his singular learning, and his very acute judgment," returned to the attack with fresh spirit, and even, it would seem, indulged in some heavy Dutch wit at the expense of his antagonist. This second letter, however, did not reach its destination; perhaps it was never sent; but it was shown by some literary friend to Sir Thomas More, who replied to it in a long epistle, in which he attacks the scholastic divinity and defends the study of Greek and of the Scriptures.[15] No breach

---

[14] *Ep. Apol. ad. Mart. Dorpium Theol.*—*Er. Op.* ix. i.
[15] *Ep.* dxiii. App.

of friendship took place between Erasmus and Dorpius ; on the contrary, the latter, who had originally entered into the contest at the instigation of others, and who really seems to have deserved a part of the praise which Erasmus bestowed upon him, deserted his party and went over to the side of the enemy. He even became such a warm supporter of the new learning, that he was actually expelled from his college for an oration which he had written in its defence.[16]

[16] This interesting circumstance is recorded in a letter of Froben's, quoted by Hess in his Life of Erasmus, vol. i. p. 168, note. "*Frobenius Zuinglio.*—Dorpius a factione Theologica summa, ob orationem editam, affectus contumelia, simulque ex suo ejectus collegio, ac nunc totus agit Erasmicum. Hanc illi ignominiam ad meliores acutissimum addituram calcar non dubito.—*Hottingeri Hist. Eccles.* t. viii. p. 261."

CHAPTER VIII.

ERASMUS AT CAMBRIDGE — AMMONIUS OF LUCCA — LETTER FROM WARHAM — THE "DE COPIA" — CORRESPONDENCE WITH COLET — THE CRUELTY OF THE SCHOOL-ROOM — ADVICE TO A COURTIER — PUBLIC AFFAIRS — CORRESPONDENCE WITH AMMONIUS — PILGRIMAGE TO WALSINGHAM — TO THE TOMB OF BECKET — ERASMUS CONDEMNS WAR — MEETING WITH CARDINAL CANOSSA.

THE correspondence with Dorpius took place in the year 1515, some four or five years after the publication of the "Praise of Folly," and we must now, therefore, go back to follow the fortunes of Erasmus in the meantime. Soon after his arrival in England he was invited to Cambridge by Fisher, Bishop of Rochester, who was then Chancellor of the University, and to whom we find him confessing many obligations in a dedicatory epistle prefixed to a translation of a part of a commentary on Isaiah, ascribed to St. Basil. This was his first work on his arrival at Cambridge, but it was never finished, because Erasmus soon became convinced, by the internal evidence, that St. Basil was not really the author.[1]

Cambridge would appear, at this time, to have been somewhat behind her sister University. She was scarcely so far advanced now as Oxford had been when Erasmus went there some fourteen years ago; and while Grocyn, Linacre, and others were doing all

[1] *Er. Op.* viii. 483.

they could to promote true learning, and especially the study of Greek, at Oxford, Cambridge still remained wholly given over to Aristotle and Scotist darkness. By degrees, however, learning began to revive there too. The study of mathematics was introduced, and the great classical authors, whose names were scarcely known before, began to be heard in the lecture-halls.[2] Fisher, who was himself a very learned man, and a warm patron of letters, was now labouring earnestly in the cause of reform ; and at his invitation Erasmus took up his abode in Queen's College, where his study is still pointed out high up in the square tower overlooking the quadrangle.

At Cambridge Erasmus gave the first lectures in Greek, and was appointed the Lady Margaret's Professor of Divinity. "Hitherto," he says, writing to a friend in London, "I have lectured on the grammar of Chrysoloras, but to a small number of students. I hope to have a better attendance when I begin the grammar of Theodore [Gaza] ; perhaps I may also undertake some Divinity lectures, for that matter is just now under consideration. The profit is too small to have any influence with me ; still, I am doing my best, in the meantime, to promote sound scholarship, and am whiling away a few months."[3]

Whether he drew a salary as Professor of Greek is

---

[2] "Ante annos ferme triginta, nihil tradebatur in schola Cantabrigiensi præter Alexandrum, parva logicalia, ut vocant, et vetera illa Aristotelis dictata, Scoticasque quæstiones. Progressu temporis accesserunt bonæ literæ ; accessit matheseos cognitio ; accessit novus, aut certe novatus Aristoteles: accessit Græcarum literarum peritia ; accesserunt auctores tam multi, quorum olim ne nomina quidem tenebantur, nec a summatibus illis Jarchis."— *Er. Op.* iii. 130, A. This letter was written in or after 1516.

[3] *Ep.* cxxiii.

uncertain. By his own account, indeed, he taught Greek and divinity for several months at Cambridge without remuneration; but this probably means that he asked no fees, as we find him elsewhere telling a correspondent that in the course of five months he had received from some of his audience just one noble, and that much against his will, while in the same space of time he had spent sixty. He would certainly have a salary as Lady Margaret's Professor—this, indeed, is implied in the passage just quoted—though it was a small one; and no doubt Fisher took care that he was paid for his Greek lectures, even if there was no endowment.[4]

At Cambridge we find Erasmus still restless and unsatisfied, but working hard at his studies, complaining bitterly of his poverty and of the expenses he was obliged to incur, and, as usual, in mortal fear of the plague. We have several entertaining letters written during these years to Andreas Ammonius, a very agreeable Italian from Lucca, whose acquaintance he had made in London, and who shortly afterwards became Latin secretary to Henry VIII.[5] To this friend we find him writing from Cambridge to complain that he does not

[4] "How long Erasmus was Greek Professor in Cambridge I know not; it is by some made a question, whether he was ever called so or not, taking him only for a reader in that language; but I think it pretty plain, by Rich. Croke's Oration in praise of Greek learning, that he was his successor in that chair," &c.—*Knight*, p. 133. It is certain that Croke calls Erasmus Professor of Greek—"quem vos olim habuistis Græcarum literarum professorem, utinamque potuissetis retinere" (Croke's oration, quoted by Hallam, *Lit. Hist.* i. 294, note)—but it is not so clear that he might not have called the first, and, at the time, the only teacher of Greek in the University, a Professor, even though there had been no formal appointment.

[5] *Er. Op.* iii. 122, F.

like the beer of the place at all, and the wine not much. Could he contrive to have a flagon of Greek wine, the best he can get, sent down to him, only it must not be too sweet? "And," he adds, "don't be anxious about the money, for I will pay beforehand if you like."[6] And Ammonius does send him some wine, and will receive nothing for it; for soon after Erasmus again writes to thank him for a very pleasant letter which he had received from him, in addition to some delicious wine. "As to your being angry at my mentioning the money, I had no doubt of your kindness, which deserves a royal income; but I supposed you would have sent a somewhat larger flagon, which would have lasted some months: though this, indeed, is too large for a modest man like myself to take without payment. . . . I wonder you keep so much at home and never take an outing. Should you ever think of paying another visit to this university, you will find many ready to welcome you, but none more so than myself. As to your advice to me to return to London, should this depression of spirits last, I know of nothing there that has any charm for me except the pleasure of meeting two or three friends. Of this, however, another time. I hear that Julius Maximus is dead. Farewell, most excellent Ammonius."[7]

The truth was, the bad wine of Cambridge had brought on an access of that painful disease to which Erasmus was now a martyr. Yet when the fit was over he was able to make a jest of it; and there is a letter to him from Warham joking with him on the subject in a style that scarcely befits the gravity of an archbishop, but accompanied with a kind of medicine which Erasmus

[6] *Ep.* cxviii.   [7] *Ep.* cxvi.

was never loth to take. "If we wish health, Erasmus," says Warham, "to those that are well, much more ought I to do so to you who are sick. Yet I presume you are now quite free of the gravel, at any rate since the purification of the Virgin. What, I should be glad to know, can be the meaning of stones in your little body? Or what would it be possible to build on such a rock as that? For you are not engaged in building magnificent houses, I fancy, or anything else of that kind. So, as pebbles are of no use to you, see and relieve yourself of the superfluous load, and pay money to have the stones carried away, not as I am paying it every day to have them brought to my buildings. To enable you to do this the more readily I have given thirty angels to the son of a certain goldsmith of London; and I wish they could be changed into ten legions of angels. This is a kind of medicine which is very potent. Use it for the recovery of your health, and I only wish I could purchase health for you for a much larger sum. For there are a great many valuable works you will have to edit, which you cannot do unless you are well. Take good care of yourself, and do not defraud me by your illness of the brilliant hopes I have entertained of you, and of the fruit of your learning."[8]

The following letter to Colet, evidently written immediately after his return from a visit to London, introduces us to Henry Bullock, then a Fellow of Queen's, and afterwards chaplain to Cardinal Wolsey, who employed him, along with Watson and Ridley, to confute Luther.[9]

[8] *Ep.* cxxxiv.   [9] KNIGHT'S *Life of Erasmus*, p. 142.

ERASMUS *to* COLET.[10]

"*Queen's College, Cambridge,*
"*August* 24, 1511.

"IF you can be amused by my misfortunes, my dear Colet, you shall have plenty of cause for laughter. For besides my mishaps in London, my servant's horse fell lame, the groom having changed the one Bullock had sent; besides, I had nothing to eat the whole way. The next day we had constant rain until dinner-time, and after dinner lightning, thunder, and showers, and my horse fell three times on his head. Bullock, having consulted the stars, says he has found out that Jupiter was angry! I am well pleased to find here the traces of Christian poverty; so far, indeed, am I from expecting any profits, that I have made up my mind that I must spend here whatever I can extract from the pockets of my patrons. There is a physician here, a countryman of my own, who, by the help of the Quintessence, is working prodigious miracles, making old men young, and bringing the dead to life; so that I have good hopes of growing young again, if only I can get a taste of the Quintessence; and should I be so fortunate, I shan't regret having come to Cambridge. As to profit, I see no hope of it; for what can I get from those who have nothing, especially as I have no impudence, and was born under the anger of Mercury. Farewell, most excellent preceptor. As soon as I enter on the duties of my professorship I will tell you how I succeed, which will give you still more amusement.

"I may venture perhaps to attack your favourite Paul. Think of the boldness of your friend Erasmus."

[10] *Ep.* cxvii.

Just about the time Erasmus was settling at Cambridge his friend Colet, now Dean of St. Paul's, was engaged in founding, entirely at his own expense, a school in St. Paul's Churchyard for the free education of 153 children; and for this school, in which he was naturally much interested, Erasmus completed, in due course, a work on Latin composition, which he had sketched while residing in Italy,[11] the object of which was to aid in the acquisition of an elegant and copious style, and to supply the young student with an abundance both of words and ideas. Hence it was entitled, in Latin, *De duplici copia verborum ac rerum*. It was sent to Colet, with a very complimentary, but not too flattering, dedication, bearing the date April 29, 1512.[12]

It was evidently before this that Erasmus had written warning Colet not to be rash in believing any reports about Linacre, who, it seems, had written for the new school a grammar which Colet had rejected as being too learned for beginners. "Though it is the nature of men," he says, "to be as fond of their writings as parents are of their children, still I have the best reason for believing that he entertains the most friendly feelings towards you, and that he is not much annoyed at the rejection of his grammar." From another sentence it appears that Erasmus was looking out for an assistant-master for the new school—a competent head-master having been already found in William Lilly—but had not yet been successful.

"I have here sometimes," he continues, "a hard battle for you with the Thomists and Scotists, but of that when we meet. I have begun a translation of

---

[11] "In Italia delinearam opus de verborum rerumque copia."—*Er. Op.* i. 487. [12] *Er. Op.* i. 1.

St. Basil on Isaiah, and I like the work very much. I intend sending a specimen of it to the Bishop of Rochester, to try whether he will reward my labour with some little present. Oh, beggary! I know you are laughing at me. But I hate myself; and I have quite determined either to secure an income sufficient to raise me above the need of begging, or to imitate Diogenes." [13]

This letter was accompanied by a short treatise on "The Method of Study," [14] in which Erasmus enumerated the qualifications required in a schoolmaster, and showed that he ought to be familiar with all that the classical, and especially the Greek authors, can teach in every department of knowledge. This, he admitted, was a heavy burden to lay upon any one's shoulders; but his object in exacting so much from the teacher was to lighten the labours of the pupil. He expressed a doubt, however, whether Colet, who despised art and method, would approve of his advice.

Colet, in reply, assured him that he thoroughly approved of everything he had said, "and," continued he, "when I came to that place at the end of your letter where you say that you could make young men moderately eloquent in both languages in fewer years than it takes those pedants to teach them to stammer, oh! Erasmus, how I wished I could have you as a teacher in my school! I hope, however, you will give us some aid in teaching our instructors, as soon as you leave those Cambridge men.

"Your papers shall be carefully preserved as you

---

[13] *Ep.* cxlix.
[14] *De Ratione Studii*. Afterwards enlarged and dedicated to Peter Viterius, Professor of *Belles Lettres* in the University of Paris.—*Er. Op.* i. 519.

request. I will take your advice about Linacre, so kindly and wisely given. Do not leave off making inquiries for an assistant-master, if you can find one in Cambridge who will not be too proud to be under the head-master. You tell me you sometimes have battles in my behalf with those soldiers of Scotus, and I can only say that I am glad to have such an excellent champion. But it is an unequal and inglorious contest; for what praise can be got by brushing away a swarm of flies? What thanks will you deserve from me for cutting down a set of reeds? It is a necessary contest rather than a glorious or a great one; but at any rate it proves your solicitude and loving care on my behalf. Persevere, Erasmus, in giving us Basil, since in so doing you will give us Isaiah. You will do well, in my opinion, to imitate Diogenes; for if you can find pleasure in poverty you will be a king of kings, and by despising money you will obtain money and fortune too. . . . If you beg humbly I have something for you; but if you ask immodestly, poverty must help poverty, to say the least, very poorly. Farewell, and pray write me often." [15]

Two other letters of Erasmus, which will now be understood, may be given at more length.

ERASMUS *to* COLET.[16]

"*Cambridge, Oct.* 29, 1513 [? 1511].

"I AM now quite taken up with finishing my *Copia*, so that I am now a living enigma, being in the midst of abundance (*copia*), and yet in the greatest want. And I wish I could end both at the same time; for I shall

[15] *Ep.* iv. App.   [16] *Ep.* cl.

bring the *Copia* to a close very shortly, if only the Muses will favour my studies more than Fortune has my worldly interests. This, indeed, has been the reason why I have answered your letters so briefly and carelessly. With the Scotists—a most invincible set, and unsurpassed for self-conceit—I do not fight much, for I would not waste oil upon them, or time; besides, why should I stir up a nest of hornets? I have nearly given up translating St. Basil, not merely because I suspect that it is not a genuine work, but because the Bishop of Rochester, to whom I sent a specimen of my translation, telling him that I was desirous that Basil should appear in Latin under his auspices and as coming from his university, did not receive the proposal very warmly; and, as I have learned from a friend, he suspects that I am not translating from the Greek, but am merely polishing up some other person's version. Strange, what notions get into men's heads!

"For your jest about Diogenes, I am glad to find I can give you pleasure in any way. But I am quite serious about acting Diogenes if Fortune continue her ill usage; not in the sense of fancying myself a king of kings, but in that of despising life altogether: how else, indeed, could I act Diogenes at my age and with my health? and what may not he despise who disregards even life? . . .

"For your offer of money I acknowledge your former kindness to me, and return you the best thanks I can. But I am rather annoyed at that expression of yours, although written in jest, 'if you beg humbly.' Perhaps you mean, and you are quite right, that my discontent with my lot proceeds entirely from human pride; for the truly meek and Christian spirit makes the best of everything. I am more surprised how you can connect humility with immodesty; for you say, 'if you beg humbly and ask immodestly.' If you call that humility which is opposed to arrogance, what agreement is there between impudence and modesty? But if by '*humbly*' you mean servilely and abjectly, you, my dear Colet, are of a very different opinion from Seneca, who thinks nothing costs us so dear as that which is bought with prayers, and that he does not act the part of a friend who expects from his friend that humiliating word 'I beg.' Socrates, once conversing with some friends, said, 'I would have bought a cloak to-day if I had had the money.' 'He gave too late,' says Seneca, 'who gave after hearing this.' Another, having a friend who was sick and in want, but who from shame would not let either be known, put some money under his pillow when he was asleep. When I used to read this in the days of my youth, I was extremely struck with the modesty of the one and the generosity of the other. But pray who could be more immodest or more abject than myself, who have lived so long in England as a public beggar? I have received so much from the Archbishop that it would be perfectly infamous to take any more from him, though he were to offer it. I asked ―― with sufficient effrontery, and he refused me with still greater impudence. Even our friend Linacre thinks me too bold, who, knowing my poor state of health, and that I was leaving London with scarce six angels in my pocket,—winter coming on, too,—yet strongly advises me to spare the Archbishop and Mountjoy, and rather to economize and learn to bear poverty with patience. A most friendly counsel! For this reason above all, I hate my hard fortune, because it will not permit me to be modest. While my strength permitted, I used to conceal my poverty; now I cannot, unless I would risk my life; though I am not yet so hardened as to ask everything from everybody. I do not ask others lest I should be refused; and with what face can I ask from you, especially as you do not abound in this kind of wealth? Still, since you approve of immodesty, I will end my letter with the most impudent sentence I can. I have not assurance enough to ask you for anything, and yet I am not so proud as to refuse a present, if such a friend as you should offer it to me, especially in my present circumstances. Farewell.

"I have forgotten the brevity which I had intended; but something has just occurred to me which, I know, will make you laugh. When I spoke of the undermaster, among some of the Masters of Arts, one of them, a man of some reputation, replied with a sneer, 'Who would endure to spend his life in a school among boys, who could possibly manage to live anywhere else?' I answered quietly that I thought it a very honourable office to instruct youth in sound morals and useful learning; that Christ did not despise the tender years of children, and that no period of life so well repaid kindness or yielded more abundant fruit, youth being indeed the seed-time on which the State depends for its future growth. I added that truly pious men would be of the opinion that in no other way could they serve God better than by bringing children to Christ. 'Whoever wishes to serve Christ,' said he, turning up his nose in derision, 'let him enter a monastery and take religious vows.' I answered that Paul made true religion consist in works of charity; and that charity consists in doing all the good we can to our neighbours. He treated this remark with disdain, as if it only showed my ignorance. 'Lo,' said he, 'we have left all; in this perfection consists.' 'He has not left all,' I answered, 'who, when he has it in his power to do good to a great many, refuses the office, because it is considered too humble.' And so, to prevent dispute, I left him. There is a specimen of Scotist wisdom for you, and a dialogue to boot!"

ERASMUS *to* JOHN COLET.[17]

"*Cambridge, July* 11, 1511 [? 1512].

"YOU answer seriously a letter written in joke. I ought not, perhaps, to have joked with so great a man, but remembering your kindness rather than your greatness, I had a fancy to amuse such an excellent friend with a little 'Attic salt.' It will prove your good-nature to take my nonsense in good part. You write that I am in your debt, whether I like it or not. Certainly, my dear Colet, 'it is hard,' as Seneca says, 'to be indebted to any one against one's will;' but I don't know any one to whom I would rather be indebted than yourself. And such has been your disposition toward me always, that even though there had been no acts of kindness, I should be very much in your debt; but there have been so many acts of kindness that if I did not acknowledge them I should be very ungrateful. About your poverty I quite believe what you say, and I am sorry for it; but my poverty, pressing very hard upon me, compelled me to trouble you. How unwillingly I did so you may infer from my having been so long in asking for the fulfilment of the promise you made long ago. I am not surprised

[17] *Ep.* cxv.

you should have forgotten your promise, considering how much engaged you have been; but once, in your garden, the conversation having turned on the *Copia*, when I mentioned my intention of dedicating the work to our young prince, as being suitable to his years, you begged me to dedicate it rather, as a new work, to your new school. I answered with a smile that your school was poor, whereas I wanted some one who would give me a small sum in my hand. You laughed. Then, when I reckoned up several items of expense, you said after a pause that you could not give me as much as my necessities required, but you would gladly give me fifteen angels. And when you repeated it with eagerness, I asked you if you thought that enough. You answered still more eagerly that you would gladly pay at least this sum; 'then,' said I, 'I will gladly accept it.' This statement will, perhaps, recall the matter to your recollection. I could confirm what I say by other proofs, only I am sure you have confidence in me. There are some who say—and they are your friends, for I hold no communication with your enemies, nor do I care one jot for what they say—that you are a little hard, and too careful in the distribution of your money; and that this comes from no close-fistedness—for it was thus I explained the statement with the approval of my informants—but from your inability, on account of your natural modesty, to refuse those who press you urgently, which makes you less liberal to friends who are not troublesome, as you cannot satisfy both. Not that this has anything to do with myself, seeing that I have always found you exceedingly kind, though I am not a very impudent or troublesome beggar. I have not, therefore, heard this from your detractors, but from those who really wish you well; still, I neither accept their opinion nor dissent from it, except so far as to acknowledge your uniform kindness to myself.

"If you can conveniently give me the rest of what you promised, considering the present state of my affairs, I will accept it, not as a debt, but as a free gift, which I will repay if I can, and for which at any rate I shall be grateful.

"I was sorry to learn from the conclusion of your letter that you are more harassed than usual with business. I would wish you as far removed as possible from worldly affairs, not because I am afraid the world may take hold of you and claim you as its own, but because I would rather your talents, eloquence, and learning were devoted wholly to Christ. But if you cannot extricate yourself, nevertheless take care that you do not become every day more deeply immersed. It were better perchance to be conquered than to purchase victory at so great a cost; for mental tranquillity is one of the greatest of blessings, and these are the thorns which accompany riches. Meantime, oppose the talk of the malevolent with an upright and sincere conscience, gather up all your powers for the service of Christ, and the world in its many forms will have less power to trouble you. But for me to advise you is very like a sow teaching Minerva, or a sick man endeavouring to prescribe for his physician. Farewell.

"I have finished the collation of the New Testament. I am now attacking St. Jerome, and as soon as I have despatched him I shall fly to you. Thomas Lupset, your pupil—and he is worthy of his master—is of great use to me, as well as a great pleasure, by his daily companionship, and by the assistance which he gives me in my critical labours. I pay him for his work by giving him mine, which I would do more freely if he had leisure from his studies, from which, however, I should be sorry to take the young man. Once more, farewell."

Erasmus, who extended his interest in education far beyond the universities, and entertained very just and enlightened views on that subject, many years afterwards wrote a treatise advocating the early and liberal education of boys, in which he embodied some of his own experience of the schools and schoolmasters of his time, and gave some instances of the shocking cruelties often perpetrated by the petty tyrants of the rod.[18] One of these, though it might unhappily be paralleled from later times, is of so revolting a nature, that without some special object one would not wish to quote it. Another is interesting because it illustrates the notions of the age, those notions which Erasmus had set himself to combat, and also because it has been supposed, though perhaps without sufficient reason, to have been supplied by Colet's new school. After remarking that no masters are so cruel as those who have nothing to teach, for they find it impossible to get through the day without flogging and storming at their pupils, Erasmus goes on to say that he was intimately acquainted with a divine of very great reputation, who never objected to any cruelty, because he believed severe measures to be necessary to conquer the spirit of boys and tame their natural wildness. "Never," he continues, "did he take dinner with his little flock, but after the meal one or another was dragged out to be flogged, and he would

[18] *Declamatio de pueris ad virtutem ac literas liberaliter instituendis.*— *Er. Op.* i. 485. Its date is 1529.

often exercise his severity even on those who had committed no offence simply to accustom them to blows. I myself once stood by when, after dinner, as usual, he called up a boy, I think about ten years old ; indeed he had come fresh from his mother to the school. He began by saying that his mother was a very pious woman and that the boy had been particularly recommended to him by her ; then, in order to find an excuse for flogging him, he began to accuse him of disorderly conduct, though the boy was perfectly innocent, and made a signal to the master whom he had entrusted with the care of the school to flog him. He immediately caught the boy, threw him down, and whipped him as if he had committed sacrilege. The divine more than once interfered, saying, 'That will do, that will do ;' but the executioner, quite deaf with excitement, went on with the punishment, until the poor boy almost fainted. Presently the divine turned to me and said, 'He had done nothing to deserve this, but it was necessary that he should be *humiliated*,' that was the word he used."[19]

In an age in which the Lord Chancellor of England could think it right to keep his flesh in subjection by the use of a hair-shirt and by scourging, it would be a folly to suppose that any cruelty of disposition or want of high principle was implied in this treatment of boys ; and that Erasmus should have so regarded it is only another example of the triumph of his common sense over the superstitions of his time. This faith in the rod as an instrument of humiliation, moreover, might seem to agree very well with Colet's ascetic notions, and it is certainly true, as Knight observes, that it would be

[19] *Er. Op.* i. 505, B, C.

difficult to apply the story to any one else.[20] On the other hand, Erasmus tells us that Colet took particular delight in the purity and simplicity of children, and there is nothing in the picture he has drawn of his character that would lead us to suspect him of undue severity to others. Perhaps it may be well to give him the benefit of the doubt.

In his frequent visits to London Erasmus was not always able to obtain a home among his many wealthy friends, and we find him accordingly negotiating with Ammonius to secure him a lodging. "At Austin Friars," writes the latter, "there is no one with whom you can live. I don't know whether you would like me to ask the blind poet; he has some disengaged bedrooms, I am told, which might be hired, but you would require to furnish them. In the lodging in which I am myself, they say all the rooms are full: besides, the table is very poor. Near St. Paul's, as you are aware, there is a college of some learned men, who, they say, live sumptuously, but I think they might as well live in a ditch. Send me word what you wish, and meantime, should you return, you will not fail of a chamber."[21]

---

[20] KNIGHT'S *Life of Colet*, p. 175. Mr. Seebohm certainly rejects this opinion of Knight's with very unnecessary indignation. "This is the story which we are told it would be difficult to apply to any one but Colet, as though Colet were the only 'divine of reputation' intimately known to Erasmus! or as though Erasmus would thus hold up his friend Colet to the scorn of the world!"—*Oxford Reformers*, p. 212. To this it is obvious to reply that every "divine of reputation" intimately known to Erasmus will not fit the conditions of the case; he must also have charge of a school, and not as master, but with a master in his pay; in short, he must be exactly in the position in which Colet was with respect to St. Paul's School: and, secondly, that Erasmus does not hold up any one to the scorn of the world, as he mentions no names.

[21] *Ep.* cxxviii.

And to this Erasmus replies that he wants only "a small comfortable room, well protected from the winds, and with a bright hearth. I shall cater for myself in my usual way. I should not wish you to say anything on this subject at present; still, if you can find out anything, I should be glad to know whether my patron has paid Bernard those twenty nobles: for this affair makes me dread coming to London, as I hate nothing so much as being dunned. Still you may treat with him for a lodging if you should happen to meet him."[22]

Bernard Andreas, the blind poet above mentioned, had been Prince Arthur's tutor, and Poet Laureate under Henry VII. He had acted very unkindly towards Linacre, having done everything he could to prejudice the King against him, and had thus incurred the hostility of Erasmus. Linacre, it seems, had written a translation of Proclus on the Sphere, which he presented to Henry VII., but Bernard having informed the King that the book had been translated before—which was literally true, only the previous translation was a miserable production—the King not only took no notice of the present, but conceived an unconquerable aversion to Linacre, whom he ever afterwards looked upon as an impostor.[23] What was the exact nature of Erasmus's obligation to Bernard does not appear. It has been assumed that he had lodged with him, and that Bernard had over-charged him for his board; and this may possibly have been the case.[24] What is certain is, that he owed him money

---

[22] *Ep.* cxli.
[23] *Er. Op.* iii. 1263, D.
[24] KNIGHT'S *Life of Erasmus*, p. 118. This, however, is merely Knight's inference from the two passages above quoted, and these passages rather point to an opposite conclusion.

which he was unable to repay, and that Mountjoy was at length obliged to come to his help and settle the claim. Erasmus took his revenge on Bernard by writing an epigram on him, in which he was cruel enough to make reference to his infirmity. At least, although his name is not mentioned, it was no doubt well understood that he was the subject of the following couplet on "a blind corrector of tragedies:"

> Cur adeo, lector, crebris offendere mendis?
> Qui castigavit, lumine captus erat. [25]

Which may be translated,—

> Complain not, reader, if some faults you find:
> The reason is, the critic's eyes were blind.

Ammonius appears to have kept Erasmus pretty well informed of what was going on in the world, and Erasmus is frequent in his requests for the latest political news. The following sentences, with their somewhat ghastly jest at the expense of the unfortunate heretics, afford us a glimpse, by no means attractive, of the London of the sixteenth century:—

"Jupiter must be very angry with us, for it is raining day and night, and hardly ever leaves off. It has, indeed, moderated the severity of the pestilence. But unless the magistrates apply a remedy, a famine will ensue, which is in no respect a lighter evil. I am not surprised that the price of wood is raised, so many heretics are offered up every day, and they are still increasing; why, even my own brother Thomas, who is more of a clod than a man, has founded a sect forsooth, and has his disciples. But let us pass to Italian affairs," and then he proceeds to give an account of the

---

[25] *Er. Op.* i. 1221, E.

league recently formed at Rome between the Pope, the King of Spain, and the Venetians.[26] This was the Holy League, formed by Julius II. towards the close of the year 1511, for the purpose of expelling the French from Italy.

These were indeed exciting times, and important events were taking place, which Erasmus, among his books at Cambridge, anxiously watched through whatever means of information—chiefly private correspondence—the age afforded. On the 17th of November, 1511, Henry VIII. joined the league, and in the course of the following year occurred the battle of Ravenna, almost equally disastrous to the defeated allies and to the French, who, though victorious, lost the flower of their army and their brilliant young general, Gaston de Foix; and in consequence of which the French were ultimately compelled to abandon their conquests in Italy and to leave the country. The year 1513, which we are now approaching, was marked by the death of Julius II., on the 27th of February, and the accession of Cardinal John de' Medici, under the name of Leo X., to the Papal throne; by renewed attempts on the part of Louis XII. of France to establish himself in Italy, and recover Milan, and his signal overthrow at the battle of Novara; and by the brilliant successes of the English arms, both in France and on the field of Flodden, where James IV., with the flower of the Scottish nobility, perished.

Meantime Ammonius was trying to make his way at Court, but not succeeding as speedily as he desired, he was sometimes inclined to regret that he had ever left Rome. Erasmus, however, assures him that with

[26] *Ep.* cxxvii.

such gifts as his he cannot fail to rise to the highest position, and in answer to his inquiries he gives him the following sarcastic advice:—" First of all, harden your brow until you have lost all sense of shame. Then mix yourself in everybody's business. Elbow aside whomsoever you can. Neither love nor hate any one in earnest, but let your interest be the universal standard, and the sole end towards which all your actions are directed. Give nothing unless you can hope to get it back with interest, and be complaisant with everybody in everything..... Have two strings to your bow. Employ people to come about you as if they were entreating your services. Threaten to leave, and get everything ready for your departure. Show letters in which you are invited with great promises, and go away sometimes in order that your loss may be felt in your absence." [27]

Ammonius, having at length obtained the post of Latin secretary to the King, accompanied his master in the short and brilliant campaign which began with the Battle of the Spurs and ended with the capture of Terouenne and Tournay. While thus employed he found time to keep his friends in England supplied with graphic pictures of camp life, at which Erasmus laughed heartily. "But pray, my dear Ammonius," he writes, "remember the advice I gave you in my last, to fight at a safe distance. Be as fierce as you please with the pen, and run through ten thousand of the enemy in one day. I am so delighted at our success that I have no words to express it." In the same letter Erasmus gives us some hint of the studies which had occupied him at Cambridge. "My mind," he says, "is in such a

[27] *Ep.* cxlii.

glow over Jerome, whose works I am emending and illustrating with notes, that I could fancy myself actually inspired. I have now emended almost the whole by the collation of a large number of old manuscripts. And I am doing this at my own expense, which I assure you is no joke."[28] And in another letter he writes, "I am fighting as hard with the misreadings of Seneca and Jerome as you are with the French."[29] The following amusing letter from Ammonius, written on his return to London, is sufficiently characteristic to deserve translation:

ANDREAS AMMONIUS *to* ERASMUS.[30]

"*London, Nov.* 24, 1515 [? 1513].

"I GOT three letters from you in the camp, which pleased me better even than the flight of the French. I answered the first in true military style; but I don't know whether you got my letter. To your last, which was delivered to me just on my departure from France, when we were marching back for the triumph, I made no reply; nevertheless I have executed your commissions. For I was very particular in giving your respects to the Abbot of St. Bertin, and I read over to him the whole long catalogue of the friends you had met at his house. He cheered up most wonderfully at the name of Erasmus; indeed I can compare it to nothing but a widowed mother hearing news of a son who had been long absent. He laid hold of me, and, as there were a good many people there, he drew me aside, and made a great many most friendly inquiries about you. At length he asked how you were getting on in Eng-

---

[28] *Ep.* cxix.   [29] *Ep.* cxxix.   [30] *Ep.* clxxxvi.

land, and I told him, what was the fact, that your success was far below your deserts. In one word, he seemed full of affection towards you. I then went to see the Master of the Rolls, and showed him what you had written about him. I gave him the book of Plutarch, for which he returned thanks in two or three words; and being very much engaged, as it seemed, he hurried off, and I had no other opportunity of speaking to him.

"As soon as I touched English soil I began asking for you, and where you were. As you wrote that you had run away from Cambridge to escape the plague, Sixtine at length told me that you had indeed left Cambridge on account of the plague, and had gone to some place where you were in great distress because you could get no wine; and that, thinking the want of wine a worse evil than the plague, you had returned to Cambridge, and were there now. O brave comrade of Bacchus, who would not abandon your general in the hour of danger! Wherefore I send you, as a present from your commander, a flagon of Cretan wine, worthy of Jupiter himself, and made of milk and nectar, which you shall have an opportunity of drinking in larger quantities if you come here soon. But as to your congratulations on my increased fortune, you do not act like a friend unless you congratulate yourself at the same time, though you do not use it as your own; and I, in my turn, congratulate you, as well on many other accounts as on those ten gold pieces which Durham gave you, not so much for the value of the gift, as because he is not wont to be so liberal except to those of whom he is particularly fond; but as to his not having answered a word when you spoke about me, I am not surprised, and yet I know not the cause. For a little before he left our camp he expressed some indignation with me, but how he came by it I cannot divine. So long, however, as I do my own duty and am without fault, I shall not be very anxious how this or the other feels towards me.

"I have a great deal more to say in answer to your letters, and, besides, a whole sackful of trifles which I want to pour into your bosom. . . . Farewell, my dearest Erasmus. Love me as ever. I shall have my revenge on you for calling me 'most valiant.'"

To this Erasmus replied in a letter from which the following extracts may suffice:—

Erasmus *to* Ammonius.[31]

"*Cambridge, Nov.* 28, 1511 [? 1513].

". . . I AM charmed that you should not have quite forgotten me in the great hurry and bustle you have been in, and that you should have paid so much attention to my foolish commands; and though that is nothing new for you, I admire your good-nature and accept your kindness to myself as much as if it were. I am quite as much obliged to you for the wine as if I had received it. I wonder, however, that you should trust anything of that kind to those rascals whose treachery you have more than once experienced. The groom who delivered the letter declares that no flagon was given to him.[32] . . . I am prevented from coming

---

[31] *Ep.* cxxxi.
[32] The words which follow here—"Respondit ὁ Δουνελμαῖος, sed οὐδὲν πρὸς ἔπος," &c.—would seem to be an interpolation from another letter, which has been lost, and are clearly referred to in the preceding letter from Ammonius.

to London before Christmas, partly by the plague, and partly by the highway robberies, of which England is now full. . . .

"Come, you call me 'most holy,' which is an outrage on the supreme Pontiff! But what epithet is there that would better fit a soldier and a conqueror than 'most valiant?' If you had whole wagon-loads of trifles, to say nothing of sackfuls, you would never satisfy me, if I should have the good luck to have a talk with you. . . . I, my dear Ammonius, have been living for some months the life of a snail, shut up at home and buried in my books. Cambridge is a complete desert; most of the men are away for fear of the plague, though, when they are all here, even then it is a desert. The expense is intolerable, and there is not a farthing to get. Now, suppose I have sworn this by everything sacred. It is not yet five months since I came here, and in that time I have spent sixty nobles. I have received just one from some of my hearers, and this much against my inclination. I am determined, in these winter months, to leave no stone unturned, and, as they say, to cast my sheet-anchor. If I succeed, I shall provide for myself some comfortable retreat; but if not, I am determined to fly hence, I know not whither; if nothing else, at least to die elsewhere. Farewell."

The Master of the Rolls mentioned in the above letter of Ammonius was Dr. John Young, Dean of York, to whom Erasmus dedicated his translation of Plutarch's "Precepts for the Preservation of Health." [33]

During his stay in England, at this time, Erasmus, it seems, would sometimes seek relief from incessant

[88] KNIGHT'S *Life of Erasmus*, p. 174. *Er. Op.* iv. 29.

toil by an occasional excursion into the country, in company with some friend or another. Thus it happened that in one of his summer vacations, curiosity led him to go on a pilgrimage to the celebrated shrine of Our Lady of Walsingham, where he hung up a votive poem in Greek in her honour. His experiences on this occasion were afterwards embodied in one of his Familiar Colloquies, in which he minutely describes the elegant but unfinished church, about three miles from the sea, with the winds sweeping through its open doors and windows, the small wooden chapel of the Virgin, dimly lighted with wax-candles and filled with a most fragrant odour, the altar adorned with gems and gold and silver, and the priest standing by to see after the offerings and to scowl on those who offered nothing. Here he was shown, on one side of the church, a small door, which it would be impossible to enter without stooping, but through which he was assured an armed knight, after invoking the aid of the Virgin, had passed on horseback; while on another side there was another small chapel filled with most precious relics, where he saw a joint of St. Peter's finger, large enough to have belonged to a giant. His profane remark that St. Peter must have been a very big man, eliciting a burst of laughter from one of his companions, might have brought him into trouble, and nearly put a stop to the exhibition. The verger, however, was appeased by a present of a few coins, and then proceeded to point out a shed in front of the church, which he said had made its appearance there quite suddenly in winter-time, when the ground was covered with snow, and under which there were two wells of exceedingly cold water, possessed of great virtue, and excellent for curing complaints of the head or stomach. On being asked whether it had been long there, he told them for some centuries. "And yet," said Erasmus, "the walls do not look very old; the thatch seems comparatively new; nor do these cross-beams look as if they had been there a great many years." To silence their doubts, the verger pointed to a very old bearskin nailed on the boards, and smiled at their dulness in being blind to so obvious a proof. Apologizing for their stupidity, the party then turned to look at the Virgin's milk, which was shown them in a glass globe. Erasmus thought it looked like chalk mixed with the white of an egg, and mischievously prompted a young Cambridge friend who accompanied him, named Robert Aldridge, to ask how he could prove it was really the Virgin's milk. At first no answer was vouchsafed, but on the question being repeated in the gentlest way, the monk exclaimed, in a tone of horror, "What need to ask such questions when you have the tablet before you to vouch for it?" at the same time pointing to a tablet above the altar; and he would at once have expelled them from the church had not a piece of silver, for the second time, allayed his rising anger.

Returning to the church after dinner, they found that the tablet told a long story of how the milk had been brought from Constantinople to Paris, where an Englishman, into whose care it was given, obtained the half of the original quantity from the canons there, and, having brought it with him to his own country, gave it to the brethren at Walsingham. This milk was peculiarly precious because it was caught direct from the Virgin's breast, and not, as in other instances, gathered from the ground. Nor did Erasmus fail to present his offering of verses. Returning on another occasion, he saw them hanging up in the church; and being questioned whether it was he who had presented a votive tablet in Hebrew characters about two years before, knowing that the monks called everything Hebrew which they did not understand, he admitted that it was. He was then assured that it had excited a great deal of curiosity among the pilgrims, one learned man having pronounced it Arabic, another declaring that the characters were fictitious, till at length one came who was able to decipher the title, which was in Roman letters. Erasmus then translated the ode into Latin verse, and refused to take the reward which was offered him, declaring that he would gladly do anything for the Virgin, even if it should be to carry her letters to Jerusalem. At last he was prevailed on to accept a fragment of wood cut from a log on which she had been known to rest.[34]

On another occasion he visited, in company with Colet, the celebrated shrine of St. Thomas à Becket at Canterbury, where he reverentially kissed the sacred rust on the spear-head with which Becket was slain, saw the martyr's skull enclosed in a silver casket, inspected his hair shirt, his girdle, and his drawers, and kissed his handkerchief; and where Colet gave great offence by asking whether Becket had not been in his

[34] *Coll. Fam.*, *Peregrinatio Religionis ergo*. The first pilgrimage to Walsingham took place in 1511, as is evident from *Ep.* cxiv., in which he announces his intention to Ammonius. It is the second, which took place two years later, when Erasmus returned to find his Greek ode mistaken for Hebrew, that is more particularly described in the Colloquy. But the incidents on either occasion would be much the same, nor would chronological exactness be observed in translating them into humorous dialogue; if, indeed, the second visit may not have been purely imaginary. The letter to Ammonius just cited contains, so far as I remember, the only reference in his epistles to the pilgrimage to Walsingham.

lifetime very kind to the poor, and suggesting that, as he could not have since changed his character except for the better, it could not fail to gratify him if the poor were permitted to help themselves to some of the wealth with which he was now surrounded.[35]

Such, then, were the experiences which Erasmus was storing up for future use during his vacation rambles, while filling the Lady Margaret's Divinity chair at Cambridge. He now, however, as appears from the following letter to his old friend, the Abbot of St. Bertin, received an intimation that his return to his own country would be agreeable to the Court of Brussels; and it was probably at the same time or soon afterwards that he was appointed Councillor to Prince Charles.

ERASMUS *to* ANTHONY À BERGIS, *Abbot of St. Bertin.*[36]

"*London, March* 14, 1513 [? 1514].

"I HAVE heard, most learned father, from the Bishop of Durham, and from Andreas Ammonius, the King's Secretary, of your affection and truly fatherly love for me: on which account I am the more anxious to return to my country, provided only the Prince can give me an income sufficient for my humble wants. Not that I am tired of England or dissatisfied with my patrons. I have here, too, a number of friends, and many of the bishops have shown me no common kindness; but particularly the Archbishop of Canterbury, who could not possibly be kinder or more affectionate if he were my father or brother. By his gift, I have a pretty good pension, which I draw from a benefice I resigned. My other patron adds as much more from his own

---

[35] *Coll. Fam., Peregrinatio Religionis ergo.*   [36] *Ep.* cxliv.

means. I get a good deal from the kindness of the nobility, and would get much more if I were willing to pay my court a little; but the genius of the people of this island is rapidly changing, owing to the preparations for war. Everything is rising in price every day, while liberality is proportionately decreasing. How, indeed, can men who are so often decimated avoid growing parsimonious? Lately, too, I nearly got my death for want of wine, having brought on a fit of the gravel by the wretched stuff I was compelled to drink. Besides, it is always a kind of banishment to live in an island, and now we are more closely confined than ever by war, so that even letters cannot pass out. I see, also, great disturbances likely to arise, the issue of which it is impossible to predict. Oh! that God would be merciful and still this storm which is raging in the Christian world. I often wonder what it is that urges, I will not say Christians, but men to such a pitch of madness that they will make every effort, incur any expense, and meet the greatest dangers, for their mutual destruction. For what else are we doing all our lives but waging war? We are worse than the dumb animals, for among them it is only the wild beasts that wage war, and even they do not fight among themselves, but with beasts of a different species, and that with the weapons with which nature has furnished them; not as we do, with machines invented by the art of the devil, nor for all manner of causes, but either in defence of their young or for food. Can we, who glory in the name of Christ, whose precepts and example taught us only gentleness, we who are members of one body, who are one flesh, and grow by the same spirit, who are nourished by the same sacraments, attached to the same head, and called to the same immortality, and who hope for that highest communion, that, as Christ and the Father are one, so we also may be one in Him—can we, I say, think anything in this world of such value that it should provoke us to war?— a thing so ruinous, so hateful, that even when it is most just, no truly good man can approve of it. Pray consider by whom it is carried on—by homicides, gamblers, scoundrels of every kind, by the lowest class of hirelings, who care more for a little gain than for their lives. It is such as these that make the best soldiers, since they only do for pay and for glory what they did before at their own risk. These off-scourings of mankind must be received into your fields, into your cities, to enable you to carry on war. In short, we must put ourselves at the mercy of these men, while we desire to revenge ourselves on some one else. Add to this the crimes which are committed under the pretext of war, since 'amid the din of arms good laws are silent,'—how many robberies, sacrileges, rapes, and other disgraceful deeds such as one is ashamed even to mention. This corruption of morals must needs last for many years, even after the war is over. Then think of the expense, so that, even if you conquer, you still lose far more than you gain;—what kingdom, indeed, could you put against the life and blood of so many thousand human beings? . . .

"This is the proper office of the Roman Pontiff, the Cardinals, the Bishops, and the Abbots, to compose the dissensions of Christian princes; they should in these cases declare their authority, and show how much power they have in virtue of the reverence paid them. Julius, who was certainly not universally esteemed, aroused this storm of war; shall not Leo, a learned, upright, and pious man, be able to allay it? . . . What do you suppose the Turks will think of us when they hear of Christian princes falling out so furiously with one another, and that for a title to empire? Italy is now delivered from the French. What has been accomplished by so much bloodshed, except that where the Gaul ruled before, some one else rules now? The country, too, was more flourishing before than it is now. But I will not go more deeply into these matters. . . . . For my own part, whatever income I have, I derive it from England; but I would willingly resign the whole of it, on this condition—that a Christian peace might be cemented among Christian princes. To this result your own influence, which has great weight with Prince Charles, and still more with Maximilian, and which is respected by the English nobility, will contribute in no small degree. Nor do I doubt that you have yourself already experienced what losses even friends may occasion while war is going on. So that you will be acting for your own interest in using your utmost efforts that this war may be brought to a conclusion, and will be well repaid for your labour. I will fly to embrace you as soon as I shall be allowed to escape from this. Meantime, farewell, most respected father."

On the whole, England had not turned out the land flowing with milk and honey which Erasmus had expected. Probably, as he was always willing to confess, he was himself to blame for his comparative want of success. It may be that if he had been somewhat more of an adept in paying his addresses personally to the great—in writing no one could flatter more elegantly—he might have reaped more ample harvests from their liberality; and that if he could have consented to leave his studies for a few months in order to dance attendance at court, he might have had any number of church-livings he chose. Yet it may well have been that the publication of the "Praise of Folly" destroyed all his chance of preferment. How *could* a man who had said such sharp things about the Church be put into high office in it? Such is not the stuff of which bishops or even deans are made. In our own days it seems impossible to promote a man who has in any way attacked or dissented from any part of the Church doctrine or discipline, or even run counter to popular opinion in these matters; and assuredly great offence would have been taken had any special favour been shown to the author of the *Moria*. It is clear that Erasmus never stood high in the good graces of the ruling favourite at the English court. Wolsey, indeed, could scarcely like a man who handled the high ecclesiastical dignitaries so freely, and taught with so much earnestness that cardinals should be humble and unostentatious. And, in fact, he seems never to have given him anything. Yet Erasmus made advances to Wolsey more than once, and sent him a piece translated from Plutarch with a flattering dedication.[37] This was apparently a year or two later than our narrative has yet carried us, and at a time when honours were coming so thick on Wolsey that Erasmus was obliged, he tells us, to alter the dedication three times before presenting it. Wolsey did, indeed, at one time promise him a prebend at Tournay, but he changed his mind and gave it to some one else, promising Erasmus a better one. This

---

[37] *De utilitate capienda ab inimicis.—Er. Op.* iv. 23.

promise, however, was never fulfilled;[38] and Erasmus, though he speaks of the singular favour which the cardinal had always shown him, says distinctly that he was never one whit the richer by his munificence.[39]

It is not altogether easy to understand what it was that Erasmus expected, or what he complained of; and perhaps he did not very well know himself. He only knew that he had allowed his imagination to run on the "heaps of gold" which were awaiting him in England, and that when he had made up his mind to settle in England the heaps of gold had vanished into thin air. It is difficult to suppose that even if a bishopric had been offered him he would have accepted it; to have fulfilled its duties would have been uncongenial to his tastes, and without a knowledge of the English language, even in those days, impossible.

Yet once, as we shall see hereafter, he had a narrow escape of being made a bishop, without his consent—not, however, in England, but in Sicily. No wonder if he thought it a good joke. It would not have suited him at all, nor, as he declared in all seriousness, would he have sacrificed his studies for the finest bishopric in the world.

Indeed, he was far too conscientious, and had the interests of the Church far too much at heart, to take any office as a mere sinecure. Accordingly, when Warham, in fulfilment of his promise, offered him the

---

[38] *Er. Op.* iii. 1523, C; 1545, E.

[39] "Cardinali Eboracensi, cui dicavimus libellum Plutarchi, puto me nihil non debere, ob singularem favorem, quo me jam olim prosequitur; et tamen hactenus ex illius munificentia non sum pilo factus ditior."—*Cat. Luc.* In regard, however, to the prebend at Tournay, compare *Er. Op.* iii. 220, C, D, from which it appears that Erasmus was unable or unwilling to fulfil the conditions attached to the benefice.

rectory of Aldington, in Kent, afterwards notorious in connection with the history of the Holy Maid of Kent, who belonged to the town, he refused it on the ground that his ignorance of the English language would prevent him from discharging the duties of a pastor, nor was he willing to draw a pension from a parish to which he rendered no service in return. The Archbishop met his scruples by assuring him that he did far more good to the Church by his books than he could by preaching to a little country congregation, and that no wrong was done if he received, in reward for his labours, a small portion of the Church's revenues. He promised, moreover, that the interests of the parish should not be neglected, and he kept his word by putting it in charge of a young priest of good character and of some learning. On this understanding Erasmus agreed to draw a pension of twenty pounds annually from the parish of Aldington, and this was the only English living from which he ever derived any income.[40]

There was, however, one way in which his wishes might have been amply gratified, and in which, it is more than probable, he himself expected to find an escape from poverty and the honourable reward of his labours for the advancement of learning. Henry VIII. might, of his own munificence, have bestowed on him

---

[40] *Er. Op.* v. 678. KNIGHT, p. 155-157. Knight tells us Erasmus was collated to the rectory of Aldington "the 22 of March, the *end* of the year 1511." I suppose this would mean 1512. See, in Knight's Appendix, the "instruments taken out of Archbishop Warham's Register, relating to the rectory of Aldyngton, in Kent, to which Erasmus was collated," from which it appears that the previous incumbent was Master John Alan, who freely resigned March 22, 1511, while, on July 31, 1512, Erasmus resigned, and got the pension of 20*l.*, John Thorneton, the Archbishop's suffragan, having been presented.

such a liberal pension as would have secured his independence, and enabled him to live in a style adequate to the place which he held in the literary world, and by so doing he might have retained in his kingdom the greatest literary luminary of the age, and would certainly have done honour to himself and to England. Erasmus frequently complains of having been induced to come to England by promises which were never fulfilled, and whether any promises had been actually made him or not, he may have referred to some particular personage who might reasonably have been expected to confer upon him some distinguished favour; and indeed in one place he speaks of having been betrayed by some one who had made him repeated promises, but whom he does not name. He cannot have referred to Warham, with whom he never finds fault, and who seems to have been lavish in his generosity, nor to Mountjoy, from whom he had a pension, nor to More, from whom he seems to have expected nothing. It was probably, then, some one too great to name, whom he considered as having especially deceived him; and Erasmus was sometimes heard to say that it was the duty of kings to aid the studies of literary men by setting them above want, but that they were too ready to save their own revenues by having recourse to church livings, which scholars were obliged to accept in order to secure the leisure they needed for their studies.[41] On the other hand, Henry, who was far too munificent

---

[41] "Sane plus semel Erasmum dicere memini, Principum esse debere officium, ut propria liberalitate studiosos juvent; sed illos suis impensis parsuros ad sacerdotiorum collationem confugere, ad quæ accipienda sectatores disciplinarum cogi, ut otium literarium tueri queant."— BEAT. RHEN. *Ep. Car. Cæs.*

to grudge the money, if he had supposed there was a real claim upon him, may have thought that Erasmus, who was no courtier, and of whom he saw but little, had done nothing to deserve a reward at his hands; and if Wolsey was unfriendly or indifferent, that would sufficiently account for the King showing him no favour. While in England, Erasmus dedicated to Henry only one unimportant work—his translation of Plutarch's treatise on distinguishing a friend from a flatterer [42]—but whether because he was himself too sparing of flattery, or the King, full of his ambitious schemes, had no leisure just then to bestow on the pursuits of literature, it would not appear that he received any acknowledgment. Some years afterwards, however, on receiving the third edition of his work, Henry sent him a present of sixty angels, besides offering him a handsome salary if he would return to his kingdom. [43]

It must not, of course, be supposed that Erasmus, notwithstanding his constant complaints, was really poor, except by comparison. But he liked to live comfortably, he was fond of good wine—indeed, he maintained that his health required it—and his frequent journeys on horseback must have been very expensive. Sometimes he begged or borrowed a horse from a friend, but while he was at Cambridge we find him once keeping two horses, which, he says, were much better cared for than their owner, as well as two servants, who were much more elegantly dressed than their master. His con-

[42] *De discrimine adulatoris et amici.*—*Er. Op.* iv. 1.

[43] *Ep.* cclxviii. cccxiii. Conf. *Cat. Luc.*—" Huic (Henrico octavo) me puto tantum debere, quantum obtulit, si voluissem accipere ; obtulit autem fortunam meis meritis longè majorem. Ceterum multo post jam oblito dedicationis illius misit Angelatos sexaginta, impulsu vel admonitu potius Joannis Coleti."

tinual correspondence must have cost him a considerable sum in those days, and associating constantly with great men, he could not make a mean appearance. So long, therefore, as he had no fixed income to depend on save Lord Mountjoy's pension of one hundred crowns, it is no wonder if he sometimes felt himself a little straitened, and looked anxiously round for a rich man whom he might make his prey. Now, however, he had also his pension from the parish of Aldington, amounting to another one hundred crowns, and he confesses to having received from the Archbishop of Canterbury more than four hundred nobles during the few years he had been in England.[44] The sale of his works, too, must have brought him in a considerable sum, which would now be increasing every year, and, besides, there were the presents which he was continually receiving from one or another of his wealthy patrons. For the present, then, Erasmus was at any rate raised above poverty and was likely to remain so, as long as Warham lived.

Whether he could have been induced to take up his residence permanently in this country, even had his utmost hopes been fulfilled, may well be doubted. At any rate he must have left it frequently to seek the advantages offered abroad for the publication of his works, and as old age drew on and health became worse, such long journeys would have been found impossible. In truth, the press in England was too far behind the press on the Continent to admit of any of his more important works being printed in this country ; and so, early in the year 1514, having completed his labours on St. Jerome, and hearing at the same time that Froben, the celebrated printer of Basle, was actually engaged in printing the

[44] *Ep. Pat. Servatio.*

entire works of that father, Erasmus packed up his manuscripts, bade farewell to his English friends, and took his departure for the Continent. It must have been immediately before leaving London that he dined in company with Cardinal Canossa, who had come over as Papal legate to endeavour to negotiate peace between the kings of France and England, and with the amusing account which Erasmus has left of this interview I shall conclude the present chapter. He had been invited to dinner by his friend Ammonius, and finding, on his arrival, a stranger in the dress of a private gentleman, with his hair tied up in a net, and attended only by one servant, he had not the least idea that he was in the presence of a person of any importance. Nor did his host undeceive him. He chatted with Ammonius, and, wondering at the military bearing of the stranger, at length asked in Greek who he was. "Oh! a great merchant," said Ammonius in the same language. "I thought so," replied Erasmus, and took no further notice of him. "We then sat down to dinner," he continues, "Canossa taking the precedency, and I sitting next him, and during the entire meal I talked familiarly with Ammonius, as my manner is, but took no pains to conceal my contempt for the merchant. At length I asked Andreas whether the report was true that a legate had come from Léo X. to put an end to the dissension between the kings of France and England, to which he answered in the affirmative. 'The supreme Pontiff,' I went on, 'has no need of my advice, but if he had asked it, it would have been different.' 'What would you have advised?' inquired Ammonius. 'It would have been better,' I answered, 'if no mention had been made of peace.' 'Why so?' 'Because,' said I, 'peace cannot be made all at once, and in the meantime, while the rulers are treating about terms, the soldiers, at the mere suspicion of peace, run into greater excesses than during war. By a truce, on the other hand, the soldiers' hands are tied at once. Now, I should propose a truce for three years, during which the terms of an enduring covenant might be discussed at leisure.' Andreas assented, and said, ' I believe that is just what the legate is doing.' I then returned to the subject, on which I had not yet got any clear answer. ' Is he a Cardinal ? ' I asked. ' What makes you think so ? ' replied he. ' Because the Italians say so.' ' And how do they know it ? ' he asked again. ' I am acquainted with you here,' I replied ; ' if, after some years, we should meet in Brabant, would you ask how I knew you ? ' Here they smiled at one another, while I had not the least suspicion. Then I pressed him to tell me whether he was really a Cardinal. Ammonius equivocated, and at last said, ' He has the mind of a Cardinal.' ' That is something,' said I, with a smile, ' to have a Cardinal's mind.' All this and much more Canossa listened to in silence ; then he said something in Italian, and presently introduced a few Latin words, but still in such a way that you might have fancied he was nothing more than a merchant with some little learning. As I made no reply, he turned to me and said, ' I am surprised that you should choose to live here among this barbarous people, unless indeed you prefer to be alone here to being first at Rome.' Astonished to hear so acute an observation from a merchant, I replied that I was living in a country where there were a great many men of distinguished learning, among whom I was content to occupy the lowest place, whereas at Rome I should be nowhere. I said this, and more to the same effect, because I felt a little nettled by the remark of the merchant, and I think some good genius must have stood my friend; otherwise Ammonius, who knew very well how freely I blurt out among my friends whatever comes to my lips, might have exposed me to the greatest risk." A few days afterwards Erasmus learned from his friend that the merchant whom he had treated with such marked disdain was no other than Canossa himself, the very legate about whom he had been making such curious inquiries; that the Cardinal had conceived the highest opinion of him, and even wished him to accompany him to Rome. Of this, however, Erasmus would not hear. It would seem that he never wished to see Canossa again after such an awkward adventure; nor was he at all pleased with Ammonius for having played him such a trick. As he very truly observed, he might have made some remark on the Pope or on the legate himself, which might have turned greatly to his disadvantage.[45] Canossa, on the other hand, was evidently much taken with his new acquaintance, and a year or two afterwards, having been made Bishop of Bayeux, he sent him a pressing invitation to come and live with him, promising him, besides a pension of two hundred ducats a year, his expenses, and the keep of two horses and a servant. This invitation, however, as all others that threatened to interfere with his liberty, Erasmus declined.[46]

[45] *Ep*. mccxxxix.   [46] *Ep*. ccxxiv. ccvi.

CHAPTER IX.

LETTER TO AMMONIUS—ERASMUS REFUSES TO RETURN TO STEYN—ADVENTURE NEAR GHENT—VISITS STRASBURG—SCHELESTADT—BASLE — ACQUAINTANCE WITH FROBEN — ZASIUS — ZWINGLE—ŒCOLAMPADIUS—PIRCKHEIMER—THE CHRISTIAN PRINCE—JOHN REUCHLIN — LETTERS TO RAPHAEL AND GRIMANI — TO POPE LEO X.

ERASMUS *to* ANDREAS AMMONIUS.[1]

"*The Castle of Hamme, July* 8, 1514.

"I CALLED at your house more than once, my dearest friend, to bid you a last farewell, and at the same time to enjoy your conversation—which, indeed, has been one of the greatest pleasures I have had in life—as long as I could. I had a very good passage, but one also which caused me some anxiety. The sea was perfectly calm, the wind in our favour, the sky clear, and the hour most convenient, for we set sail about seven o'clock. But those robbers of the sea, the custom-house officers, carried off my portmanteau, filled with my writings, into another ship. I believe they do this kind of thing purposely, in order to purloin something, should they have the opportunity, or, if not, to extort a few coins by selling you your own property. Accordingly, believing that the work of so many years was gone for ever, I was in as great grief as I should fancy the fondest parent could possibly be for the loss

[1] *Ep.* clix.

of his children. And, indeed, in all other things they treat strangers in such a way that it would be better to fall into the hands of the Turks than get into their clutches. I am often surprised that the kings of England should tolerate such scoundrels, who not only give great annoyance to strangers, but bring disgrace on the whole island, seeing that every one tells at home how inhumanly he has been treated, and others form their judgment of the nation from the doings of these robbers.

"I don't know whether I told you that I paid my respects to the King's Majesty. He received me with the most friendly looks, and the Bishop of Lincoln then bade me be of good hope and confident. He said nothing, however, about making me a present; nor did I venture to put in a word on that subject lest I should be thought impudent. Durham gave me a present of six angels as I was going away, and this, if I mistake not, is the fourth sum of like amount that I have received from him. The Archbishop sought an opportunity and gave me an equal sum. Rochester gave me a real; and that is the whole of what I have carried away with me. I wished you to know this, lest it should have been supposed that I had taken advantage of my leaving England to amass a large sum of money.

"I am now at the castle of Hamme, where I intend to stay a few days with my friend Mountjoy, after which I shall proceed to Germany, only stopping to call on two or three friends on my way. If my fortune should correspond with my own wishes and the promises of others, I shall return soon; but if not, I must adapt my plans to circumstances. God grant that I may return safe, and that I may find my friend

Ammonius not only safe, but loaded with the richest gifts of fortune. If you should ever have an opportunity of advancing the interests of your friend Erasmus, I feel sure you will do the same for him in his absence as you have always done for him whether absent or present. Farewell, dearest friend."

While Erasmus was wandering about the world, labouring hard in the cause of letters and associating with great men, meantime he was not altogether forgotten by his brethren in the humble Augustinian convent of Steyn, nor, it would seem, had they quite despaired of eventually recovering the lost sheep. At least, one of them, named Servatius, having recently become prior of the convent, thought it his duty to write him a letter, pressing him to return, and rebuking him for his unclerical habits and for having left off the dress of his order. This letter reached him while he was at the castle of Hamme. As his answer, which, of course, was a refusal, has already been made use of for some particulars in his life, it will not be necessary to reproduce the whole of it here, but a few extracts may be interesting.

After reminding the reverend father that he had originally become a monk greatly against his will, Erasmus proceeds to defend his present manner of life, and to contrast it with the habits of the monastery, to the no small disadvantage of the latter. "I have always," he says, "kept this in view, in what kind of life I should be least tempted to evil, and I think I have found it. Meantime, I have lived among sober men; I have lived in the pursuit of letters, which have saved me from many vices. I have enjoyed the opportunity of associating with men of a truly Christian spirit, by whose conversation I have been improved. I say nothing just now of my works; but many confess that they have been made, not only more learned, but better, by reading them. The love of money has never possessed me. For fame, I value it not a jot. Though I was at one time led astray by pleasure, I have never been its slave. Rioting and drunkenness I have always abhorred and avoided.

"Whenever I have thought of re-entering your fraternity there has occurred to me the envy on the part of many, and the universal contempt with which I should be overwhelmed; I remember too the sort of talk we used to have, so frigid, so silly, so far from the spirit of Christianity; our drinking bouts, so unclerical; in short, our whole manner of life, from which, if you take away what they call the ceremonies, I know not what good would be left. Finally, I remembered my bodily infirmities, which are now increased by age, disease, and toil, and which would both prevent my satisfying you and occasion my own death. For some years past I have been subject to the stone, a painful and indeed fatal disease; and during the same period I have found it impossible to drink anything but wine, nor will my disorder permit me to drink every sort of wine. I am compelled also to be particular as to my food and the climate in which I live. For this is a kind of disease which very easily returns, and which requires the utmost care; and I am acquainted with the climate of Holland, and with your way of living, to say nothing of your morals. Accordingly, if I should return, I should gain no end but to give you trouble and hasten my own death.

". . . You wish me to have a settled abode, a thing which advancing age also recommends. Yet we hear the travels of Solon, Pythagoras, and Plato spoken of approvingly. The Apostles, too, were wanderers, and especially Paul. St. Jerome was a monk at Rome, in Syria, in Africa, and in various other places, and he continued his sacred studies even when his hair was grey. I am not to be compared to him, I admit; but nevertheless I have never changed my place except to avoid the plague, or for the sake of learning, or for my health, and wherever I have lived—forgive my boasting for the sake of its truth—I have met with praise and approbation from those who were best able to bestow them. Nor is there any country, whether Spain, Italy, Germany, France, England, or Scotland, which does not invite me to share its hospitality."

Erasmus then goes on to speak of his reception at Rome, and tells how in England there was not a bishop but was glad to have a bow from him; how the King himself had written to him with his own hand; and how the Queen desired to have him as her tutor. After mentioning Warham, Mountjoy, and his other English friends, he goes on to say a few words about his writings; he next apologizes for his change of dress, and finally thanks Servatius for his offer to look out for some retreat for him where he may live in quiet and enjoy a large income. "What this is," he adds, "I can't imagine, unless you mean to set me over a nunnery, so that I, who have never consented to serve kings or archbishops, must become the slave of women. As to an income, that is no inducement to me, for I don't want to become rich, provided I have as much as my health and my studies require, and I am not a burden to any one. . . .

I am now on my way to Germany, that is to say, to Basle, where I intend to publish my works. Possibly I may spend this winter in Rome. On my return I shall try and see you somewhere; but that is impossible at present, as the summer is almost over, and I have a long journey before me.

"... Farewell, my reverend father, as you now are, my once very genial companion." [2]

So far indeed was he from thinking of again submitting his neck to the monastic yoke, that, on the contrary, he applied to Leo X. for a dispensation from his vows. His letter, addressed to Lambertus Grunnius, the apostolic secretary, in which, under the name of Florentius, he describes how he was entrapped into a monastery against his will, and when he was too young to be able to judge for himself, was now sent to the Pope, who expressed his indignation against the man-stealers, and willingly granted the request. Along with this letter Erasmus forwarded all necessary information for the drawing up of the diploma, and desired the secretary to be at his ease about the expenses, which he pledged himself to pay; the Pope, however, had given directions that no charge should be made. The letter to Grunnius is without a date, so that we cannot fix the exact time when this transaction took place.[3]

Leaving Hamme, Erasmus spent two days with his friend the Abbot of St. Bertin, after which he went on to Ghent and Antwerp, in each of which cities he stayed

---

[2] *Ep.* viii. App. The letter to Father Servatius appears in two forms slightly different. The other will be found in the first volume of Le Clerc's *Erasmus*.

[3] *Ep.* ccccxlii., ccccxliii. App. The letter to Grunnius is also printed by Jortin in his Appendix—*Life of Erasmus*, iii. 1.

a few days to see his friends, and thence he proceeded to Bergen, where he visited the Prince de Vere and his mother.

On the way to Ghent he met with an adventure of which he has given a humorous account in a letter written to Mountjoy. "Scarcely," he tells him, "had he left the inn where he had spent the night when his horse shied at some clothes which were spread on the ground to dry, and having happened to stoop to one side to speak to his servant just at the very moment that his horse started to the other side, in his effort to keep his seat, he gave his spine a wrench which was like to have broken it. Finding it impossible to ride farther, he tried to dismount, but so excruciating was the pain that he succeeded only with the help of his attendant. He was now six long miles from his destination, in the open country, and with no inn at which even tolerable entertainment could be found within sight. To walk such a distance would have been difficult for him at any time; in his present condition it was impossible. In this extremity he called in the aid of St. Paul, and vowed that, if he might only escape the present danger, he would finish the commentary he had begun on his Epistle to the Romans. Presently, finding he could walk no further, he tried if he could mount his horse, and unexpectedly succeeded. By moving quietly on he was able to get to his journey's end, but on retiring to his bed-room on his arrival he found he could not stand without support on both sides. The physician and apothecary were sent for, and all his thoughts were turned on death. On wakening the next morning, however, he found he could raise himself without difficulty, and presently it appeared that his pain was gone. Whereupon he returned thanks to God and St. Paul.[4]

If this vow was actually made with any serious belief in its efficacy—and it is only a parallel case to the vow of St. Geneviève—it is another curious illustration how difficult it is for even the most rational minds to escape entirely from the influences of an age of superstition, and shows that if Erasmus could set these influences at defiance when he was well, he was obliged to yield to them when disease or pain made his will less resolute. The whole story, however, has such a comic aspect that one is half-inclined to suspect that the vow may have been an after-thought, designed for the amusement of those who know its author's way, or as a satire on the usual conduct of religious persons when placed in disagreeable circumstances. On the other hand, it is unquestionable that the least superstitious people will, under stress of pain, have recourse to expedients which they would be ashamed to acknowledge, and the practice of making vows was so inveterate in that age that even those who had least faith in their efficacy may sometimes have found themselves instinctively turning to so easy a relief. Probably the truth is that Erasmus actually called in the aid of St. Paul. The levity with which he treats the subject shows either that he did not really believe his rapid recovery to be due to the assistance of the saint, or that he was ashamed of doing so. The best practical com-

---

[4] *Ep.* clxxxii. This letter is correctly dated Aug. 29, 1515. In the postscript, the only part written after the arrival of Erasmus in Basle, we must undoubtedly read "Basiliam veni post Assumptionis," instead of "Annunciationis," the Assumption of the Virgin being August 15, and the Annunciation March 25, when Erasmus was still in England.

mentary on the incident is that the vow was never fulfilled.

From Holland he proceeded to Strasburg, where he found a congenial society of learned men who received him with acclamation, the most prominent of whom were Sebastian Brandt, the celebrated author of the "Ship of Fools," and James Wimphelingus. The latter, who was now a venerable old man, had been formerly a professor of divinity at Heidelberg, where he underwent a bitter persecution from the Augustinians, to whom he had given mortal offence by declaring that St. Augustine was no monk, at least not after the fashion of those who then professed to represent him. Julius II., however, with the approval of all enlightened people, had delivered him from his enemies.[5]

At Schelestadt, his next halting-place, the magistrates, hearing of his arrival, sent him a present of three jars of the choicest wine, and invited him to a dinner, from which he excused himself on the plea of haste. He was not, however, ungrateful for their attention, but celebrated the praises of the city, which was the birthplace of Beatus Rhenanus and other well-known men of the time, in a short elegiac poem.[6] A young friend named John Sapidus accompanied him hence to Basle, where the first whom he met were Beatus Rhenanus, from this time forth one of his most intimate and best-loved friends; Gerard Listrius, the learned physician, who has been already mentioned as having written the commentary on the *Moria;* and Bruno Amerbach, one of the three sons of John Amerbach, Froben's predecessor in the printing-office. The day after his arrival he called on Froben. The honest

---

[5] *Er. Op.* iii. 1141.   [6] *Encomium Slestadii.—Er. Op.* i. 1223.

printer, whose plain, well-marked features still live on
Holbein's canvas, and about the corners of whose mouth
there lurks that spice of dry humour which made him a
fit companion for Erasmus, was not at that moment
expecting his visit; and the latter, remembering, perhaps, his first meeting with Aldus, could not forbear
indulging in a little of his customary pleasantry. He
told him, accordingly, that he had brought with him a
letter from Erasmus, with whom, he added, he was on
terms of the closest intimacy. He had been charged by
him with the duty of superintending the publication of
his writings, and anything he undertook would be sure
to meet with his approval. "In short," he continued,
to relieve the printer's perplexity, "I am so like him
that whoever sees me sees Erasmus." Froben laughed
and welcomed him, and Froben's father-in-law carried
him away to his home, having first paid his reckoning
at the inn. Two days afterwards the professors of the
University, through the Dean of the Theological
Faculty, invited him to supper for the following evening,
when he was introduced to all the learned men of the
place. They would have overwhelmed him with atten-
tions had he permitted it. But he had hard work before
him, and was compelled to beg that they would leave
him to himself. The next eight months were spent in
labour so incessant that, as he tells one of his correspondents, he had scarcely time to eat. He had worked
so hard, as he tells another, that he had almost killed
himself in the endeavour to bring St. Jerome to life. A
complete edition of the works of Seneca, whose text he
had corrected with enormous labour, an edition of the
"Adages," so enlarged as to be almost a new work,
an improved edition of the *De Copia*, his "Book of

Similes," and his translations from Plutarch—these works, together with the continued preparations for the "Jerome" and the New Testament, might well have exhausted the energies of any less indefatigable student. They were apparently too much for the press of Froben. The *De Copia* and the "Similes" were sent to Matthias Schurer, the printer of Strasburg. The "Jerome" did not make its appearance for about a year, while the New Testament was not yet even begun.[7]

Another friend whom he made during his stay in Basle was Udalric Zasius, Professor of Imperial Law at Friburg. Zasius wrote to him one or two playful letters in which he addressed him as "Great Man," and told him he intended to mention his name in a work he was then preparing on the Imperial Law.[8] Erasmus of course replied in the same strain. He thanked him for his intention of immortalizing him. "But, pray," he adds, "do not continue to load me with invidious titles, lest you may give occasion to sarcastic people to ridicule me. For who but must laugh to hear Erasmus called 'Great,' seeing how small he is, in every sense of the word; or 'Fortunate,' seeing that Fortune has bestowed upon him no favours whatever?"[9]

While he was staying at Basle he also made the acquaintance of two men who afterwards played a distinguished part in the history of the Reformation. Zwingle, who had an intense admiration for him, and never went to sleep without reading some pages from his writings, came to Basle on purpose to see him. He afterwards thought it a great matter to be able to boast

---

[7] *Ep. ad Jac. Wimphelingum.* Conf. *Ep.* xi. und xiii. App.
[8] *Ep.* x., xxvii. App.   [9] *Ep.* xi. App.

that he had seen Erasmus.[10] The other was the mild and amiable Œcolampadius, who, by his knowledge of Hebrew, was of great assistance to him, a year later, in editing the Greek Testament. For him he seems, at this time, to have conceived an affectionate regard, which, amid the differences of after years, was never wholly obliterated. He gave him as a mark of his friendship a manuscript containing the beginning of St. John, which Œcolampadius attached to his crucifix, and would often reverently kiss.[11] It was probably at this time too that he became acquainted with Bilibald Pirckheimer, the learned senator of Nuremberg, who continued till his death one of his most attached friends. Pirckheimer wrote a book in defence of Reuchlin, with which Erasmus declared he had only one fault to find, and that was the list which he had appended to it, of those who supported Reuchlin; "for who," asked he, "that has any pretensions to learning or piety does not support him?"[12]

Erasmus, as we have seen, had intended proceeding into Italy this winter, but he found plenty of work to keep him at Basle, where accordingly he remained till the following spring, and before the end of March, 1515, we find him once more among his English friends. As I have already mentioned, he had been invited about a year before to the court of Brussels, and made a councillor to Prince Charles of Austria, the Arch-Duke of Burgundy, then a lad of fifteen, but destined soon to succeed to the throne of Spain, and eventually to become Emperor of Germany as Charles V. To this Prince, who was the son of his old friend Philip the Fair, he dedicated, as the first fruits of his new office,

[10] *Er. Op.* iii. 1538, C, D.   [11] *Ib.* 235, C, D.   [12] *Ib.* 270, A.

a treatise which he wrote about this time, perhaps in the intervals of his journey, on the education of a Christian Prince.[13] This little work, applauded though it was, and deservedly so, at the time of its appearance, cannot be said to have retained much of its value. It abounds, indeed, in admirable precepts, but most of them are tolerably obvious; and as the chief motives which it supplies for good government are those of virtue, a bad king possessed of absolute power might naturally ask why he should obey them. True, he is told he will be hated by his subjects, but he sets their hatred at defiance; and that tyrannies never endure, but he hopes that his own case will prove an exception. Again, the philosopher in his study easily sees that to capture a city costs infinitely more, both in treasure and in men, than to build one; but what if the monarch's passion be for military glory, and not for his people's welfare? Another objection to such a treatise might be that while, with praiseworthy fulness, it treats of the means of despotism, one might derive from it the maxims of tyranny, as easily as learn how to govern well. Probably, however, Erasmus has said upon the subject nearly all that could be said by one who relied chiefly on ancient wisdom and classical illustration, and indeed, I ought to add, on the sympathies of a generous

---

[13] *Institutio Principis Christiani.*—*Er. Op.* iv. 561. We find it first mentioned under the date March 31, 1515, in the following terms:— "Est in manibus libellus de instituendo Principe, quem illustrissimo Carolo, archiduci Burgundiæ, Maximiliani nepoti, destinavimus."—*Er. Op.* ii. 144, A. I would gladly fix the exact date of his appointment to the dignity of councillor, but Erasmus has not thought it of sufficient importance to refer to it particularly in any of his letters. He notices it only in the *Cat. Luc.*, and in a tract against Lee, but without any precise indication of date.—Jortin, iii. 187.

nature. His own political opinions may not be of much importance, especially if they were derived from books rather than founded upon observation; and yet he had ample opportunity for bringing his shrewd sense to bear on the relations between kings and people. It does not, however, add much to our knowledge to find that he considers the best form of government to be a monarchy tempered by a certain proportion of the aristocratical and democratical elements. If his testimony in favour of free trade be thought of any value it may be found here: for he protests against the imposition of duties upon the necessaries of life, such as corn, bread, wine, beer, and clothing. The treatise was printed at Basle in the following year, accompanied by a translation of the work of Isocrates on the administration of a kingdom.

During this year the interest in the cause of the learned and high-minded John Reuchlin, the greatest Hebrew scholar of that age, and an earnest and enthusiastic investigator of the mysteries of the Cabbala, on which he had published one or two curious works, had reached its height. Persecuted by the Dominicans, under the Inquisitor, the ignorant and bigoted Hochstraten, for his opposition to the diabolical proposal to destroy all existing Jewish literature, the Scriptures alone excepted, Reuchlin had defended himself in a book which he called the "Eyeglass," and on a mandate being issued by Hochstraten to burn it, had appealed from the Inquisitor to the Pope. The Bishop of Spire, to whom Leo committed the case, on the 14th of April, 1514, gave sentence against the enemies of Reuchlin and imposed on them perpetual silence, and then it became their turn to insist that the matter must be carried to Rome to be decided there. Meantime, the persecution continued more bitterly than ever; Reuchlin was formally condemned by the Universities of Paris, Maintz, Erfurt, and Louvain; and weary of the strife, and anxious for some decisive sentence, he, too, for the second time, appealed to Rome.

Such was the state of the case while Erasmus was at Basle, and on his journey thither and back again to England, he must have heard it eagerly discussed in the towns along the Rhine. It was probably on his return journey that he met the great scholar himself, and was asked by him to use his influence in Rome on his behalf.[14] Erasmus, who must have seen in the persecution against Reuchlin, an image of what he himself had to expect from the hostility of the monks, did not forget the request. He had, besides, other reasons for writing to Rome. He had, perhaps, not yet given up all thoughts of returning thither, and had he received sufficient encouragement, it is possible he might have done so. He wished also to bespeak the interest of his powerful friends there, and especially of the Pope, on behalf of the important works which were soon to make their appearance at Basle. Accordingly, with these three objects in view, we find him writing from London to his friends, Raphael, Cardinal of St. George, and Cardinal Grimani, two letters of very similar purport, in which he begins by complaining that in England his fortune has not been such as he had been led to expect, adding that he almost regrets having left Rome, especially when he remembers its liberty, its splendour, its enlightenment, its libraries, the intercourse he had enjoyed there with the learned and the great. But

[14] *Er. Op.* ix. 1642, B.

what could he do? His friends had promised him mountains of gold. Lord Mountjoy had led him to expect an ample revenue, combined with leisure for study, and liberty to live as he pleased. To the late King there had succeeded a youth of almost angelic virtue, an accomplished scholar, and who loved him so, that shortly before his father's death he had written to him with his own hand. Thus encouraged, he had dreamt of a second age of gold, or of a residence in the Fortunate Islands. Erasmus, however, here admits that he was himself partly answerable for the disappointment of his expectations. It was not that fortune had not come in his way, but he had been wanting to his opportunities, having such a distaste for public business, being so entirely without ambition, and besides so lazy, that unless fortune should flow in upon him as he slept, there was little chance of his attaining it by his own efforts. He was far, therefore, from blaming his friends, especially as the trumpet of Julius, in summoning them all to war, had drowned the voice of the Muses. He then proceeds to give an account of his literary labours, for which he hopes a more favourable consideration now that peace has been restored to the world, and especially calls attention to the St. Jerome. He is in doubt whether to dedicate this great work to the Archbishop of Canterbury, to whom, he says, he owes everything, or to the Pope; but he promises to be guided by the advice of the Cardinals. And then he proceeds to make a most earnest appeal on behalf of the brother scholar, who, as we have just seen, had requested his interposition. "I pray and beseech you," he writes, "by your regard for learning, which your Highness has always singularly favoured, that that admirable man, John Reuchlin, may have your goodwill in his present trouble. By aiding him you will render a service to literature and to all literary men, whose interest in him is in proportion to their own learning. All Germany is indebted to him, for he was the first to give an impulse to the study of Greek and Hebrew in that country. He is a man profoundly versed in many languages, of very various accomplishments, known to the whole Christian world by the books which he has published, high in favour with the Emperor Maximilian, one of whose councillors he is, esteemed and honoured in his own country, where he holds the office of judge (*duumvir*), and of a character on which no one has hitherto cast a stain. Besides, his old age and grey hairs deserve respect. At his time of life he had earned the right to enjoy the fruits of those studies he had so honourably pursued, while it was hoped, too, that he would publish, for the common good, the labours in which he has been engaged for so many years. It is considered, then, by all good men, not only in Germany, but in England and France, a most unworthy thing that so excellent and so gifted a man should be harassed with odious litigations, and that about a matter which, in my judgment, is utterly paltry. The arms of kings have been confined by your wisdom—let the same wisdom restore peace to the students of letters. Far hence be all that savours of rancour or of feud. Now that kings have returned to harmony at your bidding, it is monstrous that learned men should engage in mutual conflict with books and abuse, and that, while the former are content with harmless weapons, they should fight with pens dipped in poison. How much better had it been that this man should have bestowed upon literary pursuits of the highest class the toil, the money, and the time which he has spent on these pettifogging lawsuits. Julius II. is remembered by many with gratitude because, by his own voice, he released James Wimphelingus, a man not only estimable for his learning and piety, but also of venerable age, from litigations of this kind, and imposed silence upon his calumniators. Whoever, believe me, shall restore John Reuchlin to literature and the Muses, will oblige a very large number of persons."

The letter to Raphael, from which this extract is taken, together with the companion letter to Grimani, is dated London, March 31, 1515.[15]

The Cardinals were in favour of the dedication to Leo, but without waiting for their reply, Erasmus wrote to the Pope, about a month later, to ask his permission. The daring satirist, who had not scrupled to attack the Pontiffs themselves for their degeneracy from the example of the Apostle whose successors they professed to be, addressed Leo in a more servile tone than might have been expected, telling him he surpasses the rest of mankind in majesty as much as men surpass the brutes. He then descends to a style of more reasonable flattery, recalling the blessings which had come upon the Christian world, and especially upon the world of letters, from the accession to the chair of St. Peter of so great a ruler, a member of the family of the Medici, ever the patrons and friends of men distinguished for their learning and their virtue. "Of that house," he continues, "you are no degenerate offspring; on the contrary, you outshine its glory by your own superior virtues, and by the splendour of those accomplishments

[15] *Ep.* clxvii., clxviii.

by which you cast its former brilliancy into the shade you render it the more illustrious." He takes occasion, however, it must be added, to utter a few useful truths, and in congratulating Leo on the restoration of peace, reminds him that the chief warfare of the head of the Church should ever be with moral evil. There was, no doubt, he admits, another kind of warfare, viz., with the barbarous and impious enemies of the Christian religion and of the Roman See. But the former was by far the more necessary of the two, as well as the more difficult; and when we had conquered on that field we might hope to fight successfully on the other. There was, besides, this great difference between these two kinds of warfare, that while the one was disapproved of by some good men, the other was universally applauded. For there can be no doubt that Christ and Paul exhort us to make war on sin, but neither Christ nor his Apostles urge us to take up arms against the Turks. "And indeed," he adds, "I am not sure whether, as Christ with the Apostles and Martyrs conquered the whole world by their beneficence, patience, and holy teaching, it would not be better to subdue the Turks by setting them a good example than by arms." He is assured, however, that his Holiness is doing everything in his power for the restoration of religion, which has recently gone sadly to decay; and by the reconciliation of the sovereigns of Christendom he has prepared the surest means for the subjection of the impious Turks. "Those savage beasts will fly so soon as they shall hear the roar of our Lion; they shall feel, they shall feel, ferocious though they are, the invincible strength of the meek Leo; nor shall they be able to withstand a Pontiff whose power shall consist in his piety rather than in the number of his troops, and who shall carry all the power of heaven with him to the war."

After this burst of rodomontade, Erasmus continues in a more sober strain. He assures the Pope that his strongest desire is now to complete some work by means of which the services of his Holiness towards the Christian world may be held in everlasting honour; and as he is convinced that such a task exceeds his unaided powers, he has resolved, as the surest means of attaining his end, to make use of some name already immortal. Seeing, then, that St. Jerome was the greatest of the Latin theologians, and that his works were so corrupted that they had become almost unintelligible; encouraged, moreover, by the sympathy of so many learned men, especially the Lord Archbishop of Canterbury, and Father John Peter Caraffa, his Holiness's ambassador in England, who urged him to a task from which his own modesty would have made him shrink; and especially relying upon *His* aid, who never fails to assist our pious efforts, he had at length resumed a labour which other occupations had interrupted, and had undertaken to restore the text of Jerome's Epistles, that being the part of his works of which he had assumed the special charge. He then gives a particular account of his labours upon Jerome, which, however, to avoid repetition, as we must return to the subject presently, may be omitted here. The following extract from the conclusion of his letter describes his fellow-labourers in this important undertaking, and will serve as an introduction to some account of the edition of St. Jerome, which will be noticed at length in another chapter:—

" For a considerable time past this great work has

been in progress at Basle, at the printing-office of Froben, so well known for its accuracy and for the number of excellent works, especially those bearing on sacred subjects, which have issued from it. I need scarcely say that this work, as well as its expenses, are shared among several persons. For in those parts of Jerome which I have not taken in hand, but in which I occasionally give my assistance, several learned men have been diligently employed for some time past; among whom I must mention first that distinguished man, John Reuchlin, of Phorzheim, who knows Greek, Latin, and Hebrew almost equally well, and, besides, can hold his ground in every branch of science with the very foremost men of the time. It is with good reason, then, that all Germany looks up to him as a kind of Phœnix, and as the greatest glory of which it can boast. Conon of Nuremberg, also, a theologian of the Preaching Order of Friars, as they are vulgarly called, has been of no small service to our undertaking. He is a man whose acquaintance with Greek literature is most extensive, and who has ever shown the most unwearied industry in promoting the cause of learning. And with these must be named Beatus Rhenanus, of Schelestadt, a young man whose profound learning is equalled only by his exquisite critical taste. But it is to the brothers Amerbach, with whom Froben shares the expenses and the toil, that the praise of this undertaking is chiefly due. Indeed, one might fancy that it was the express destiny of this family that Jerome should be restored to life by their means. The father, a most worthy man, had his three sons taught Greek, Latin, and Hebrew expressly for this purpose. On his death he bequeathed the task to his children, dedicating to it all the wealth he had. And now these excellent young men are devoting themselves to the accomplishment of their worthy father's intentions thus entrusted to their hands, dividing St. Jerome with me on this principle, that whatever is not included in those books which are written in the epistolary form, shall be their special charge. But your Holiness will doubtless ask why I trouble you with these details? I was about to say, most Holy Father, that while there is no name better known or more revered than that of Jerome, I see, nevertheless, how much splendour, weight, and authority shall be added to it ;—and while the glory of Leo is unapproachable, it will yet gain, if I mistake not, no little lustre ;—if so rare, so great, and so renowned a work shall pass into the public hands under the happy auspices of your name. It is but fitting that all good literature which is the offspring of peace, should flourish under a Pontiff by whom repose and peace, without whose fostering care learning must perish, have been restored to the world. Fitting too that the chief teacher of the Christian religion should be dedicated to that religion's High Priest, and the best of all theologians to the best of all Popes. I am not indeed ignorant that the dedication of anything to your Holiness is a subject on which the most scrupulous consideration is called for ; that which is consecrated to Deity should be worthy of Deity. If, however, in this undertaking I shall obtain your Majesty's favour, it will be my desire to consecrate to Leo not merely these labours, but all the fruits of my studies. For myself I expect no other reward for such excessive toil than that the works of Jerome restored by my industry may be of some service to the cause of Christian piety.

He whose grace I seek as the reward of my labour will most abundantly recompense me. Jerome will find more readers according as he is rendered more intelligible. He will be the more acceptable to all if his works appear under the sanction of so great a Pontiff." [16]

Leo's reply to this letter was extremely gracious. He not only declared himself highly pleased with the labours of Erasmus, but addressed a letter to the King of England, specially recommending him to his favour.[17] These letters, which bear the date of July 10, 1515, did not reach England till Erasmus had again left it, to return to Basle. After all the St. Jerome was not dedicated to the Pope. Erasmus had not foreseen that the other great work which he had in contemplation, and for which it was even more important to have the sanction of the Pontiff's name, would appear first. The New Testament, as we shall see, was dedicated to Leo, and the Jerome to the Archbishop of Canterbury.

[16] *Ep.* clxxiv.   [17] *Ep.* clxxviii., clxxix.

CHAPTER X.

The "Adages"—History of the Work—First Edition—Discussion with Polydore Virgil—Aldine Edition—Reprinted by Froben—Definition of a Proverb—Examples—Erasmus rails at Kings and Priests—The Sileni of Alcibiades—The Scarabæus.

The few years immediately preceding the ever memorable day, October 31, 1517, on which Luther posted up his theses on the church door at Wittenberg, and thus gave the signal for the Reformation, were a period of great literary activity, and were distinguished by the publication of several remarkable works, which themselves must have done much to prepare the world for coming events; and among the rest, certainly not the least remarkable were three by Erasmus—viz., the new and greatly enlarged edition of his "Adages," his "St. Jerome," and his New Testament. These I shall now proceed to notice in order, and at some length. The "Adages" first claim our attention.

This, which, in its latest form, fills one of the largest of the eleven folio volumes which constitute Le Clerc's edition of "Erasmus," is a most singular work, and, though it may be supposed that few would have patience to read it in these days, it is, nevertheless, well worthy of study. Not only is it a monument of vast learning, but it is a rich repository of anecdotes, quotations, and historical and biographical sketches.

What a boon it must have been to the student in an age when books were rare and expensive, supplying him, as it did, with apt and elegant phraseology on all sorts of subjects, serving as an introduction to the Greek and Latin classics, and furnishing besides eloquent declamations against kings and monks, war and priestcraft! To those, too, who desired an easy method of learning Greek, it must have been a valuable aid, all the Greek quotations, of which there were several thousand, being carefully rendered into Latin.[1] Thus, besides to a great extent serving the purpose of a dictionary and a grammar, it is a common-place book, a journal and a book of travels, all in one.

This is true, however, only of the later editions, in which the adages number 4,151, and are each followed by a commentary explaining their meaning and origin, and illustrating their use, and in some instances digressing into long rhetorical essays in which the vices of the age are keenly satirised or boldly denounced. Compared with these later editions the first, which appeared in the year 1500, was indeed, as Erasmus himself described it, an *opus jejunum atque inops*,—a poor miserable production.[2]

The history of this celebrated work is as follows. When Erasmus was at Oxford, or possibly before he went there, the idea occurred to him of making a collection of proverbs from the writings of the ancients. Some Greek writers who were then considered "not

---

[1] The title-page to the Aldine edition of 1508, states that there are in the work about 10,000 verses from Homer, Euripides, and other Greek writers, literally translated in the metre of the original, besides many quotations from Plato, Demosthenes, and others.

[2] *Er. Op.* iii. 96, B. See above, p. 139.

obscure," but whom nobody knows now, had previously attempted the same kind of thing; but their works were so mutilated, besides having no references, that they had proved of little service to him.³ Latin writers, such as Aulus Gellius, Macrobius, and others, had shown their appreciation of the value of proverbs by noting and explaining them whenever they came in their way, while among the moderns, such masters of classical Latinity as Pico and Politiano, had endeavoured to give grace to their style by the interspersion of ancient adages; " but as yet," says Erasmus, " no one had made any formal collection of them." The plan was discussed at Oxford with the University men, and due encouragement given, Charnock being particularly urgent that the work should be undertaken.⁴ The earliest conception of the work was a very modest one, but from the first Erasmus appears to have foreseen to what it was likely to grow. " I intend," he says in a letter to Battus shortly after his return to Paris, " writing a collection of ancient adages. I foresee there will be some thousands, but it is my purpose to publish only two, or at the most, three hundred."⁵ Indeed, he felt that he was not yet enough of a Greek scholar for any greater undertaking. A little farther on in the same letter we find him complaining that Greek nearly kills him, and that he has no money either to purchase books or to hire a teacher.

³ " Adde huc quod apud Græcos complures extiterunt non obscuri nominis auctores, qui proverbiorum collectanea vel ex professo conscripserunt. Veluti Apostolius Bizantius, Stephanus Diogenianus. Quorum nos quidem, præter nomina, nihil adhuc nancisci quivimus, nisi ex Diogeniani collectaneis fragmenta quædam, verum adeo mutila, adeoque nuda nulla auctorum nomenclatura, nullis locorum indiciis, ut ex his nobis non multum accederit."—Preface to the first edition.
⁴ *Ib.*
⁵ *Ep.* lxxx.

Afterwards he took some lessons from Hermonymus, already referred to as the Professor of Greek at Paris, and of whom he speaks with such contempt as one "who was incapable of teaching even if he had been willing to do so, and who would not if he could."[6] He was, he wittily complains, "twice a Greek; for he was always hungry, and he demanded heavy fees."

The first edition of the "Adages," which was published at Paris in the year 1500,[7] consisted of about eight hundred proverbs, and was dedicated to Lord Mountjoy. The explanatory remarks are in this edition extremely brief, sometimes not extending beyond two or three words; and a few proverbs which subsequently suggested long dissertations are found here with no more comment than is barely sufficient to explain their meaning. Nor is there any great display of learning. There are very few Greek references, and these are probably at second hand. And there are perhaps nearly as many citations from previous collectors, or from such writers as the grammarian Donatus,

---

[6] See above, p. 33, note.

[7] *Desiderii Herasmi Roterodami veterum maximeque insignium paræmiarum id est adagiorum collectanea: opus qum novum tum ad omne vel scripturæ vel sermonis genus venustandum insigniendumque mirum in modum conducibile. Id quod ita demum intelligetis adolescentes optimi si hujus modi deliciis et literas vestras et orationem quotidianam assuescetis aspergere. Sapete ergo et hunc tam rarum thesaurum tantillo nummulo venalem vobis redimite, multo præstantiora propediem accepturi, si hec boni consulueritis. Valete. In noie scte trinitatis. Venalis invenietur hic liber in officina: Magistri Johannis Philippi, cujus quidem tum industria: tum sumptu nitidissimis formulis est emendatissime impressus: In via divi Marcelli ad divinæ trinitatis signum.* Such is the title-page, evidently the composition of the printer, of the oldest edition I have seen. Its date, however, is 1505. On the opposite side there is a letter from Faustus Andrelinus, expressing his approval of the work, which bears the date June 15, 1500.

as from original authorities. Erasmus himself makes very light of the labour expended on this work, and speaks of it as having been merely the occupation of his leisure hours. He had put together these proverbs, he says, in a very few days, and without strict regard to accuracy, intending them to serve as a private assistance to his pupil and friend Lord Mountjoy; and eventually certain persons had printed them, but so badly that it might have been supposed errors were introduced intentionally. And in the original dedication to Mountjoy, in which he quotes from Pliny the sentiment which should be the motto of every student, that he considered all time lost which was not devoted to study, he says he had dictated the work rather than written it, at a time when he was suffering from fever, and had been forbidden by his physician to touch a book. Accordingly, abandoning severer studies, he had roamed for a time through various authors, gathering from their works all sorts of flowers, which he then wove into a garland. That he published the volume of Adages sooner than he had intended, and while conscious of its imperfections, is undeniable; but he is careful to disclaim all responsibility as to the correctness of the press, the book having been printed, he says, when he was absent from Paris.[8] Twenty-four years afterwards he gave a somewhat whimsical account of the motives which led him to publish thus prematurely. We have seen how, in consequence of the absurd law prohibiting the removal of coin from the realm, he had been deprived of

---

[8] "Eam quidam, sedulo quidem illi, sed sinistro nimioque studio mei, publicandam etiam ac formulis excudendam curarunt."—Preface to the Aldine edition. Cf. *Er. Op.* iii. 671, F.—" Meus [liber] absente me excusus est Lutetiæ."

his little all at Dover, and had arrived on the other side of the Channel almost in a state of destitution. Now, it seems, the natural thing for an indignant scholar to do, under those circumstances and in those times, would have been to seize his pen and write a book full of abuse of England and the English. Erasmus, wishing to show that he bore no malice, determined, on the contrary, to publish something in which there should be no reference to his misadventure. In such a case he seems to have thought that silence would be accepted as conclusive evidence of a forgiving disposition; and as Mountjoy might be supposed to have incurred his special wrath, he resolved to dedicate the volume to him.[9] All this, however, may have been purely imaginary so far as regards the publication of the "Adages." It does not seem very probable that Erasmus would attack a country in which he had been so kindly received and made so many valuable friends; and still less that he would quarrel with Mountjoy, on whom he was dependent for a pension. It is much more likely that he sought to recruit his exhausted finances by the publication of a work which was pretty sure to sell.

The little book was received with favour, accompanied as it was by a recommendatory letter from Faustus Andrelinus, the Poet Laureate. This letter Erasmus had himself asked for, on the plea that the worse a man's goods are the more they need commendation: yet he afterwards found it convenient to say that the printer had extorted it.[10] In England, it would seem, the work was less in demand than might have been expected, considering the connections the author had established there, for we find him regretting

[9] *Cat. Luc.*   [10] Cf. *Ep.* lxxi. and dcii.

that he had sent any copies to this country, since they sold better and for a higher price in France; and it will be remembered how he complained to Colet that, after three years, he had received no account of one hundred copies which had been sent to England.[11] That "somebody must have got the money" seemed clear enough, but what was still more certain—as has happened occasionally even since the sixteenth century—was, that the author had not got it.

Several years afterwards he had a good-humoured discussion with Polydore Virgil, who had also published a book of Adages, as to which of them was first in the field. Polydore charged his eminent contemporary with having stolen from him; while Erasmus declares that at the time his "Adages" were published he had never heard of any Polydore, except the one killed by Polymnestor in the Tragedies. He was at Louvain, he says, (a place to which he had always felt an objection, he knew not why, though he discovered it afterwards,) when he first heard of the rival work. There a certain theologian named Luke had spread a report that he had come before the world dressed in borrowed feathers; that Polydore had written a work of the same kind as his, only far better, and that he was no more than Polydore's ape. He immediately made inquiries. No such book was to be had in any of the shops, but at last he chanced upon a copy in the library of a most inveterate book-collector named Busleiden. Eagerly he compared the dates; found that his own was published on the 15th of June, 1500, and Polydore's in Italy three months later. Such an argument, one would suppose, was decisive, provided the facts were correctly

[11] See above, p. 138.

stated. But Erasmus, as if he was aware that this was not the case, goes on, in his letter to Polydore on the subject, to urge additional proofs of his ignorance.[12] Polydore's book, he says, contained some good proverbs which were not to be found in his own; but such an admirable plagiarist as he was accused of being would certainly not have omitted any. Besides, supposing he had known of the book, why should he have cited Polydore, seeing that his proverbs are taken from the commonest sources, when he might have referred to the original sources themselves? After all, he concludes, there is not much merit in a compilation, but such as there is they had better divide between them.[13]

Indeed, the question was not worth disputing about, for the fame of Erasmus in no respect rests upon his first edition. This was reprinted at Paris and Strasburg in the course of the next few years; but the first appearance of the work in anything like the shape in which it is now known was at Venice in 1508,[14] though the digressions, which are to us the most curious and interesting part of the book, were not added till a still later period. During these eight years Erasmus had collected a vast number of adages, both Greek and Latin, which he was now prepared to add with comments and illustrations; and in the splendid library of Aldus he enjoyed ample means for completing his work to the best advantage. He has himself, under the

---

[12] There is no doubt, I believe, that Polydore Virgil published his book of Adages in 1498. It is unfortunate that Erasmus should have allowed himself thus to misstate a plain fact, rather than acknowledge that another was first in the field.

[13] *Ep.* dcii.

[14] *Erasmi Roterodami Adagiorum Chiliades Tres, ac Centuriæ fere totidem. Venetiis in Ædibus Aldi. Mense Sept. mdviii.*

proverb *Festina lente*, given a most interesting account of his labours, and bears generous testimony to the kindness which he received from his Italian friends. He had, he tells us, brought nothing with him to Venice but a confused mass of materials derived from authors already printed; but, notwithstanding his being a foreigner, he found every one ready to lend him all the aid in their power. Aldus withheld none of his treasures. Other learned men, such as Lascar, Marcus Musurus the poet, and Aleander, sent him their manuscripts, and some even whose names he did not know proffered their assistance. Thus he was enabled by a comparison of good manuscripts to bring his work to a perfection which would otherwise have been impossible. The work went merrily on, Aldus printing while Erasmus wrote, and the bulk of it was completed in the course of about nine months. The number of proverbs collected now amounted to 3,260, and a vast mass of learning drawn from the most various sources was thus given to the world. In the same essay in which he records these particulars Erasmus contrasts the generous encouragement shown by the Italians to a Dutchman with the illiberal conduct of some more nearly akin to him, and from whom, therefore, better things might have been expected. He had applied to a friend of his —of what country he does not say, using the general term Cisalpine—for the loan of a Suidas which he knew him to possess, and which had the Proverbs noted on the margin. He wished to have it merely for a few hours, until his amanuensis should copy some sentences into his note-book. The owner of the Suidas refused, in spite of repeated applications. Erasmus, having tried in vain to overcome his obstinacy, suggested that perhaps, he intended publishing a collection of proverbs himself. No: he vowed he had no such notion in his head. At last the admission was forced from him that he was afraid that learned men would be held in less esteem if what had hitherto been their monopoly should be made public property.[15]

This, the first great edition of the "Adages," was received with immense applause by the literary world, though the sale of such an expensive work as it must have been could not be very rapid. In course of time, however, other editions followed. Froben brought out a splendid one, almost rivalling the Aldine, at Basle, in 1513, and it was this which first drew the attention of Erasmus to the merits of that enterprising printer. In 1515 he printed another, under the superintendence of the author; and it was in this that there first appeared those remarkable essays, containing such fierce attacks on monks and kings, to which reference has already been made. Afterwards, the "Adages" were reprinted repeatedly by Froben, and always with some additional matter, as well as at Strasburg, Paris, and elsewhere; and altogether the demand was such as not only to be commensurate with the merits of the work, but to have satisfied or surpassed the utmost expectations of its author.

In proceeding to give some more detailed account of this great work in its completed form, it is obvious to remark that there are many of the so-called adages which do not strictly come under that name. What is a proverb? According to Le Clerc, it is the essence of the proverb that it shall be figurative, and he, therefore, defines it "a short moral sentence which indicates something different from what the words seem at first

[15] *Er. Op.* ii. 397—407.

to mean."[16] We need not, however, tie down Erasmus to any definition except his own. He has shown that some proverbs are not moral, and that others are not metaphorical, and he is surely entitled to say what extent of ground he wishes to be covered by his work. His own definition is that a proverb is "a saying often repeated, and with something uncommon in the mode of expression;"[17] but this, it must be confessed, would by no means include his entire collection, and in order to complete his number of four thousand and upwards, mere phrases, idiomatic expressions, and sometimes even single words are called into requisition. Probably, however, of recognized proverbs occurring in the classical writers of antiquity, there are few or none omitted; and it is interesting to observe that there are many which were familiar when Socrates talked wisdom in the market-place of Athens, or when Cicero thundered in the Roman Senate-house, which are equally common now, either in precisely the same form or one slightly altered. Thus we have "Many a slip 'twixt the cup and the lip," which is expressed in Latin in the following hexameter,—

Multa cadunt inter calicem supremaque labra;

and this again is a translation from the Greek:—

Πολλὰ μεταξὺ πέλει κύλικος καὶ χείλεος ἄκρου.[18]

Again, *Fumum fugiens in ignem incidi*, which may be translated "Out of the frying-pan into the fire;"[19] "one swallow doesn't make a summer," only the Greeks and Romans naturally said "spring."[20] "As like as two

---

[16] *Bibliothèque Choisie*, i. p. 391.
[17] "Paræmia est celebre dictum, scita quapiam novitate insigne." —*Er. Op.* ii. 2, B.
[18] *Er. Op.* ii. 181, A.
[19] *Ib.* 184, C.
[20] *Ib.* 299, C.

eggs;[21] *ne quid nimis,* "too much of one thing,"[22] the authorship of which is disputed, some ascribing it to Pythagoras, others to Bias, though one would not think it quite beyond the bounds of possibility that two such great men might have hit upon it severally without suspicion of plagiarism; *duabus sedere sellis,*[23] suggesting sitting between two stools, though it is really equivalent to having two strings to one's bow; "pigeons' milk," of which the classical form, however, was hens' milk;[24] *alterum pedem in cymba Charontis habere,* "to have one foot in the grave,"[25] and so on. Shakspeare's—

> At lovers' perjuries
> They say Jove laughs—

is, of course, but a literal translation of Ovid's—

> Jupiter ex alto perjuria ridet amantum,—

and of Tibullus's—

> Perjuria ridet amantum
> Jupiter.[26]

Pages might be filled with similar examples, all amply illustrated with learned remarks, classical quotations and allusions, or, perhaps, fables, accounting for the origin of the proverbs, and explaining their use.

But undoubtedly by far the most curious and interesting part of the "Adages" consists of those digressions, sometimes simply narrative or descriptive, sometimes keenly sarcastic, sometimes full of vehement rhetoric, in which Erasmus delights his readers with his knowledge of his own times, and with various scraps of

[21] *Er. Op.* ii. 186, A.
[22] *Ib.* 259, E.
[23] *Ib.* 262, F.
[24] *Ib.* 222, D.
[25] *Ib.* 427, B.
[26] *Ib.* 549, C.

information or anecdote, exposes the vices of his age, and launches out into unmerciful attacks on monks, theologians, and kings. The monks, of course, furnish ample materials for wit and sarcasm, and assuredly they are not spared; but Erasmus seems also to have been the earliest of those writers who during the course of the sixteenth century vindicated the right of subjects to rebel, and even defended tyrannicide. Indeed, he plainly suggests assassination as the best means of ridding the world of a bad ruler; for what else is it but to suggest assassination to speak of princes and the Bruti in the same breath? I shall presently give an analysis of one or two of the more celebrated of these rhetorical pieces. Meantime, a few examples of the way in which Erasmus makes his proverbs the vehicles of his attacks on contemporary abuses may be found interesting.

Rudius ac planius—that is, "speak with less refinement, and you will be better understood." This proverb, derived from the practice of the ancient philosophers of wrapping up their wisdom in language unintelligible to the multitude, suggests a side-blow at the would-be philosophers of the day. "Even to this day," says Erasmus, "some professors of philosophy and theology, while teaching things in no way beyond the capacity of a woman or a clown to utter, wrap up the question in obscure phraseology and monstrous big words." [27]

Quot homines, tot sententiæ—"many men, many minds." Erasmus wish... would hearken to this a... case... not be so much co...points of no importance. [28]

[27] *Er. Op.* ii. 42,... 114, A.

A mortuo tributum exigere—applied to those who gather riches by unscrupulous means. We have here some vigorous railing against merchants, kings, and priests. "I would sooner," he says, "have a usurer than the mean traders of these days who hunt up gain from every source, by tricks, lies, impostures, misrepresentations, buying here in order to sell elsewhere at double the price, or by their monopolies plundering the miserable common people; and yet we think these are almost the only honest men. . . . . Now, the rage for ownership has gone to such extremes that there is nothing in the world, sacred or profane, that is not beaten into money. Once, even under tyrants, who, however, did not yet fully know their own power, the seas, the rivers, the roads, and wild animals were common property. Now, certain noblemen, as if they were the only men in the world, or rather as if they were gods, claim everything as their own. The unhappy sailor is compelled at a great risk to steer out of his direct course, and to submit to anything he may be ordered by those insolent robbers, as if it was not enough for him to battle with the winds and waves but such storms as these must be let loose upon him. No sooner is the harbour reached than extortions begin; you cannot cross a bridge but you must pay toll; you cannot pass over a river but you feel the prince's might; if you have any baggage you must redeem it from those accu   bbers; and, what is most cruel of all, the wretc   mon people are defrauded, and   ssary   rtailed, by innumerable tithes   gh, surely! But ecclesiastical   bitterest language, and the greediness   erely handled. "You cannot be baptized, that is to say, you cannot become a Christian, without paying for it; such are the splendid auspices under which you enter the doors of the Church. They will not marry you unless you put your hand into your pocket; they will not confess you but to get something by it. They celebrate the mass for hire; they will not sing for nothing, they will not pray for nothing, they will not lay on a hand for nothing. Hardly will they bless you from a distance by the motion of their hand unless you give them something. They will not consecrate a stone or a cup but for hire. Nay, even that truly pontifical office of teaching the people has not escaped the contagion of money-making. To sum up all, however, in one word, they will not so much as impart Christ's body unless you are willing to pay for it. I say nothing of the harvest which is gathered from litigations and dispensations, as they call them; from pardons, vulgarly called indulgences; from conferring priesthoods, from confirming Bishops and Abbots. But what could you expect to get gratuitously from people who make even the burial of the dead a matter of buying and selling, and that in ground which does not belong to them? Among the Gentiles there was a common sepulchre for the miserable plebeians; there was a place where you might bury whom you would gratis. Among Christians the earth may not even be opened to receive the dead unless you hire what ground you want from a priest, and according to the amount you pay will be the sort of place provided for you. If you like to pay handsomely you shall have the privilege of rotting in the church close by the high altar; but if you can afford only a moderate sum you must be content to return to your kindred elements among plebeians and under the open sky."[29]

After all this does not seem so very unfair. It was right that those who wanted a handsome burial should pay for it, and far better surely that the priests should make a moderate charge for their services than live on alms like the mendicant friars. But the morality of the time was that of the convent, from whose atmosphere it would seem that even Erasmus was not entirely free; commerce, even as applied to the things of this life, was hardly thought of as honourable, while political economy was unknown.

"A head without a tongue"—spoken of those who have no advice to offer themselves, but nod their head in assent to the opinions of others. "The crocodile," Erasmus caustically adds, "also has a head without a tongue, but armed with teeth, like many we meet with now, who, although they have no talent for speaking, can yet give a deadly bite. The Nile is far away, but this kind of crocodile may be found everywhere."[30]

Under the head of *Virum improbum vel mus mordeat*, "even a mouse would bite a wicked man," meaning that the slightest thing may be made the occasion of a quarrel, he takes occasion to relate an instance of base ingratitude which had come within his own knowledge. A wealthy citizen of London, a man held in universal respect, had been cured of a dangerous disease by a German physician, to whom he continued to make the most extravagant promises as long as his life was in danger. On his recovery the physician modestly reminded him of the debt. The other put him off, observing that his wife had the key of his

[29] *Er. Op.* ii. 336, *sqq.* [30] *Ib.* 390, E.

money chest: "and you know," he added, "the nature of women; I don't want her to know that I am giving away so large a sum of money." A few days afterwards the physician, meeting his patient, who by this time had lost every trace of his malady, renewed his application, when he was told by the citizen that his wife had paid the money by his orders. The physician assured him it was not so, but happening to address him in the singular number, the other immediately seized the opportunity to consider himself grossly affronted. "Do you, a vulgar German," he exclaimed, "presume to *thou* an Englishman?" and he darted away, apparently beside himself with rage. "I could not help laughing at the story," says Erasmus, "and yet I was sorry for the disappointment of my friend, as well as amazed that any one could be guilty of such monstrous ingratitude. It would not be right, however, to judge all Britons by this scoundrel." [31]

Festina lente, "hasten slowly"—one of the most valuable of all mottoes, is the explanation of the well-known anchor and dolphin of the Aldine editions; the dolphin, being, as was supposed, the swiftest of all creatures, expresses the haste, while the anchor round which it is twisted supplies the qualifying adverb. The emblem itself is borrowed from a coin of the Emperor Vespasian, with whom, as well as with Augustus, this saying was a great favourite; and when Erasmus was at Venice, the coin was shown him by his friend and entertainer, Aldus Manutius. The dolphin and anchor having been explained at somewhat tedious length, the occasion is taken for passing a well-deserved eulogium on the great printer. "If some deity friendly to literature,"

[31] *Er. Op.* ii. 332.

Erasmus exclaims, "would but favour the fair and truly royal vows of Aldus, I can promise that within a few years the studious will possess, by his work alone, all the good authors there are in the four languages, Latin, Greek, Hebrew, and Chaldee, in a complete and accurate form, and no one need have any lack of literary material. And then we shall see how many excellent manuscripts there are still hidden, which are either kept back through ignorance, or suppressed, owing to the ambition of certain persons who care for nothing except that they may be thought the only wise men. Then we shall know, too, with what prodigious errors those authors abound who are now considered tolerably correct. . . . . The library of Ptolemy," he finely adds, "was contained within the walls of a house, but Aldus is constructing a library which shall have no limits but those of the world." [32]

Under *Ne puero gladium*, we have an anecdote of Henry VII. "This monarch," Erasmus says, "was distinguished for his sound good sense and his laconic speeches;" and once, having been listening to a theologian of one of the mendicant orders haranguing in the most unmeasured terms against princes, he exclaimed, "It was very like putting a sword into the hands of a madman." The saying was, perhaps, hardly worth recording, but surely Erasmus had forgotten how aptly it might have been applied to himself.[33]

These are a few flowers out of this immense bouquet, and they may suffice to give some idea of the variety and richness of the collection. But the author himself has furnished the best description of the difficulties of his undertaking—difficulties so great in that age, when

[32] *Er. Op.* ii. 397, *sqq.*   [33] *Ib.* 559, B—E.

many of the best classics still existed only in manuscript, and when the best manuscripts were scattered far and wide through Europe, often lying hid in obscure corners where they were by no means easy of access, that nothing but the most unconquerable zeal for learning could have carried him over them in triumph. This description is appropriately introduced under *Herculei labores*, the "labours of Hercules," a proverb applicable to toil, not only immense, but also unrequited, and hence in a special degree to literary work. "For," as Erasmus complains —though in his own case, it must be owned, without much reason—"there is no kind of labour which is repaid with so much ingratitude; and the reward of the scholar, after he has lost his sight, brought on premature old age, and worn out his life in study, neglecting for its sake sleep, health, and personal appearance, is to find that he has only succeeded in making himself an object of detestation and envy. The unlearned neglect him; the half-learned laugh at him; and the learned, with the exception of a few, are so filled with envy, that, overlooking all his merits, they have the sharpest eyes for detecting any mistakes into which he may chance to have fallen." To write a book like the "Adages" obviously requires a far more extensive range of reading than any other sort of literary production. For most ordinary subjects the author would have before him a certain limited number of books which it would be necessary for him to consult. But for a work like this there was not a book, ancient or modern, in either Greek or Latin, that had not to be read, and read too with the utmost care and minuteness; "since adages, being very small, sometimes escape the most searching eye. Can any one now form an idea how infinite is the toil of hunting through every country in the world for such tiny things as these? Human life is hardly long enough for turning over the pages of so many poets, grammarians, orators, logicians, sophists, historians, mathematicians, philosophers, and theologians. Every one, I think, must admit this. But how small a part is even this of our toil!" Erasmus now describes the commentators, whose ignorance and carelessness, he says, made no small addition to his labours; and then he proceeds to speak of the "prodigious corruption of the manuscripts, which was such that it was impossible to select a passage for quotation but some obvious blunder would meet the eye, or else there would be one lurking in secret. Think of this, too," he continues: "in the composition of other works the mind has an ample range, so that, wherever you may happen to be, you may be putting the finishing strokes to some portion of your work by keeping your thoughts constantly in motion; whereas here you are so tied down that you cannot depart one foot's breadth, so to speak, from the manuscripts. For your only hope of success depends on your having a number of manuscripts, especially Greek ones; and how rare these are everybody knows. Consequently you must spoil your sight among decayed volumes, thick with the dust of ages, torn and mutilated, and eaten through and through by moths and worms; which are, besides, extremely difficult to read; and, in brief, are of such sort that any one who was long employed among them would soon begin to feel in himself the effects of old age and decay, as well as to make others feel them too." And all the pleasure there may be in this kind of work is the reader's; the writer has none whatever. "In other studies you may indulge your imagination, you may expatiate sometimes among the flowers of eloquence. There are pleasant nooks in which you may rest when weary, and recruit your exhausted strength. But here it is not merely 'cold cabbage hot again,' to use the Greek proverb, but the same things have to be repeated thousands of times—the meaning of an adage, its origin and its application." In the sequel of this essay, which he prolongs to such an extent that he fears, not without reason, lest the reader may consider it a Herculean labour to finish it, Erasmus offers an elaborate apology for any imperfections his work may be supposed to contain; for having completed it so hastily; and, finally, for having undertaken it at all. If any of the charges to which he refers were brought against his book—we know at least that Budæus and he had some epistolary quarrelling as to the propriety of the digressions—it has long survived them; and Erasmus has not only, as he says himself, surpassed Hercules, who was unable to grapple with two monsters at once, whereas he brought out his edition of St. Jerome and an enlarged one of the "Adages" simultaneously at Basle, but he has overcome the greatest enemy of the works of man, Time, which is continually devouring its own offspring.[34]

I shall now conclude this notice of the "Adages" of Erasmus with some account of two of the best known and most characteristic of the longer essays introduced in the edition of 1515. These are the "Sileni of Alcibiades" and the *Scarabæus*.

Every one knows that Silenus was the rakish god who nursed the infant Bacchus, and that Alcibiades, in

---

[34] *Er. Op.* ii. 707, C. *sqq.*

the Banquet of Plato, compares Socrates to a Silenus. The force of the comparison lies in the fact that the Greeks had little images called Sileni, which outwardly portrayed the thick lips and flat nose of the fosterparent of Bacchus, but which were so constructed that the outside could be removed, when the features of a true denizen of Olympus would suddenly be disclosed to view. Hence "the Sileni of Alcibiades" passed into a proverb used of persons or things apparently worthless or ridiculous, but concealing something infinitely precious under their uninviting exterior. Erasmus makes the happiest use of this proverb, applying it in the first instance to the ancient philosophers, such as Diogenes, who, though he was vulgarly looked on as no better than a dog, yet had something within him which drew from Alexander the Great the exclamation, "If I were not Alexander I should wish to be Diogenes;" or Epictetus, who, though a slave, poor and lame, yet possessed the only qualities which give a man any value in the sight of Heaven—uprightness united with wisdom. Then, with a boldness which to some may seem startling, if not even wanting in reverence, he applies it to Christ, remarking that, in this instance, if we look to the outside only, it would be impossible to find any condition more abject or contemptible. "His parents were obscure, his home humble, himself poor, his followers a few fishermen and a publican. His life, to which all pleasures were unknown, led through hunger, weariness, reproaches, and mockeries to a cross. . . . But if the Silenus be opened and we look within, that is to say, if, the eyes of our understanding being enlightened, he shall condescend to reveal himself, what an inestimable treasure will you find : a pearl of so great price under so vile an exterior, so great majesty under such deep humility, such boundless riches under such poverty, such unimaginable virtue under such weakness, so great glory under such ignominy, such absolute repose amid such excessive toils, and, to conclude all, an unfailing fount of immortality in so bitter a death." The Prophets, the Apostles, and John the Baptist are treated in a similar way, and it is shown by various illustrations that all through nature the most obvious things are usually the least valuable. How far Erasmus was from accepting any hard literal method of interpreting the Bible is clear from the following passage, in which he shows that there, too, the same rule prevails. "To speak first of the Old Testament, if you do not look deeper than the mere historical clothing, and read how Adam was made of clay, how his wife was taken secretly from his side as he slept, how the serpent tempted the woman with an apple, how God walked in the garden in the cool of the evening, how the gates of Paradise were guarded by a sword to prevent the return of our first parents,—is there not danger lest you may suppose all this to be a fable forged in the workshop of Homer?[35] Yet, under these external wrappings, what splendid wisdom lies hid! The parables of the Gospel might well be supposed to be the work of some illiterate peasant if you consider only the outside shell. But crack the nut,

---

[35] Compare the *Enchiridion Militis Christiani* for a very similar passage, where also the Sileni of Alcibiades are introduced :— "Maxime vero scripturæ divinæ, quæ fere Silenis illis Alcibiadeis similes, sub tectorio sordido ac pene ridiculo, merum numen claudunt. Alioqui, si sine allegoria legeris, Adæ simulachrum de argilla uda formatum," &c.

and you will not fail to find that ancient and truly divine wisdom, the very counterpart of Christ himself." Beside the Sileni already described, there is another class, who present just the opposite characteristics, looking fair upon the outside, but inwardly full of corruption; and these are called inverse Sileni. "Such are those who, by their sceptre, their guards, their splendid titles, would seem to be no less than gods come down upon the earth; but who, if they could be opened, would be found to be, not kings, but tyrants, robbers, and public enemies. Such are those bishops whose mitre, sparkling with gold and gems, and all their mystic panoply, proclaim them more than men, while, in reality, they have the heart of soldiers or of traders. Such are they—and one meets them everywhere—whose rugged beard and pale face, the hood and the girdle, and their sour looks might lead you to think them the holiest of men, whereas, if you could only peep inside, you would find their heart a sink of selfishness and greed. The great difference between the man of the world and the Christian is that the former looks exclusively to those things which lie upon the surface and at once meet the eye—such as riches, birth, and personal advantages—whereas the latter seeks for those qualities which the eye cannot see, and which have the least possible connection with material objects. Hence, in the vulgar estimate, gold is set above learning, a noble birth is preferred to virtue, the decrees of men to the precepts of Christ, the shadow to the substance, things temporal to things eternal. And closely connected with this false view of things is the practice of using false names. Thus, men call it justice when evil is overcome with evil and crime with crime, or when an injury is repaid with abundant interest. They call him a traitor and an enemy of his sovereign who wishes that his sovereign should govern according to law, that is, who wishes that he should be truly a king, and not a tyrant. And, on the other hand, he is called his sovereign's friend who corrupts him by bad education, poisons his mind with false opinions, mocks him with flattery, and by his evil counsels makes him hateful to his people, and involves him in perpetual wars. They say that the king's majesty is exalted when he has gained any accession of irresponsible power. They say his empire is extended when he has acquired the right to one or two petty townships, albeit it may have been purchased at a vast expenditure of blood, and at the cost of making thousands of his subjects widows and orphans. In the same way they call the priests, bishops, and supreme pontiffs the Church, whereas they are in reality no more than the Church's ministers. The Church is the Christian People, whom Christ himself calls greater, because it is they who sit at meat, while the bishops are they that serve; and yet, though less in this respect, in all others they would be greater if, not merely in their office, but in their life and character, they resembled Christ, who, though he was Lord and Master of all, took upon him the form of a servant. They say the Church is adorned and honoured, not when piety increases among the people, vice diminishes, and holy doctrine flourishes, but when her altars shine with gold and jewels; nay, even when her priests rival the satraps of the East in their estates and the multitude of their servants, in their luxury, their mules, their horses, their sumptuous palaces, and whatever else contributes to the stir and splendour of life." These are a few of the examples which Erasmus gives of the abuse of words, and of the way in which the majority of men permit themselves to be deceived by outward appearance.

He then proceeds to show that in all this he was far from desiring to despoil either kings of their power or priests of their dignity. On the contrary, he who would have kings resemble God, whose image they bear, by the possession of wisdom and superiority to sordid affections, has a far higher idea of regal excellence than those who pander to their pleasures, and make them slaves to their own passions. He, who would have bishops pure from every earthly stain, as the vicar of Christ and guardian of Christ's heavenly spouse, has formed a higher estimate of episcopal dignity than those who load them with worldly wealth, entangle them in mean cares, and expose them to the storms of war. "I am willing," he continues, "that priests should reign, but I think earthly dominion is unworthy of their heavenly calling. I am willing that Popes should triumph, but it must not be in such sanguinary triumphs as were celebrated by a crime-stained Marius or an impious Julius. I desire that they should be rich, but it must be with the Gospel pearl, the heavenly riches, in which they shall the more abound the more they bestow them upon others. I wish that they should be securely guarded, but with apostolic arms, with the shield of faith, the breast-plate of righteousness, and the sword of salvation, which is the word of God. I am willing that they should be most warlike, but against the true enemies of the Church, simony, pride, lust, ambition, anger, and impiety. Wilt thou know what are the true riches for a Pope? Listen to the first of

Popes: 'Silver and gold have I none, but such as I have give I thee; in the name of Jesus rise and walk.'" From this the transition is easy to attack the temporal power. "Why dost thou value the successor of St. Peter on that wealth which Peter himself boasts that he did not possess? Why dost thou wish to see the apostolic princes dressed in those ornaments which the Apostles trampled under foot? Why dost thou call that the patrimony of Peter which Peter himself boasted that he had not?" After showing that temporal sovereignty, with all that it involves, is most unsuitable to the priestly character, Erasmus remarks that it never prospers so well in the hands of a priest as in those of a layman. And for this there are two reasons. The first is, that the majority of men submit more readily to secular than to ecclesiastical rulers; and the second, that while the former, having children to succeed them, bestow all their care to improve their dominions, the latter, being without heirs, and generally called to the throne in their old age, try to make the most of their time by spoliation and plunder. Besides, when a secular ruler rises to the head of affairs, the battle for the throne, having been once fought, is at an end, and his favourites, having been exalted and rewarded, are no more a drain upon the resources of the people. But it is quite different in the other case, in which the battle must be perpetually renewed, and where there is a constant succession of new men, all demanding to be enriched at the nation's expense. Another consideration of some importance is that the people more readily submit to the authority to which they have been accustomed; and in the event of their king's death, they are content to see that authority revived in his natural heir;

whereas, in the case of ecclesiastical rule, every transference of power necessarily implies a total revolution. Besides, the secular prince is instructed from his earliest childhood in all the arts which will qualify him for the exercise of authority; the priest may have been designed by nature for the oar, and may be raised to the Papal throne by the mere caprice of Fortune.[36] Lastly, it is scarcely possible that one man should be equal to two such difficult administrations. It is extremely difficult to be a good prince. But it is even more difficult, though at the same time more honourable, to be a good priest. Why, then, unite the two? Christ will not gain in power by being made a partaker of earthly sovereignty, nor in dignity by being loaded with its trappings. After all this, it was probably not much to the purpose for Erasmus to declare as he does, in bringing his essay to a close, that he did not wish that the priests should be forcibly deprived of any wealth or dominion they at present possessed; he only desired that they should surrender them voluntarily, or at least rise superior to them, and, as Paul enjoins, possess them as though they possessed not. The note of war upon the temporal power of the Church was too clearly struck to permit any such modifying expressions to be accepted as an atonement.[37]

As though he thought that in attacking the Church he had been too sparing of the secular power, Erasmus wrote another treatise in which kings are the special objects of his wrath. "The beetle pursues the eagle," is the proverb which he makes the occasion of this declamation.

---

[36] There is a reference here to Julius II., who was said to have been the son of a sailor.—Froben's *Scholium*.

[37] *Er. Op.* ii. 770, C. *sqq.*

The *Scarabæus* is nothing but the old Æsopian fable of the beetle and the eagle, only told by Erasmus with all the wit of which he was so great a master, and with the most pointed reference to the tyrannical arts practised by contemporaneous sovereigns. He introduces the subject in the most humorous way, announcing in mock heroic style his purpose of recounting the causes which led to war between the great king of the birds and the humble insect, and calling upon the Muses, who disdained not to inspire Homer to sing the battle of the frogs and mice, to condescend to lend him their assistance. First, however, he proposes to give some account of the nature, character, and habits of the combatants upon either side ; and it is in describing the eagle that he finds the opportunity for launching forth into a fierce denunciation against tyranny. The eagle has been designated by common consent the king of the birds, no doubt because, being formed for rapine and plunder, he is the aptest type that could be found of the regal character. If this be disputed on the ground that a king's highest praise is clemency, and to do injury to no man, however great his power, it must be answered that such kings exist chiefly in the dreams of philosophers, and that history supplies hardly any examples of them. In our times, at least, there is scarcely one to be found to whom the Homeric epithet of "people-devouring king" will not apply. And they are now not even satisfied with the title of king, unless there be added to it a long list of splendid lies, calling them gods, though they hardly deserve the name of men ; invincible, though they have never left a battle-field without being beaten; august, though everything about them is mean an narrow; serene, though they are ever shaking the world with the storms of war; Catholic Christian, though Christ is never in their thoughts. But now examine the eagle more minutely. Look at his greedy and wicked eyes, his threatening beak, his savage jaws, his fierce brow. Consider, further, his dark and death-like hue; then his voice, harsh, terrible and awe-inspiring, and that threatening, dissatisfied shriek which puts all the animals to flight. No sooner is this cry heard than all the world trembles; the senate shrinks into itself, the nobility becomes obsequious, the judges fawn, the theologians are silent, the lawyers assent, the laws give way; nothing remains unshaken, not even religion, nor natural affection, nor justice, nor humanity. And though there are so many tuneful birds whose various and melodious notes might move the very stones, yet the shrill and unmusical cry of the eagle is enough to put them all to silence. There are many other particulars in which the comparison holds good. Thus, a pair of eagles require an ample space for their depredations, and will not suffer any other robber in their neighbourhood. And do not *our* eagles, too, love broad lands? Are they not ever striving to extend their empire, and going to war continually with the neighbouring eagles or kites about the bounds of their kingdom, which means simply the limits within which they have the right to plunder? Only there is this difference, that the bird never preys upon his neighbour, but carries his booty from a distance to his nest. Tyrants, on the contrary, do not spare even their closest connections, but the nearer the throne the greater is the danger. But the eagle would not be armed in a sufficiently *royal* manner were he provided only with hooked beak and hooked talons; he has eyes also which are sharper than any lynx's, and which can brave the sun's fiercest beams, and indeed it is said that by this test they prove the legitimacy of their offspring. Accordingly they see from a great distance the prey on which they intend to pounce. But the king of the birds has only two eyes, one beak, and a few claws. The human eagle has at his command myriads of watchful eyes, innumerable beaks and claws in the persons of his officials and subordinates, and is besides of an insatiable hunger from which nothing is secure, be it secreted where it may. Do but consider the various arts, the tricks, the wiles, the machinery with which wicked princes are provided to enable them to pillage their subjects, as gainful laws, fines, false titles, pretended wars, the accusations of the informer, and the claims of relatives, and you must confess that the eagle is hardly worthy the name of king. After describing the enemies of the eagle, and the various modes by which they are vanquished, Erasmus comes next to the beetle. His description is exceedingly witty, but from the nature of the subject—seeing that he is dealing with a creature of unclean habits—is not altogether nice, and may therefore be passed by. Only that the beetle is a warrior no one need doubt, who will consider his bright scales so closely knit together that no part of his body is unprotected, and his horrible hum not more musical than the braying of a military trumpet. The manner in which war fell out between these redoubtable chiefs is now unfolded somewhat as follows:—Once, upon Mount Ætna, an eagle was pursuing a hare, and was on the point of pouncing upon her, when the frightened creature took refuge in the hole of a beetle which happened to be near; for in such an extremity any refuge is welcome. Now, this beetle was a mighty man of war; for on that mountain, it is said, the nation of the beetles is of a peculiarly excellent stock, so that on account of their great size "the beetle of Mount Ætna" has become a kind of proverbial phrase. The hare, then, taking refuge in this beetle's cave, threw herself at his feet imploring protection against her merciless foe. Flattered to find that any one should suppose him capable of yielding such protection, and pleased that his poor abode, which men seldom passed without stopping their noses and muttering a curse, should be made a harbour of safety precisely as if it had been holy ground or the statue of a king, the beetle went out to meet the eagle and endeavoured to stay his wrath in such words as these: "The greater is thy power, the more incumbent is it upon thee to spare the innocent. Pollute not my house with the blood of an unoffending creature; so may thy nest be ever free from such calamity. It is the part of a generous and royal mind to grant indulgence even to the unworthy. Let reverence for the sanctities of home, which are founded upon natural justice, protected by law and allowed by custom, prevail with thee to spare the innocent; let thy suppliant's love, if not his authority, prevail. But if thou despisest our race and the beetle's arms, at least expect that the gods will remember right and wrong. If it nothing moves thee that the outrage of a violated home will rebound upon thine own head, at least revere supreme Jupiter, whom by this one deed thou wilt thrice offend. This is my guest,—thou wilt break the laws of hospitality; this is my suppliant,—thou wilt violate the laws which protect suppliants. Finally, I am thy friend, interceding with a friend;—thou wilt therefore break the laws of friendship. Thou who holdest the thunderbolts of Jupiter knowest how sure is his anger, and how terrible his vengeance." But the eagle would wait to hear no more. Contemptuously spurning the beetle from him, he pounced upon the hare and tore her to pieces before his eyes. Neither the prayers nor the threats of the beetle availed, though perhaps he would not have despised him so much had he remembered how the king of the beasts was once saved by a mouse, or how an ant, in return for some kindness, saved the life of a dove when actually in the fangs of a hawk. So true is it that there is no creature so weak or so abject, but it may find occasion to benefit or to injure those infinitely stronger than itself. No such reflections, however, occurred to the eagle, engrossed as he was with the immediate enjoyment of his prey. The outrage sank more deeply into the heart of the magnanimous beetle than any one could have believed, and urged by shame, pity, and anger, and foreseeing that if such a crime were allowed to pass unpunished, beetles would never more be able to hold up their heads in the world, he resolved upon a terrible revenge. He did not, however, dare to encounter the eagle in person, not merely because he was inferior in strength, but because Mars, being a stupid god, and as blind as Cupid or Plutus, generally favours the worse cause. But knowing the love which parents generally have for their children, and believing that the eagle was not altogether a stranger to such natural affections, he determined to attack him in his offspring. Besides, he considered that it would be for his own greater safety if he could root out the entire race, and he cherished also the fond hope that in the event of success he himself might ascend the throne. Armed with this resolution he proceeded to the eagle's nest. Whether he flew or crept is a disputed point; some authors maintain that he contrived to be carried thither by the eagle himself, having clung to him unobserved, as he sprang from the ground. Once arrived, he watched his opportunity, and then thrust out the eggs one by one until he had destroyed them all. The rest of the story may be told more briefly. The eagle built her nest—for here it will be advisable to change the sex of our bird—in a more remote and inaccessible spot, but the beetle still pursued her. Another and another was tried, but in vain. At length she appealed to Jupiter, who permitted her if she pleased to lay her eggs in his lap. The bird obeys and deposits there the last hope of her race. And now what follows is almost past belief. The unconquered beetle flies to the palace of supreme Jupiter, and drops into his lap a ball of dirt which he had prepared for the purpose. Jupiter, who cannot bear dirt, seeing that he dwells in the purest region of the world, and far from all earthly contagion, and offended by the smell, in endeavouring to free himself from the pollution, sweeps away the eagle's eggs, which, falling from so great a height, were destroyed long before they reached the ground. By this act the beetle, who had hitherto carried on his operations in secret, was at length discovered, and thus, besides satisfying his vengeance, gained the additional pleasure of having his power acknowledged; while the rage of the eagle was proportionately increased when he found he had been defeated by so contemptible an antagonist. Hence arose dire war between them, the eagle pursuing and destroying the race of beetles wherever they were to be found, the beetle stretching every nerve for the destruction of the eagle. Nor would there have been any end until both species were utterly destroyed, had not Jupiter called a council of the gods, by whom it was decreed that during the thirty days of the eagle's incubation the beetle must abstain from hostilities, and for that period not be seen in public at all. This decree was proclaimed by Mercury and engraven on brass by Vulcan. It endures to the present day, and will endure to the end of time. The deadly war continues between the beetles and the eagles, but during the time that the eagle is sitting the children of the beetle are nowhere to be seen.—Such is a brief account of this excellent satire, which would necessarily lose much in any translation, but of course loses far more in so curtailed an analysis. Erasmus does not conclude without turning upon the poor beetle whose cause he had so long defended, but in whom, as his humour altered, he appears to have seen a type of his own tormentors. The fable warns us that no one should despise any enemy, however mean. "For there is a class of men, of the lowest condition indeed, and yet whose malice is to be feared, not less black than beetles, nor less offensive, nor less vile, who, nevertheless, by the obstinate malice of their nature, as they are incapable of doing good to any one, often give a great deal of annoyance, even to persons in high positions. They terrify us by their black dress and blacker looks, stun us with their clatter, and drive us mad with their stench; they buzz round us, settle upon us, pierce us with their stings, so that it were far better to engage in feud with **really powerful** men than to provoke those beetles, **whom one** is ashamed even to have conquered, and **whom you can** neither shake off nor encounter in battle without contamination." [38]

[38] *Er. Op.* ii. 869, A. *sqq.*

CHAPTER XI.

LAURENTIUS VALLA'S ANNOTATIONS ON THE NEW TESTAMENT—ERASMUS EDITS THE NEW TESTAMENT—WRATH OF THE MONKS—CONTROVERSY WITH FABER — LATOMUS — LEE — STUNICA—CARANZA — EDITION OF ST. JEROME—SPURIOUS WORKS—JEROME'S LIFE BY ERASMUS—DEDICATION TO WARHAM.

FOR years past it had been a cherished object with Erasmus to print an edition of the New Testament in the original tongue, and with this view he had been collating manuscripts whenever he had opportunity. As early, indeed, as the year 1505 he had appeared as a critic of the Greek text, not, however, in his own name, but as editor of the Annotations of Laurentius Valla,[1] to whom must be ascribed the honour of having been the first to attempt a revision of the text by a comparison of authorities. Having found by chance a copy of this work on the shelves of an old library, and thinking its publication would be a great boon to the studious, he consulted Christopher Fisher, Apostolic Protonotary, on the subject. He was perfectly sensible that such a work would provoke hostile remark, but Fisher desired him not to permit himself to be deterred from a useful labour by the mutterings of a few monks, and himself undertook the responsibility of the publication by becoming its patron.[2]

[1] *Laurentii Vallæ, viri tam Græcæ quam Latinæ linguæ doctissimi, in Novum Testamentum annotationes apprime utiles.—Basileæ*, 1526.
[2] *Ep.* ciii.

The time was now come when Erasmus was not merely to tread in the footsteps of Valla, whose work, however creditable at the time, did not extend beyond a few brief notes, but to leave him far behind by his own infinitely more extended labours. On the 17th of April, 1515, Beatus Rhenanus wrote to him from Basle: "Froben wants to have your New Testament, for which he promises that he will give as much as anybody."[3] This was joyful news. It would save him the fatigue and inconvenience of a journey to Italy, and it promised to secure for Germany the credit of the first publication of the New Testament in the original Greek. If it was known that at this very time the New Testament had been actually in print for more than a year, though not yet published, as part of the Complutensian Polyglott, which was preparing under the auspices of Cardinal Ximenes, there was the more need for despatch. Soon after receiving this news Erasmus was on his way to Basle.

It will now be convenient to embrace in one review the several editions of the Greek Testament of Erasmus, and to follow rapidly the controversies to which it gave rise, returning by-and-by to notice his connection with other events which were transpiring at the same time, and which undoubtedly made those controversies more bitter than they might otherwise have been.

At the time that Erasmus thus undertook to edit the New Testament in Greek, as well as for centuries before, the Latin translation of the Greek and Hebrew Scriptures and the Apocrypha was the sacred book of the Church. This, with many slight variations in the manuscripts, was substantially Jerome's version, and it

[3] *Ep.* xxi. App.

was upon this that the text subsequently authorized by the Council of Trent was founded. To the monks and theologians of that day it was the Bible as much as if no originals had existed, or as if Hebrew Prophets and Galilean Apostles had written in Latin; it was the Bible as much as the authorized English version is the Bible to the average church-goer of our own times. From this preachers declaimed, and from this controversialists reasoned. Such was the passing ignorance of the monks that it is probable many of them had not the faintest conception of any original by which the Latin might be tested, and even respectable theologians did not think it necessary to look beyond it.[4] It is not surprising, then, that the earliest book printed was the Latin Bible. That was about the middle of the fifteenth century, and before the close of that century several other editions had appeared; among the rest a neat one in octavo, by John Froben, bearing the date 1491. Nor were the modern languages neglected. Before the end of the fifteenth century there were translations of the Bible in German, Italian, Dutch, French, and Bohemian —all, of course, from the Latin; and at the beginning of the sixteenth century there was even a Spanish one. But all this time, and even while splendid editions of the Greek classics were issuing from the press of Aldus in Venice, as well as from a few other centres of literary activity, no one had been sufficiently enterprising or sufficiently zealous in the cause of religious progress to edit or to print the Christian Scriptures in their original tongue. The truth is, that those who were interested in religion cared very little for learning; while most of those who were interested in learning cared not at all

[4] See above, p. 81.

for religion. The monks did not wish for the Greek Testament, because they could not have read it, and, if they could, would not have trusted it against the Latin; and the learned men, of Italy in particular, where the greatest number of books were printed, did not wish for it, because they were not Christians. Erasmus, however, differed both from the monks and from the learned men. He cared for literature and for religion too; and for him accordingly was reserved the honour of being the first to give to the world an edition of the New Testament in Greek.

It was a great triumph for Germany, when, on the 1st of March, 1516, there appeared at Basle, from the press of Froben, the whole New Testament in Greek, printed side by side with an improved Latin translation, and with annotations by Erasmus.[5] It was dedicated to Pope Leo X., and the title-page announced that the text was after several ancient and excellent manuscripts, in both Greek and Latin, with the citations in the Fathers compared. In reality, however, owing, it may be supposed, to the haste with which the work was hurried through the press, not more than five Greek

---

[5] *Novum Instrumentum omne, diligenter ab Erasmo Roterodamo recognitum et emendatum, non solum ad græcam veritatem, verum etiam ad multorum utriusque linguæ codicum eorumque veterum simul et emendatorum fidem, postremo ad probatissimorum autorum citationem, emendationem, et interpretationem, præcipue Origenis, Chrysostomi, Cyrilli, Vulgarii, Hieronymi, Cypriani, Ambrosii, Hilarii, Augustini, una cum annotationibus quæ lectorem doceant quid qua ratione mutatum sit. Quisquis igitur amas veram Theologiam, lege, cognosce, et deinde judica. Neque statim offendere, si quid mutatum offenderis, sed expende, num in melius mutatum sit.*

And on the colophon: *Basileæ, in ædibus Ioannis Frobenii Hammelburgensis, mense Februario. Anno M.D. XVI. Regnante Imp. Cæs. Maximiliano P. F. Augusto.*

manuscripts, which happened to be at hand, or which Erasmus had brought with him, were used as his principal authorities; and these were neither very old nor very valuable.[6] The oldest, which contained the whole of the New Testament, except the book of Revelation, has been assigned to the tenth century, and allowed by the great critics to be of considerable authority. But the other four, which included only parts of the canon, were of quite recent date and comparatively little worth. Amongst them all there was but one copy of the Apocalypse, and that wanted the last six verses, which, accordingly, Erasmus was obliged to supply from the Latin—a task in which he succeeded so ill, that in that short passage he deviated from the true text no less than thirty times. Otherwise, as was to be expected in one who was conscious that there were very few who could rival him in a knowledge of Greek, his prejudices seem to have been against the Latin; and though he sometimes followed it when it was wrong, he more frequently deviated from it when it was right. Nevertheless, the work was a marvel of genius and industry.

[6] This at least is the usual statement. Erasmus himself, however, seems to say that he used at least nine manuscripts, as he says in the *Apologia* prefixed to his first edition:—" Nos in prima recognitione quatuor Græcis adjuti sumus : in secunda quinque," &c. It is clear, moreover, from several references, that he had been collating manuscripts wherever he had opportunity. Thus in a letter to Colet, from Cambridge, which I have referred to the year 1512 (*Ep.* cxv.—see above, p. 220), he says, "Absolvi collationem Novi Testamenti;" and again, in his *Responsio ad Notationes novas Ed. Lei*, we have these words,—" Primum sic agit Leus quasi mihi non fuerit nisi unicum exemplar, cum tam multis sim usus, primum in Anglia, mox in Brabantia, postremo Basileæ non semel," &c. Probably, however, his notes were not much used for the first edition, which, indeed, according to his own well-known expression, was *præcipitatum verius quam editum.*

Many things conspired to make the sale more **rapid** than might have been anticipated. The fame of the editor, now known either personally or by reputation to all the learned men, as well as the princes and nobility, of Holland, France, Germany, Italy, and England, the increasing number of students of Greek, the desire to know something of the Scriptures in the original—all these things raised the interest to its height. The friends of Erasmus bought the book for his sake, or for its own; his enemies bought it to discover the heresies and errors which they had determined beforehand it must contain. Within three years there was a demand for another edition, and this also was speedily exhausted, although the two together consisted of 3,300 folio copies. The second edition appeared in the beginning of 1519, with a greatly improved text, and with the Vulgate so altered as to be substantially a new translation. This edition was fortified with a Papal Brief, a copy of the Nicene Creed,[7] and an engraving of the Trinity, which, one would think, ought to have been effectual, though they by no means proved so, in protecting the work against charges of heresy. Right above the Pope's letter, which spoke in the highest terms both of the scholarship and the orthodoxy of the work, there appeared a sufficiently quaint device, which curiously illustrates the zeal with which the great literary warfare was carried on—a woodcut representing the victorious Germans under Arminius overthrowing the legions of Quinctilius and Varus, with a tablet in one corner inscribed with the words—*Tandem, Vipera, sibilare*

---

[7] It is a singular circumstance that the creed is here given in its Eastern form, that is, it makes the Holy Spirit proceed from the Father only, instead of from the Father and the Son.

desiste. This was of course the printer's doing, but it was certainly no great compliment to Leo.

From the time that the New Testament was announced, great murmurings were heard among the cowled heads, and probably curses, "not loud, but deep," proceeded from many lips that ought to have been used only to bless. The sweets of labour, however, may have come first. The friends of Erasmus hastened to send him their congratulations on this great achievement, and those who were determined to cavil may have thought it necessary to examine his work before they began their attack. At first, some gentle passages of arms took place with men not really hostile, or who did not despair of retaining the great scholar in the service of the Church; and these were conducted with wonderful courtesy, for Erasmus enjoyed the respect of all competent persons, and he himself entertained the notion, not very common in any age, that the precepts of Christianity were applicable even to the conduct of theological controversy. But by-and-by more bitterness infused itself into the strife. Accusations of heresy and Arianism were heard. Erasmus, it was said, had charged the Apostles with lapses of memory and with writing bad Greek; he had altered texts which were important for proving the Deity of Christ, and he had omitted altogether the testimony of the Three Witnesses in the First Epistle of John. Some of these faults it may have required a little learning to detect; at all events, they could not have been discovered without reading the book. But one thing was clear to the commonest understanding: he had departed from the Vulgate translation, and had substituted comparatively pure Latin for its intolerable

barbarisms. Evidently the common Bible of Christendom was not good enough for him, and priests and preachers must now be called upon to give up the words they had so long been accustomed to regard as divine. This raised the wrath of the monks to its height. "Solecisms," they cried, "are not offensive to the Almighty." "Well, but," replied Erasmus, "neither are they pleasing to Him." "It is too bad," they said, "that the Holy Scriptures should be made subject to the rules of grammar." "The Vulgate," it was answered, "is not Holy Scripture, but a translation of Scripture; and those who do not like the revised translation are not obliged to use it." Some were ignorant and impudent enough to say that it was an intolerable crime for any one to presume to correct the Gospels. "Is every fool, then," retorted Erasmus, "to be permitted to corrupt the manuscripts of the Gospels, and is it an impiety to restore what has been corrupted?" To those who feared that the authority of the Bible might be called in question if any variations from the received standard should be acknowledged, he replied that for more than a thousand years there had been no complete agreement either in the Greek or the Latin copies.[8] Perhaps it was to conciliate the monks that the common title, *Novum Testamentum*, was restored in the second edition, instead of *Instrumentum*, which had been preferred in the first, on the ground that it was the more proper word to express the deed, or written document, containing the Testament. This title was also defended on

---

[8] See the *Apologia* prefixed to the first edition; also the preface to the fourth and fifth editions. The New Testament, with Erasmus's translation and annotations, and the prefatory matter, occupies the sixth volume of Le Clerc's *Erasmus*.

the authority of Jerome and Augustine; but it does not seem to have occurred to Erasmus that the word Testament, which in Latin, as in English, properly implied the decease of one of the contracting parties, was altogether a misnomer.

The New Testament of Erasmus was, in fact, as may easily be supposed, by no means a faultless production. The first edition abounded in typographical errors, and there were a few of a more serious nature, which, however, may be excused on the ground of the great haste with which the work was finished—the printing and much of the editing having occupied only five or six months.[9] The very title-page contained a sufficiently glaring and rather ridiculous blunder. This was the mention, in the list of the Fathers whose works had been used in the preparation of the text, of Vulgarius, a writer no one had ever heard of before. The mistake arose in the following way. Erasmus had a copy of Theophylact on Matthew, with this title: Τοῦ Θεοφιλεστάτου Ἀρχιεπισκόπου Βουλγαρίας κυρίου Θεοφυλάκτου ἐξήγησις εἰς τὸ κατὰ Ματθαῖον Εὐαγγέλιον; in his haste he took Θεοφυλάκτου for an epithet, while for Βουλγαρίας he must have read Βουλγαρίου, which he converted from the name of a country into the name of a man, and translated "Vulgarius;" and under this name Theophylact was quoted in his notes. To make matters worse, he attributed to Vulgarius a reading which is not to be found in Theophylact, and in one place grossly misconstrued him. Another blunder, scarcely pardonable even at a time when geography was a mystery

---

[9] On the 2nd of October, 1515, Erasmus wrote, "Novum Testamentum jam aggressi sunt."—*Er.* *Op.* iii. 1523, B., where the date 1513 is a palpable blunder.

which few had attempted to penetrate, was the statement that the port of Neapolis, where Paul arrived on his journey from Samothrace to Philippi, was a town in Caria. Nor was Erasmus at all thankful to those who pointed out, in no friendly spirit certainly, such slips as these. Gentle and temperate as he was, compared with the more energetic spirits who were preparing to shake the world, his pride as a scholar was obstinate in refusing, wherever that was possible, to acknowledge an error. He was willing enough indeed to confess, in general, that, being human, he had made mistakes, but all particular mistakes he thought himself bound notwithstanding to defend. He was obliged, however, to apologize for the haste which had led him to give a new Father to the Church, which he did by asserting (untruly, it would appear) that the name Theophylact was almost illegible in the manuscript he had made use of. But he stuck to it to the last that the Herodians mentioned in Matthew xxii. 16, were the soldiers of Herod the Great; sheltering himself here under the authority of Jerome, whose shield he thought ample enough to defend him against all the darts of malice. His final edition of the note on Acts xvi. 11 is a curious example of human or theological weakness. It may be translated thus: "*Neapolis.* Not the city of that name now held by the Spaniards in Italy, but another in Caria, in Asia. This seems to be the opinion of Jerome in his list of the names of places in the Acts, but I think wrongly. Some will have it that Neapolis is in Thrace or Macedonia, near Ptolemæus, and not far from Philippi. And this opinion is the more probable one, as there are several cities of that name."

Such real blunders as these were of course eagerly

seized upon by the calumniators of Erasmus in order to increase the outcry against him. But the principal objects of attack were the merits rather than the faults of his work. There is throughout his annotations a boldness and freedom of criticism which in our own day would be denounced as daringly rationalistic; and if his text is not always correct, which indeed was not to be expected, it was at least honestly constructed. A few examples will give the best idea of the character of his criticism. Of Luke's style, he remarks that it is purer than that of the rest of the Evangelists, owing to his acquaintance with Greek literature. The Epistle to the Hebrews, he says, breathes the spirit of Paul, but is not at all in his style. He doubts whether the Apocalypse be the work of John the Apostle. On this book, chap. i. 4, he remarks, "It must be honestly confessed the Greek has no meaning whatever." Rom. ix. 5, he points in the usual way to make it agree with the Latin, but intimates in his note that the sentence might be pointed in three different ways, adding that there is here no complete refutation of the Arians, as the final clause, "who is over all, God blessed for ever," may be referred to the Father and not to Christ. So on 1 Tim. iii. 16, "God manifest in the flesh," he suspects that the word "God" was introduced against the Arians, and that the true reading was not Θεὸς but Ὅ, referring to μυστήριον in the preceding sentence. There his common sense led him to a conclusion which the more thorough criticism of after times has fully confirmed.[10] That was quite true too, or very nearly true, which his enemies had brought as a charge against him,

---

[10] Here, however, he has the support of the Vulgate, which actually reads *quod*.

that he had accused the Evangelists of lapses of memory. For on Matt. ii. 7, "And thou, Bethlehem," &c., after quoting the remarks of Jerome that the prophecy as given here does not agree with the words of Micah, and that the Evangelist must either give the words as quoted by the Scribes and Pharisees, or else must himself have made a mistake through a lapse of memory, he shows that the first of these opinions will not hold, and then proceeds, but very cautiously and without admitting that he entertained it, to justify the second. That that was really his own view we may very fairly suspect, but it was scarcely fair to charge him with it, especially as he finally suggests another alternative, namely, that the Evangelist may have intentionally altered the sense of the original to adapt it to the novel circumstances. But the best proof of the courage and honesty of Erasmus might be thought to be the omission of 1 John v. 7. Yet, what else could he have done but omit it? The words were not in his manuscripts. The omission, accordingly, was no act of his, and the proper way to state the case would be to say that he forbore to insert it. Even for that, however, much credit is due to him, especially as he persevered in that honest course in his second edition, after the clamour against him had begun. How he came to yield at last, and insert this notable forgery in his third and subsequent editions, we shall see presently.

But the notes on the New Testament were by no means confined to questions of textual criticism. There was other matter in them which was sure to give offence, and which might seem to have been introduced on purpose to offend. They were made the vehicle, perhaps to an unwarrantable extent, for conveying the opinions of the writer upon the manners of the time, and especially for uttering sarcastic allusions to the various abuses which prevailed in the Church. In fact the *Encomium Moriæ* was here repeated, only in a somewhat more serious form. And on many points — for example, on the dress of the priests and the ceremonies observed in public worship, on fasts and feasts, on the monastic life, on vows, penance, the worship of relics, on marriage and divorce, — opinions were expressed which, if they were not at variance with the authorized doctrines of the Church, were at all events in direct conflict with popular ideas, and with the teachings and practice of the most zealous upholders of the ecclesiastical system. It is an evidence of the boldness of Erasmus, and shows how little he was of a Papist in the strict sense of the word, that he altogether denies the primacy of Peter, and in his note on the famous text, Matt. xvi. 18, "Upon this rock I will build my church," expresses his surprise that any should have so perverted the meaning as to refer the words exclusively to the Roman Pontiff, "to whom," he adds, in his second edition, "they undoubtedly apply first of all, seeing that he is the head of the Christian Church; but they apply not to him only, but to all Christians," &c. On Matt. xvii. 5, "Hear ye Him," he remarks, "Christ is the only teacher who has been appointed by God himself. Such authority has been committed to no theologian, to no Bishop, to no Pope or Prince. Not that we ought not to obey them, but we ought to obey Christ first of all."[11] Here are some remarks upon the superstitious respect for pretended relics, introduced in a note on Matt. xxiii. 5, "That they may be seen of men."

[11] These words are not in first edition.

"Jerome, on this passage, condemns the superstition of certain women who, like the Pharisees with their phylacteries, used to carry about little copies of the Gospel, and pieces of the wood of the true cross, and other things of the same kind, which, he says, have a zeal of God but not according to knowledge. If that most holy man entertained such sentiments with regard to weak women who might fairly have claimed some little indulgence, what would he say were he to return to the world now, and see Mary's milk exhibited in our churches for money, and almost as much honour paid to it as to the consecrated body of Christ; miraculous oil, and fragments of the true cross in such quantities, that if they could be brought together it would take a merchant vessel to hold them all; if he were to see Francis's hood exhibited at one altar, and the Virgin Mary's shift at another, in one church Anna's comb, in another Joseph's boot, in another Thomas of Canterbury's slipper, in another," [12]—but here the translator must break off, for the next relic mentioned is, in fact, unmentionable. The statement in Acts ix. 43, that Peter lodged "with one Simon a tanner," calls forth the exclamation, "Oh! how great a guest—the very chief of the Apostles—to lodge with so humble an entertainer! In our days, three royal palaces scarce suffice to receive Peter's vicar."[13] In reference to the language of Scripture, we are told on Acts x. 38, that "the Apostles learned Greek, not from the orations of Demosthenes, but from common conversation."[14] Again, St. Paul's statement that he preached the Gospel without charge (1 Cor. ix. 18) gives occasion to a sneer at

---

[12] Not in the first edition.   [13] In the first edition.
[14] In the first edition.

the greediness of the clergy. "That," says Erasmus, "was a boast truly worthy of an Apostle, but one which no one in our days is ambitious of making. Nothing is to be had now gratuitously. You cannot even get buried free of cost." But there were yet other and more important questions on which it is clear that Erasmus held opinions very different from those which prevailed among the majority of the clergy and the monks, and by his views on which he might well have seemed to have done something to occasion the now rapidly approaching schism in the Catholic Church. Such was his avowed wish, directly in opposition to the Council of Toulouse, which had forbidden the Bible to the laity, that the Scriptures might be translated into all tongues, so that even Turks and Saracens, to say nothing of Scotch and Irishmen, might read them, and Christians take from them the subjects of their daily conversation.[15] Such, still more, were the doubts which he expressed as to whether the sacrament of matrimony was known to the early Church—to the Church of St. Jerome and St. Augustine—amounting, of course, to a doubt, or at least suggesting one, whether marriage was a sacrament at all; the similar doubts which he expressed regarding auricular confession; and when he further proceeded to attack the celibacy of the clergy, and argued how much better it would be, considering the gross immorality which it occasioned, if marriage were not altogether forbidden, it is not wonderful if all whose interests or feelings attached them to the old system felt bound to oppose and denounce him.

Such a book, appearing at such a time, could not fail to be bitterly attacked. The strife began even

[15] *Paraclesis ad pium lectorem*, prefixed to the *Novum Testamentum*.

before its publication, when Martin Dorpius, in the letter which has been already noticed in connection with the *Moria*,[16] remonstrated with Erasmus on his design, and maintained that there was no fault to be found with the Vulgate; but it was not till after the appearance of the second edition, when men's minds were exasperated by the bold defiance which Luther had hurled at Rome, that the more formidable and systematic attacks upon it commenced. Meantime, however, Erasmus had a controversy of a comparatively friendly kind, which indeed he had himself provoked, with the French theologian, James Lefevre of Etaples, or Faber Stapulensis, as he was called in Latin. Faber was a man of undoubted learning, and had already made one important contribution to theological study.[17] He and Erasmus had known one another intimately at Paris, where they had many long conversations on subjects of common interest, but strangely enough neither of them had happened to mention that he was meditating a work upon the New Testament.[18] It was therefore with surprise that Erasmus learned, while he was making arrangements for his own work at Basle, that Faber had partly anticipated him—it was in reality to a very small extent—by the publication of a commentary on the epistles of Paul with a new translation of his own printed side by side with the Vulgate version.[19] In this

---

[16] See above, p. 203.

[17] His *Quincuplex Psalterium*, printed at Paris by Henry Stephens, in 1509.

[18] "Sæpe mecum admiratus sum, quinam evenerit, ut in tam crebris, tam prolixis, tamque familiaribus colloquiis, quibus Lutetiæ fueramus conflictati, ne casu quidem inciderit ulla mentio, quid vel meum, vel tuum studium parturiret ac moliretur."—*Apologia ad Jac. Fab. Stap. Er. Op.* ix. 19, C.

[19] *Jacobi Fabri Stapulensis in omnes D. Pauli epistolas commentariorum libri XIIII.*

work Faber undoubtedly laid himself open to attack. His Latin was far from Ciceronian. His Greek was often defective.[20] His want of judgment was shown in the fact that he assumed the genuineness of Paul's epistles to Seneca and printed them as a kind of supplement to his commentary on Philemon. In truth Faber was guilty of some egregious blunders, such as would now be simply impossible, but were at that time more pardonable; and two or three of these Erasmus took the opportunity of pointing out in his own notes, not however without apologizing for his dissent and paying many compliments to the learning of his friend. But theologians are proverbially a combative race, and to express a difference of opinion, still more to convict of an error, is sometimes to bring upon oneself a charge of blasphemy. So it proved in the present instance. In a second edition of his commentaries which speedily appeared, Faber, without altogether throwing off the garb of friendship, attacked Erasmus with considerable warmth, and even charged him with impiety. The question turned on the proper meaning of Heb. ii. 7, which Faber, assuming that the epistle was originally written in Hebrew, and afterwards translated (not always correctly) into Greek, proposed to render, "Thou hast made him a little lower than God," according to Jerome's interpretation of Psalm viii., while Erasmus thought that this rendering, besides being inadmissible for either psalm or epistle, solved no difficulty in the latter. Christ, he argued, in his Divine nature, was never made

---

[20] As an example of his Latin it may be mentioned that he headed his translation — *Intelligentia ex Græco*;—of his Greek, or rather of both, that he rendered παραβουλευσάμενος—*ex deliberatione positurus est animam.*

lower than the angels, nor could he be said to have been made lower than God. In his human nature, on the other hand, he was made not *a little*, but a great deal lower than the angels, and lower even than the most abject of the human race. From the dilemma thus raised he proposed to escape by rendering, " Thou hast made him " (not "a little" but) "for a little time, lower than the angels."[21] Faber, with perfect propriety, as regards the Hebrew, disputed the translation, but not satisfied with this, he hastened to charge the sentiment, certainly somewhat harsh in its expression, but quite innocent in intention—that Christ had been made lower than the most abject of the human race, as impious and most unworthy both of God and Christ. Besides Erasmus, in the course of his remarks, took occasion to state that doubts had been entertained as to the authorship of the Epistle to the Hebrews, that it was received late by the Roman Church, and that Jerome had said that there were some who did not receive it on the ground that its descriptions of Jewish customs were not always strictly correct, and for these surely very cautious and perfectly true allegations, he was accused by his friend of folly, vanity, and ignorance. It was a year and a half before he was aware that these formidable charges were in circulation against him. He was getting into his carriage to start for Louvain when a friend mentioned to him that a second edition of Faber's commentaries had appeared, and

---

[21] As regards the meaning of Heb. ii. 7, Erasmus may have been quite right in rendering $\beta\rho\alpha\chi\acute{u}$ $\tau\iota$ "for a little time," and for this meaning he relies on Acts v. 34, where he maintains that it is the only possible one. Faber was probably a better Hebraist, but both were mistaken in supposing that the Psalmist and the author of the Epistle must necessarily have meant the same thing.

referred him to the passage in which he was attacked.[22] He immediately procured the book from his bookseller, read it as he travelled, and on his arrival, in the course of the following fourteen days, wrote his Defence,[23] in which, while treating his opponent with the greatest courtesy, he carefully reviews the controversy between them, and reads Faber an admirable lecture on Christian charity and forbearance.[24]

Another attack was called forth by a short essay on the right method of the study of Scripture, which

---

[22] "Cum essedum (*sic*) conscenderem, eruditissime Faber, Lovanium commigraturus, id enim malui quam principem in Hispanias comitari, commodum submonuit me quidam amiculus Commentarios in Paulum iterum abs te editos," &c.—*Er. Op.* ix. 17, A.

[23] "Quatuordecem dumtaxat diecularum spatio."— *Io. Frobenius Lectori*. As a curious example of the way in which printers in the sixteenth century thought themselves entitled to recommend authors and their works to the public, and also as a proof how they themselves stood in the ranks of learning, this whole preface of Froben's may be quoted: "Jacobus Faber Stapulensis in secunda suarum in Paulum Annotationum æditione, ERASMUM nostrum erroris notavit, ipse fœdissime hallucinatus. At hic (o divinam ingenii promptitudinem) etiamdum ab officina calente opera, quatuordecem dumtaxat diecularum spatio, hanc Apologiam effudit verius quam scripsit. Ex ea tametsi brevi, sed mire docta, velut leonem (ut aiunt) ab unguiculis, æstimare licet, quam sit ERASMUS theologicarum etiam argutiarum non ignarus, quibus nunc Theologi passim in scholis utuntur. Adjecit quidam apud nos, pauculas in marginibus adnotatiunculas, ut lectori consuleret. Eme, lege, et ERASMUM θεολογικώτατον καὶ διαλεκτικώτατον, hoc est, summum Theologum et acerrimum disputatorem deprehendis. Argumentum Apologiæ sequens pagella copiosius explicabit. Bene Vale."

I certainly cannot reconcile Froben's statement that Erasmus wrote his Reply while Faber's work was warm from the press, with the following words of Erasmus himself:—"Quin de hac quoque proxima editione mirum ubique silentium, quæ jam sesquiannum per omnes regiones volitat, me uno omnium inscio."—*Apol. ad Fab.*

[24] *Apologia Des. Erasmi Roterodami ad Insignem Philosophum, Jacobum Fabrum Stapulensem.* Lovanii, 1517. *Er. Op.* ix. 17.

Erasmus had prefixed to his Greek Testament, and in which he maintained that the first thing required was a knowledge of the three tongues, Greek, Latin, and Hebrew.[25] In the course of his remarks, he incidentally mentions that he himself, though within a year of fifty, returned to the study of Hebrew whenever he had an opportunity. He also inculcated the advantage of having as much general knowledge as possible, especially of the objects named in Scripture, so that the student may not, like some ignorant commentators, make a quadruped of a tree, or a fish of a precious stone. Nor were poetry and good letters to be despised. Christ clothed all his teachings in parables, and that was poetry. Paul quotes from the poets, but there is nothing in his writing to remind one of Aristotle and Averroes. It is difficult for those who are imbued with the scholastic philosophy to appreciate the simplicity of the Scriptures, but if it be maintained that without it one cannot be a theologian, Erasmus will console himself with the example of so many famous men, Chrysostom, Jerome, Ambrose, Augustine, Clement, nay, of Peter and Paul, who were utterly ignorant of it, and even condemned it. It was probably this attack on the divinity of the schools which gave the most offence, and James Latomus, a doctor and professor of divinity at Louvain, took up the cause of scholasticism, and, at the same time, jealous for the authority of the Vulgate, attacked the principle that a knowledge of Greek and Hebrew was necessary for the study of Scripture. In the dialogues which he wrote

---

[25] *Erasmi Roterodami Methodus.* This treatise, which was afterwards considerably expanded and printed as a separate work, under the title of *Ratio Veræ Theologiæ* (*Er. Op.* v. 75, *sqq.*), was not repeated in the later editions of the New Testament.

on this subject he did not name Erasmus, but it was evident that he had him in view, and the latter, fearing lest he might be misconstrued, wrote a defence of himself in two books, in which he declared that he had never intended to condemn the scholastic divinity : he merely preferred to it the study of the Scriptures, as he believed the Church had always done.[26] He was himself residing at Louvain at the time, but the controversy was carried on in an amicable spirit, and no breach of friendship took place between the disputants.

But it was our own country, where he had found his best friends, which furnished also his bitterest enemies. And among those who took up arms against his New Testament none was more bitter or more unrelenting in his persecutions than Edward Lee, afterwards chaplain and almoner to Henry VIII., and eventually Archbishop of York. At this time he was a comparatively young and still unknown man, and, as Erasmus believed, actuated in his hostility to himself by nothing but ambition and the love of notoriety. Such a vain creature was he, according to Pirckheimer, that you would have thought everything he trod upon must needs turn into a rose, and in his own estimation no one could compare with him for beauty, learning, and sanctity.[27] His attack, which began about a year after the first appearance of the New Testament, was of the most vexatious kind, being carried on by private whispers rather than on the open field of fair controversy, while neither his age nor his learning entitled him to enter into conflict with a scholar of such established reputation. Erasmus speaks of him in his letters

---

[26] *Apologia in dialogum Jac. Latomi.—Er. Op.* ix. 79.
[27] *Er. Op.* iii. 550, A.

with the utmost contempt, or rather with an anger which shows that he could not afford to despise him, declaring that "a creature more arrogant, ignorant, and venomous the world had never seen;" and when his book, which was kept back, as we are assured, by mere cowardice for more than two years, at length came out, "mendacious," "foolish," "ignorant," are among the epithets he applies to it. Lee, he tells us, had learned all the Greek and Hebrew he knew in a few months on purpose to write his criticisms. He had adopted the most underhand means to excite an interest in his book, bribing the monks with entertainments, and with presents of wine and fruit; and with the same view he had written not less than six hundred letters, for which he had been obliged to employ several amanuenses.[28] Nor could he be prevailed upon, though often entreated, to furnish his antagonist with a copy of his criticisms. When the second edition of the New Testament was going through the press, and a considerable part had already been printed off, Erasmus met Lee, showed him the sheets, and offered, if he would point out anything in them contrary to the orthodox faith or to good morals, to reprint them, notwithstanding the great expense it would cost him, and to make honourable mention of Lee as the author of the amendments.[29] Such an offer it was, no doubt, easy to make, if Erasmus had resolved beforehand on no account to acknowledge an error, and it is scarcely to be wondered at if Lee refused to comply. Lee, however, maintains that he did send the manuscript of his notes to Erasmus; but that, finding he took no notice of it, he was compelled to print it; and he adds that Erasmus bribed or threatened the printer in

[28] *Er. Op.* iii. 575, F. [29] *Ib.* 655, B.

Antwerp to whom he had applied to prevent him from undertaking the work.[30] Nor does Erasmus altogether deny the first part of this statement. His account of the matter is that Lee, having called upon him at Louvain, insinuated himself into his confidence, and was taken into his sleeping apartment, where he was shown the preparations for the second edition of the New Testament, already far advanced towards completion, and that he then began to study the first edition, having by this time acquired sufficient Greek for that purpose, and some time after confessed that he had made some notes upon it. Erasmus begged him to let him see them; but he would never send more than half a page at once, and always insisted on its being returned before he would let him have another, as though he were afraid it should be copied; and Erasmus, finding that most of his criticisms were worthless, and that he had already anticipated the few that were sound, took no further notice, except to write a word of admonition on the margin of one of his papers. At this Lee seemed to take great offence. He looked daggers at Erasmus, and on the departure of the latter for Basle, he spread a report everywhere that he had detected no less than 300 errors in the Greek Testament. When, at length, his notes were published, they were found to be full of the most scurrilous abuse.[31] "At last," wrote Erasmus to Capito, "the British viper has broken loose! Edward Lee, the everlasting disgrace of that famous island, has come forth into the light. . . . I would describe the monster to you, but I am afraid

---

[30] See *Apologia Edouardi Leei ad diluendas quorundam calumnias.*
[31] *Annotationes Edouardi Leei in Annotationes novi testamenti Desiderii Erasmi. Prostant Parrhisiis.*

posterity would not believe that such a beast ever wore the form of humanity."[32] Erasmus was in some doubt whether he should notice this attack, and his friends were also divided on the subject. Rejecting, however, what reports had been spread to his disadvantage, and fearing lest his silence might be construed into a confession of defeat, he determined to reply, but briefly. His answer cost him forty days' labour.[33]

Lee's criticisms were principally textual, and had for their object the defence of the Vulgate; but he also took occasion to charge Erasmus with favouring Arianism and Pelagianism, with undermining the authority of Holy Scripture, and other offences against the Catholic faith. I shall notice at some length only one of these criticisms, which happens to have a special interest—that on 1 John v. 7. Lee based his defence of the authenticity of this celebrated passage on the fact that Laurentius Valla, in his annotations on the New Testament, had not noticed its omission from any of his manuscripts; on Jerome's Preface to the canonical Epistles, in which he said it was stated that the text had been corrupted by the heretics; and on an insinuation which he chose to make to the effect that Erasmus had consulted only one manuscript. Besides—and this no doubt made a deeper impression on those who were likely to take his side of the question than any learned arguments—the consequence of omitting words so important to the orthodox faith would be the revival of

---

[32] *Erasmus Capitoni* in the appendix to Hess, vol. ii. p. 545, *sqq.*

[33] *Des. Erasmi Roterodami Liber quo respondet annotationibus Eduardi Lei, quibus ille locos aliquot taxare conatus est in quatuor evangeliis.*—*Er. Op.* ix. 123. *Liber alter quo respondet reliquis annotationibus Eduardi Lei.*—*Ib.* 199.

the Arian heresy and a schism in the Church. Lee's arguments, such as they were, were not very difficult to dispose of. Laurentius Valla was but human; he may have been guilty of an oversight, or he may have found the words in question in his manuscripts. It was not true that Jerome had said this passage had been corrupted by the heretics; and even if he had said so, Jerome was not infallible; on the contrary, he was a man of a warm and even violent temper, and often made assertions much more positively than facts seemed to warrant. Jerome's language, however, really implied that he had changed the public reading of the Church, and that accordingly the Latin must have previously agreed with the Greek.[34] Nor was it the case that the disputed words had been omitted by none but heretics; for Cyril, an orthodox Father, in collecting all the texts he could find against the Arians, quotes the testimony of the Spirit, the water and the blood, but not that of the Three in heaven, which he certainly would not have omitted had he found it in his copies. As to the charge that Erasmus had been guilty of carelessness and dishonesty in not consulting more than one manuscript, it was simply absurd. He had, in fact, consulted many in England, in Brabant, and at Basle, and at different times had had in his hands a greater number than Valla. Had he found the words in a single copy, he would, he says, have inserted them; but that not having been the case, he followed the only course that was open to him—pointed out what was wanting in his Greek manuscript. Probably that was an aggravation of his offence; could he not have printed the Greek as it stood

---

[34] Erasmus does not appear to have questioned the authenticity of the Preface to the canonical Epistles.

without calling special attention to it, and might he not at least have retained the usual Latin reading? Having disposed of the critical part of the question, Erasmus proceeds to relieve the mind of his opponent of his apprehensions of heresy. He reminds him that others besides himself can read Greek, and that soon every one pretending to scholarship will be able to do so. To what purpose, then, would he have concealed the real reading of the Greek manuscripts? *There is* the reading, for the Arians, as well as everybody else, to see for themselves, and he is not responsible for the fact. And how can Lee suppose that the mouth of the Arians, if there *were* any Arians, would be stopped at once by the testimony of the Three Witnesses? Are there not other passages in which the word "one" means not one in substance, but one in consent? Must it not, indeed, have this meaning in the case of the three that bear witness on earth; and might it not be made to bear this sense also in the words under dispute? But, in fact, there *are* no Arians. No heresy more completely extinguished! And as to the disturbances which Lee anticipates, why, the New Testament has now been in the hands of the public for more than three years, and none of these dreadful results have followed. By-and-by, Erasmus becomes pleasantly severe. The unlucky Lee had broken into a strain of solemn admonition, foretelling the evils that would come upon the world from this corruption of Scripture, and calling upon the Shepherd of the Church to awake. "There is still hope," he exclaims, "with the help of God, since the smoke has not yet burst into a flame. The Guardian of Israel will not slumber nor sleep, if the watchman in Israel slumbers not nor sleeps." Rather insulting to the Pope, replies Erasmus, to suppose he does nothing but snore and yawn. "But let Lee be comforted. The watchman in Israel will not always slumber and sleep, but will at last put to silence such wild and seditious calumnies, and shut the mouth of all who, by their foolish clamour, would excite among the people the trouble which seems to be the element in which they live themselves. For should any disturbance arise in the Church of God, it will be entirely their doing; we have no desire either to promote sedition or to advocate unsound doctrine. If, however, we fall into any unintentional errors, certainly it was not for Lee to find fault with our mistakes, seeing how many disgraceful blunders he is guilty of himself in that little pamphlet of his; much less to abuse and calumniate us. However, I am ready to acknowledge the justice of all the reproaches he has heaped upon me, if, in all my many works, some of which are of great length and fill more than one volume, while some were produced in great haste, I am guilty of so many flagrant blunders, or so often inconsistent, if I misquote or show that I do not understand my own language, as often as he has done in that little pamphlet which he drew up two years ago, with the aid of his friends, and when he was able to give to it the whole of his attention."

It might seem that there could be no doubt with whom the victory would remain in a contest of this kind between learning and capacity upon the one side, and ignorance and dulness on the other; but, unfortunately, treachery supplied the place of knowledge, and Lee carried away the most substantial fruits of a conflict in which he was otherwise completely defeated. Erasmus in his reply had twice professed his willingness to insert the testimony of the Three Witnesses if a single manuscript could be produced containing it. Lee must in due time have satisfied himself that none such could be found at Oxford or Cambridge, nor probably anywhere else. But what then? Were there no amanuenses living? Was it impossible to have a manuscript written on purpose which should contain the disputed words, and satisfy the scruples of this troublesome Grecian? That the *Codex Montfortianus* was written under the direction of Lee, with the express object of deceiving his opponent and exacting from him the fulfilment of his promise, there is indeed no positive proof; but its opportune appearance at this particular juncture lends a countenance to the supposition, and there was nothing in the character of Lee to make it probable that he would have hesitated to commit a pious fraud which he thought so important to the orthodox faith. One only wonders that he should have gone such a long way round to accomplish his purpose, instead of simply affirming the existence of the manuscript; but no doubt he had a tender conscience, and found it more agreeable to equivocate than to lie; and besides, how did he know but Erasmus would run over to England to have a sight of this newly-discovered treasure? Erasmus, however, was very easily satisfied. It does not appear that he ever even saw the *Codex Britannicus*, as he calls it. He desired peace, and shrunk from the clamour that was raised against him on all sides. Having been informed, therefore, that a manuscript had been found containing the testimony of the Heavenly Witnesses, although he suspected, and with good reason, that it had been corrected after the Latin, he inserted the spurious words in his third edition, which appeared in 1522. There the text corresponds exactly with the reading of the *Codex Montfortianus*, which is now deposited in the Library of Trinity College, Dublin, proving its identity with the *Codex Britannicus* of Erasmus.[15] In the subsequent editions it was altered into better Greek.

Another antagonist, of a very similar temper to Edward Lee, but of greater pretensions to learning, whom the attacks of Erasmus on all the favourite prejudices of the time summoned into the field, was the Spanish theologian, James Lopez Stunica. An adept in the three languages, and having spent many years in the study of the original text of the Old and New Testaments and in the comparison of manuscripts, he

---

[15] The *exact* agreement, it must be understood, applies only to the interpolated clause; but it is remarkable that for the *eighth* verse Erasmus had a better text in his second than in his third edition, where he altered it after the *Codex Britannicus*, the only differences being the insertion of καί before ὕδωρ, and the retention of the clause, καὶ οἱ τρεῖς εἰς τὸ ἕν εἰσιν, which the *Codex Britannicus omitted*, and which *the Dublin MS. also omits*. That this clause was omitted by the *Codex Britannicus*, we have the express testimony of Erasmus himself twice repeated,—in the *Apologia ad Stunicam*, and in the note on 1 John, v. 7, in the later editions of his Testament—in both of which places, after giving the whole seventh and eighth verses, he remarks that it may be merely accidental that the καὶ οἱ τρεῖς εἰς τὸ ἕν εἰσιν is not repeated. It is important to notice this, because a little lower down, in the very same note, Erasmus contradicts himself (possibly owing to a mere printer's blunder) by stating that the *British MS. adds* to the witness upon earth, καὶ οἱ τρεῖς εἰς τὸ ἕν εἰσιν. The text of the *Codex Britannicus* in verses 7 and 8, as quoted by Erasmus, certainly deviates from that of the *Dublin MS.* in the omission of the ἅγιον after Πνεῦμα, and the οἱ before the second μαρτυροῦντες; but that these are mere slips in copying is clear from their re-appearance in the text of the third edition, which text, be it remembered, has been in other respects altered for the worse—viz. by the omission of the article three times—in order to make it agree with the newly discovered authority.

thought himself well qualified to sit in judgment on the work of his Dutch contemporary.[36] Accordingly he published a series of criticisms,[37] in the preface to which he treats Erasmus with high disdain, as a man of letters who had gained some reputation—more than he deserved—by his literary and grammatical labours;—he mentions particularly his translations from Lucian and Euripides, and his "Adages,"—and who had been tempted on to the audacious design of publishing a new translation of the Scriptures, to which he added a volume of annotations in the style of Laurentius Valla. Nor will he allow him any higher motive than the love of notoriety and the pleasure of finding fault with the old translation and its author. How elegant he could sometimes be in his language may be inferred from a single passage, in which he speaks of Erasmus as so "steeped in the beer and butter of his country" as to be incapable of clear thought.[38] He charges him repeatedly with gross ignorance of the Holy Scriptures, with ignorance of Greek, with ignorance of the writings of the Fathers. He defends some of the worst solecisms of the Vulgate; and, above all, he is indignant because Erasmus had expressed a doubt whether the name of God was applied to Christ in the writings of the Apostles and Evangelists in more than two or three places, and asserts that to those who seek diligently it must be apparent that the name is so applied in

---

[36] "Quippe qui non paucos annos in sanctis scripturis veteris ac novi testamenti hebraice, græce et latine perlegendis consumpsimus," &c.—Preface to Annotations.

[37] *Annotationes Jacobi Lopidis Stunicæ contra Erasmum Rotero-* *damum in defensionem Tralationis Novi Testamenti.* It was printed at the Complutensian University in the year 1520.

[38] "Ut Erasmus butiro et cervisia patria obrutus somniaverit."—Note on Gal. iii.

many passages; after which he proceeds to enumerate the texts usually advanced in proof of the supreme deity of Christ. Stunica, however, while guilty of some gross blunders himself, was undoubtedly successful in detecting several serious errors in the notes of his antagonist, and had he entered into the controversy in a better spirit, and shown himself less captious and more concerned for the interests of truth, he might have been considered no unworthy opponent.

More than three years had elapsed between the appearance of the first edition of the Greek Testament and the attack of the Spanish theologian—a fact for which Stunica offers no other explanation than the statement that the new translation was some time in reaching him. Erasmus, however, gives a very different account of the matter. According to him, Cardinal Ximenes was highly pleased with his edition of the New Testament, and when Stunica expressed his surprise to him that he should pay any attention to a work teeming with such monstrous errors, he nobly replied in the language of Scripture—"Would that all were such prophets! Go thou and do better if thou canst, but disparage not another man's labour."[39] It was not, accordingly, till after the Cardinal's death that Stunica ventured to publish his attack. Erasmus, who pathetically complains that at his time of life he should be compelled to enter into a controversy by which his peace of mind will be destroyed, as well as the pleasure of his studies, replied in a careful, and, on the whole, pretty temperate apology.[40] Point by point he foils the

---

[39] *Er. Op.* ix. 284, D.

[40] *Des. Erasmi Roterodami Apologia respondens ad ea quæ in Novo Testamento taxaverat Jacobus Lopes Stunica.—Er. Op.* ix. 283, *sqq.* This work is without a date.

attack of his enemy, exposing his mistakes, defending his own positions, showing that in one or two instances the corrections of Stunica have been anticipated in the second edition of his Greek Testament, but with these exceptions never of course admitting that he has been wrong. He indignantly repels the charge of having treated the old translator with contempt; on the contrary, he had often praised him, and sometimes even defended him against Faber and Valla. Still more audacious was it to assert that he had condemned the translation of the Church, seeing that he had protested so often that he was merely translating the Greek copies, but had never said that he approved their readings. Nor will he admit that the translation now in use is St. Jerome's, as Stunica assumes. The contrary, he thinks, he has abundantly proved in his notes.

But his adversary's hints at heresy fairly roused his anger. If he had expressed a doubt whether the epithet, "servant," could be applied to Christ, he was in danger of falling into the error of Apollinaris, who denied the human nature. If he had added that, though Christ was subject to his Father, it was as a son, not as a servant, he must beware of seeming to favour the heresy of Arius, who denied the equality of the Son with the Father. "*I*," he exclaims, "deny Christ's human nature, who adore it in so many of my books! *I* make Christ in His divine nature inferior to the Father, who so often express my detestation of the Arians! I have defended myself from the charge of heresy; let Stunica defend himself from the suspicion of perverse and wicked calumny. Let him call me a Dutchman, rude, coarse, stupid, ignorant, a block, a dolt, a fool, and I shall not be greatly moved; but who can bear to have the suspicion of heresy fastened upon him by a brazen-faced buffoon—and such heresy, too, as affects not the honour of the Pope, nor the dogmas of the schools, but Christ himself?"[41]

It is a difficult matter fighting when you cannot see your adversary's weapons; but Erasmus was under this disadvantage with regard to the famous Rhodian manuscript, to which Stunica frequently appealed in condemnation of his text. "This Greek manuscript of the apostolic epistles," he says, "is of very great antiquity, and was brought from the island of Rhodes to Spain, where it was presented to Cardinal Ximenes, and by him deposited in the public library of this Complutensian Academy." Erasmus, however, would not permit himself to be crushed by its authority. He opposed to its readings the numerous ancient copies which he had consulted in England, in Holland, and at Basle, and besides even ventured to suspect that, like some other Greek manuscripts he had met with, it was corrected after the Latin, in which case it would of course be valueless as an instrument of criticism. "I would have more confidence," he caustically remarks, "in a copy which did not always agree with the Latin."[42]

---

[41] *Er. Op.* ix. 317, C, D.

[42] The Rhodian manuscript has never been seen since the sixteenth century. Stunica first introduces it in reference to 2 Cor. ii. 3, where Erasmus had remarked "*Super tristitiam* superest;" and gives the reading of the Rhodian manuscript as follows:—ἵνα μὴ ἐλθὼν ἐπὶ λύπης σχῶ, ἀφ' ὧν ἔδει με χαίρειν. Erasmus replies—"At ego illi Rhodiensi oppono tot vetusta exemplaria, quae nos vidimus partim in Anglia, partim in Brabantia, partim Basileæ, quorum nonnulla Cardinalis quidam Roma secum advexerat, cum illic esset synodus, et in itinere moriens legavit totam bibliothecam, quæ Græca erat, monasterio Carthusiensium; ac deprehendi quosdam Græcos codices ad nostros esse castigatos, quo de numero suspicor esse Rhodiensem illum. Quod si verum est, codex ille nihil aliud est, quam

On 1 John, v. 7, however, of the genuineness of which Stunica, following in the footsteps of Lee, was an advocate, the Rhodian manuscript would seem to have failed. Like his predecessor, Stunica relies exclusively on the Preface of Jerome, and on his own assumption that the Greek copies are evidently corrupt. He does not of course quote a single Greek authority, and Erasmus accordingly is able to ask triumphantly, "Where has your Rhodian manuscript gone to sleep?"[43] All other arguments he points out were beside the purpose, since he had never undertaken to emend the Greek manuscripts, but only to render them faithfully. Nevertheless he certainly did not believe that the Latin copies in this instance represented the original text; and he proceeds to show once more, by the same arguments which he had employed against Lee, that the words under discussion were unknown to the early Church. He adds, moreover, that he had recently consulted two (Latin) manuscripts of remarkable antiquity at Bruges, in which they were wanting.

Stunica, it may be supposed, was neither convinced nor pacified by this reply. He pursued his adversary with unrelenting animosity, and two years afterwards (1522) published a rejoinder, in which he resumed some of the principal points in the controversy between them —especially that regarding the title of Deity as applied to Christ—and openly charged him with Arianism.[44] He had at first, it would seem, really supposed that the

amussis alba in albo lapide. Ego magis fiderem exemplari Græco, quod non usquequaque consentiret cum nostris."—*Er. Op.* ix. 333, A, B.

[43] "Ubi dormit codex ille Rhodiensis?"—a question which the world has been asking ever since.

[44] *Jacobi Lopidis Stunicæ Libellus trium illorum voluminum præcursor quibus Erasmicas impietates ac blasphemias redarguit. Romæ*, 1522.

statement of Erasmus on that head arose from ignorance of Scripture, but when he found him putting another construction on the passages adduced to show that the name of God is frequently applied to Christ, he no longer hesitated to bring the terrible charge of heresy. About the same time he published a collection of the "blasphemies and impieties" of Erasmus, taken from his various works, and principally from the notes to the New Testament, and the edition of Jerome.[45] Stunica was at that time residing at Rome, and so highly was Erasmus esteemed there, that he found considerable difficulty in bringing out these attacks, two decrees of the conclave having been actually issued to prevent it, nor was it until after the death of Leo X., when he probably took advantage of the interval which elapsed before the arrival of the new Pope, Adrian VI., that he succeeded in his design. In reply to these works, Erasmus also wrote an apology, which, however, it will not be necessary to notice at length.[46]

Stunica was followed by another Spanish divine, Sanctius Caranza, who undertook the defence of his countryman against Erasmus, especially with reference to those passages to which the latter was supposed to have given an Arian interpretation. Erasmus again replied that he had no doubt that the Deity of Christ might be proved from Scripture, but he protested against straining particular texts to meanings which could not properly be put into them. Caranza would seem to

---

[45] *Erasmi Roterodami Blasphemiæ et Impietates per Jacobum Lopidem Stunicam nunc primum propalatæ ac proprio volumine alias redargutæ. Romæ,* 1522.

[46] *Des. Erasmi Roterodami Apologia adversus libellum Jacobi Stunicæ, cui titulum fecit, Blasphemia et impietates Erasmi.* Basiliæ, 13 Jun. Anno 1522.

have been a fairer and more moderate disputant than Lee and Stunica.[47]

Such were the more serious controversies which followed the publication of the New Testament. Sometimes, in the hands of the ignorant monks, the attacks upon it assumed a sufficiently comic aspect, and Erasmus has not failed to record one or two instances of this in his usual humorous style. There was, for example, a certain Dr. Standish, Bishop of St. Asaph—St. Ass, Erasmus calls it—who was terribly distressed because Erasmus, following Laurentius Valla, had substituted the masculine word *Sermo* for the neuter *Verbum* in the first chapter of St. John's Gospel.

On a certain occasion he was preaching in St. Paul's Churchyard, and having begun a sermon upon Charity, all of a sudden he broke out into a furious attack upon Erasmus, declaring that the Christian religion must be ruined unless all new translations were abolished, and that it was intolerable that this man should have corrupted the Gospel of St. John by putting *Sermo* in the place of *Verbum* which had been the reading of the Church for so many centuries. Then he began to appeal to the feelings of his audience, bewailing his own unhappy lot, to think that he who all his life had been accustomed to read, "*In principio erat verbum,*" must henceforth read, "*In principio erat sermo;*" and finally he appealed to the mayor, the aldermen, and the whole body of citizens to come to the rescue of Christianity in this its hour of

---

[47] "Post longas et inutiles rixas, tandem mihi res esse cœpit cum homine vere Theologo, qui, si credendum est amicorum litteris, et disputat erudite, et docet modeste, et admonet amanter."—*Desiderii Erasmi Apologia de tribus locis, quos ut recte taxatos a Stunica defenderat Sanctius Caranza Theologus.*—*Er. Op.* ix. 401, *sqq.*

peril. No one, however, took notice of his rodomontade except to laugh at it. It happened the same day that Standish was to dine at the palace, and two of his hearers—one of whom was a bachelor, and profoundly versed in the scholastic philosophy as well as in the modern learning, the other a married man, but of the most heavenly mind (no doubt, as Knight conjectures, Master Richard Pace and Sir Thomas More)—were to meet him. They were no sooner seated, than one of them remarked how glad he was to find he had been reading the Commentaries of Erasmus. Standish, perceiving that a trap was laid for him to compel him to confess that he had been attacking a book which he had not read, replied bluntly, " Perhaps I have read as much as I chose to read." " I have no doubt you have," replied the other. " Pray, may I ask on what arguments or authorities does Erasmus rely, that he has ventured to change the common reading in John's Gospel?" To this question, of course, the Bishop was unable to make any reply. He said he was content with the authority of Augustine, who affirms that *verbum* was a better word than *ratio* as an appellation of the Son of God. "Yes," said More, "than *ratio;* but what has that to do with *sermo?*" "Why, they are the same thing." "Nay," replied his tormentor, "they are very different; and it is not very wise in you to attack a man who has rendered such good service to the cause of letters, without having either read the passage you criticise, or made yourself master of the subject." Some time afterwards, made no wiser by his defeat, Standish surprised the Court by dropping reverently upon his knees in presence of the King and Queen, and a large assemblage of the nobility and of learned men. Every one was eager to hear what so eminent a theologian had to say, supposing it must be something of great importance. He began by pronouncing an eulogium, in English, upon the ancestors of the King and Queen for having ever defended the Catholic Church against heretics and schismatics, and then proceeded to exhort and adjure their Majesties to follow in the footsteps of their progenitors, warning them that most dangerous times were at hand, and that unless the books of Erasmus could be suppressed, the religion of Christ was ruined. Then, raising his hands and eyes to heaven, he prayed that Christ would condescend himself to aid his spouse if no one on earth would come to her defence. While he was still on his knees, one of his two tormentors on the previous occasion (Sir Thomas More) stepped forward, and having said how much he admired the pious harangue of the reverend father, begged that, as he had alarmed their Majesties so much, he would now be good enough to point out what it was in the books of Erasmus from which he apprehended such terrible consequences. He replied he would do so at once, and, reckoning on his fingers, proceeded: "First, Erasmus denies the resurrection. Second, he makes the sacrament of matrimony of no account. Lastly, he is unsound on the Eucharist." More commended the clearness of his statement, and observed that nothing now remained but that he should prove his assertions. "Certainly," replied the other; and beginning upon his thumb, "First," said he, "that he denies the resurrection I prove thus: Paul in his Epistle to the Colossians (he meant Corinthians) writes thus: 'We shall all rise, but we shall not all be changed' (the reading of the Vulgate); but Erasmus has altered the reading of the Church, and from his Greek copies reads as follows: 'We shall not all sleep, but we shall all be changed.' It is clear that he denies the resurrection." Presently the poor Bishop was led into a still greater absurdity, if that were possible, and said that Jerome had restored the true reading from the Hebrew; till at length the King took pity on his incurable stupidity, and diverted the conversation to some other subject.[48]

Three editions of the Greek Testament by Erasmus have now been mentioned. The fourth appeared in 1527, and the fifth in 1535, the year before his death. On all of them, except the last, which hardly differs from its predecessor, much labour was spent.

In estimating the merits of Erasmus as an editor of the New Testament, it ought surely to be considered sufficient if he can fairly claim to have been the first. And this he can do with very little qualification. Cardinal Ximenes is indeed entitled to equal honour, as having planned the Complutensian Polyglott, in which the New Testament, it would seem, was printed by the beginning of the year 1514; but the whole work was not ready till 1517, nor was it published before 1522. The name of Laurentius Valla also must not be forgotten as the very first, so far as is known, who collated different manuscripts of the New Testament. But Erasmus was the first who edited, printed, and published the Christian Scriptures in their original tongue, and for that the world owes him a debt which it would not be easy to repay. His text, indeed, was far from perfect; and yet a chapter from his last edition, compared with the text of Griesbach or Tischendorf, pre-

[48] *Ep.* clxvi.

sents wonderfully few variations, and these generally such as in any less important book might well be thought trifling. It is ever to be regretted, for his own credit's sake, that Erasmus should have given way about 1 John v. 7; yet there was much excuse for him; and there can be no doubt that the clergy would never have rested till they had secured its insertion.

The edition of the works of St. Jerome, which, as we have seen, had been in progress long before the New Testament was begun, and to which we must now give our attention, was delayed till after the completion of the latter work. At length on the 1st of July, 1516, it came out in nine splendid folio volumes, sumptuously printed, a worthy monument of the learning of the editors, and of the industry and spirit of the printer and publisher. It was dedicated to Archbishop Warham, in one of the most finished compositions of the pen of Erasmus. The epistle dedicatory prefixed to the first volume is dated April 1, 1516, precisely a month after the publication of the New Testament.

Of all the Fathers of the Church, Jerome was the one for whom Erasmus had the warmest admiration, whose writings he had studied most diligently, and with whose mind his own had the closest affinity. In some respects, it is true, the resemblance was not great. The grim old Father, dwelling in the deserts of Syria, the companion of wild beasts and scorpions, his face pale with fasting, his mind fevered with passions which all his austerity had not been able completely to subdue, his spare person lacerated with self-inflicted stripes, lying naked on the ground or clad only in the coarsest sackcloth, visited by horrible visions, and hearing ever the sound of the last trumpet ringing in his ears, certainly differed in not a few important points from the self-satisfied and by no means ascetic German man of letters. Jerome believed firmly in the virtue of the monastic life, and in the excellence of virginity. Erasmus denied both. It was the former who wrote that "marriage peoples the earth, but virginity paradise;"[49] Erasmus maintained that an old maid was a monster.[50] Jerome had the deepest reverence for sacred relics and sacred places; Erasmus constantly made them the subjects of his wit. The former was probably much more superstitious than the latter; yet Erasmus pronounced St. Geneviève a better physician than Dr. Copus: and Jerome, in his old age, referring to the supernatural flagellation inflicted on him for reading the classics, declared that to be a dream, which, when a young man, he had solemnly averred was a reality. Making allowance, however, for the difference between an age of increasing darkness and one of increasing light, there is probably sufficient similarity in the characters of these two eminent men to convince us that Erasmus would have been a Jerome had he lived in the fourth century, and Jerome an Erasmus had he lived in the sixteenth. Certainly the eulogies which Erasmus writes on the father, and in which he praises particularly his vast and varied learning, his acquaintance with profane literature, his antiquarian skill, his linguistic accomplishments, his eloquence, his fervour, the grace which tempers the severity of his style, his judgment, his memory, his power of happy combina-

---

[49] Adv. Jov. L. i. c. 9.
[50] *Coll. Fam. Proci et Puella.*—"Quid juxta naturam prodigiosius anu virgine?" It is true the sentiment is put in the mouth of a fictitious character, but it need not be doubted that it was that of Erasmus himself.

tion, might almost have been written of himself.[51] There was, besides, one other respect in which they closely resembled one another: they both inclined to moderate and common-sense views of religion; and if Augustine was the master of Luther, Jerome was the master of Erasmus. He had read his works with enthusiasm from his boyhood, and as he advanced in life he continued to read them, perhaps with greater judgment, but not with less devotion. Jerome, he declares, holds the first place in the best kind of theology; certainly among the Latins, but even Greece can hardly furnish his equal.[52] "Jerome," he exclaims elsewhere, with still greater enthusiasm, "Jerome is a river of gold; he who has Jerome alone needs no more ample library."[53]

The task of editing the works of this Father was one of no small difficulty. There were manuscripts, moth-eaten and mutilated, and covered with filth, to be deciphered. The very letters in which these manuscripts were written, strange Gothic characters, had to be learned like a new alphabet. There was a text,

---

[51] "Tantam uno in homine reperias secularium ut vocant literarum cognitionem, tantam omnis antiquitatis peritiam, tot linguarum absolutam scientiam, tam admirandam locorum et historiarum omnium notitiam, tam non vulgarem mysticorum voluminum eruditionem, tantum inimitabilis eloquentiæ, tam exactum ubique judicium, tam sacrum afflati pectoris ardorem, rerum adeo diversarum tam digestam ac præsentem memoriam, tam felicem juxta ac divitem mixturam, denique tanto lepore conditam severitatem, ut quemadmodum per se facundi, si cum Cicerone conferantur, protinus videntur obmutescere, ita coeteri doctores quos ultra collationem suspicimus, cum Hieronymo compositi, vix sapere, vix loqui, vix vivere videantur." Pref. to vol. ii. *Divinarum literarum studiosis omnibus.* Conf. *Ded.* to Warham.

[52] Pref. to vol. ii.

[53] "Aureum flumen habet, locupletissimam bibliothecam habet, quisquis unum habet Hieronymum." —*Ep. Ded.*

corrupted partly by the carelessness or the ignorance, partly by the wilful dishonesty of transcribers, to be restored. Finally, there were spurious works to be separated from the genuine, in which, however, the imposture was so gross that it was much more easy to detect it than to overcome the prejudices by which it had hitherto been sustained. Into such a miserable state indeed had these precious remains been suffered to fall, that if Jerome could have returned to life he would have been unable either to recognize or to read his own works.[54] Erasmus, however, found himself equal to all these difficulties. He not only furnished a text which left very little work for future editors,[55] but he accompanied his text with learned *scholia*, or brief critical and explanatory notes, in which all the resources of his great learning were called into requisition, to elucidate every obscure or doubtful point. While printing the spurious works in obedience to a prejudice which he believed would probably demand them, he relegated them to a place by themselves, and warned the reader not to waste time on their perusal. He supplied a life of his author which contained no statement that could not be substantiated from his own writings; and he roused the attention or rather the enthusiasm of his readers by eloquent dissertations in his praise.

It seems a pity that Erasmus should have thought

---

[54] *Ep. Ded.*

[55] It is true that Marianus, the next editor of St. Jerome, claims to have restored the true reading in about 1,500 places which Erasmus had either corrupted, or through ignorance failed to correct. It would be strange if with far more resources at his command he had not produced a better text, but the number of reliable corrections may probably be overstated. What is more certain is that this author, who loses no opportunity of assailing Erasmus, has sometimes availed himself of his learning without acknowledgment. The editors of the Benedictine edition do him more justice.

it necessary even to print, instead of discarding altogether, such miserable trash as "Jerome's Life by an unknown Author," or "Cyril's Letter to Augustine on the Miracles of Jerome;" but it was impossible to avoid it without giving unnecessary offence. At least he thought so, and in his preface to the spurious works addressed to all students of theology,[56] he justifies himself at considerable length for his boldness in venturing to question the genuineness of any work hitherto received as Jerome's, observing that the Church, from whose judgment he would never willingly depart a single hair's breadth, has left the point undecided. He then enters upon a learned and elaborate discussion, showing the way in which spurious works obtain currency, and remarking that in proportion as an author is known and revered, it is the more probable that his name will be abused. In heathen literature, both Greek and Latin, there are abundant examples. There are verses in Homer which Homer never wrote. There are spurious plays of Euripides and Aristophanes. There are spurious dialogues of Plato and Lucian. Of the great number of plays bearing the name of Plautus, Varro admits only twenty-one to be genuine. The "Precepts of Rhetoric," for ages past ascribed to Cicero, are proved by the style not to be Cicero's. Nor have the sacred writers been spared. The Epistles of Paul to Seneca and of Seneca to Paul contain nothing worthy of either. Some books of the Old Testament are not received by the Hebrews, and of those which they do receive, the author is not always certain. St. Jerome himself marks with an obelisk some parts of Daniel,

---

[56] *Des. Erasmus R. Divinarum literarum studiosis omnibus*, prefixed to vol. ii. containing the spurious works attributed to Jerome.

and rejects third and fourth Esdras as apocryphal. In Jerome's lifetime the Epistle to the Hebrews was rejected by the Roman Church, and the Apocalypse by the Greeks. The Epistle of James was believed by many not to be by the Apostle, but by another of the same name. Many rejected the second Epistle of Peter, with whom St. Jerome sometimes agrees, though he elsewhere accounts for the diversity of style by supposing that the Apostle had made use of a different interpreter. There are now three epistles received as John's, though Jerome testifies that only the first is from the Apostle. There are various ways in which spurious works may be ascribed to well-known authors. It may happen through the mere accident of an identity or similarity of names. It may happen through the mistake or caprice of the bookbinder. Sometimes when a work is anonymous the reader makes an unfortunate guess, and ascribes a false name. Sometimes a fictitious name is used without any design of misleading, but nevertheless gains currency as the real one. This was the case with the Epistles of Phalaris, and of Paul to Seneca. But finally there are those who use great names with the worst possible intention, in order to propagate heresy and recommend their own pestilent dogmas to the reader. Hence such impudent forgeries as the letter of Jesus to Agbarus, the Gospel of Peter, the Gospel of Nicodemus, and other similar works. It is not wonderful, then, if the great name of Jerome has been made use of in order to gain acceptance for writings in which there is no trace of his hand. That such was actually the case Erasmus, judging from internal evidence, has no doubt whatever. He is convinced, he says, that there was some one—the style proves that it was always the same person—whose principal occupation it was to interpolate his own worthless compositions in the works of others, but particularly in those of Ambrose, Augustine, and Jerome. This impostor had an extraordinary passion, amounting almost to insanity, for corrupting the writings of St. Jerome in every conceivable way, so that, not satisfied with forging whole books and epistles in his name, he would even introduce some drivelling of his own into the interpretation of a prophecy or a psalm, thus not merely sewing his own rotten rags upon Jerome's fine purple, but spoiling his good wine by pouring into it his own vinegar. There is, however, one grand touchstone by which the genuine may ever be distinguished from the spurious, and that is the style.[57] But then stupid people answer that the same author has not always the same style. Certainly not, replies Erasmus; there will, of course, be variations according to the nature of the subject, the age of the author, the progress he has made in his studies, or the particular state of mind in which he writes. The Philippics of Cicero, for example, which he wrote in his old age, are not in the same style as the Orations against Verres which he wrote in his youth. The phraseology of the defence of Milo is very different from that of the treatise on moral duty. Sometimes we vary our style intentionally to adapt it to different subjects; and as we improve in facility of expression, some alteration will naturally follow. Nevertheless, authors have their identity just as persons have; and if it is easy to recognize a well-known face under all changes of expression, if the features of the old man at once recall the friend of one's youth, if no two

---

[57] "Character orationis et habitus."

brothers or two sisters are ever so like that they cannot readily be distinguished from one another, it is always possible to recognize the same writer, however much he may vary his style. In Jerome especially there can be no difficulty, because so many and so remarkable were his gifts that the presence of any one of them would suffice for his identification. In those which he enjoyed in common with others, such as force of intellect, fertility of fancy, fervour, eloquence, knowledge of Scripture, zeal for learning, he was so superior to others that he might at once be distinguished by his pre-eminence. But Jerome had also gifts peculiar to himself, of which the principal was that remarkable power of combination by which he was enabled to enrich his compositions with quotations from the most varied sources, Greek, Latin, and Hebrew, ancient and modern, yet without violating the unity of the subject. Another was that pleasantry (*festivitas*) which the learned admire so much in Marcus Tully. Besides— but this is certainly very inconclusive reasoning— Jerome has written no work which he does not himself somewhere cite; he has, however, cited none of those which Erasmus rejects. To the argument founded upon the style of the suspected compositions, it is added that some of them are not found in the oldest copies, while others do not even pretend to be Jerome's. Finally, there are some of them in which Jerome's authorship is so frequently insisted upon, that this very circumstance of itself excites suspicion.

Erasmus, whose great fault was that he never knew when he had done with a subject, thought it necessary to follow up this beautiful piece of criticism with another preface, also addressed to students of theology,[58] in which the same arguments are further illustrated, and which he himself confesses is needlessly verbose. There is nothing in it, I believe, worth repeating, except one or two anecdotes which he narrates in order to show how people are often led astray by their prepossessions. While living with the Bishop of Cambray he made the acquaintance of a Sicilian named Peter Sauteranus. This gentleman, who was no less witty than learned, used to tell how he had once in Paris written the following epigram—

> Tempora fatalis quoniam sic limitis itis
> Tristia concentu funere solor olor—

to which he gave the title of *Cygnus moriens pro specu*. Having then engaged a skilful penman to copy it out in antique characters, and taking care that some of the letters should be left imperfect as if defaced by time, he presented it to the Poet Laureate, Faustus Andrelinus, telling him he had found it among some old relics he happened to have by him. Andrelinus received the paper with the utmost reverence; he read it and re-read it, and all but worshipped it, till the other put an end to his admiration, or changed it into laughter, by acknowledging the deception. A somewhat similar practical joke was once played by Dr. Cop, who, at a supper-party where a number of physicians were present, singled out from the vegetables on the table a very common kind of parsley, and holding it up—"Come!" cried he, "physicians ought to know something about the nature and virtue of plants. Say, who can, what is the name of this herb?" No one

---

[58] *Erasmus Roterodamus Divinarum studiosis literarum*, prefixed to the third series of vol. ii.

ventured to express an opinion, so convinced were they all that it must be some rare and foreign herb about which so eminent a man was making such grave inquiries, until he solved the problem by calling the cook, who at once answered for the doctors. The last anecdote is of one of the most learned of the Italian scholars, whose name, however, is suppressed. Some one presented to him a fragment torn from a manuscript, observing casually that he fancied it to be quite recent. The Italian, who was one of those who despise anything modern, immediately began to find fault with it, denouncing the barbarian who had wasted paper on such miserable stuff. It was then announced that the fragment was Cicero's. The moral of these stories is, of course, that "even with learned men a strong prepossession sometimes completely blinds the judgment," and that, consequently, the mere habit of accepting certain works as Jerome's is no proof that they are really his.

The "Life of Jerome," notwithstanding the mistake of placing his birth under Constantine, instead of Constantius his son, is probably the best that has ever been written. Discarding the fables of the old writer, to whom, however, it should in gratitude be remembered we are indebted for the immortal lion which, in all worthy representations, attends upon the saint, Erasmus uses Jerome himself as his principal authority, and from the fulness of his acquaintance with his writings gives a vivid sketch of the main events of his life. Nor does he forget to infuse into the narrative a little of his own philosophy. Thus, where he records how Jerome, after much hesitation, decides upon adopting the monastic life, he is careful to remind us that the monk of those days was very different from the monk of more recent times. To be a monk then was to be released from family ties, from worldly duties, and, consequently, to possess greater freedom than in any other state. He could change his residence as he pleased. His dress was simple, and such as convenience prescribed, rather than any inflexible rule. He was bound by no vows, and if he repented of his resolve, his worst punishment was to bear the character of inconstancy. The famous story of Jerome's supernatural flagellation naturally comes under discussion here, and it is worthy of note, and a proof, perhaps, how small was the store set upon simple truth either in the fourth century or the sixteenth, that, if the saint could deliberately lie, his biographer evidently saw no sin in a lie which was told with a pious object. The story itself is so well known that it may be superfluous to repeat it. Jerome —such is his own account of the matter—had been unable, on his retirement from the world, to bring himself to part with the library which he had collected with so much care at Rome, and had, consequently, been tempted to indulge in the study of the profane writers until his taste revolted from the rude style of the prophets. One day, when he was reduced almost to the point of death by a fever, he was suddenly hurried before the eternal judgment-seat, and being examined as to his condition, he replied that he was a Christian. The answer was stern and terrible,—"Thou liest; thou art a Ciceronian, and not a Christian, for where thy treasure is, there will thy heart be also." Thereupon, he was immediately seized and subjected to a castigation so severe that he cried for mercy, nor was he delivered until the bystanders, flinging themselves at the feet of the Judge, besought him to spare his youth and his ignorance, on the understanding that the offence should never be repeated. That this was no vain dream, but a reality, was proved by the pain which he felt upon awaking, by the marks of the stripes upon his shoulders, and by the zeal with which from that time forth he pursued the study of the Holy Scriptures. An obvious explanation, which would go some way to vindicate the character of the saint, would be, no doubt, that a vivid dream, acting upon a strong imagination, and especially during an access of fever, might leave upon the memory all the effects of an actual occurrence. But the difficulty is that Jerome related the circumstance with a solemn asseveration of its truth after a sufficient interval had elapsed to enable him to review it calmly, and yet, after a much longer interval, ridiculed an adversary who had referred to it for not being satisfied with replying to his serious arguments, but he must notice also his dreams. Nor need we scruple to suppose that the saint was guilty of falsehood when we find him, in his commentary on the Galatians, interpreting the difference between the apostle of the Gentiles and the apostle of the circumcision as " economical" and not real. And it further illustrates the looseness of Jerome's code of morals that, in reply to Augustine, who objected to this interpretation that, by attributing falsehood to an apostle, it invalidated the whole authority of Scripture, he justified it on the plea that it was introduced to refute Porphyry's blasphemy, who charged Paul with rudeness in rebuking the chief of the apostles; as if any interpretation of Scripture were admissible provided it was adapted to silence an antagonist, and without regard to its truth. Erasmus, however, does not concern himself much with the question of right or wrong. He merely remarks that a falsehood which had for its object to deter a young lady from the excessive study of the classics, was justifiable on the same principle on which it is generally considered allowable for parents to frighten their children from doing wrong by fictitious threats. But he labours hard to prove that a story the moral of which was so unpalatable to a classical scholar, was not merely a falsehood, but was acknowledged by its author to be nothing more. One argument which he uses will probably be considered abundantly conclusive. If, he says, it be a crime to possess profane authors, and if to read them be to deny Christ, why should Jerome alone be flogged? "For my own part," he concludes, "I had rather be whipped with Jerome, than anointed with honey in company with the men who are so scared by Jerome's dream that they abstain from all literature; though," he caustically adds, "they do not keep themselves from the vices of those whose books they are afraid to touch."

In this biographical essay, Erasmus clearly places Jerome above Augustine, both for eloquence and for logic. In reply to the charge—"as arrogant as it is impious"—that he was no theologian, he remarks that as it can be founded only on the fact that he does not indulge in sophistical subtleties, or talk of majors and minors like the scholastics, it would exclude from that honourable title all who have lived more than four hundred years ago, and among the rest the Apostles themselves. But if learning, eloquence, a knowledge of the Holy Scriptures, and other such qualities constitute a theologian, then assuredly Jerome is one of the greatest. And as to his style, so far from assenting to the witticism of Theodore Gaza, that if Jerome was whipped for being a Ciceronian, he had certainly not deserved it, he seems inclined to place him above Cicero himself. " Cicero speaks; but Jerome thunders and lightens. We admire the language of the one; but the feeling as well as the language of the other." [59]

To restore the text, and illustrate with ample learning, the writings of St. Jerome, was a task which could not but redound to the honour of the scholar who accomplished it successfully. The epistles of Jerome indeed had been printed before in the splendid edition of 1470, published at Rome in two large folios, but with a less pure text, the Greek and Hebrew words omitted, without systematic arrangement, and with too little attention to the distinction between the genuine and the spurious. But Froben's edition was in every respect worthy both of the esteem in which Jerome was held in that age, and of the learning and reputation of his editor. The brothers Amerbach, it is true, share with Erasmus the credit of this great work, but the foregoing review will have made it evident that he superintended, and made himself responsible for every part. It was a worthy offering to lay before the Primate of England, to whom, as he had already presented the New Testament to the Pope, it was natural that Erasmus should wish to dedicate it. The greatest of theologians, he remarks, might well congratulate himself on being restored under the auspices of one who was second to

---

[59] "Loquitur Cicero; tonat ac fulminat Hieronymus. Illius linguam miramur; hujus etiam pectus."

none among Bishops; for, as Jerome was a perfect master of every branch of learning, so did Warham unite in his own person, in due harmony and proportion, all episcopal graces. A second edition of the Jerome was called for in 1524, and a third in 1533, the year following that in which Warham died.

CHAPTER XII.

ERASMUS AT BRUGES—MEETING WITH MORE—INVITED TO INGOLDSTADT—LETTER TO FISHER—JOHN WATSON—ERASMUS NEARLY MADE A BISHOP—INVITED TO PARIS—BUDÆUS—CORRESPONDENCE WITH HIM—LOUVAIN—ATENSIS—VIVES—COLLEGE OF BUSLEIDEN—HUTTEN—DEATH OF AMMONIUS—OF COLET—ENGLISH DWELLING-HOUSES—LETTER TO LAURINUS—TO BEATUS—WRITINGS OF ERASMUS—THE COMPLAINT OF PEACE—THE PARAPHRASE OF THE NEW TESTAMENT.

WE have seen that Erasmus left England on his way to Basle, some time between the 17th of April, 1515, the day on which Rhenanus wrote to him that Froben had decided on printing the New Testament, and the middle of July, when he ought to have received the Pope's letter, in reply to his request that he might dedicate his St. Jerome to his Holiness. We have no means of deciding exactly when he arrived in Basle, but it was probably not till the season was considerably more advanced. His new office of councillor to Prince Charles made it necessary that he should now present himself at the Flemish court, and it was no doubt with this view that he went to Bruges, where we find him enjoying the society of Cuthbert Tonstall, the learned and amiable Bishop of London, of Richard Sampson, afterwards Bishop of Chichester, and of Sir Thomas More, and reckoning up with them the advantages and disadvantages of a benefice at Tournay, which Wolsey was then willing to give him, and which Sampson was anxious that he should accept.¹ It so happened that More, Tonstall, and Sampson were part of an embassy from the English king, to settle some commercial difficulties with Flanders, and as they left home in May it is more than probable that Erasmus accompanied them. No doubt he left them at Bruges, where they were detained four months; nor were they able to return home till toward the close of the year. It was while on this embassy that More wrote his "Utopia," and it may be considered fortunate that he found the time hang somewhat heavy on his hands, otherwise we might never have possessed that admirable plea for religious toleration. In a letter written shortly after his return home More complains to his friend that he had been absent for more than six months, when he had expected to return within two. We can understand that to a man of his strong domestic feelings such a severance of the home ties must have been exceedingly trying, and it is no wonder if he adds that he never liked the office of an ambassador. His next remark, though merely intended as a joke, was, I fear, more true than flattering. "Such an office," he says, "does not suit us laymen; it is much fitter for you priests, who either have no wife and children at home, or find them wherever you go."²

The office of councillor did not bring very much profit to Erasmus. He tells us indeed that a salary had been promised him out of the Prince's treasury, but this implies that at the time of writing at least he had received none; and in the meantime he "was living on his own juice like a snail, or rather like a polyp gnawing his own limbs;"³ but he confesses to having got a prebend which

---

[1] *Er. Op.* iii. 220, A, D.   [2] *Ep.* ccxxvii.
[3] "Hactenus quidem hic sementem facio, cujusmodi messem facturus,

he had turned into an annual pension. His engagements to the Prince at all events furnished him with a fair excuse for declining any invitations with which he was honoured from other quarters. While at Basle he received a most flattering invitation from Ernest, Duke of Bavaria, who was most anxious to secure his services for his university at Ingoldstadt, and determined to spare no expense for that object. If he pleaded old age, he was assured of the greatest comfort and quiet, as the intention was not that he should wear himself out with toil, but simply give the light of his presence to the university. The delightful situation and healthy atmosphere of the place were held out as further inducements; a handsome salary was promised if he would accept, and he was encouraged to expect that rich livings would be put at his disposal. If he would not take up his residence among them, it was hoped that he would at least pay a visit to Ingoldstadt and give the Duke an opportunity of meeting and conversing with him. The expenses of his journey would be paid in the most liberal manner and a handsome present made him. Erasmus, however, does not seem to have complied with the Duke's invitation even in this modified form.[4] He had never intended remaining so long at Basle, and as soon as he could get away from his work he returned down the Rhine to Flanders, and thence it would seem crossed the Channel for a short visit to England. From St. Omer we have the following note to his friend Ursewick, dated June 5, 1516:—

incertus: meo etiamnum succo victito, ad cochlearum exemplum; imo polyporum in modum, arrosis meis ipsius brachiis, me ipsum pasco," &c.—*Er. Op.* iii. 180, C.

[4] *Ep.* ccxxix. ccxxx.

ERASMUS *to* URSEWICK.[5]

"*St. Omer, June* 5, 1517 [? 1516].

"I HAVE been exceedingly fortunate in the horse you gave me, for he has carried me in safety to Basle twice and back again, a very long and most dangerous journey. He is now as wise as Homer's Ulysses—

Mores hominum multorum vidit et urbes—

to say nothing of his visiting so many universities. While I was almost killing myself at Basle for ten months, in the meantime he was perfectly idle, and has grown so fat that he can hardly walk. Upper Germany has pleased me amazingly, and Erasmus was immensely popular there. Of course you have seen the New Testament? The whole of 'Jerome' will appear shortly, together with the little book on the education of a Christian Prince. I have sent the Archbishop of Canterbury four volumes of the 'Jerome' by your *protégé*, the one-eyed Peter, whom I found so busy writing books that he has almost killed himself with toil. I think he must be under some fatality, he has become so unlike what he used to be. He has got quite abstemious and hates wine, and hence has become unwontedly pale. In whatever corner of the world I may dwell, I shall always remember your kindness. Farewell."

Another letter of the same date, addressed to the Bishop of Rochester, contains some interesting references to his New Testament. "This work," he says, "was feared before its appearance, but now that it is published

[5] *Ep.* cclv.

it meets with the approval of all divines who have the least spark of either learning or honesty. The Prior of Friburg, a man of the greatest authority among his own people, the author of 'The Philosophical Pearl,' as soon as he had dipped into the work, declared that he would rather have it than two hundred golden florins. Louis Berd, a Paris divine, a man of the first eminence in that department, is in perfect raptures with it, and laments having wasted so many years in those scholastic disputations. Such also is the opinion of Wolfgang Capito, public preacher at Basle, a most learned Hebraist and practised theologian. Both these men are diligent students of Greek. To omit the rest, the Bishop of Basle, a man now well up in years and of the most unblemished life, has shown me the greatest kindness, and although I refused all his offers, he at length compelled me to accept a horse, which, on my departure from the city, I was able to sell again for fifty golden florins. Ernest, Duke of Bavaria, sent a special messenger to Basle to offer me two hundred gulden a year, besides splendid presents and the prospect of some good livings if I would take up my residence at Ingoldstadt, the university of Bavaria. And a German Bishop, whose name I do not at present recollect, has done the same thing. But I must leave off boasting, though I might give many other similar instances with the most perfect truth.

"I know that I deserve none of these favours, but I am glad to find that my labours, such as they are, meet with the approval of good men. Many are by this means induced to read the Scriptures, who otherwise never would have read them, as they themselves confess; many have begun to learn Greek,—indeed, that is the case everywhere. The whole of 'St. Jerome' will appear at the next Frankfort fair. I am now sending to the Archbishop of Canterbury, by the one-eyed Peter, who is sent for this purpose at my own expense and risk, the four volumes of 'Epistles,' which he will be glad to lend to you. I had come as far as St. Omer with the intention of crossing to England, but a feverish attack made me unwilling to risk a sea voyage. As soon as I can I shall take some means of proving that I am not altogether unmindful of the very great kindness you have shown me.

"Prince Charles, they say, is succeeding to no less than nineteen kingdoms. What wonderful good fortune! but I trust it may prove to be for the happiness of my country and not of the Prince only. When, on leaving Basle, I was preparing to travel through Lorraine, I met soldiers everywhere, and saw the country-people carrying their furniture into the nearest towns; there was a report that they intended attacking the people, but it was unknown by whom they were sent. I have a notion they had been disbanded by the Emperor, and were looking for some other employer who might give them their pay in his stead. Oh! the strange games of Christian princes! It is thus we fill the world with tumult, and stake everything on the hazard of war, and yet we think ourselves Christians! But I and the like of me can do no more than lament that it should be so. Would that all Popes, cardinals, magnates and divines would conspire together at length to put a stop to these disgraceful evils; but that will never be till the interests of individuals shall be postponed to the public advantage and the latter alone be regarded. By this means even the private condition of every one would be improved.

Farewell. I shall be better if I shall have earned the favour of a letter from you." [6]

That Erasmus a little later in the season fulfilled his intention of crossing to England, is clear from a letter which he wrote from Brussels to John Watson. He gives us, however, no particulars of this visit, merely remarking that he had mounted his horse to go to Cambridge when some one told him the Bishop of Rochester was expected in London that very day, and consequently he had waited for him there.[7] Watson was a young Cambridge divine who had been very intimate with Erasmus at that University, and entertained the greatest admiration for him. He had recently been travelling in his footsteps in Italy, and had written to him on his return, telling him in what esteem he was held by the learned there, and how his "Folly" was regarded among them as the very height of wisdom. At Venice they were particularly loud in his praises, and were very anxious that he should return.[8] Watson was one of those who were able to appreciate the labours of Erasmus. Perhaps that may partly explain why he never attained any high preferment in the Church.[9]

While in London Erasmus received the Pope's letter, which must have been waiting for him nearly a year, and wrote to say that if it had reached him when he was still in Basle, no dangers would have deterred him from hastening to throw himself at his most blessed feet. As it was, however, he had now returned to his own country, where increasing years, as well as the kindness of his own Prince, detained him. Charles—he writes here in a rather different spirit from

[6] *Ep.* cclvi.
[7] *Ep.* cxcii.
[8] *Ep.* clxxxiii.
[9] KNIGHT: p. 145-6.

his language previously quoted in another letter [10]—had most kindly invited him in his absence, and without any solicitation on his part, and had at once bestowed on him a very rich and honourable preferment. He expresses great obligations to his Holiness for the additional favour he had experienced in consequence of his letters, from the King of England, the Cardinal of York, and the Archbishop of Canterbury.[11]

On his return to Brussels in autumn, Erasmus waited on the Chancellor Sylvagius, by whom he was informed, much to his surprise, and still more, it would seem, to his amusement, that Charles, who had now, by the death of his grandfather, Ferdinand of Spain, succeeded to the title and the possessions of the Catholic King, was anxious to make him a Bishop. "Here is a man," said the Chancellor, addressing the assembled councillors, "who does not yet know what a great man he is." Then turning to Erasmus, he continued, "The Prince wants to make you a Bishop; and he had actually conferred on you a most desirable bishopric in Sicily, but since discovering that it is not in the list of those reserved for the Crown, he has written to the Pope, begging him to give it you." Erasmus thought the affair a good joke, and wrote a humorous letter on the occasion to Ammonius. "Nevertheless," he adds, "I am pleased with the Prince's good-will towards me, or rather with the Chancellor's, who, in fact, is the Prince. I only hope this comedy may end well."[12] It ended exactly as he wished, for no more was heard of the Sicilian bishopric. In another letter he

---

[10] See above, p. 362.   [11] *Ep.* clxxxi.
[12] *Ep.* clx. This letter should evidently be dated Oct. 6, 1516, and not 1514.

says, "The mistake was a fortunate one. On my friends congratulating me, I could not help laughing. However, I thanked them heartily for their kindness, but begged them not to engage in such an unavailing enterprise again, as I would not exchange my leisure for any bishopric however splendid."[13] We may well believe that the *Nolo episcopari* was never more honestly spoken; and though, as he remarks, the Sicilians were originally Greeks, and were still celebrated for their wit, he might almost as well have been made a bishop in India, as be compelled to reside so far from all the seats of learning.

At Brussels, where a part of this winter was spent, there was some difficulty about procuring a lodging on account of the crowded state of the city. He succeeded, however, in finding a small room, which had the advantage of being near the Court, and what he considered a greater recommendation, not far from where his friend Tonstall, the English Ambassador, was residing. It was while here that he received another invitation, which he seems to have had more hesitation in declining than that of Duke Ernest. Francis I. was desirous of adding to the glory of his reign by surrounding himself with learned men, whom he proposed to invite to his kingdom by the offer of splendid rewards; and on one occasion, having expressed this intention in the presence of William Petit, his confessor, and some others interested in learning, the opportunity was seized to mention the name of Erasmus, and accordingly the great scholar Budæus, who was known to be already in friendly correspondence with him, was commissioned to invite him in the King's name, and promise him a preferment, with

[13] *Ep.* ccxix.

a thousand francs or more. Even allowing for the difference in the value of coin, the pecuniary reward does not seem very ample; but a residence in Paris, and connection with so splendid a Court, would not have been without its attractions for any one ambitious of that kind of distinction. Budæus, though it may be doubted whether he cordially wished Erasmus to come —indeed in the very letter which he wrote on this occasion, he candidly confessed that he was jealous of his fame—perhaps said all he could to induce him to accept the invitation of Francis. He praised the generosity of the King, and described him as eloquent in speech, easy of access, and endowed with rare gifts of mind and body. He dwelt upon the honour of being invited by such an illustrious Prince. He told him how high he stood in the esteem of Stephen Poncher, the Bishop of Paris, who was then the Ambassador of the King of France at Brussels. "I have seen your New Testament," he said, "open in his bedroom." At the same time he very properly took care to explain that he could guarantee nothing, and advised him, if he thought the offer worth considering, to write either to himself or to some other friend, to ask for some distinct pledge on the part of the King. Poncher, according to Budæus, was a most accomplished scholar and statesman, well known on both sides of the Alps, both as a diplomatist, and as a friend and patron of literary men. He made the acquaintance of Erasmus at Brussels, frequently sought his society, and returned to Paris full of his praises. Neither his persuasions, however, nor the arguments of Budæus, availed to bring Erasmus into France. In his reply to Budæus he excused himself from giving any definite answer until the Chancellor, who was then absent, should have returned. He left Poncher with the impression that had his faith not been pledged to his own Prince, he would certainly have accepted the invitation of the French monarch; and he wrote a graceful letter to Francis himself, in which he congratulated him on the proof he was giving of his right to the name of "Most Christian King" by his efforts for the maintenance of peace, and which he concluded, while he avoided making any promise, by devoting himself entirely to his Majesty's service.[14] These letters, no doubt, were regarded as a refusal, and the invitation was not pressed. Nor is there any reason to regret that the summons of Francis was not responded to. The atmosphere of Paris was not as favourable to liberty as that of Germany; the Sorbonne was active and energetic in the extirpation of heresy, and the bold destroyer of abuses might in time have found himself surrounded by enemies too powerful to resist, and who would either have silenced or destroyed him.

The letter noticed above was not, as has been already hinted, the first which Erasmus received from Budæus. There remains, in fact, a very lengthy correspondence between these two eminent scholars which forms a kind of episode in the literary history of the period, and which now demands a brief notice.

William Budé, or Budæus, was a native of Paris, and was a year or two younger than his illustrious contemporary. Of a wealthy family, he was fortunate in having a father who was fond of learning and a great buyer of books. In his boyhood he had the advantage of such schooling as the times afforded; he then studied law, but on his

[14] *Ep.* cxcvii. cciii. cciv. ccxii.

return home bade farewell for a time to letters and gave himself up to idleness and pleasure. After some years thus wasted, the good influences of home prevailed, and he determined to devote himself to private study in his father's library. Hence he used to say he had been "self-taught and late-taught." He received, indeed, some lessons in Greek from an old man to whom he was obliged to pay an extravagant fee for teaching him many things he had afterwards to unlearn, but who, he admits, read and pronounced well. As Budæus says that this old man was the only Greek in France, he must of course have been no other than Hermonymus of Sparta, of whom we have already found Erasmus speaking in such contemptuous terms.[15] Budæus afterwards twice visited Rome and the other principal cities of Italy, where he saw many of the learned men, but without having much opportunity of benefiting by their intercourse; and on his return home he made the acquaintance of John Lascar, who, he says, did what he could for him by occasionally reading with him and lending him his manuscripts. The first important work of Budæus was his Annotations on the twenty-four books of the Pandects, of which however he disowned the first edition of 1508. But the work which had hitherto done most for his fame (though not so important as his much later Commentaries on the Greek language, which became the kernel of the new *Thesaurus Linguæ Græcæ* of Henry Stephens), was that on the not very inviting subject of the Roman *As* and its parts, in which he reduced the ancient monies to their modern equivalents, and cleared up many obscure points in classical literature. This work, which is said to be very

[15] See above, p. 274.

diffuse, and sometimes difficult to understand, nevertheless produced the most astonishing effect in Europe, and the name of Budæus speedily became celebrated everywhere as that of the only scholar who could have any pretension to dispute the palm of learning with Erasmus.[16]

It was therefore with some sense of rivalry and with a consciousness of the eyes of the world being on them, that these two learned men began to address one another in long and elaborate epistles written alternately in Latin and Greek, in which they mingled extravagant praises of one another's learning with captious censures of one another's faults, and insinuated each his own merits while affecting the utmost degree of self-depreciation. Erasmus, it so happened, had inserted a note in his Greek Testament, in which, after speaking in the highest terms of Budæus, he took occasion to point out an error into which he had fallen in his explanation of the word παρηκολουθηκότι in the proem to Luke's gospel, and Budæus had freely confessed himself wrong, but without admitting Erasmus to be altogether right. Budæus again had invited the criticisms of his rival on his great work, and the latter having found fault with him for his digressions, which he thought only served to obscure still more a very difficult subject and one which required minute and careful handling, Budæus retorted that every one could not be expected to be as eloquent as Erasmus, and complained that the latter occupied himself so much with works on small and trivial subjects.[17] The Greek word which he used to express this idea (λεπτολογήματα), though withdrawn and apologized for, rankled long in the mind of his correspondent, who

[16] *Ep.* cccxlix. *Biog. Un.* art. Budé.   [17] *Ep.* cc. ccl.

declared that he could not conceive what particular works he referred to, as none of his books made any extraordinary pretensions, though they had all some good aim, and it might be hoped had been found of some little use in the world.[18] Then they took to abusing one another's handwriting. "Pray don't give me so much trouble in future," says Budæus, "seeing with what pleasure I read your letters; but use your customary handwriting, which I know to be clear and beautiful. You have surely sent me the first rough draft, instead of a clean copy. If you continue to write so carelessly, mind that this fault does not bring you into disgrace; for I not only keep your letters among my literary treasures, but show them round among my friends, because I think it is for my own character that the world should know that I have such intimacy with you."[19]

To which Erasmus replies,—"You certainly act the part of an intimate friend in thus finding fault with me for my bad writing. I think, however, I can partly clear myself of this charge, as well as retort it upon you. For in the first place it is scarcely civil to expect one whose time is taken up in copying out large volumes, and who sometimes has twenty letters to write in a day, to write as neatly as if he had nothing else to do. As to my copying out my letters, I should be quite unequal to the task, and were I to employ others to do so, I should require five servants at least. And yet my wife"—(in a former letter, Erasmus referring to the complaint of Budæus that owing to his family cares he had little time for study, had declared that for his part he was married to Poverty)—"and yet my wife, about whom

[18] *Ep.* ccli.   [19] *F*

you make yourself so merry, hardly allows me to keep one, so imperiously does she rule my house, proving herself my mistress more truly than my wife. How much trouble what you call my draft may have given you I do not know. This I know, that I had so much difficulty in deciphering your clean letter, that I was obliged to write it all over again with my own hand, to make it legible, first to myself, and then to my learned friends; for, before, I could scarcely read it myself, while others could not at all; not so much because you had written carelessly, as on account of the peculiarity of your writing. This, however, is an inconvenience which you can easily cure by taking care to send us plenty of letters, for thus your hand will become familiar to us." [20]

But the most serious difference, which almost led to a breach of friendship, between these two eminent men, arose out of Erasmus's controversy with Faber. Budæus warmly espoused the cause of his countryman, and told Erasmus that considering the greatness of his own fame, he might have afforded to pass over Faber's attack. Erasmus replied, very justly, that he could not submit in silence to be called impious and a blasphemer, and that he had written his apology more in sorrow than in anger; and he appealed to those who were intimate with him whether he had ever, even when the wound was fresh, said an unkind word of Faber. Finally, he was quite ready, he said, to retract his defence, if Faber would set the example by withdrawing the attack. Indeed, the controversy with Faber seems really to have given him some pain, and he constantly speaks of it as a quarrel with a friend. In one of his letters he offers

[20] *Ep.* ccxxi.

to make Budæus arbiter in the dispute, provided he will read his apology with care, and complains that many had found fault with him who had read neither the attack nor the defence. The example of Jerome and Augustine, both of whom had proved themselves sharp controversialists when attacked, he thought amply justified him in defending himself. There cannot be a quarrel without two, and on this occasion Erasmus was determined not to quarrel with Budæus, and the latter having given him to understand that henceforth there could be no terms between them, he replied in a long letter, in which he declared himself his everlasting friend, and in the course of which, as preparatory to some pretty hard knocks, he took occasion to say, amid much more in the same style, "Though my writings shall perish with their author, or rather perish before him, yet posterity shall say that there was one Erasmus whom the great Budæus neither hated nor utterly despised."[21] The correspondence between the two scholars was kept up for many years after this, but on a very reduced scale, and it may be doubted whether there was ever any real cordiality between them. The Frenchman carefully abstained from mentioning his great rival in any of his works, though it is said he was often entreated to do so,[22] and subsequently, as we shall find, Erasmus gave fresh offence by comparing Budæus, in his *Ciceronianus*, with Badius the printer of Paris, also a learned man, however, and the author of many works. This last offence, it is probable that Budæus never forgave.

The correspondence between these two famous scholars might fairly claim a place among the quarrels of authors. The reader of our days, indeed, is apt to

---

[21] *Ep.* cclxxxv. cccv. cccx.   [22] BAYLE: art. Budæus.

find the letters a little tedious, and those of Budæus, in particular, somewhat heavy and laboured; but at the time when France and Germany seemed to be pitted against one another in the persons of their respective champions, the friendly discussion was watched with eager interest.[23] Even yet it is impossible not to admire the literary skill displayed on either side, the dexterity with which the darts of irony are shot under the appearance of almost worshipping admiration, and the easy manner in which the most extravagant praise is made to pass into downright censure. As to the comparative merits of the two men, it seems to be admitted that Budæus possessed the more accurate knowledge of the Greek tongue. In breadth of scholarship, extent of reading, and general vigour of mind, as well as in grace and eloquence of style, Erasmus was unquestionably his superior, as he was the superior of all the other learned men of the time.[24]

Meantime, the authorities of the University of Louvain, and especially the members of the theological faculty, were desirous that Erasmus should once more take up his residence among them.[25] Although it

[23] The correspondence between Erasmus and Budæus was printed, along with some other letters, at Louvain, in 1517, under the following title:—*Aliquot Epistolæ sane quam elegantes Erasmi Roterodami, et ad hunc aliorum eruditissimorum hominum antehac nunquam excusæ præter unam et alteram.*

[24] I am surprised that Mr. Hallam (*Lit. Hist.* i. p. 284, ed. 1855) should have insinuated that this was not also the judgment of contemporaries. The words of Budæus himself on this point are plain enough: — "Erasmo . . . . cui ego jam invidere cœpi ob nimiam istam gloriam, qua non modo Germaniam (de reliquis Provinciis nunc silebo), sed Galliam etiam nostram ita irradiat, ut gloriolam nostram præradiet, et jam nobis esse obscuris ac videri necesse sit."—*Er. Op.* iii. 168–169.

[25] *Er. Op.* iii. 191, C.

seemed natural that he should do so while his connection with the Court of Brussels lasted, there were considerations which made him hesitate. Louvain was a noted seat of the enemies of learning, and was one of the four universities which had joined in the persecution against the excellent and learned John Reuchlin. The influence of the Emperor had not protected that eminent man from the hostility of the monks, and in going to Louvain, Erasmus might seem to be thrusting his head into the lion's mouth. Besides he dreaded the annoyance which his reputation might bring upon him on the part of the students. It was with these things in his mind that he wrote to Ammonius in the letter from Brussels already quoted:—"I don't like the idea of going to Louvain. I should be obliged while there to show attention to the scholastics at my own expense: the young men would come crowding about me continually, begging me to criticise this poem, to correct that letter; one would ask for one author, and another for another; nor is there any one there whose friendship would be either useful or ornamental. Besides I should be obliged to listen sometimes to the yelpings of the pseudo-divines—the most disagreeable kind of people I know; among whom an individual has recently appeared who almost succeeded in embroiling me in a quarrel, and I am now in the position of holding the wolf by the ears, neither able to gain the mastery, nor yet to escape myself. He flatters me when I am present, but abuses me behind my back: his promises are most friendly, but he acts like an enemy. Oh! that great Jupiter would melt down and re-cast all this sort of people, who, though they contribute nothing to make us either better or more learned, yet give trouble and annoyance to everybody!"[26] Nevertheless he removed to Louvain in the course of the winter, and there were his head-quarters for the next few years. Whether it was that by his conciliatory manners he was able to disarm opposition, or to overawe it by the greatness of his fame, or whether the obstructives were not so strong as had been supposed, he seems to have found himself at first comfortable enough, and was well satisfied with his reception. "I find the divines of Louvain," he writes to Tonstall, "frank and agreeable, and especially John Atensis, a man of incomparable learning and the greatest possible kindness. There is not less theological learning here than at Paris, but there is less sophistry and less pride."[27]

Atensis, who was the Vice-Chancellor of the University, somewhat disappointed the expectations which Erasmus had formed of him. He says elsewhere that he was indeed no enemy of good letters, but of an irritable temper, and supposes that in any hostility he showed to himself he acted at the instigation of others. Indeed, the anxieties of his position between the two parties, the men of culture and the obscurantists, hastened his death, which took place not long afterwards, and as it was not till after this that the advocates of the old theology began to grow violent in their abuse, he does him the justice to suppose that he must have exerted his influence to keep them somewhat in check.[28]

At Louvain he was received with open arms by Dorpius, now quite a convert to the good cause. There, too, he formed a close intimacy with Ludovicus Vives, a young Spaniard from Valencia, of whose abilities he

[26] *Ep.* clxxx.   [27] *Ep.* ccxciii.   [28] *Er. Op.* ix. 1649, A.

formed a very high estimate, saying that he was one of those who would eclipse his own fame. "He has," he observed in a letter to More, "an extremely philosophical mind; nor do I know any one who is better qualified to break the ranks of the sophists, in whose tactics he is thoroughly disciplined." [29] Nor did he overrate the powers of Vives, who afterwards gained a high reputation as a scholar, and was invited to England by Cardinal Wolsey, where he read lectures at Oxford, and was subsequently appointed tutor to the Princess Mary.[30]

Louvain was at this time one of the most frequented of all the Universities, rivalling even Paris itself, and Erasmus estimates the number of students at no less than three thousand. While he was there a great impulse was given to liberal studies by the munificence of Jerome Busleiden, who, by his will of June 22, 1517, bequeathed several thousand ducats to found a college for the three learned languages. In the formation of this institution Erasmus, it may be supposed, took a lively interest, and it was on his recommendation that one Adrian, a converted Jew, and possessed of a knowledge of Hebrew literature which few in that age could rival, was appointed professor of Hebrew.[31] To him also was committed the charge of looking out for a competent teacher of Greek, and the next year we find him writing to John Lascar, of Constantinople, to beg that if he knew any one he could recommend he would send him at once. There were many candidates, he said, but he and those with whom he was acting were anxious to secure a native Greek who might teach the correct pronunciation. The salary was to be about seventy ducats,

[29] *Er. Op.* iii. 542, C. [30] JORTIN: i. 191-2. [31] *E*

besides the pupils' fees ; and the expenses of the journey from Constantinople, and a dwelling-house, were guaranteed.[32] The chair, it would appear, was offered to James Ceratinus, so called from his native place, Horn, in Holland, one of the most accomplished Grecians of the day, and a man of unblemished character, as well as of extraordinary modesty, who in 1525 succeeded Mosellanus at the University of Leipsic.[33] He was previously professor of Greek at Tournay in the new college there, but having been driven thence by " war and the plague, the two greatest evils which afflict humanity," he was now resident at Louvain.[34] He could not, however, be prevailed upon to accept the professorship, and it was accordingly given to Rutgerus Rescius, whom Erasmus commends as a man of pure character, and most diligent in the discharge of his duties.[35]

The Latin professor was Conrad Goclenius, a Westphalian, whom Erasmus seems to have taken completely into his confidence, and whom he afterwards, at a time when he thought he was going to die, entrusted with his will, in which he left a considerable sum to himself. We find him introducing Goclenius to More as one whom he might love with his whole heart. "He has plenty of wit," he tells him, "but of the most refined sort; and in story-telling you will find him nearly a match for yourself. He has quite a special talent for poetry, and is always clear and sweet, nor is there any subject, however unattractive, round which he cannot throw a charm. And yet he writes prose so admirably

[32] *Ep.* cccxiv.
[33] *Ep.* dccxxxvii. dccxxxviii.
[34] *Er. Op.* iii. 667, A.
[35] *Ep.* cccclxxx.

that you would think it quite impossible for him to write a verse." [36]

With such friends as these, and there were others whom he also mentions with honour, Erasmus could not want for congenial society. It was not, however, to be expected that the enemies of culture should witness these proceedings with indifference, or look favourably on an institution designed to facilitate the study of such dangerous languages as Greek and Hebrew. There were some accordingly, who, by secret intrigue, or open clamour, offered all the opposition they could to the success of "the college of the three tongues." "The old parrots!" exclaims Erasmus, bitterly, "they would rather be *double*-tongued, as in truth they are; it is hopeless to think of teaching them a new language." [37] "Let them dissemble as they will," he says again, "they detest it." [38] It is to be feared that Rescius must have yielded at length to these adverse influences, for we find Erasmus, in the very last letter he ever wrote, in the year 1536, complaining that instead of reading Demosthenes and Lucian, and other classical authors, he was translating back into Latin, ecclesiastical institutions which had been first rendered into Greek. Such was the influence of men whom jealousy for their own useless studies would not even permit geography to be taught in their university!

It was probably not long after his settlement at Louvain that Erasmus first made the acquaintance of

---

[36] *Er. Op.* iii. 615, A, B.

[37] "Instituitur hic collegium trilingue, ex legato Buslidii. Sed obstrepunt nonnulli, qui, quod sunt, bilinguem esse malunt; jam vetuli psittaci, quibus mutandae linguae spes non sit."—*Er. Op.* iii. 367, C.

[38] "Dissimulent quantum libet, hoc collegium illos pessime habet."—*Ib.* 523, C.

Ulrich von Hutten, the celebrated German reformer and man of letters, of whom we shall have more to say by-and-by. Hutten, coming to Louvain, would of course call on Erasmus, for whom he entertained the greatest admiration, and no doubt they congratulated one another on the victory of Reuchlin, who, on the 2nd of July, 1516, had been acquitted by the commission appointed to try him at Rome. "And when," Erasmus would sometimes ask, " is Hochstraten to be hung ?" to which Hutten would reply that he would attend to that matter shortly. Many a laugh too they must have had over the famous *Epistolæ Obscurorum Virorum*, or Letters of Obscure Persons, of which Hutten is known to have been in part the author, and which almost rivalled the *Moria* itself, both in popularity and in the effects which they produced. These letters, written in a language which amusingly exaggerates the barbarous Latin of the monks, under pretence of defending Hochstraten and his party, in reality turn them into infinite ridicule, and hold them up to the scorn and contempt of the world. Erasmus, Hutten tells us, and it can be easily believed, was in ecstasies with this satire, and declared that such an admirable way of turning the barbarians into ridicule had never before been invented.[39] Afterwards, however, on being himself suspected of the authorship, and thinking that it was quite enough for him to bear the odium of the works to which he had put his name, he found it convenient to change his tone, and took several oppor-

---

[39] "Maxime omnium laudabas et applaudebas, autori prope triumphum decernebas, negabas unquam excogitatam compendiosiorem illos insectandi viam, hanc demum optimam esse initam rationem, barbare ridendi barbaros," &c.—*Expostulatio.*—*Hut. Op.* Münch, vol. iv. p. 356.

tunities of speaking disparagingly of it, as a work of which he disapproved. Able to adapt himself to every society, Erasmus was at this time on the best of terms with Hutten, notwithstanding their very opposite characters. Under no circumstances is it probable that a close friendship could have been established between them. As it was, they became, as we shall find, bitterly hostile.

In the spring of this year (1517) Erasmus had been in England, where the King and Wolsey, at length, it would seem, sensible of the honour which would be reflected on their country by the presence of so eminent a man, received him with the greatest kindness, and offered him a splendid dwelling-house together with a pension of six hundred florins to induce him to remain. For some time he kept this promise before his eyes, and on the death of the Chancellor Sylvagius in the following year, he seemed inclined to accept it. His other connections in England might well have drawn him to this country, and in a letter written about this time, we find him saying that were it not for the help he received from Britain he would still be a beggar.[40] He had objections to Germany on account of the stoves, whose dry heat disagreed with his constitution, and the frequent highway robberies which made the roads dangerous, and he felt no inclination to accompany his master to Spain, though invited thither by the Archbishop of Toledo. Eventually, however, he decided against England. "I am afraid of the troubles that may happen there," he wrote to More, "and I dread the slavery to which I should be subject."[41]

And when we remember what troubles actually

[40] *Ep.* clxxxv. App.   [41] *Er. Op.* iii. 1658, E.

came, no doubt we shall admit that he was right. Other considerations, too, may have influenced him. Though Warham long survived, old friends were beginning to drop away into the land of shadows. In 1517, Ammonius of Lucca, whose memory he ever continued to cherish as that of a most gifted man and faithful friend, was cut off, when not yet forty, by the sweating sickness, notwithstanding his temperate habits, which he had boasted to More only a few hours before his death were a sufficient protection against contagion.[42] A loss which Erasmus felt even more was that of Colet, who died on the 16th of September, 1519, and these two much-loved friends being gone, it may be that his inclination to make London the home of his old age was greatly diminished in strength. "For thirty years," he wrote to Thomas Lupset, "I have not felt any one's death so much; I am resolved to consecrate his memory to posterity."[43] And nobly he kept his word in the admirable portrait he has left us of his friend.[44]

The sweating sickness which carried off Ammonius, was a contagious fever of a most pestilent character, which, having first broken out in Henry VII.'s army on his landing at Milford-Haven in 1483, subsequently ravaged England five different times, ultimately disappearing in 1551. The presence of such an enemy, in addition to the ordinary plague to which England was subject in common with other countries, though apparently to a greater degree, might well have terrified any one even less careful of himself than Erasmus. Moreover, at this time England was certainly not before, and was probably considerably behind, other countries in the ordinary comforts and decencies of life, and in

[42] *Ep.* dxxii.   [43] *Er. Op.* iii. 508, B.   [44] *Ep.* ccccxxxv.

a well-known letter addressed to Francis, Cardinal Wolsey's physician, Erasmus, no doubt quite justly, attributes the prevalence of the plague in our own country to the filthy habits which then prevailed. His details are not altogether nice, but for the sake of the unpleasant truth they will be pardoned. The letter has no date, but certainly belongs to 1518 or 1519, and is as follows:—

ERASMUS *to* FRANCIS, *Physician to the Cardinal of York.*[45]

"I OFTEN wonder and lament how it happens that for so many years Great Britain has been afflicted with pestilence without intermission, particularly with the sweating sickness, a malady which seems peculiar to itself. We read of a city being delivered from a pestilence which had long ravaged it by the destruction and renewal of its buildings in accordance with the advice of some philosopher. Either I am greatly deceived, or by some such plan must England be delivered. In the first place they never think whether their doors and windows face north, south, east, or west; and in the second place the rooms are generally so constructed that, contrary to Galen's rule, no thorough draft can be sent through them. Then they have a large part of the wall fitted with sheets of glass which admit the light but keep out the air, and yet there are chinks through which they admit that filtered air which is all the more pestilential because it has been lying there a long time. Then the floors are generally strewed with clay, and that covered with rushes which are now and then

[45] *Ep.* ccccxxxii. App.

renewed, but so as not to disturb the foundation, which sometimes remains for twenty years nursing a collection of spittle, vomits, excrements of dogs and human beings, spilt beer and fishes' bones, and other filth that I need not mention. From this, on any elevation of temperature, there is exhaled a vapour which, in my judgment, is by no means beneficial to the human constitution. Besides, England is not only surrounded on all sides by the sea, but many parts of it are very marshy, and it is intersected with salt rivers, to say nothing just now of the salt fish, of which the common people are wonderfully fond. I should have confidence in the island becoming more healthy if the use of rushes could be abolished, and the bed-rooms so built as to be open to the sky on two or three sides; and if all the glass windows were so made as to open or shut all at once, and shut so fast as to leave no chinks through which noxious winds could force a passage; since, as it is sometimes healthy to admit the air, so is it also sometimes healthy to exclude it. The vulgar laugh if you complain of their cloudy sky: I can only say that for thirty years past, if I entered a room in which no one had been for some months, I would immediately begin to feel feverish. It would be an advantage if the vulgar could be persuaded to live more sparingly and to be more moderate in the use of salt-fish. Then there might be policemen who should have the charge of seeing that the streets were kept clean from filth; and they should also look after the neighbourhood of the city. I know you will laugh at me for making myself anxious about these matters; but I do so out of friendship for a country which has so long afforded me hospitality, and where I would willingly spend the remainder of my life if I could. I doubt not that you in your wisdom know far more about these things than I do, but I wished to mention them in order that, if my judgment should accord with yours, you may commend them to the consideration of the leading men of the country; for these things used to be the care of monarchs. I would very gladly have written to his Reverence my Lord Cardinal, but I had neither time nor anything to say; and I know well how immersed he is in the affairs of state."

After reading the above no one will wonder that Erasmus declined the hospitality of England and preferred to reside in a country where they did not indulge in the luxury of rushes.

After a winter of more than usually hard work,—no winter he complained had ever seemed so long to him,—he was ready about Easter to start once more for Basle, with the materials he had prepared for the second edition of the New Testament. These constant journeys, undertaken though they were for the public advantage, were, it seems, made a subject of reproach against him by the monks, ever ready to seize an opportunity of attacking the friends of that learning which they so much hated. Their complaint that the need of a revision of his Greek Testament implied that the first edition was far from perfect, would have been more just if it had not been merely spiteful. Nettled by some remarks to this effect which had reached his ears, Erasmus could not forbear administering a severe rebuke to his tormentors before leaving Louvain, as will appear from the following extracts from a long letter to Marcus Laurinus, a canon of Bruges, who appears to have been one of his most confidential friends.

Erasmus *to* Marcus Laurinus.[46]

"Louvain, Easter Monday, 1518.

". . . It is hard indeed to bear the obstinate and perverse ingratitude of mankind. None are more in need of my labours than those who thus bark at my studies; nor do any bark more furiously than those who have never seen the cover of one of my books. Try the experiment, my dear Marcus, and you will find that what I say is true. The first time you meet with any person of that kind, let him rave on against my New Testament, until he has quite exhausted his fury and is so hoarse that he can say no more, and then just ask him if he has ever read the work. If he is impudent enough to say he has, press him to produce the passage with which he finds fault. You won't find one of them who can do it.

". . . As to their cavil that I am preparing a new edition because I am dissatisfied with the first, suppose it were so, what is there to blame in that? What fault can they find if I study to surpass myself and to do what Origen, Augustine, and Jerome did, especially when I candidly promised, in my first edition, that I would do so if necessary?

". . . But these men of severe life find fault with me for my want of steadiness, because they have heard that I am going to Basle; as if forsooth I went to Basle, or had done so before, for my amusement. It was there I edited St. Jerome and the New Testament, besides many other works; and to serve the public interest, I undertook a most dangerous journey, and thought nothing

[46] *Ep.* ccclvi.

of the expense or the toil by which I have worn out a good part of my life and my health. A strange unsteadiness, if I did not choose to drink away my time with them instead of going to Basle! They run hither and thither, up and down the world, and fly over land and sea, not at their own expense, seeing that they make a profession of beggary, but with money got, by cheating and scraping together, from widows whom they drive mad by descanting on their sins, by robbing nuns, and lastly by imposing on the good-nature of simple brothers, and this that they may injure and cast a stain on men who have done good service to the Christian commonwealth. And they, forsooth, are esteemed steady and grave, while I, because I make myself a slave to the public interest with my own money and to my own loss, am unsteady. 'Let him choose,' they cry, 'a city in which to live.' What! do they think I live here in a Scythian desert? Do they suppose that every one is blotted out of existence whom they do not see continually at their compotations? To my thinking, I have a home wherever I have my library and any little furniture I possess. But if the public advantage demands that I should change my place, it would be better, if I mistake not, to praise my public spirit than to condemn my unsteadiness. If I could have released myself from the necessity for this journey at a cost of three hundred gold pieces, I would willingly have paid down that sum. As the case stood I was obliged to go. Nor did I ever change my abode except for fear of the plague, or on account of my health, or to make an honest penny. Italy is the only country I ever visited of my own accord, and I went there partly to visit the holy places at least once, partly to benefit by the libraries of that country and enjoy the society of its learned men. I have not yet repented of that instance of my unsteadiness. I am now here for about two years without a break. I might have followed the Catholic King into Spain with the very best prospects. I have received an invitation from the King of France, who promised me mountains of gold; also a most kind one from the King of England and the Cardinal of York, and from Francis, Archbishop of Toledo, lately deceased. I have received invitations from the Bishop of Paris, from the Bishop of Bayonne, from the Archbishop of Maintz, from the Bishops of Liege, Utrecht, Basle, and Rochester, and from the Dukes of Bavaria and Saxony. This is no lie; the fact is known to many and is clear from their own letters to me. Neglecting all these invitations, I have persevered with the work I had on hand; and yet I must be called unsteady, though my sole desire is to finish what I have begun at the cost of so many sleepless nights!

"If the virtue of steadiness consists in your occupying the same place as long as possible, stones and the trunks of trees must claim the first rank of merit, and next to these come shells and sponges. It is no vice to change one's abode; the vice would consist in changing it from bad motives. Nor is it a virtue to remain long in the same place, but to have lived in a praiseworthy manner. Socrates is praised because he always lived as a good citizen in Athens. Yet Plato's travelling is not deemed a vice. John the Baptist never went beyond Judæa; Christ merely touched its confines: yet we do not on that account condemn the apostles for unsteadiness because they wandered up and down through the world. No one condemns Hilarion for his wanderings because Paul never left his cave. Yet why bring forward such examples for those who are not steady even-while living in the same city, but are continually changing their stall and their feeding-ground, and wherever the kitchen sends up a richer steam and a more savoury smell, thither they crowd. They say I have no steadiness because I have not gone on drinking with them for five-and-forty years in the same city, like a sponge, which, once it is fixed, lives only to drink; because I have not made free with the nuns, gambled, or played the sycophant. In truth, I vastly prefer my unsteadiness to their steadiness. For I think it is far more creditable to have lived in many places in such a way that, no matter where you may be, the best men of the place wish you back again, than to have lived in the same city in such a way as to bring disgrace upon yourself, or even to make it a matter of indifference whether you have lived there at all. What if my health compels me to change my place? Will they make no allowance for the duty of paying attention to one's health? As it is, they condemn me because I prefer the public advantage to everything else. But they can do without my labours. Let them; only let the cultivated and the learned have the benefit of them. I don't want to compel any one to be wiser than he wishes to be. But a truce with these fellows, my dear Marcus. Let us, in the spirit of pure Christianity, love the good, and tolerate the bad, if they refuse to be overcome even by kindness. Like to like, as the proverb says. A hard knot requires a hard wedge to split it; and while they are attempting to fix their teeth in a soft and brittle substance, they may chance to break them against something solid. As for me, I have neither time nor strength to fight with these ruffians.

"I hope you will not inconvenience yourself to come here, though otherwise I should be delighted to see you. I shall visit you, I hope, in a short time, and spend some days with you, to enjoy your society, before I leave this. Even if I do leave this, I shall not be long away. If I go to Basle I shall return next autumn; if to Venice, next spring. . . . Farewell, excellent friend."

At Basle Erasmus remained till the autumn. He arrived there about the middle of May, but had not been longer than ten days in the city when he was seized by an infectious disorder, the symptoms of which were cough, violent headache, and pains in the bowels, and which, in the course of the summer, proved fatal to a large number of persons. From this he was fortunate enough to recover in the course of some days, but he was afterwards attacked by dysentery, and during the whole summer, which was an extremely hot one, he enjoyed scarcely a moment's health. Nevertheless, he was able to see some important works through the press; but he would not wait for the completion of his second edition of the New Testament, which he was obliged to leave to the care of Froben and the brothers Amerbach, and which did not appear till the following March (1519). His restless habits, and perhaps the state of his health, required change, and by October he was on his way back to Louvain. A letter to his friend Beatus describes his return journey, and gives very minute details as to his physical sufferings—details far more fit, as Jortin has remarked, to be poured into the ears of his physician in the privacy of the bedchamber, than to be committed to writing and handed round the circle of admiring friends and acquaintances.[47] So at least the taste of our times would say ; but, in truth, anything that Erasmus might choose to write was welcome in Basle, and, indeed, wherever Latin was understood or there was any pretension to literature. The first part of the letter, however, is a lively description of the difficulties and discomforts of travel in the sixteenth century, and as such will probably interest the reader.

ERASMUS *to* RHENANUS.[48]

"*Louvain*, 1518.

"I MUST give you, my dear Beatus, a full account of my journey, which was a complete tragi-comedy. I was feeling rather weak and ill, as you know, when I left Basle, not having yet become reconciled to the open air after my long confinement to the house, and the constant work in which I was engaged. The voyage was pleasant enough, except that about noon the heat of the sun was rather annoying. We stopped for dinner at Brisach, but I never had a worse dinner in my life. The smell was enough to kill you, but the flies were even worse than the smell. We sat for more than half-an-hour at the table doing nothing, waiting for dinner to be served. At last it was put on the table, but there was positively nothing fit to eat—soup with bits of meat so dirty that the mere sight of them was enough to make you sick, and salt fish which had evidently done duty more than once before. . . . . Towards night we were landed in some village, where it felt very cold, but the name of which I don't want to

---

[47] JORTIN : vol. i. p. 130.   [48] *Ep.* ccclvii.

know, nor, if I knew, should I care to mention it. I was nearly killed there. We had supper in a small room heated by a stove, where there were more than sixty of us, I think, a most miscellaneous set of people, and it was not over till nearly ten o'clock. Oh! the stench! the noise! especially as they began to grow warm with wine; and yet we were obliged to take our time from their watches. In the morning, while it was still quite dark, we were routed from our beds by the shouts of the sailors, and I was obliged to go on board both supperless and sleepless. We got to Strasburg before breakfast at about nine o'clock, and then we found ourselves more comfortable, especially as Schurer supplied us with wine. Some of our friends were waiting for us, and soon they all came to make us welcome. Thence we went on horseback to Spire, nor did we see anywhere so much as the shadow of a soldier, notwithstanding the formidable reports which had reached us. My English horse broke down completely, and could scarcely drag himself to Spire, that wicked blacksmith having used him so badly that both his ears had to be burnt with a red-hot iron. At Spire I stole away from the inn and went to a neighbouring village, where I had been before, where the dean, a kind and learned man, entertained us hospitably for a couple of days, and where, as good luck would have it, we fell in with Hermann Busch. Thence I proceeded by carriage to Worms, and from there on to Maintz. It so happened that a secretary of the Emperor, named Ulrich Farnbul, got into the same carriage with me, and paid me the greatest possible attention all the way to Maintz, where he would not suffer me to go to the inn, but brought me to the house of a certain Canon, and when I was going away accompanied me to the boat. The voyage was pleasant, the weather being fine, but it was rather longer than it need have been, owing to the carelessness of the sailors. The smell of the horses, too, was disagreeable. . . . On arriving at Popard, as we were walking up and down on the bank, some one, I don't know who, recognized me and pointed me out to the Customs' collector. The collector's name, if I remember right, is Christopher Cinicampius, vulgarly Eschenfelder. You would not believe how overjoyed the man was to see me. He dragged me into his house, and there, on a table, among his business papers, were lying the works of Erasmus. He called his wife and children and all his friends, shouting aloud that he was now indeed happy; and meanwhile he sent two bottles of wine to the sailors, and afterwards, as they continued to vociferate, two more, promising that on his return he would remit the tax to whoever had brought him such a man.

"Hence, in order to show us respect, John Flaminius, the superior of the convent, a man of angelic purity, of sound and sober judgment, and of no common learning, accompanied us as far as Coblentz, where we were carried home by Matthias, the Bishop's chaplain, a young man, but of very composed manners, and an excellent Latin scholar, besides being deeply versed in the law. There we were very merry over our supper. At Bonn the Canon left us, in order to avoid the city of Cologne, which I also wished to do, but my servants had gone on there with the horses, and there was no one in the boat on whom I could depend to go and fetch him back—I could not trust the sailors. Accordingly, the next morning—it was now Sunday, and the weather was thick and unwholesome—we arrived at Cologne before six o'clock. I went into the inn, gave directions to the servants, to see about hiring a two-horse carriage, and ordered breakfast to be ready at ten. I then went to mass, and on my return found breakfast not yet ready. Not a carriage was to be had. I then tried to get a horse, for my own were useless, but with as little success. I saw that they were doing all they could to keep me there, so I instantly ordered my own horses to be saddled, put one of my valises on one of them, gave the other in charge to my host, and set off on my lame horse to the Count of New Eagle, a journey of five hours. He was living at Bedburium, and I spent with him five most delightful days, in so much quietness and comfort, that I was able to finish a good part of my proof; for I had brought part of the New Testament with me. I wish you knew this man, my dear Beatus. He is young, but has all the wisdom of age; he is sparing of words, but when he speaks it is very sweetly and from his heart; he is learned in more than one branch of study, but without ostentation, and is altogether a most unaffected and most lovable man. I was now feeling much stronger, and better satisfied with myself, and was hoping to be well enough to visit the Bishop of Liege and to return to my friends in Brabant in good health. What feastings, what greetings, what talks I was promising myself! I had determined, if the autumn should prove favourable, to go to England, and accept the offer which the King has so often repeated. But, oh, the deceitfulness of human hopes! the uncertainty of life! From these dreams of happiness I was suddenly hurled down to the very brink of destruction. Already a two-horse carriage had been hired for the next day. The Count, who was unwilling to bid me farewell before night, told me he would come and see me before I left in the morning. That night a violent storm of wind arose, which had been blowing also the night before; nevertheless I got up in the middle of the night to say something to the Count, and having waited till seven o'clock, and the Count not making his appearance, I ordered him to be called. He came, and being an extremely modest young man, he asked me whether it was still my intention to leave in such unfavourable weather, adding that he was anxious about me. Thereupon, my dear Beatus, Jupiter, or some evil genius, took from me, not half my reason, as Hesiod says, but all I had left; for the half was gone when I ventured to Cologne. And I would that he had either warned his friend more impressively, or I had been more attentive to his modest but friendly advice. I was carried away by the power of destiny; for what else shall I call it? I got into the carriage, an open one, the wind blowing so that it might have torn up an oak; it was a south wind, and was loaded with pestilence. I thought I was well protected by my cloak, but its force penetrated everywhere. Towards night rain came on, which was even more pestilential than the wind which carried it. I arrived at Aix, tired with the shaking of the carriage, which was so unpleasant to me, especially as it was over a stony road, that I would rather ride on a horse no matter how lame. Here I was carried from the inn by a Canon to whom the Count had introduced me, to the house of the precentor, where we found some other canons at dinner. A very poor breakfast had sharpened my appetite; but these worthy people had nothing to give me but some carps, and they were cold. However, I took my fill; and supper being prolonged with various talk till far on in the night—for it was late when they sat down—I excused myself, and went to bed, having slept very little the night before.

"The next day I was taken to the house of the sub-prior, for it was now his turn to entertain. As there was no fresh fish there except eel, the weather must assuredly have been in fault, for otherwise he keeps a sumptuous table. I filled myself with some fish dried in the air. It was that kind which the Germans call from the stick with which it is pounded, and which I usually like well enough; but I found part of this was still raw. After breakfast, the atmosphere being then most pestilential, I went into my bed-room, and ordered a fire to be lighted. The Canon, who was a very kind man, chatted with me for about an hour and a half. Meantime I felt my stomach turn sick, and when this lasted, I dismissed him; and——"

But here Erasmus becomes so disagreeably minute that it may be as well to break off. He proceeds to narrate, with many particulars, how he at length arrived at Louvain, with several ulcers breaking out on his body, and a strong suspicion that now at last he had caught the plague. Instead of going at once to his chambers in the University, he took refuge at the house of his friend Theodoric Martin, the printer, and immediately sent for a surgeon, who confirmed his fears, and having promised to send some soothing lotions, declined himself to return for fear of infection. Some physicians, however, who were consulted declared that there was no disease, and a Hebrew doctor said he wished he had

as healthy a body. Other conflicting opinions were pronounced; but, meantime, Erasmus recovered sufficiently to return to his studies, and resolved to make an effort to throw off his trouble by mental exertion. It was nearly four weeks, however, before he was able to leave the house of the friendly printer, and, meantime, Dorpius, Atensis, and other friends, notwithstanding his warnings that no one should come near him, insisted on visiting him, and made his time pass pleasantly by their conversation. "My dear Beatus,"—thus the letter concludes,—"who would believe that, after the fatigue of so many journeys and such severe study, this thin and delicate frame of mine, on which age, too, has now set its seal, would be able to bear up also against so many diseases? For you know how seriously ill I was at Basle not long ago, and, indeed, more than once. I could not escape the suspicion that this year would be fatal to me, one misfortune followed another in such rapid succession, and each one more difficult to bear than its predecessor. Yet such was my frame of mind that, even in the lowest depression of disease, I was neither tormented with a wish to live nor did I tremble with fear of death. In Christ alone was all my hope, from whom I prayed for nothing but that he would give me what he himself might judge to be for my good. When I was a young man, I remember I used to shiver all over at the very name of death; but I have gained this much at least by years, that I fear death very little, nor do I measure human happiness by length of life. I am now past my fiftieth year, and when I consider how few are permitted to reach that age, I cannot complain that I have not lived long; besides, if this has anything to do with the matter, a monument is even now ready by which I may testify to posterity that I have lived. And, perchance, from the pyre, as the poets say, when envious tongues shall be silent, my glory shall shine the more brightly. Yet human glory must not come near the heart of a Christian. I pray that we may have the true glory of being accepted with Christ."

While Erasmus was thus lying ill at the house of his friend Martin, in the meantime his enemies began somewhat prematurely to rejoice over his death, and a preaching friar at Cologne announced with great glee to his applauding companions that he had not only died, but died, as he expressed it in his wretched monkish Latin, *sine lux, sine crux, sine Deus,*—without candles, crucifix, or God.[49] To die without the visible means of grace provided by the Church would be, of course, in the eyes of all good Catholics, to be utterly lost, and if that fate had indeed befallen the great leader of the new crusade against the cherished ignorance and superstition of the monks, he had only got his deserts, and the world was well rid of him. Nay, the imagination of some had even carried them so far that a report was spread—only, however, in the distant city of Prague—that he had been burned at Cologne, along with his books:[50] no doubt, the wish was father to the thought. Fortunately, however, Erasmus disappointed the hopes of his monkish adversaries. He recovered from his disease, whatever it was, and lived to plant many another pointed shaft in their sides.

But it is now time to glance at the literary labours on which he was engaged during his residence at Louvain, for the editing of the New Testament by no

---

[49] *Er. Op.* iii. 432, E.   [50] *Ib.* 432, D.

means sufficed to exhaust his energies. It must have been shortly after his arrival that he wrote a declamation against war, which he called *Querela Pacis*, or The Complaint of Peace,[51] and which he dedicated to Philip, Bishop of Utrecht, another natural son of Philip the Fair, and brother of David, the late Bishop.[52] The subject was one on which Erasmus felt strongly, and wrote earnestly and eloquently. No member of the Society of Friends ever detested war more cordially than he did, and in that warlike age he never feared to lift up his voice boldly against it.

As in the "Praise of Folly," Folly is the speaker, so in this essay Peace utters her own complaint, bewailing her unhappy fortune that she can find no resting-place anywhere. She has tried the cities, but found the private houses full of quarrelling and dissension; she has tried the courts, but found the courteous salutations and ceremonies, which at first promised so well, mere hypocrisy; she then tries the theologians, the priests, and, last of all, convinced that here at least she must find a secure asylum, the monks; but, need it be said, without success. "School contends with school, and, as though the nature of truth varied in different places, there are some doctrines which never cross the sea, the Alps, or the Rhine; nay, in the same University the logician is at war with the rhetorician, the lawyer with the divine. And still further, even in the same profes-

---

[51] *Querela Pacis undique gentium ejectæ profligatæque.—Er. Op.* iv. 625.

[52] BURIGNI (i. 145) says, on the authority of Calkreuter, that Erasmus composed this piece at Rome. But this only shows that he had not read it. Doubtless it may embody parts of the *Anti-polemus*, which he wrote at the request of Julius II., but as Leo X. is mentioned more than once, it was evidently written under the latter Pontiff.

sion, the Scotist fights with the Thomist, the Nominalist with the Realist, the Platonist with the Peripatetic, so that they cannot agree even in the most minute particular, and often they will fight most desperately for a mere straw, until, in the heat of the discussion, they proceed from arguments to abuse, and from abuse to blows, and, if the affair is not settled with daggers and lances, they stab one another with pens dipped in poison, tear each other in pieces on paper, and brandish against one another's fame tongues armed with death. But none revolted me more than the monks, among whom there are as many factions as there are societies, while Dominicans dispute with Franciscans, Benedictines with the followers of St. Bernard; there are so many names, dresses, ceremonies, studiously diverse, so as to exclude all possibility of agreement, while each order is in love with itself, but condemns and hates every other. And yet nothing can be more utterly at variance with Christianity, whose founder is emphatically called the Prince of Peace." Erasmus here does not forget that in the Old Testament, God is called the God of hosts and the God of vengeance, and I am not sure whether he is strictly orthodox when he remarks in explanation that there is a great difference between the God of the Jews and the God of the Christians, "though," he hastens to add, "in his own nature God is one and the same." He has, however, no difficulty in proving from the New Testament the unchristian nature of war.

Well might he be honestly indignant at the conduct of the clergy in flattering the passions of princes and people. The Franciscans and Dominicans, he says, when England and France were about to engage in war, a few years before, instead of restraining this mad fury, did all they could to increase it. Priests and Bishops leave their churches and follow the armies to the field, while above the contending hosts waves the holy cross, whose mission it is before all things else to preach peace to mankind, but which is now made the symbol of war. "What hast thou to do with the cross, thou wicked soldier? It is the sign of him who conquered not by fighting but by dying, and who saved and not destroyed. Dost thou carry the sign of salvation, while thou art hastening to kill thy brother, and with the cross destroyest him who by the cross was saved?" Nor does he fail to notice the absurdity of the fact that the same holy symbol is present in *both* camps. "What a monstrous thing is this! Can the cross fight with the cross, Christ carry on war against Christ? The prayers which are offered up for peace must be regarded as a mere mockery of God, so long as the princes of the earth rush to arms on the flimsiest pretences, and while prompt to answer to the call of the warlike Pope Julius, pay no attention to the voice of Leo summoning the world to peace and concord. Hence it is clear that they call in the aid of religion as a mere cloak to conceal their impiety." The mockery of Christianity becomes almost grotesque when we learn that the guns were often called after the Apostles and engraved with images of the Saints.

Erasmus goes the length of scarcely permitting even defensive war, except indeed against the incursions of Turks and other barbarians. Among Christians he thinks all war intolerable, and unequivocally contends for peace at any price, on the plain mercantile principle that to purchase peace will always cost less than to carry on war. It would be unjust, however, not to add that he urges also the higher motive that it is more Christian to forgive than to take vengeance. Yet it may be doubted whether the chivalrous Francis I., if he ever read this treatise, would have felt greatly flattered on finding it said of him that he did not scruple to purchase a peace, even though the next sentence explains that he did so in order to prove that the good of the human race was the object most worthy of a king. But, in truth, Erasmus was not careful to flatter the great, nor mindful of what kings might think of him; otherwise he would never have been so bold in his attacks upon their conduct. In this very essay he disposes of the "divine right" of kings in the most offhand way, asking what great difference it can make *who* reigns, so long as the public interests are properly attended to.[53]

The treatise concludes with an earnest appeal to Kings, Bishops, and all in authority to follow the things that make for peace, pointing out that the greatest sovereigns of the day, Francis, Charles, Maximilian, and Henry, and above all the Pope himself, "the pacific and meek Leo," are in its favour, and urging that thus "the empire of kings will be more august, when they shall rule over a pious and prosperous people, the priests will have more time for the performance of their sacred duties, the Christian name will be more formidable to the enemies of the cross; while, above all, they will gain the favour of Christ, to please whom is the sum of all human happiness."

Some part of the year 1517 was employed by Erasmus in preparing editions of Suetonius and Quintus

---

[53] "Quasi vero ita magni referat, quis regnum administret, modo publicis commodis recte consulatur."—*Er. Op.* iv. 633, C.

Curtius, both of which were afterwards printed by Froben. The latter he dedicated to Ernest Duke of Bavaria, in an elegant epistle, in which he says that he had always, from his very boyhood, been a great admirer of this author for his singular fairness and correctness, as well as the terseness of his style, and had taken him with him as the companion of his voyage when he visited England the preceding spring. He was, however, he adds, no admirer of the subject of the history, regarding Alexander the Great as no more than a successful robber.[54] The Suetonius was edited from a very old manuscript, which Mountjoy had found in a monastery at Tournay, when he was governor of that city. It was dedicated, in a very long epistle, to Frederic, Elector of Saxony, and his cousin George.[55]

During this same winter at Louvain (1517–1518), which he had found so long, Erasmus made a valuable contribution to Greek learning, by translating the grammar of Theodore Gaza, and thus supplying students with the best Greek grammar that had yet appeared.[56] He also enlarged and printed in a separate form the short treatise on the proper method of theological study, prefixed to the first edition of his Greek Testament, and of which some account has already been given.[57] It was dedicated, in its new form, to the Archbishop Elector of Maintz and Magdeburg, who had been recently made a Cardinal.

Among other works printed at Basle in the course of the summer (1518), Erasmus now published for the first

[54] *Ep.* cclxxvi.
[55] *Ep.* cccviii.
[56] *Theodori Gazæ Grammaticis, libri duo.*—*Er. Op.* i. 111.
[57] *Ratio, seu Methodus, compendio perveniendi ad veram theologiam.*—*Er. Op.* v. 75. See above, p. 325. The dedication bears the date Dec. 26, 1517.

time the first book of his youthful treatise, the Anti-Barbarians, to which reference has been already made.[58] The original design, as I have said, had extended to four books, of which the first and second were completed, but having been entrusted to the care of Richard Pace, when the author was about to leave Italy, they were unfortunately lost. On taking up his residence at Louvain, however, Erasmus found that the first book, in its original youthful form, had got into circulation to such an extent that he deemed it advisable, lest it should be published by others, himself to take it in hand, and prepare it for the press. The work, thus revised, was dedicated to John Sapidus. Another youthful work, also published this year, was the " Praise of Medicine,"[59] an essay which the author said he had written long ago, at a time when he was trying his hand at everything. One can easily believe that it was printed without much revision. It is a mere declamation, with very little substance, giving, however, some significant hints as to the superstitions which then prevailed, and especially as to the belief in astrology. It was dedicated to one Henry Affinius, a distinguished physician of the day.

Up to this time the *Enchiridion* had been frequently reprinted. A new edition was now published by Froben with a defence of the work by its author, in the form of a letter addressed to Paulus Volzius, the devout abbot of a monastery near Schelestadt. In this letter Erasmus sharply attacks the scholastic divinity, and contrasts with it the practical teaching of Christ and His Apostles. Referring to the war which was just then contemplated against the Turks, he asks what would be the result if, after conquering them, in order to convert the survivors

[58] See above, p. 25. [59] *De Laude Medicinæ.—Er. Op.* v. 521.

to Christianity—"for I suppose," he adds, "we do not intend to put them all to the sword"—the works of Occam, Scotus, and the rest, were put into their hands. "What," he asks, "will they think when they hear of those thorny and inextricable subtleties about instants, formalities, quiddities, and relations; especially when they observe that the great professors of our religion agree so little among themselves, that they often resort to abuse and contempt, and sometimes even to blows? .... The most effectual way of conquering the Turks would be if they were to see the spirit and teaching of Christ expressed in our lives; if they perceived that we were not aiming at empire over them, thirsting for their gold, coveting their possessions, or desiring anything whatever save their salvation and the glory of Christ. .... And unless this spirit animates us, I am afraid we shall sooner degenerate into Turks ourselves, than bring over the Turks to our side." Erasmus then proceeds at some length to justify his little work against the attacks which had been made upon it, showing that in exposing and condemning abuses, he had not intended to find fault with any of the institutions or customs of the Church, so long as they were kept in due subordination to the precepts of Christ. "If any one utters a warning that it is safer to trust in good deeds than in the Pope's pardons, he does not therefore condemn those pardons, but he prefers that which is more certainly in accordance with the doctrine of Christ."—"I find no fault if some live on fish, others on herbs and vegetables, and others on eggs: but I warn those who, in a Jewish spirit, persuade themselves that they can be made righteous by these things, that they are grievously mistaken; who pride themselves on such trifles, the inventions of men, while yet they think it no sin to take away another's good name by their lying calumnies." In his condemnation of the monastic orders, whose origin and degeneracy he rapidly sketches, he is unsparing enough, though affecting to find fault only with abuses. "I utter no reproaches," he says, "because the Franciscans and Benedictines follow their own rule; but only because some of them prefer it to the Gospel." Doubtless he was thinking of his own early experience when he expressed the wish that no one should be permitted by law to take monastic vows before his thirtieth year. "But," he continues, "those who, like the Pharisees, compass sea and land to make one proselyte, will never want for young men ignorant of the world to allure into their nets and make a prey of. There is a large abundance of fools and simpletons everywhere. For my part I could wish, and I doubt not that all truly pious men would wish the same thing, that the Gospel religion was so dear to all, that, content with this, no one should bind himself to the Benedictine or Franciscan rule; nor do I doubt that Benedict and Francis themselves would wish so too. . . . . I could wish that all Christians lived in such a manner that those who are now alone called religious might no longer be thought so."[60] The letter to Volzius bears the date August 14, 1518. We are informed elsewhere that this new preface injured the sale of the work by offending a number of the Dominicans, who had previously commended it.[61]

Previous to the third visit of Erasmus to Basle, Froben had printed, in the beginning of the year 1518, a collection of his letters enlarged from one which had appeared the preceding year at Louvain, and another

[60] *Ep.* cccxxix.   [61] *Cat. Luc.* See

was issued under the superintendence of the author himself before he left Basle in the autumn. Thus the readers of that time—and their numbers were increasing every day—were already put in possession of a series of letters perhaps the most entertaining that has ever been given to the world, unsurpassed for their flowing easy style, their biting satire, their graphic powers of description, their wit, eloquence, and learning, and constituting now, with the additions that were subsequently made, one of the most interesting and delightful autobiographical sketches that it would be possible to name. Among so many—they now fill two folio volumes and number upwards of eighteen hundred, of which far the greater part are by Erasmus himself—some, no doubt, are of little intrinsic value. There are others which one would have thought the author would be far more anxious to destroy than to publish. Nevertheless, as the correspondence of the most brilliant literary man of his day, we could not wish that one had been lost. These letters were read with delight and eagerness at the time of their first appearance, and they will continue to be read as long as any interest is felt in the great men and the great events of the time to which they belong.

One other work, the composition of which, however, extended over several years, may be most conveniently noticed here. At Louvain Erasmus had written a Paraphrase of the Epistle to the Romans, which towards the close of 1517 he published, and dedicated to his old friend Cardinal Grimani. This was followed, after about a year and a half, by the two epistles to the Corinthians and the Galatians, and then, in due time, by the rest of the canonical epistles. The two epistles to Peter, we may notice, were dedicated to Cardinal Wolsey. The idea of making Paul write as Erasmus would have written is not one that by any means commends itself to the taste of our age, nor, indeed, to the good taste of any age. It should be remembered, however, that the Paraphrases were written at a time when Erasmus was much better appreciated than St. Paul. The work accordingly was received with universal favour; and when we find such a man as Richard Pace writing that, by the help of the Paraphrase on the Corinthians, he had been enabled to understand better than ever before both the language and the meaning of St. Paul, it may be supposed that such a work was needed.[62] Erasmus himself had not intended to go beyond the epistles of Peter and Paul, but the persuasions of his learned friends had induced him to persevere. His own good sense, it seems, would have withheld him from paraphrasing the Gospels, but having gone to Brussels to meet the Cardinal of Sion, on his return from the Diet of Worms, that dignitary, being particularly interested in the work, and to whom a part of it had been dedicated, besought him to do for St. Matthew's Gospel what he had already done for the Epistles. Erasmus replied, very justly, as we may think, that to paraphrase so simple a narrative would be like lighting a candle at noon-day; besides, he urged, if he undertook St. Matthew, he would be expected to paraphrase the rest also, and must go over the same

---

[62] "Tuam in duas Pauli ad Corinthios Epistolas paraphrasim diligentissime perlegi : et ex hoc tuo labore tantum me fructus percepisse fateor, ut nunc tandem (quod antehac mihi contigit nunquam) audeam affirmare, me aliquatenus (ne nimium meo ipsius tribuam ingenio) cum quid dicat, tum quid sentiat divus Paulus, intelligere."—*Er. Op.* iii. 308, F.

ground repeatedly wherever the Evangelists agree. Eventually, however, he yielded. The simple story of the Evangelists passed into the wordy rhetoric of Erasmus, and the result was dedicated to his four principal patrons—Matthew to Charles V.; John, which followed next in order, to Ferdinand, Charles's brother; Luke to Henry VIII.; and Mark to Francis I. Last of all, he paraphrased the Acts of the Apostles, which he dedicated in the beginning of the year 1524 to the new Pope, Clement VII., thus having completed, or rather completely transformed, the New Testament, with the exception of the Apocalypse, a book which seems to have had little attraction for the Reformers of that time. The work, when complete, was accompanied by an address to the pious reader, advocating the propriety of making the Scriptures accessible to the most illiterate, and of translating them into the vulgar tongue.[63]

The Paraphrase of the New Testament cannot be counted among the most permanently interesting of the works of Erasmus. Yet there was none which gave such universal satisfaction, or which so entirely escaped censure.[64] Doubtless it did good work in promoting the study of the Scriptures, and so preparing the way for the coming Reformation. It is well known that it was so highly appreciated in England that a copy of it, translated into English, was ordered to be placed in every parish church beside the Bible.

---

[63] The Paraphrase of the New Testament fills the seventh volume of Le Clerc's *Erasmus*.

[64] "Absolvi Paraphrases in omnes Epistolas divi Pauli germanas, opus, ni fallor, victurum, et adeo felix, ut illis quoque probetur, quibus nihil placet Erasmicum."—*Er. Op.* iii. 414, D.

But we have now once more passed, and must accordingly return to, that point of time which forms an epoch not merely in the life of Erasmus, but in the history of the world. The great movement generally known as the Protestant Reformation is so intimately connected in its origin and progress with his life, he himself was so peculiarly related to it, as having, on the one hand, done more, by his assaults on the superstitions of the time, than almost any other individual, to prepare the way for it, and, on the other, as having never openly espoused it or gone hand-in-hand with its leaders;—his conduct, on this account, was so misrepresented at the time, and has been so misunderstood since, that it will be necessary to treat of this part of his life with special fulness. In presenting the views and feelings of Erasmus in regard to the Lutheran movement, I shall adopt the plan I have hitherto followed, of permitting him to speak for himself; but it will be advisable first to try to understand accurately the nature of that movement itself.

END OF VOL. I.

LONDON: PRINTED BY
SPOTTISWOODE AND CO., NEW-STREET SQUARE,
AND PARLIAMENT STREET.

This book should be returned to the Library on or before the last date stamped below.

A fine is incurred by retaining it beyond the specified time.

Please return promptly.

Check Out More Titles From HardPress Classics Series In this collection we are offering thousands of classic and hard to find books. This series spans a vast array of subjects – so you are bound to find something of interest to enjoy reading and learning about.

Subjects:
Architecture
Art
Biography & Autobiography
Body, Mind &Spirit
Children & Young Adult
Dramas
Education
Fiction
History
Language Arts & Disciplines
Law
Literary Collections
Music
Poetry
Psychology
Science
…and many more.

Visit us at www.hardpress.net

Im TheStory
personalised classic books

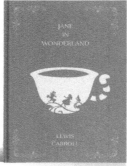

"Beautiful gift.. lovely finish. My Niece loves it, so precious!"

Helen R Brumfieldon

★★★★★

UNIQUE GIFT

FOR KIDS, PARTNERS AND FRIENDS

Timeless books such as:

 Kids

Alice in Wonderland • The Jungle Book • The Wonderful Wizard of Oz
Peter and Wendy • Robin Hood • The Prince and The Pauper
The Railway Children • Treasure Island • A Christmas Carol

 Adults

Romeo and Juliet • Dracula

Highly Customizable • **Change** Books Title • **Replace** Characters Names with yours • **Upload** Photo (for inside page) • **Add** Inscriptions

Visit
ImTheStory.com
and order yours today!